NUCLEAR STRATEGY AND WORLD SECURITY

OTHER PUGWASH PUBLICATIONS

Preventing the Spread of Nuclear Weapons (C. F. Barnaby, ed., Souvenir Press, 1968)

Implications of Anti-Ballistic Missile Systems (C. F. Barnaby and A. Boserup, eds, Souvenir Press, 1969)

Impact of New Technologies on the Arms Race (B. T. Feld, T. Greenwood, G. W. Rathjens and S. Weinberg, eds, The Massachusetts Institute of Technology, 1971)

J. Rotblat, Scientists in the Quest for Peace: a History of the Pugwash Conferences (The MIT Press, 1972)

Pugwash on Self-Reliance (W. K. Chagula, B. T. Feld and A. Parthasarathi, eds, Ankur Publishing House, 1977)

A New Design for Nuclear Disarmament (W. Epstein and T. Toyoda, eds, Spokesman, 1977)

International Arrangements for Nuclear Fuel Reprocessing (A. Chayes and W. Bennett Lewis, eds, Ballinger, 1977)

Feeding Africa (Pan-African Pugwash Group, 1978)

The Dangers of Nuclear War (F. Griffiths and J. C. Polanyi, eds, University of Toronto Press, 1979)

Appropriate Technology and Social Values (F. A. Long and A. Oleson, eds, Ballinger, 1980)

New Directions in Disarmament (W. Epstein and B. T. Feld, eds, Praeger, 1981)

European Security, Nuclear Weapons and Public Confidence (W. Gutteridge, ed., Macmillan, 1982)

Scientists, the Arms Race and Disarmament (J. Rotblat, ed., Taylor and Francis, 1982)

Proceedings of the First Pugwash Conference on Science and World Affairs (J. Rotblat, ed., Pugwash Council, 1982)

The Dangers of New Weapon Systems (W. Gutteridge and T. Taylor, eds, Macmillan, 1983)

The Arms Race at a Time of Decision: Annals of Pugwash 1983 (J. Rotblat and A. Pascolini, eds, Macmillan, 1984)

NUCLEAR STRATEGY AND WORLD SECURITY
Annals of Pugwash 1984

Edited by

JOSEPH ROTBLAT AND SVEN HELLMAN

© Pugwash Conferences on Science and World Affairs 1985

All rights reserved. No reproduction, copy or transmission
of this publication may be made without written permission.

No paragraph of this publication may be reproduced, copied
or transmitted save with written permission or in accordance
with the provisions of the Copyright Act 1956 (as amended).

Any person who does any unauthorised act in relation to
this publication may be liable to criminal prosecution and
civil claims for damages.

First published 1985

Published by
THE MACMILLAN PRESS LTD
Houndmills, Basingstoke, Hampshire RG21 2XS
and London
Companies and representatives
throughout the world

British Library Cataloguing in Publication Data
Nuclear strategy and world security: annals of
Pugwash 1984.
1. Nuclear arms control
I. Rotblat, Joseph II. Hellman, Sven
327.1'74   JX1974.7
ISBN 978-0-333-39668-1   ISBN 978-1-349-17878-0 (eBook)
DOI 10.1007/978-1-349-17878-0

Contents

Preface: Editors		ix
Notes on the Contributors		xiii
Acronyms		xvii
Glossary		xx

Part One. The Strategic Arms Race

1	R. L. Garwin	Technological Developments and their Implications	3
2	M. A. Milstein	The Problem of Strategic Stability	14
3	L. Freedman	Escalation and Arms Control	18
4	R. Smoke	Crisis Control Measures	28
5	J. P. Holdren	Nuclear Forces and Proposals for a Nuclear Weapons Freeze	40
6	W. B. Slocombe	Proposals for a Nuclear Freeze	55
7	J. C. Mark	Implications of a Comprehensive Test Ban for a Stockpile of Nuclear Weapons	60
8	W. Epstein and R. J. Leng	The Point Count Plan for Nuclear Arms Reduction	70
9	J. Prawitz	The Naval Arms Race and Arms Control	76

Part Two. Military Aspects of Space

10	G. E. Perry	Extent of Militarisation of Outer Space	83
11	A. G. Arbatov	Prevention of the Militarisation of Space	99
12	J. Ruina	The ABM Problem Revisited	103
13	B. Jasani	Restricting Anti-satellite Technology	107
14	T. Orhaug	An International and Regional Satellite Monitoring Agency	124
15	C. Voûte	A Space Policy for Peace	143

Part Three. Prohibition of Chemical Warfare

16	J. P. Perry Robinson	Chemical Warfare: Status of Technological Developments and Deployments	155
17	S. J. Lundin	Negotiations on a Chemical Weapons Ban	176
18	Mayaten Rautio and Miettinen	Verification of Chemical Disarmament	186
19	E. Ezz	Chemical Weapons Verification	195
20	K. Lohs and Karin Meier	A Chemical-Weapon-Free Zone in Europe	202

Part Four. Problems of European Security

21	L. V. Sigal	The Euromissiles: Negotiating a Way Out?	209
22	S. Lodgaard and P. Berg	Disengagement in Central Europe	242
23	A. D. Rotfeld	The Stockholm Conference on Confidence- and Security-building Measures and Disarmament in Europe	260
24	A. A. C. von Müller	Confidence-building by Hardware Measures	275
25	A. Boserup	Conventional Forces in Europe – Report from Pugwash Symposium, Vedbaek, Denmark	287

Part Five. Security of Developing Countries

26	M. S. Wionczek	Emergence of Military Industries in the South and Their Longer Term Implications	295
27	U. D'Ambrosio	The Rise of Militarism: Effects on Third World Countries	307
28	E. E. Galal	Arms Control and Crisis 'Management': Feasibility and Complexities in the Third World	313
29	K. S. Subrahmanyam	Regional Conflicts and Their Linkage to Strategic Confrontation	320
30	I. Ahmad	Impact of the Global Arms Race on Prospects for Development	328

Part Six. Scientists, Public Opinion and the Arms Race

31	B. T. Feld	Public Opinion and Arms Control	343
32	H. Alfvén	Terminology of Nuclear Issues	348
33	S. P. Kapitza	Scientists and Public Opinion	351
34	S. Hellman	Scientists and Public Opinion – Differences between East and West	355
35	E. L. Tollefson	Role of Universities in the Campaign to Suffocate the Nuclear Arms Race	360
36	Patricia J. Lindop	Pugwash and the Scientific Community	367
Appendix		Statement from Pugwash Council '1984 and Beyond: Science, Security and Public Opinion'	377
Index			385

Preface

This volume of the Pugwash Annals is the second in the series - begun last year with the publication of 'The Arms Race at a Time of Decision: Annals of Pugwash 1983' - which aims at making available to a wider audience the ideas and issues debated at the Pugwash Conferences.

These conferences are held in private so that the debate can be frank and uninhibited. Most of the work is done in small groups with about 25-35 participants sitting around a table and conversing with each other rather than making speeches or giving lectures. The discussion is generally based on the papers commissioned by the Pugwash Council and circulated well in advance of the meeting; usually there are also other papers proffered by participants. It is the belief of the Council that the independent contributions by expert scholars, and the consensus reached by them, would be of interest to members of the community who share with Pugwash the desire to create a safer but less armed world.

Apart from providing information the book is also an auspicious testimony to the fact that even in a climate of mistrust and fear, like the one prevailing now, scientists from all parts of the world, holding widely different political views, can and do work together to find solutions to the most pressing problems of the day.

As is to be expected from the calibre of the authors, their contributions are the result of original thinking; this is reflected in the difference of approach and in a divergence of views not necessarily due to political convictions. The views expressed in the papers are those held personally by the individual authors, because those participating in Pugwash meetings come in their personal capacity and not as representatives of the institution with which they are affiliated. This freedom from prior commitment and absence of briefing ensure that the discussion is conducted in the scientific spirit of objectivity, and often leads to a conciliation of diverse opinions. Indeed, some of the papers presented in this book include modifications made by the authors in the light of the discussions.

In addition to the Annual Conferences, the Pugwash Council organises every year several other types of meetings: workshops, symposia and study groups. A selection of papers presented at these meetings, or a summary of them, is included in this volume. Thus, Chapters 6 and 7 were discussed at the Tenth Workshop on Nuclear Forces held in Geneva in June 1984, and Chapter 5 is a summary and critical review of that Workshop. A similar review of the Symposium on Conventional Forces in Europe, held in Vedbaek in March 1984, is given in Chapter 25. All the remaining chapters are from papers presented at the Annual Pugwash Conference, held in Björkliden in July 1984. The agenda of this Conference was divided into six Working Groups, and these correspond to the six Parts of this book.

Part One is on the main topic on the Pugwash agenda: the strategic nuclear arms race and the ways to stop and reverse it. The Conference was held at a time when all negotiations on these issues between the superpowers have broken down, with no prospect in sight for a resumption of official talks on the nuclear arms race, which meanwhile continued unabated, and new nuclear weapon systems being deployed and stationed in more countries. The Pugwash forum was one of the very few to maintain the dialogue between the two sides on these problems. Despite the depressing atmosphere created by the deadlock in official negotiations, the debate was positive and productive in its aim to elucidate and recommend ways and means to facilitate a resumption of talks, and suggesting topics to be taken up at these talks. All this was not just wishful thinking. As will become clear from reading the papers, the obstacles to reaching agreement are assessed critically and realistically, but out of the detailed analysis of the situation there emerge specific proposals for the avoidance of future crises, and concrete measures to reduce nuclear arsenals which should be acceptable to both sides.

Part Two, on the military aspects of space, is concerned with the latest menace: an extension of the nuclear arms race by the militarisation of space, and the development of a third generation of nuclear weapons. Military satellites have been an integral, and to some extent stabilising, element of nuclear weapon systems; their reconnaissance function, for example, plays an important part in the verification of agreements. However, the development of improved antisatellite weapons, coupled with the projected use of space-based weapons to destroy ballistic missiles in flight - the star wars concept - constitute a threat to the

ABM Treaty, a new danger of a war in space, and is likely to add a further spiral to the nuclear arms race. A moratorium on testing and deployment of anti-satellite weapons is considered to be an essential first step to avert these perils. An important confidence-building measure in this area - which was discussed in two previous Pugwash Symposia - would be a satellite monitoring agency, set up in the first instance on a regional basis with the initiative coming from Europe.

Problems of verification are also the major concern in another area of impending military developments, namely, chemical warfare, which is the subject of **Part Three**. The present status of technological developments and deployments is extensively reviewed in the papers. The possibility of reaching an agreement on a Convention on Chemical Weapons, which would prohibit the development, production and stockpiling of such weapons, had generated a hopeful atmosphere and encouraged the search for mutually-agreed methods of verifying adherence to the Convention. The many obstacles on the way are not minimised, but several concrete proposals to overcome them are put forward.

Part Four, on European security, is related to the nuclear issue discussed in Part One, and to the breakdown of the negotiations on Euromissiles. The technical and political problems connected with the control of these weapons, particularly after the deployment of new systems, are analysed in great depth, and some options for the future are outlined. It is the general feeling that confidence-building measures are needed to create the necessary environment for technical solutions. The relevant history of the meetings on confidence- and security-building measures is described in detail. Apart from some specific confidence-building measures, the importance of détente, at present dormant, is strongly emphasised; a recognition of arms control as an integral part of international affairs would strengthen the elements of political and military détente.

The linkage problem is also stressed in **Part Five**, in relation to the security of the developing countries. The arms race has become a global issue by drawing the Third World into East-West confrontations. New trends are discernible in military-economic interchanges in the whole world. There has been a remarkable emergence of military industries in some Third World countries; the far-reaching implications of this phenomenon for the future of these countries are analysed in the papers.

In **Part Six** Pugwash scientists inquire how they might enhance their own efforts to tackle the many problems on the agenda of the other groups, in particular, how they could enlist for this purpose the help of a larger segment of the scientific community, in addition to measures aimed at influencing public opinion. Although Pugwash never intended to be a mass movement, it can contribute to the shaping of public opinion by providing information and by promoting systematic education on relevant issues. The introduction of regular University courses on the arms race and the consequences of a nuclear war might be one method. Other specific ways of augmenting the Pugwash influence, especially in the scientific community, are recommended.

While the papers in the six Parts of this volume represent individual views, the discussion on them at the meetings usually produces a consensus on some issues. This consensus, together with the resulting recommendations, is made public in statements issued by the Pugwash Council or its Executive Committee. The statement issued after the Geneva Workshop in June 1984 is appended to Chapter 5 (pp.50-54). The statement issued after the Björkliden Conference is given as an Appendix at the end of the book (pp.377-84).

* * * *

In editing this volume we were assisted by many colleagues. We wish to express our gratitude to Dr. Bhupendra Jasani, Dr. Martin Kaplan, Professor Patricia Lindop, Mr. Sven Lodgaard, Dr. Johan Lundin and Mr. Manne Wängborg. We are also greatly indebted to Jean Egerton and Edith Salt for technical assistance, and especially to Jennifer Mills for her heroic measures to prepare the camera-ready copy of the book in a remarkably short time.

Joseph Rotblat
Sven Hellman

December, 1984.

Notes on the Contributors

I. **Ahmad** (Pakistan) physics. Member of the Pakistan Atomic Energy Commission, Islamabad.

H. **Alfvén** (Sweden) physics. Nobel Laureate. Emeritus Professor in plasma physics at the Royal Institute of Technology in Stockholm.

A.G. **Arbatov** (USSR) political science. Section leader at the Institute of World Economy and International Relations, USSR Academy of Sciences, Moscow.

P. **Berg** (Norway) political science. Research Assistant, European Security and Disarmament Programme at SIPRI, Stockholm.

A. **Boserup** (Denmark) peace and conflict research. Professor at the Institute of Sociology, University of Copenhagen.

U. **D'Ambrosio** (Brazil) mathematics. Professor of Mathematics at the Institute of Mathematics, Statistics and Computer Science of the State University of Campinas.

W. **Epstein** (Canada) disarmament and international security. Senior Research Fellow at the United Nations Institute for Training and Research, New York.

E. **Ezz** (Egypt) nuclear and chemical defence. Retired Major General. Director of Scientific Research Branch, Cairo.

B.T. **Feld** (USA) physics. Professor of Physics at the Massachusetts Institute of Technology, Cambridge.

L. **Freedman** (UK) international security. Professor of War Studies at King's College, University of London.

NOTES ON THE CONTRIBUTORS

E.E. Galal (Egypt) medical practice and pharmacology. Adviser to the Academy of Science Research and Technology, Cairo.

R.L. Garwin (USA) physics. IBM Fellow and Adjunct Professor of Physics at Columbia University, New York.

S. Hellman (Sweden) technology. Adviser on national security affairs, Ministry of Defence; President Swedish Engineers for the Prevention of Nuclear War, Stockholm.

J.P. Holdren (USA) energy, environment and arms control. Professor of Energy and Resources, University of California, Berkeley. President of the Federation of American Scientists.

B. Jasani (Sweden) nuclear and medical physics. Research Fellow, SIPRI, Stockholm; technical UN-consultant on an International Satellite Monitoring Agency (ISMA).

S.P. Kapitza (USSR) physics. Professor of Physics at the Physical Technical Institute in Moscow.

R.J. Leng (USA) political science. Professor of Political Science and Chairman of the Division of Social Sciences, Middlebury College, Middlebury, Vermont.

Patricia J. Lindop (UK) radiation biology and medicine. Professor Emeritus of Radiation Biology in the University of London.

S. Lodgaard (Norway) peace research. Director of European Studies, SIPRI, Stockholm.

K. Lohs (GDR) chemical toxicology. Director of the Research Department of Chemical Toxicology in Leipzig.

S.J. Lundin (Sweden) security policy, disarmament and arms control. Director of Research, Swedish National Defence Research Institute, Stockholm.

J.C. Mark (USA) physics and nuclear weapons design. Former Head of the Theoretical Division of the Los Alamos Scientific Laboratory, New Mexico.

Karin Meier (GDR) international law. Assistant Professor of International Law at the Karl Marx University, Leipzig.

NOTES ON THE CONTRIBUTORS xv

J.K. Miettinen (Finland) radiochemistry. Professor of Radiochemistry at the University of Helsinki.

M.A. Milstein (USSR) military policy and arms control. Retired General. Section Chief at the Institute of the USA and Canada Studies of the USSR Academy of Sciences, Moscow.

A.A.C. von Müller (FRG) philosophy and policy-advising. Research Associate at the Max-Planck-Institute For Social Sciences, Starnberg.

T. Orhaug (Sweden) information technology. Senior scientist at the National Defence Research Institute, Stockholm.

G.E. Perry (UK) physics. Former Head of Physics and Senior Teacher, Kettering Boys School, Kettering.

J.P. Perry Robinson (UK) chemist. Senior Fellow of the Social Policy Research Unit, University of Sussex, Brighton.

J. Prawitz (Sweden) arms control. Special Assistant for Disarmament, Swedish Ministry of Defence, Stockholm.

Mayaten Rautio (Finland) chemistry. Coordinator of the Finnish Project on Verification of Chemical Disarmament, University of Helsinki.

J. Rotblat (UK) physics. Professor Emeritus of Physics in the University of London.

A.D. Rotfeld (Poland) international relations. Head of the European Security Department at the Polish Institute of International Affairs, Warsaw.

J. Ruina (USA) electrical engineering and arms control. Professor of Electrical Engineering and Computer Studies, and Director of the Arms Control Programme at the Massachusetts Institute of Technology, Cambridge.

L.V. Sigal (USA) political science. Professor of Government at Wesleyan University in Middletown, Connecticut.

W.B. Slocombe (USA) international law. Former Deputy Assistant Secretary of Defense for International Security Affairs and member of the task force on the SALT-II negotiations, Washington.

NOTES ON THE CONTRIBUTORS

R. Smoke (USA) political science and psychology. Research Director of the Center for Foreign Policy Development and Professor of Political Science, Brown University, Providence, RI.

K.S. Subrahmanyam (India) international security. Director of the Institute for Defence Studies and Analyses, New Delhi.

E.L. Tollefson (Canada) physical chemistry. Professor of Chemical and Petroleum Engineering at the University of Calgary.

C. Voûte (Netherlands) geology. Professor of General and Applied Geology, International Institute for Aerospace Surveys and Earth Science, Enschede.

M.S. Wionczek (Mexico) energy economics. Senior Research Associate in Economics at the University of Mexico, Mexico City.

Acronyms

ABM	anti-ballistic missile
ACE	Allied Command Europe
ALCM	air-launched cruise missile
ALL	airborne laser laboratory
APT	automatic picture transmission
ARPA	Advanced Research Projects Agency
ASAT	anti-satellite weapon
ASBM	air-to-surface ballistic missile
ASW	anti-submarine warfare
AW&ST	Aviation Week and Space Technology
BMD	ballistic missile defence
CBM	confidence-building measures
CBW	chemical and biological warfare
CCD	Conference of the Committee on Disarmament
CCM	conventionally-armed cruise missile
CCRC	conditional conventional retaliation capability
CD	Committee on Disarmament
CDE	Conference on Disarmament in Europe
CEP	circular error probable
C^3I	command, control, communications, and intelligence
COMINT	communications intelligence
CSBM	confidence- and security-building measures
CSCE	Conference on Security and Cooperation in Europe
CTB	comprehensive test ban
CW	chemical warfare
CWFZ	chemical weapon-free zone
DABM	defence against ballistic missiles
DARPA	Defense Advance Research Project Agency
DC	Disarmament Conference
DEW	directed-energy weapon
DMSP	Defense Meteorological Satellite Program
DoD	Department of Defense
DSCS	defence satellite communications system
DSP	Defence Support Program
EDC	European Disarmament Conference

ACRONYMS

EEC	European Economic Community
ELINT	electronic intelligence
EMP	electromagnetic pulse
ENDC	Eighteen Nation Disarmament Committee
EORSAT	ELINT ocean reconnaissance satellite
ESA	European Space Agency
FEBA	forward edge of the battle area
FEL	free electron laser
FOFA	follow-on forces attack
GDP	gross domestic product
GEO	geosynchronous orbit
GLCM	ground-launched cruise missile
GLONASS	global navigation satellite system
GNP	gross national product
GPS	global positioning system
GSO	geostationary orbit
IAEA	International Atomic Energy Agency
ICBM	intercontinental ballistic missile
ICDSI	Independent Commission on Disarmament and Security Issues
IDCSP	Interim Defense Communications Satellite Program
IDM	integrated defence model
IFRB	International Frequency Registration Board
IISS	International Institute for Strategic Studies
INF	intermediate nuclear forces
IONDS	integrated operational nuclear detection system
IRBM	intermediate range ballistic missile
ISMA	International Satellite Monitoring Agency
IVA	intermediate-volatility agent
LEO	low earth orbit
LODE	large optical demonstration experiment
MAD	mutually assured destruction
MBFR	mutual and balanced force reduction
MFR	mutual force reduction
MHV	miniature homing vehicle
MIRV	multiple independently targetable re-entry vehicle
MRBM	medium range ballistic missile
MX	missile experimental
NASA	National Aeronautics and Space Agency
NATO	North Atlantic Treaty Organisation
NAVSTAR	navigation satellite timing and ranging
NIC	newly industrialising country
NORAD	North American Air Defense Command
NOSS	navy ocean surveillance satellite
NPB	neutral particle beam
NTM	national technical means
NWFZ	nuclear weapon-free zone
OECD	Organisation for Economic Cooperation and Development

ACRONYMS

OPEC	Organisation of Petroleum Exporting Countries
OSHA	Occupationl Safety and Health Administration
OTA	Office of Technology Assessment
OTH	over the horizon
OTRAG	Orbital Transport Raketen Gesellschaft
PAL	permissible action link
PGM	precision-guided munitions
PTBT	Partial Test Ban Treaty
R&D	research and development
RORSAT	radar ocean reconnaissance satellite
RPV	remotely piloted vehicle
RSMA	Regional Satellite Monitoring Agency
RV	re-entry vehicle
SAC	Strategic Air Command
SAINT	satellite inspection technique
SALT	Strategic Arms Limitation Talks
SAR	synthetic airborne radar
SDI	strategic defense initiative
SDS	satellite data system
SIPRI	Stockholm International Peace Research Institute
SLAR	side-looking airborne radar
SLBM	submarine-launched ballistic missile
SMA	Satellite Monitoring Agency
SPIN	space intercept
SPOT	Système Probatoire d'Observation de la Terre
SRAM	short-range attack missile
START	Strategic Arms Reduction Talks
STS	space transportation system
TEL	transporter-erector launcher
TOE	tonnes of oil equivalent
TRW	Thompson Ramo Wooldridge Inc.
UNCLOS	UN Convention on the Law of the Sea
UNSSD	United Nations Special Session on Disarmament
VTOL	vertical take-off and landing
WEU	Western European Union
WTO	Warsaw Treaty Organisation

Glossary

Accuracy	The ability of a warhead to hit near its intended aim point, usually measured in terms of the probability of hitting within a distance (CEP) from that point.
AirLand Battle	New NATO scenario involving deep interdiction into Eastern Europe by integrated Western forces.
Anti-ballistic missile (ABM) system	Weapon system for intercepting and destroying ballistic missiles.
Anti-satellite (ASAT) system	Weapon system for destroying, damaging or disturbing the normal function of artificial satellites.
Anti-submarine warfare (ASW)	The detection, identification, tracking, and destruction of hostile submarines.
Argument of perigee	The angle measured round the eliptical orbit from the north-bound equator crossing to the perigee point.
Ballistic missile	Missile which follows a ballistic trajectory when thrust is terminated.
Circular error probable (CEP)	A measure of accuracy of a weapon delivery system; the radius of a circle, centred on the target, within which 50 per cent of the weapons are expected to fall.

GLOSSARY

Command control and communications (C^3)	The system for authorising and transmitting to the missile the command to launch.
Counter-silo capability	The ability of a missile warhead to destroy a hardened ballistic missile silo.
Cruise missile	Missile which can fly at very low altitudes along programmed paths. It can be air-, ground- or sea-launched and carry a conventional or a nuclear warhead.
Deterrence	The ability to prevent another nation from acting in a hostile manner.
Directed energy weapon (DEW)	Weapon system based on the delivery on the target of destructive energy in the form of a beam of light or of particles with nearly the speed of light.
First-strike capability	Capability to destroy within a very short period of time all or a very substantial portion of an adversary's strategic forces.
Fission	Process whereby the nucleus of a heavy atom splits into lighter nuclei with the release of substantial amounts of energy.
Flexible response capability	Capability to react to an attack with a full range of military options, including a limited use of nuclear weapons.
Fusion	Process whereby light atoms, especially those of the isotopes of hydrogen - deuterium and tritium - combine to form a heavy atom with the release of very substantial amounts of energy.

GLOSSARY

Geostationary orbit	A geosynchronous orbit which is in the same plane as the Earth's euqator so that the satellite remains stationary relative to a fixed point on the Earth's surface.
Geosynchronous orbit	The orbit of a satellite which makes one revolution each sidereal day (1436 minutes).
Gross domestic product (GDP)	The GNP minus transactions with other countries.
Gross national product (GNP)	Annual total value of goods produced and services provided in a country.
Intercontinental ballistic missile (ICBM)	Ballistic missile with a range in excess of 5500 km.
Intermediate nuclear forces (INF)	US designation for long-range and possibly medium-range theatre nuclear weapons. See also: Theatre nuclear weapons.
Kiloton (kt)	Measure of the explosive yield of a nuclear weapon equivalent to 1000 metric tonnes of trinitrotoluene (TNT) high explosive.
Launch-on-warning	A strategic doctrine under which a nation's bombers and land-based missiles would be launched on receipt of warning (from early-warning systems) that an opponent had launched its missiles.
Manoeuvrable re-entry vehicle (MARV)	Re-entry vehicle whose flight can be adjusted so that it may evade ballistic missile defences and/or acquire increased accuracy.
Medium-range nuclear weapons	Soviet designation for long-range theatre nuclear weapons. See also: Theatre nuclear weapons.
Megaton (Mt)	Measure of the explosive yield of a nuclear weapon equivalent to one thousand kilotons.

GLOSSARY   xxiii

Multiple independently targetable re-entry vehicles (MIRV)	Re-entry vehicles, carried by one missile, which can be directed to separate targets.
Mutual assured destruction (MAD)	Concept of reciprocal deterrence which rests on the ability of the nuclear weapon powers to inflict intolerable damage on one another after surviving a nuclear first strike.
Mutual reduction of forces and armaments and associated measures in Central Europe (MFR or MBFR)	Subject of negotiations between NATO and the Warsaw Treaty Organisation, which began in Vienna in 1973. Often referred to as mutual (balanced) force reduction.
National technical means (NTM)	The use of technical intelligence collection means for verifying compliance with negotiated arms control agreements. These means must be consistent with the recognised provisions of international law.
Nuclear weapon-free zone (NWFZ)	Zone which a group of states may establish by a treaty whereby a state of total absence of nuclear weapons to which the zone shall be subject is defined, and a system of verification and control is set up to guarantee compliance.
Pixel (picture image)	Smallest resolution unit in a digitally recorded image.
Precision-guided munition (PGM)	Non-nuclear weapon system characterised by high accuracy achieved by in-flight remote control, usually accompanied by high explosive effects.
Re-entry vehicle (RV)	Portion of a strategic ballistic missile designed to carry a nuclear warhead and to re-enter the earth's atmosphere in the terminal phase of the trajectory.

GLOSSARY

Silo	A missile shelter including a vertical hole in the ground with facilities for launching the missile.
Strategic Arms Limitation Talks (SALT)	Negotiations between the Soviet Union and the United States, initiated in 1969, which seek to limit the strategic nuclear forces, both offensive and defensive, of both sides.
Strategic Arms Reduction Talks (START)	Negotiations between the Soviet Union and United States initiated in 1983 for reduction of strategic arsenals.
Strategic Defence Initiative (Star Wars)	A concept of defence against nuclear ballistic missiles by their interception and destruction in flight.
Strategic nuclear forces	Strategic nuclear forces ICBMs, SLBMs, ASBMs and bomber aircraft of intercontinental range.
Tactical nuclear weapons	See: Theatre nuclear weapons.
Theatre nuclear weapons	Nuclear weapons of a range less than 5500 km. Often divided into long-range (over 1000 km, for instance, so-called Eurostrategic weapons), medium-range, and short-range (up to 200 km, also referred to as tactical or battlefield nuclear weapons).
Transponder	Electronic apparatus which returns a pre-determined signal in answer to a calling one.
Warhead	The part of a missile, rocket or other munition which contains the explosive or other material intended to inflict damage.
Yield	Released nuclear explosive energy expressed as the equivalent of the energy produced by a given number of metric tonnes of trinitrotoluene (TNT) high explosive.

Part I
The Strategic Arms Race

1 Technological Developments and their Implications
RICHARD GARWIN

Introduction

Even the definition of strategic arms and the strategic arms race seems to be out of date. According to the US view as expressed in SALT, strategic arms are those nuclear weapons and delivery systems with sufficient range to reach from the territory of the USA to that of the Soviet Union (or vice versa), plus nuclear-armed submarine-launched ballistic missiles. The Soviet Union maintains (notwithstanding the SALT agreements) that US strategic weapons include all USA nuclear weapons, wherever deployed, capable of reaching the Soviet Union. Whatever the definition, the evolution of technology, together with deployment choices, means that the US and the USSR will be threatened by ground-launched nuclear-armed cruise missiles, sea-launched cruise missiles, and the like.

But strategic arms do not constitute a strategic arms **race**. Such a race may be defined by observers, or it may simply be a challenge by one side to the other to modernise and to expend resources without increasing either the threat to the other side or its own security. As suggested by the analysis presented in the report of the President's Commission on Strategic Forces (Scowcroft Commission)[1] **stability** at reduced levels of strategic forces is the goal. In that report, and in its final report[2] the Scowcroft Commission emphasised regarding the 1972 ABM Treaty '..the criticality of the ABM Treaty to further arms control agreements,' and said that this dictated 'extreme caution in proceeding to engineering development in this sensitive area.'

Thus, if one **defines** the use of strategic arms as limited, for instance, only to attack on strategic arms of the other side; if one imposes constraints on the use one might consider making of strategic arms in response to a strike by the other side; and if one imputes to the other side irrationality, unconcern for the survival of its population or society, one can find fears everywhere and security nowhere.

Nevertheless, if one takes the apparent position of the Scowcroft Commission, and that which is more and more expressed in the United States even by those in favour of deploying strategic defence - that the primary goal of strategic forces and arms control is to reduce the probability of nuclear war by strengthening **deterrence**, that is, not by eliminating the potential of the other side to destroy or damage one's own country, but to convince the other side that it has nothing to gain and a lot to lose by undertaking such an enterprise, the problem can in fact be tackled.

What, then, is the impact of technological evolution on this statement of strategic deterrence?

Nuclear Offence

In a recent publication[3] by the Department of Defense, it is stated that the Soviet SS-18 Mod4 is 'at least as accurate and possibly more accurate' than the Minuteman-III, and that the force of SS-18 Mod4s currently deployed 'has the capability to destroy more than 80 per cent of the US ICBM silo launchers using two nuclear warheads against each US silo'. The increase of accuracy of ICBM and SLBM, in itself, can lead to the capability for destruction of the ICBM retaliatory force, if it is based in fixed silos and if there is no possibility of launching it 'under attack', before it is destroyed. Nevertheless, as emphasised in the 1983 Scowcroft Commission Report, this fixed-silo ICBM vulnerability does not lead to strategic instability so long as there are invulnerably based submarine forces, and so long as bombers with cruise missiles can take off from their bases before destruction and can penetrate any defences.

Nevertheless, continued evolution of accuracy and reliability of strategic ballistic missiles increases concern about the survivability of the submarine and air-breathing strategic forces, especially when combined with a commitment to pose threats to the strategic offence force in order to encourage the other side to have an interest in arms control and reductions. Indeed, it may make those very reductions less achievable.

Mobility of the land-based ICBM force is a result of improvement in guidance system accuracy and flexibility, and of the introduction of solid-fuel missiles. Mobility improves survivability, under some circumstances, but it also leads to problems in **counting** the number of weapons, and hence

TECHNOLOGICAL DEVELOPMENTS 5

tends to impede progress towards reductions.

Strategic Defence

Gradual evolution of technology from vacuum tubes to solid-state circuits has now extended to the regime of radars, and makes possible effective, reliable, solid-state phased-array radars which can contribute to the ABM role. Such radars can have track-while-scan capability, so that they can allocate their resources effectively to make a greater contribution for a given investment to strategic defence.

Interceptors armed with nuclear warheads are available on both sides with high acceleration, thereby allowing a longer delay before launch of an interceptor to destroy an offensive warhead at a distance which will not destroy even a soft target. Nevertheless, valuable targets such as cities or powerful ABM radars can be destroyed by 'ladder-down tactics', in which offensive warheads are exploded at lower and lower altitudes, masking successive warheads by the fireball of the earlier nuclear explosions.

Not so much new technology but the wider **discussion** of defence technology in the United States has brought to public consciousness the utility of destroying opposing strategic ballistic missiles in boost phase, or even before they can be launched. This defence against ballistic missiles (DABM) and especially boost-phase intercept poses the serious problem of where to base the ABM system. Basing in space is evidently vulnerable to antisatellite (ASAT) capabilities, whereas basing on the ground with a view to launching into space at the outbreak of war poses an insuperable problem (at long standoff) of reaching a high enough altitude within the burn time of a booster in order to see over the curve of the earth and to destroy that booster. Furthermore, the development of systems other than the fixed, land-based ABM is forbidden by the 1972 ABM Treaty.

Observation of large strategic boosters is clearly possible from distant satellites, such as exist on both sides in the strategic warning systems. Nevertheless, prospect for boost-phase intercept could clearly be countered by shortening the duration of boost, and conventional solid-fuel missile technology can clearly be utilised to shorten the duration to 40-50 seconds and thus the burnout altitude to 80 km or so. According to studies provided by Martin Marietta[4] to the Fletcher Commission, such a missile can be produced with one warhead or several MIRVs, and the weight (and cost) might be of the order of 10-15 per cent greater than that of a missile of least cost, which would correspond to perhaps a 150 second burn time.

THE STRATEGIC ARMS RACE

Some of the candidates most favoured for boost-phase intercept – X-ray laser weapons based in space and neutral-particle beams (hydrogen-atom beams) – are totally countered by burnout at 80 km altitude. Similarly, kinetic-energy kill vehicles deployed from satellites carrying tens or hundreds of them cannot respond in such a short time from durable satellite orbits.

Technology for intercept of RVs in mid-course poses the usual difficulty of distinguishing the RVs from light decoys, which in the form of multi-layer aluminised plastic balloons look simultaneously to radar, optical and infra-red sensors like similar balloons around the RVs themselves. The 30-minute flight time allows many more opportunities for destruction of these RVs (and decoys) by beam weapons or by kinetic-energy kill. However, weapons deployed in space seem to be vulnerable to space mines accompanying them for weeks or months in peacetime, and to beam-ASAT capability if such existed.

Terminal defence of large soft targets such as cities has always suffered from the inability of the defence to attack the myriad decoys above the atmosphere and to attack the re-entry vehicles in the short time available after the decoys have been stripped off by the atmosphere. This problem would be aided by having available much cheaper interceptors, so that they could be launched to intercept at reasonable altitudes all those trajectories which appear threatening, even though many of the 'RVs' will turn out to have been decoys and need not have been intercepted.

Furthermore, it is possible in principle (although perhaps not in wartime) to use space-borne or airborne optical or infra-red systems rather than radars to observe the threat cloud, and these passive observations may be less vulnerable to destruction than a costly radar itself. Nevertheless, aircraft are far larger and more vulnerable than re-entry vehicles and are subject to attack, and the effectiveness of the sensors themselves may be reduced by nuclear explosions in space, by belts of space 'junk', or by saturating the ability of the defence to **track** each possible threat cloud. Furthermore, all of the techniques proposed for evasion or defeat of a terminal defensive system remain available, including anti-simulation, the use of manoeuvering re-entry vehicles to re-enter outside the bundle of threat trajectories and to run in at high velocity at low altitude.

Terminal defence of many hundreds of equivalent hard targets is feasible and has been feasible for 10 or 20 years. Here the defence takes advantage of the fact that a large nuclear warhead must come closer than 500 m in order to destroy the silo, and if only enough silos need survive to house the strategic retaliatory weapons, the other side cannot with comparable forces apply many warheads to **each** silo. Thus effective silo defences may follow the SWARMJET model, in which tens of thousands of non-nuclear unguided rockets are launched to intercept an incoming RV at 500-1000 m standoff. Or the defender may bury a nuclear explosive charge 1 km north of each of the silos, with the resulting hundreds of thousands of tonnes of earth thrown into the air being an effective barrier to an RV attacking the silo.

Thus it is **easy** to ascribe a role for ABM in defeating a stylised attack, but what is difficult is to eliminate the capacity of the other side to destroy the society, and thus to 'render nuclear weapons impotent and obsolete'.

A lot of technological evolution for strategic defence is thus plainly **irrelevant** to changing the reality of strategic deterrence of nuclear war by threat of retaliation.

Anti-satellite Weapons

These are covered in other papers (see pp.99-123) but I note here that the technologies advanced for use as defence against ballistic missiles almost all have greater (and sometimes real) effectiveness in the ASAT role. For instance, satellites move in general for very long periods on well-defined trajectories. There is no air surrounding satellites, so that X-ray laser and neutral-particle beam weapons have unimpeded access to the satellites.

Furthermore, a totally different and effective ASAT is at hand, using not new technology but **old** technology - the 'space mine'. A space mine is a small satellite equipped with a sensor and manoeuvering capability, and with a communication link to its headquarters. It is placed in orbit with the aid of ground-based radars and other sensors, and after being so emplaced within lethal range of its quarry (perhaps 1 km or less), its job is simply to accompany its quarry at a suitable distance, for the most part passively accommodating to the laws of orbital dynamics, and gently manoeuvering if the quarry manoeuvres, in order to remain within range. The space mine is likely to be more dense than the quarry satellite, even though smaller, so that at low altitudes it may have to augment its drag by firing a retrograde drag make-up engine in order to stay within range of the quarry satellite.

In an era of free navigation in space, such as exists on the oceans, there would be no bar to the emplacement of space mines. On the other hand, if the quarry satellite launched a blinding attack against the space mine, the space mine would immediately destroy the quarry satellite in peacetime. It is clear also that defensive satellites accompanied by space mines would be destroyed when offensive missiles were launched against the defender.

Satellites at low altitude are already vulnerable to ABM systems and in wartime to nuclear-armed ICBMs. They are vulnerable to the Soviet ASAT weapon tested 20 times since 1968, and to the (nominally ABM) US Homing Overlay Experiment Interceptor demonstrated on 10 June 1984, at Kwajalein. Satellites at low altitude will soon be vulnerable to the US ASAT weapon to be launched from a small two-stage rocket carried by a US F-15 aircraft.

In general, destroying a few satellites over a period of a day or so is a far simpler task than destroying thousands of ICBM boosters during a minute or less, or tens or hundreds of thousands of RVs and decoys during their flight of 30 minutes.

Non-nuclear Weapons and Delivery Means

In the context of the strategic arms race, either the USA or the Soviet Union might achieve the capability to destroy the other by use of strategic biological weapons, but that act (even assuming it were contemplated) could be deterred by threat of nuclear retaliation. Nevertheless, one can imagine non-nuclear strategic weapons (capable of reaching the territory of a nation), such as highly accurate ICBM or space-based weapons, guided to an accuracy of 1 metre or better, and therefore capable of destroying ICBMs in their silos, oil storage tanks, individual rooms in buildings, and the like. One could also imagine lasers in orbit capable of melting ICBM boosters in the lower atmosphere, which would clearly be capable also of igniting oil storage tanks, buildings, and the like. Of course, particular countermeasures are available to these non-nuclear weapons. Individual silos could have stand-off armour some tens of metres above, and a pond of water overhanging the roof of a building would do nicely to render space-based lasers 'impotent and obsolete'. So would a space mine.

The main point, however, is that these non-nuclear strategic weapons, if they threatened the survival of a nation, could be deterred by the use of nuclear weapons.

Navigation

Terminal homing is one type of navigation incorporated in the US Pershing II missile. Additional navigation aids are available in the US Navstar (Global Positioning System - GPS) satellite system, and in a similar Soviet system. The US system will give navigation accuracy to 10 metres in 3 dimensions anywhere in the world, and it would allow far more flexibility in basing inexpensive strategic missiles as mobile systems. It would also allow dormant basing without loss of accuracy. Ground-based transmitters of similar format could be used in the missile launch areas in order to avoid the potential loss of accuracy accompanying destruction of the navigation satellite system.

Improved navigation accuracy increases the threat to small hard targets, but it does not increase the threat against military-industrial targets. Lower-cost guidance systems can add to stability by allowing the economical redeployment of accurate RVs as single-warhead weapons.

Beam Weapons

It is essential to recognise the destabilising aspects of space weaponry. Because satellites are so vulnerable to space mines and other space weapons, the contemplation of space defences is likely to lead to a battle for control over space in peacetime.

In this regard, it is important to note the prospect for developing ABM weapons as effective ASAT weapons, as apparently advocated by Keyworth[5], and it is useful to note that some weapons which would be very difficult to employ in the ABM mode could be perfectly good and quite effective ASAT systems.

Take, for instance, a neutral-particle beam (NPB) weapon, consisting of an accelerator of negative hydrogen ions to an energy of about 100 MeV. Such an accelerator might produce a beam current of 0.1 ampere (of protons neutralised by their bound electrons), for a beam power of 10 MW.

At a 2 microradian beam divergence, a NPB accelerator in low earth orbit (LEO) might produce an irradiated region at geosynchronous (GEO) of some 100 m diameter, and at a level of radiation suitable for upset of electronics (100 Jkg^{-1}), irradiation for 20 seconds at a power level of 10 MW would suffice.

Note that the NPB for **ASAT use need not solve the problem** of discriminating mid-course RVs from decoys; it need not be frustrated by burn-out of boosters within the atmosphere in the boost-phase intercept mode, and need not be equipped with highly capable beam switching and bending systems, but need only point the accelerator and traverse it at a predetermined rate in order to irradiate the target satellite.

In the absence of a ban on ASAT tests and on weapons in space, a nation deploying such an NPB device is sure to find it accompanied by space mines, whether the other side is capable of neutral-particle-beam technology in space or not.

Command and Control

In regard to the strategic forces, the most important requirement for command and control is to **restrain** the forces when they are not to be used. To perform even the minimal deterrent role of retaliation after receipt of a strategic attack, the forces **must** be capable of being launched. If only procedural safeguards keep them from launching in peacetime, it is all too easy to imagine either hardware failures, failures of procedure, or misunderstandings which will result in the launch and explosion of nuclear weapons. So an important application of technology in strategic command and control is the so-called permissibe action link (PAL) which was introduced into US forces in the 1960s. Independent of the launch vehicle, the PAL requires that a correct sequence of digits be entered into the warhead via an electrical communication, in order that the warhead be enabled to explode. Launch without the correct code will result in no nuclear explosion at all.

Of course, if one side is contemplating a first strike against the other, knowing that the retaliatory strike cannot effectively take place without the availability of the PAL codes, it becomes a matter of high priority to interdict the communications which bring the PAL codes. It is possible, however, to hold the codes at various levels, and with various safeguards, so that if they cannot be transmitted from their central repository, they can with some time delay be made available from physical repositories in the field.

Even without PAL, a responsible strategic posture requires that the political leader, and not the military leadership, prescribe the nature and time of retaliation. It is a matter of survival for the nation itself to ensure that the strategic forces are not launched in peacetime (inevitably bringing retaliation) and that they are credibly promised to be launched themselves in retaliation. It is possible to contemplate interfering with this response (by 'decapitation'), but such interference can be prevented. The death of the leader (the US President) is countered by 'devolution' – the process by which successor presidents are chosen with the same powers of leadership. Each of these successors has the same power as the President, and it is, of course, essential that communications and information be available to the successor so that a retaliatory strike can eventually be mounted.

It is possible to imagine a second case, however, in which

the communication links to or from the leader are severed, so that it is not constitutionally possible for another to assume the responsibilities of President. Nevertheless, in my opinion, it is both possible and essential that the leader be able to **pre-delegate** authority for control of the strategic forces. Thus one sees the necessity for a system which enables people to assume responsibility for launch of the force, while enabling the leader himself to reliably **restrain** any other launch command so long as the leader is in communication.

Technology for command and control of strategic forces at the minimal required level can be made robust against the effects of the electromagnetic pulse (EMP) from nuclear explosions, and can be provided with sufficient redundancy so that it survives a nuclear attack. Nevertheless, nuclear war can reduce very much the reliability of the assessments involved in control of the strategic forces, and the attempt to decapitate the other side will surely result only in less responsible control over the retaliatory force. The technology of fibre-optic communication, mobile satellite ground terminals, and the like, can help to preserve a greater degree of flexibility and assessment, but the primary lesson to be learned is that attack on the command and control system will reduce the restraint on the forces of the other side.

If one imagines building specialised forces to attack hardened communication sites and thus to eliminate the command and control system, one faces at any time the ability of the other side to launch its forces in a less responsible fashion. Over the long run, all that can be done is to drive the other side to intersperse its command and control system with the society itself - by using vans or buses containing highly redundant mobile satellite ground terminals, and thus to ensure that so long as the society itself survives, the command and control will as well.

Treaty Verification

The advanced technology of sensors, communications, and processing has given increased confidence in warning of threatening moves on the other side, in verification of compliance with arms control treaties, and the like.

The technology of seismic detection is very largely in the public domain, and here the results of Everendon[6] regarding the unexpectedly good propagation of high frequency seismic waves (in the 30 Hz range) are of importance. These have apparently been detected in nordic seismic arrays from Soviet underground tests at Semipalatinsk and these high frequencies provide an improved discriminant between small explosions and earthquakes.

In verifying other possible arms control treaties, the information is not available publicly, but authoritative statements from individuals long involved in such activities must bear some weight. An article by R. Jeffrey Smith[7] quotes Leslie Dirks and others as optimistic on the verifiability of a ban on ASAT tests, despite an Administration report of 31 March 1984 to the US Congress emphasising difficulties of verification in any case and the impossibility of verifying a 'comprehensive ASAT ban'. The draft treaty presented to the Senate Foreign Relations Committee on 18 May 1983, bans ASAT **tests** as well as test or deployment of space weapons and is thus verifiable; it does not ban **possession** of all ASAT capabilities.

Summary

As has been the case for many years, the maintenance of superpower security by deterrence of nuclear war by threat of retaliation remains feasible. The technological arms race for the most part involves the assertion of capabilities which cannot in reality be exercised, and the denial of capabilities which were probably not useful or practical in the first place. Nevertheless, the interests of technologists on both sides spur this technological arms race, as does the claim that there is some relevance to the notion that one side or the other is 'ahead' in some measurement of force structure.

In my opinion, a small part of the effort put into the technological arms race could better be applied to rapidly achieving the following posture between the United States and the Soviet Union, with corresponding reductions and restraint to follow as the major change in attitude is reflected in agreements of broader adherence:

- 1000 nuclear warheads for US and Soviet forces.
- Assured survival of society by threat of retaliation – no counterforce against strategic forces.
- Preserve ABM treaty.
- Ban ASAT and space weapons.
- Emphasise non-proliferation of nuclear weapons, using all available national sanctions. (A comprehensive test ban treaty is essential).

The technological arms race, though unnecessary, is not benign. It will stop only when the leadership and the citizenry recognise its danger and that there is a safer alternative.

References

1. General Brent Scowcroft, Report of the President's Commission on Strategic Forces, US Government Printing Office, 11 April 1983.
2. General Brent Scowcroft, Report of the President's Commission on Strategic Forces, US Government Printing Office, 21 March 1984.
3. C. Weinberger, Soviet Military Power - 1984, US Department of Defense, April 1984.
4. M. Marietta, 'Short Burn-time ICBM Characteristics and Considerations' (Briefing to the Fletcher Commission), 20 July 1983, also E.A. Fitzgerald, 29 July 1983.
5. G.A. Keyworth, 'Reassessing Strategic Defense'. Remarks to the Council on Foreign Relations, 15 February 1984.
6. J. Everendon, 'Seismic Methods of Verification', presentation to the Conference on the Technical Means of Verification of Compliance With Arms Control Agreements, MIT, 1 February 1984.
7. R.J. Smith, 'Aerospace Experts Challenge ASAT Decisions', Science (18 May 1984) 693.

2 The Problem of Strategic Stability
MIKHAIL MILSTEIN

Though the problem of strategic stability is not a new one, we do not have a common and comprehensive definition of it. Partially this is due to the fact that we are dealing with a very complex and, to a certain extent, broad and even controversial issue that touches upon the most important aspect of the relations between the two sides. The controversial part lies in the different approaches to the conditions under which it is possible to achieve strategic stability. Roughly speaking, strategic stability should be defined as the state of politico-military relations and conditions which create mutual interest in peaceful co-existence between the two sides; settling disputes and managing crises in a peaceful way, so that the use of force shall be excluded or restrained in settling disputes, preventing them from growing into military conflicts. This can be achieved only on the basis of mutual interest in such a state, taking into account the security interests of both sides, mutual constraint, mutual concessions that do not affect the interests of national security of either side. Strategic stability cannot be one-sided.

Strategic stability is created through the interaction of many political, politico-military and military factors, among which the decisive role belongs to political factors. It is these that can create favourable conditions and the necessary pre-conditions for mutually acceptable concrete measures, directed at reaching strategic stability; the same factors may act the other way round: - hampering its achievement.

In an atmosphere of total lack of trust in each other, tense relations, hostile policy and hostile intentions - as we witnessed on the part of the present US Administration - it is extremely difficult, if not impossible, to solve the problem of strategic stability. In other words, stable political relations circumscribe stability.

That is why a better political climate, relaxation of international tension, measures capable of lessening mistrust

STRATEGIC STABILITY

between the two states, must be a necessary common condition for strategic stability.
Concretely speaking this calls for the following measures:

- renounce the policy of negotiating 'from a position of strength';
- take on a mutually acceptable and negotiated commitment of no-first-use of either nuclear or conventional forces, that is no-first-use of military force as a whole against each other;
- renounce attempts to achieve military superiority;
- strictly observe the principle of equality and equal security of both sides;
- lower the levels of military confrontation;
- accept definite negotiated norms of behaviour in the interests of averting nuclear war.

This list, of course, does not cover all measures necessary to lay the foundation for strategic stability. It can and should be extended. But one point is clear: as far as the Soviet Union is concerned, it has proposed more than once to reach an agreement on a complex of measures, capable of really lowering the level of military confrontation, to exclude the use of force, and the threat to use it from international life and thus strengthen strategic stability. These proposals are well known. But the US Administration still lays great hopes on military force, strives to achieve military superiority, and force its will on other nations. This leads to a sharp destabilisation of strategic relations, hinders reaching an agreement which would strengthen strategic stability, and increases the risk of a war.

Agreements on strategic offensive arms limitation and reduction, and continuity of this process, are of great importance for strengthening strategic stability. It was not by chance that in the joint Soviet-American declaration on principles and main directions, following the SALT II negotiations (18 June 1979), both sides pledged themselves to continue efforts 'to seek measures strengthening strategic stability, including the limitation of strategic offensive arms, which are most destabilizing to the strategic balance, and lower and avert the risk of a surprise attack' in order to lower and avert the threat of a nuclear war.

Unfortunately, these negotiations were broken off because of the USA, thus adversely affecting the creation of the necessary conditions to strengthen strategic stability in relations between the USA and the USSR. As already stated, one cannot isolate arms limitation from political relations and political conditions. They are closely interconnected and affect each other.

In this connection, one should mention the role of confidence-building measures in strengthening strategic stability. It is very important to have clarity on this issue, especially when this problem of confidence-building measures is widely discussed at the Stockholm Conference on Confidence- and Security-Building measures.

The importance of creating a climate of mutual trust by strengthening broad confidence-building measures in the politico-military field cannot be overestimated. But at the same time we must not restrict confidence-building measures to some military and technical measures only, for example, in the field of exchanging information on manoeuvres, changes of location, building lines of communication, some joint mechanisms, and so on. All this is certainly important for the strengthening of strategic stability. But confidence-building measures should not be viewed from a strictly technical point of view only. Would not a good strategic arms limitation treaty based on the principle of equality and equal security be the best confidence-building measure? Or such politico-military measure as no-first-use of military force, and an agreement on sustaining peaceful relations between states belonging to the two military alliances? The same can be attributed to an agreement on no-first-use of nuclear weapons, and certain norms of behaviour. Without doubt, these are very serious confidence-building measures. Such agreements lay down definite obligations, create a framework for better relations, making it possible to examine problems and find new approaches to strategic interrelations. Technical measures are important, but to give full attention only to the technical side may create a feeling of false security.

If the situation remains as it is now, if the arms race keeps on going intensely and rapidly along the same lines, and if there are no common steps to prevent crises, we may find ourselves involved in conflicts and a war, even if we had technical confidence-building measures. That is why it is necessary to improve substantially the political situation and political relations so as to create the genuine strategic stability needed to revive détente. In this context the Soviet point of view, in contrast to the American, is based on the assumption that it is necessary to take into consideration both political and pure military-technical measures, while focusing mainly on political measures and decisions.

Let us now discuss how the development of arms and military-strategic concepts affect strategic stability. It goes without saying that the main destabilising factor, which erodes strategic stability, is the attempt by the United States to break the existing military parity - which is the basis of strategic stability - and gain military superiority. The greatest danger of destabilising the strategic situation lies in the development and the deployment of weapon systems (for example, with high accuracy or short flight-time) which create the illusion of being able to wage and win a nuclear war, and the possibility to carry out a 'first'-disarming strike. Such weapons are not only land-based; the American sea-launched (SLBM) 'Trident-II' system, or 'Pershing-II' can be treated as 'first-strike' weapons.

Another destabilising factor can be the introduction of weapons which start new dangerous trends in the arms race (for example, the creation and deployment of weapons in outer space). The wide-scale development of ballistic missile defence with the use of outer space for this purpose, and the renunciation of the existing ABM agreement, must be viewed as serious and dangerous factors, destabilising the strategic balance.

In this connection, the development, acceptance and approval of military-strategic concepts, which contain the possibility of waging and winning a nuclear war; concepts of limited or protracted nuclear war; and the possibility of a first-disarming strike, should be also attributed to the factors which in fact nullify the complex and delicate efforts undertaken to create and strengthen strategic stability.

These considerations on the issue of strategic stability are mainly raised in order to stimulate a discussion on this important problem.

The working out of a common definition of the term 'strategic stability' and what it should include, may lead to a better understanding of each other's intentions and to the taking of effective measures to strengthen real and not false strategic stability.

3 Escalation and Arms Control
LAWRENCE FREEDMAN

Escalation is the dominant concept in contemporary strategic studies. If arms control is to have the relationship with strategic theory expected of it then it must fit in somehow with this concept. The obvious connection is with the movement from the MBFR talks through INF to START, for this can be seen to mirror the movement up from conventional to intercontinental nuclear war. A better understanding of the mechanism of escalation might therefore help us work out how these separate negotiating efforts can or should fit together. Unfortunately, there are tensions within the concept which, in the end, help more to highlight than to resolve the tensions within arms control.

Escalation refers to the process of qualitative change in the character of a war. It involves transcending limits and is therefore to be distinguished from straightforward increases in the intensity of warfare being fought within those limits (though there will be points where the increased scale and tempo of the fighting must change its character). Historically the key thresholds, in addition to the rather fundamental first step of opening hostilities, have related to a dramatic extension of the combat zone, the use of unusually unpleasant weapons, the breakdown of distinctions between the civilian and the military, and the various means by which extra belligerents are drawn into a war. Since 1945 the movement from the use of conventional to nuclear munitions has become the main preoccupation, but in any discussion of the subject it is important not to lose sight of the more traditional forms of escalation.

Identifying the Process of Escalation

In deterring, planning or conducting a war it is clearly vital that the possible processes of escalation be properly identified and understood. Part of this understanding will be whether the thresholds in question are likely to be passed deliberately or inadvertently. Is escalation likely to occur as a result of considered judgment and choice, or through some essentially uncontrollable process, propelled forward in the confusion and uncertainty of battle? If it is the former, then the course of a war can be controlled and it may therefore become a tolerable prospect; if the latter, then the risks of things getting badly out of control may be just too great. Thus uncontrollable escalation offers the greatest deterrent to war, but it also threatens to make the experience much more frightening should deterrence fail.

This dilemma is, of course, central to all thinking about nuclear war and peace. It is reflected in arms control in the tension between the two classic aims of reducing the risk of war but keeping the violence in check should war, nevertheless, occur. The traditional concept of disarmament attempts to reconcile these two objectives by assuming that the risks of war are in some way related to the amount of weaponry available for fighting them. This notion is surprisingly resilient despite impressive evidence to contradict it. The sources of war are political. It is the failure of the disarmers to come to grips with this fact that has been responsible for much of their past grief. It may be the case that conscious arms racing sends unfortunate political signals to the other side. However, it may also be the case that a stress on the military relationship as the key to a more amicable political relationship may end up exaggerating the importance of the military factor, with consequences utterly opposed to those intended. This question is beyond the scope of this paper but it is fair to note that it is as much a problem for arms control as for disarmament.

The disarmers' basic objective of removing war as a feasible option for the settlement of disputes can only work at all if it works absolutely. Partial disarmament will leave sufficient wherewithal to start a war and cannot prevent rapid rearmament once war has begun. With conventional war, the disarmers can at least make the initial killing more restricted than it might otherwise have been, though possibly not that much unless inroads have been made into stocks of small arms. In the nuclear area partial disarmament offers no hope of containing the violence, given the destructive capacity of just a few weapons. This is true whether the disarmament has been achieved through international negotiations or in a nuclear first strike.

As complete nuclear disarmament is a remote possibility, to say the least, the international community, despite its better instincts, has been forced to follow the logic of arms control and seek to prevent war not by removing the instrumentalities but by emphasizing the likelihood of an unescapable catastrophe. There remains a hankering after reductions in the cost of building up and sustaining surplus military capacity. Again this particular objective for arms control is beyond the scope of this paper. All we need note here is that if financial savings are the main concern then conventional forces should be the area of concentration.

Crossing the Threshold

For the purposes of this paper the central objective is the avoidance of war. According to the conventional wisdom, this objective can be secured through an understanding of the escalation process. First, it is vital that the movement from peace to war is not governed by escalatory pressures. That is any decision to open hostilities should be based on the exhaustion of diplomacy and not on the possibilities for achieving a quick victory or, more likely, the fear of the other side stealing a decisive advantage by anything from speedy mobilisation to a nuclear first strike. Some arms control activity is relevant here. The ABM Treaty helps deny the possibility of a nuclear first strike; CBMs should ensure that nothing untoward develops out of military manoeuvres; the Hotlines provide a means of ensuring that if something untoward did seem to be developing lines of communication would be available to sort it out before having to jump to hasty conclusions.

Having established as many mechanisms as possible to ensure that escalation is firmly controlled at this stage, this effort is capped by insisting that if war did start then further control of escalation would be virtually impossible. There is one large exception to this judgement. The threshold that divides conventional from nuclear warfare is recognised to be so fundamental that it would not be passed lightly. Such a step would be a matter for political decision. This can be clearly seen in the mechanisms set up to control nuclear use. These are tight, centralised and inhibitive, reflecting an anxiety probably felt as much among political leaderships as among their populations that nuclear war should not be entered into as a result either of accident or inadvertence. Some have argued that these procedural safeguards should be reinforced by solemn pledges not to be the first to use nuclear weapons. Aside from the dubious value of promises that would have to be kept in circumstances much more uncertain and desperate than those in which they are made, it is not altogether clear that the primary war-avoidance function of arms control is served by encouraging the view that a future war would be significantly less horrific than would probably be the case.

NATO, of course, puts great emphasis in its deterrent posture on the probability that the nuclear threshold will be passed. Forces have been structured on this assumption. Nevertheless, in its actual organisation and procedures for conflict, NATO does not follow through this logic to the point of actively facilitating passing the nuclear threshold through, for example, making it easy for field commanders to get access to nuclear stocks and release authority.

Peacetime activity, therefore, focuses on the two great thresholds - peace to war and conventional to nuclear. There is debate concerning other thresholds and their likely resilience in war, but the arms control implications of these debates have not been fully worked out. The greatest speculation has concerned the viability of thresholds once nuclear engagements have begun. In particular, there has been great interest in the possibility of conducting a limited nuclear war, which is normally taken to mean nuclear exchanges either confined to the battlefield or to the allies of the superpowers. There are two points to be made on this issue. First, nobody can accurately anticipate the course of a nuclear war. It might very well be limited in some of the ways discussed in the specialist literature, though how limited it would appear to those involved is another matter. But it would be unwise to rely on such limitations holding. The second point is that because of this uncertainty, the discussion of the processes of nuclear escalation tends very much to reflect peacetime pre-occupations - especially the balance of risk among allies. When it is firmly stated in Europe that it would be impossible to control nuclear escalation, this reflects not so much analytical judgement as a worry that the Americans (or the USSR) might take unwarranted risks in the belief that they could escape the full consequences. In terms of the general deterrence to war this is clearly the view to encourage. If the perceptions that the culmination of the escalation process would be all-out counter-city exchanges between the superpowers - and that the process could be stopped well before this point - were correct then war might appear as a less dangerous option.

There seems to be comparatively little interest as to whether there might be distinct thresholds within the conventional phase. In part this must reflect the understandable obsession with nuclear warfare that leads to anything that might come before paling into insignificance, yet we know enough now about the conduct of conventional war to recognise that it can pass through a number of stages. To take one current example: as the Iran-Iraq war moves on to serious attacks on oil installations, the use of chemical agents and the threatened expansion to other Gulf states, it is getting harder to control and bring to an end.

All the experience with conventional war in fact tends to cast doubt on the simpler versions of the concept of escalation. If wars are actually to take the form of a series of definite steps through known boundaries, with each side anxious to avoid responsibility for taking such steps, then this normally requires at least one side to have sufficient military superiority to control the pace of the conflict and the fighting to be clearly linked to a political bargaining process. So long as military moves are expected to have their main value as a source of pressure in the search for a political settlement then there is some hope of controlling escalation. However, even here, it may well be that extra pressure calls for a degree of escalation. An even greater risk comes when one or both belligerents fear that any delay or restraint could lose them victory or cause them defeat. Another factor likely to interfere with attempts to limit escalation is the 'fog of war'. A local commander taking the initiative or feeling his hand forced by an enemy presence; failures of communication or intelligence; an inadvertent attack on the assets of a neutral.

A final supposition concerning the nature of escalation that is worth considering is the notion that the process picks up speed as each stage is passed until it reaches such a pace that no brakes can effectively be applied. Again this notion may only have slight relevance to actual war. In the early stages of a war, a military logic can suddenly be let rip after being held in check by a political logic. At this early stage the fighting can be fast and furious, with probing actions serving to set the parameters of the conflict. After that things may settle down as both sides take stock before picking up later on. So there is no inevitable pattern to war and it is as well not to be surprised when events move faster than expected in the early stages - as happened, for example, in the Falklands. Moreover, the standards set in these early stages are likely to influence the readiness to consider restraint during the later stages. If a series of atrocities are believed to have occurred and peacetime agreements ignored then there is unlikely to be much response to calls for restraint and magnanimity.

The Case of Europe

What relevance does this analysis have for arms control? It suggests a number of factors that might aggravate a conflict, even one in Europe where the battle-lines are clearly drawn and the battle-plans have been carefully scripted. Taking the

case of Europe, which is the continent that has been the most subject to the attentions of arms controllers (which does not necessarily mean the most subject to the risks of war), a number of questions can be asked concerning the possibilities of a conflict getting out of hand:
- Does the anticipated path of escalation reflect what it makes most sense to say in peacetime or to do in war?
- Do agreements struck in happier times coincide with military logic and can observance be verified? If not, is there a danger that apparent non-observance will exacerbate the conflict?
- Are there means for ensuring that diplomatic activity continues even after the outbreak of hostilities? How resilient are they likely to prove?
- What are the most likely strategies to be adopted during the build-up to a war and its early stages? To what extent have these strategies been designed with regard to:

  - the impression their initiation is likely to make on the other side;
  - the degree to which they will trigger counter-measures;
  - the amount of early contact with adversary forces likely to be involved;
  - the extent to which once set in motion they can be stopped, reversed or redirected;
  - their implications for the neutral and non-aligned and the geographic spread of the war?

- How fixed is the pattern of alliances, and what factors are likely to affect decisions on belligerence or non-belligerence?
- To what extent will it be possible to shield civilians from the direct effects of the conflict?

A certain amount of analysis and intuition is available to help us answer most of these questions. There have been studies looking at, for example, the likelihood of early naval engagements around the northern waters, the pressures on the Warsaw Pact to move quickly once hostilities have begun, the possible impact of early use of deep-strike weapons, the ambiguity of the role of chemical weapons, the loyalty of various countries to their particular alliances. What is notable, however, is how little these issues are discussed in an arms control context.

Grand Accounting Exercise

Before moving on to discuss the sort of lessons that might be drawn for arms control from this analysis it might be useful to discuss first the features of arms control, as it has been practised up to now, that make it insensitive to these issues. The form arms control took in the 1970s was of a grand accounting exercise. The major effort involved drawing up inventories of the arsenals of East and West so as to be able to undertake a close comparison and eventually, through hard bargaining, iron out the differences. Such an exercise is intended more to create a visible equality which is believed to have important political connotations, than to reflect purist notions of strategic stability. Its relevance to the objectives of either preventing the outbreak of war, or limiting the costs should war occur, is therefore slight, except to the extent that the exercise can contribute to better political relations, something which in fact it has notably failed to do.

As an accounting exercise, arms control is best applied to forces which are distinctive and easy to count, which are found in broadly comparable numbers on both sides and which are readily understood in political as much as military terms. Given this, it is not surprising that arms controllers have felt most at home, and come closest to success at the strategic nuclear level. However, in practice it has proved to be not only difficult to reach a satisfactory agreement at this level, but it has also been difficult to hold the discussions at this higher strategic level. Nuclear arms control is subject to a persistent downward push.

This downward push is a result of the inherent problems in drawing mutually acceptable lines around the systems to be discussed. Are strategic weapons defined by their range or what they can hit? Are only superpower forces to be included or also those of allies? Is the formal role assigned to particular weapons relevant or is it necessary to look at what they might do if their role was changed? Despite a determined resistance, questions such as these have forced nuclear arms control away from the clear categories of ICBMs, SLBMs and long-range bombers into the more complex areas of the whole panoply of American 'forward-based systems' (medium-range dual-capable aircraft, carrier-based aircraft, and now cruise and Pershing-II missiles), British and French forces, and Soviet systems directed against Western Europe and Asia.

If the Soviet Union is now presenting its shorter-range SS-22s as a response to the new American missiles, then presumably they will have to be discussed as well; indeed many in the West are already anxious to throw battlefield nuclear weapons into the negotiating pot. And once one is into the areas of dual-capable aircraft and cruise missiles, and nuclear systems whose purported military functions might be met just as easily by new conventional weapons, then are we not caught by the unavoidable facts that everything is related to everything else, that all boundaries are hopelessly arbitrary? Eventually, sheer consistency demands that all weapons are to be included until some grand and comprehensive audit can be concluded.

Apart from battlefield nuclear weapons, which have so far been confined to bit parts in the main talks, all types of forces are being discussed at the negotiating table (or have been until recently). But the principles governing discussions of conventional forces are quite different from those which govern talks on nuclear forces. At the Vienna talks on Mutual Force Reductions, it did not prove possible to develop general rules for counting equipment; the basic unit of account is numbers of fighting men. Even with quite generous margins of error, it has not proved possible to agree on a common data base, and it is not altogether clear what it would prove if agreement were reached and a common ceiling achieved. A simple head count reveals little about the durability of deterrence, let alone the outcome of battle. This requires consideration of equipment, training, stamina and doctrine as well as geography and terrain. Moreover, the guidelines area within which the head count is taking place bears little relationship to the areas within which the main movements of forces would take place in war. The most useful outcome of the Vienna talks, apart from releasing scarce diplomatic resources which ought to be put to more productive uses, would be in providing scope for a reduction in defence spending. Any impact on the security of nations would be indirect.

From this discussion it can be seen that whereas wars start from the bottom up, arms control has worked from the top down. Neither the upward movement of war nor the downward movement of arms control is smooth and unilinear. However, because the relevant factors and their relative weight are quite different in each, the thresholds that combat forces and negotiators come up against bear little relation to each other. Furthermore, while deterrence requires that governments contemplating war lack confidence that any thresholds can be sustained, arms control only prospers to the extent that divisions, however artificial, can be established and forces thereby dealt with in discrete and manageable lumps.

Political Approach

The first conclusion to emerge from this analysis is that if our basic objective is to save resources in the defence area, then the activity should be organised with this objective in mind. The artificiality of the exercise should be recognised and the main effort redirected towards areas where the forces of the two sides are comparable and susceptible to the requisite accounting procedures. It is probably the case that strategic arms remain the area best suited to this sort of treatment, even though conventional forces are by far the most expensive.

If, however, the main objective is to prevent war, then we need to look at arms control in a different light. For a start we need to purge ourselves of the idea that we can control wars by controlling arms. It would be better if a lot of the effort devoted to arms control were put into ensuring that there are robust international institutions capable of sustaining diplomatic activity in times of tension and even through the early stages of war. As was argued earlier, any hope of controlling the pace of escalation during its early stages depends on continuing diplomatic activity.

Perceptions of the likely course and consequences of war are relevant to its likely outbreak. In shaping these perceptions, arms control has played a marginal and sometimes perverse role. In part, this is because the balance of terror is essentially so formidable and awe-inspiring that there is slight risk of political leaders failing to take it into account in their calculations. In helping to undermine any lingering prospects of first strikes, the 1972 ABM Treaty helped to reinforce this perception; in encouraging arguments that the balance is dangerously delicate and that visible numerical disparities really matter (used by both supporters and opponents of arms control) the discussions on offensive arms may have had a negative effect.

The separation of negotiations on 'intermediate' from 'strategic' nuclear forces, as if these really were distinct classes of weapons and so presumably occupying distinct stages in the ladder of escalation, has been particularly unfortunate. Not only has this separation made the negotiations themselves more difficult, but also the view of the escalation process implied is unhelpful. As the history of the negotiations amply illustrates, the separation between these two types of forces is as difficult to maintain in arms control as it would be in war. If they are ever to make progress, this will only be through either an informal or a formal merger.

Agreements at this level, so long as they can actually be concluded, can make a contribution by strengthening the sense of nuclear risk associated with any great power conflict. But a comparable contribution would not be made by agreements taking the same form but covering systems (nuclear as well as conventional) designed for the battlefield. If controls are to be exercised at this level, then they should be firmly based on at least some analysis of the processes of escalation and the implications of alternative military strategies. Such an analysis points us away from 'bean-counting'. Instead, we need to look at questions relating to command and control of forces in crisis and conflict, the inter-actions at such times between the preparatory moves of the two sides (mobilisation and manoeuvre), the impact of terrain and geography at possible points of contact, the complications resulting from the use of dual-capable systems and so on. In these terms, the new Stockholm negotiations are much more promising that MBFR. The confidence-building measures, such as notification of out-of-garrison movements, with which they are currently concerned, are of limited strategic significance, but they at least point in the right direction. It would be extremely unfortunate if these talks were actually allowed to turn to Conventional Disarmament in Europe, instead of moving on to discuss, if not legislate upon, the important linkages between strategy and crisis management.

Conclusion

The argument of this paper is that both arms control and disarmament as currently conceived and practiced, are mainly irrelevant to the fundamental issues of war and peace in Europe and elsewhere. This is largely because the basic military relations are far more stable than they are normally given credit for. The sources of instability are therefore largely political and this is where the most intensive and constant activity is required. The high priority tended to be accorded to arms control should not be allowed to detract from more traditional forms of diplomatic activity. The most useful development in international discussions on military matters would be a re-orientation away from issues of numerical balance to those connected with the actual preparations for the deployment and employment of armed forces in crisis and in conflict.

4 Crisis Control Measures
RICHARD SMOKE

Introduction

The recent years have witnessed mounting interest, at least in the West, in measures intended to improve both superpowers' capacity to retain full control of events in any future global crisis, and to terminate the crisis short of nuclear war. These measures, and accompanying practices and perspectives, are generally referred to in the United States as 'crisis control' or 'crisis management'. Representative measures now being discussed or hypothesised include: improvements in the Hotline, the addition of further high-speed communications links, the creation of some type of joint 'crisis control centre', various kinds of information-exchange arrangements, and other pre-arranged crisis procedures.

This paper attempts to show both the analytic and the social sources of the rising interest in crisis control; to sketch the history of how the topic has developed in the West; and to illuminate the relationships between crisis control, confidence-building measures, and related ideas. Throughout, the focus is on measures that the superpowers could agree upon to take jointly or in parallel. Steps that could be taken unilaterally are somewhat tangential to the current focus of American 'crisis control' studies.

Sources

Growing interest in crisis control springs both from analytic arguments that at least some kinds of crises may be growing more likely, and from social developments of the last four years. It is useful to examine these sources separately.

(1) There has been no Soviet-American confrontation, posing the risk of a military clash in the perception of either capital, for more than ten years. (The last occurred during the 1973 Middle East War.) This absence of crisis is the more

noteworthy because the Soviet-American relationship overall has steadily worsened during that time, and now is chillier than at any time since the depth of the Cold War. From this interesting fact opposite conclusions can be drawn.

Proponents in Washington of the 'peace through strength' perspective argue that this result is not surprising, and indeed is to be expected. In this analysis, the US military buildup of the last 8 years, greatly accelerated by the Reagan Administration, and the resolute declaratory policy of that Administration, discourage Soviet aggression of all kinds and hence reduce the probability of crisis. Similar arguments are made by 'peace through strength' proponents in Moscow, who assert that Soviet power had the effect of curbing American adventurism.

Proponents of détente, and many arms control advocates, in both capitals conclude from the state of superpower relations that the probability of a serious crisis is rising, and that we may have been fortunate to have avoided one for this long. This group ascribes the absence of crisis to secure and roughly equivalent deterrent forces, to a somewhat greater degree of mutual understanding of 'ground rules' achieved during the détente period, to rational restraint, and to other factors. In this view, however, sustained strong hostility and an accelerated arms race can only raise the likelihood of some kind of confrontation.

Hence **one** analytic argument holds that the probability of crisis rises in tandem with the hostility of the Soviet-American relationship. Unquestionably, the interest of some specialists, institutes, foundations and others in America, in crisis control measures, results in fact from their concern that current trends in that relationship may be making a crisis dangerously possible.

A second analytic argument, or class of arguments, focuses not on the bilateral relationship but on the gradual rise of other dangers. The possible categories of scenarios include:

- **Third World crises and wars.** They can engage the superpowers, draw them in, and become the occasion of a major global crisis. In the Western perspective, the Middle East and the Persian Gulf are obvious candidates.
- **Nth-party nuclear wars.** As weapons proliferate in coming decades, there is a rising probability of 'small' nuclear wars occurring between other nations, the origins and goals of which would not, in the first instance, be part of the East-West competition. An India-Pakistan, Argentina-Brazil, or Israel-Syria/Iraq nuclear war might be examples. Such an event might not trigger a Soviet-American confrontation, but it is not clear that it would

not.
- **Nuclear terrorism.** The threat or actual destruction of a US, Soviet, or allied city by a terrorist group possessing one or more nuclear weapons is also increasingly worrisome. Here too, it is far from certain that such an event would trigger a superpower confrontation, but far from certain that it would not.
- **Agent provocateur attacks.** Also called 'disguised third-party attacks'. In one version, an 'irresponsible' nation or terrorist group might wish to try deliberately to trigger a Soviet-American war, perhaps by the use of one or more nuclear weapons, from a belief that their own group or nation would be in a relatively better position in a post-World War III world. In another version, a third party who was involved in a regional war in which the superpowers were intervening might explode a nuclear weapon within the homeland of either superpower in an effort to trigger that superpower's immediate, overwhelming intervention in the regional war.
- **Detonations of unknown origin.** Also unlikely but possible, a detonation could occur whose origin and purpose was not immediately clear.

These categories are not mutually exclusive and more than one scenario could occur almost simultaneously. For instance, the 'best' time for an agent provocateur attack is when a sharp superpower crisis is already ongoing for other reasons. Needless to say there are other ways of breaking down the problem. (See for instance Frei[1])

In short, analytic arguments have developed that some kinds of crises, strictly bilateral or otherwise, may be growing more likely, suggesting therefore that new means of controlling crises might well be examined.

(2) The last four years have witnessed an enormous change in the social environment in which arms control and strategic issues are addressed.

Fear of nuclear war has motivated, at least temporarily, mass public movements in the West, including large peace demonstrations, huge audiences for television shows depicting the aftermath of nuclear war, uncountable numbers of workshops, conferences and other public education activities, and determined campaigns to halt several specific American weapons systems.

Some groups and some thinkers have sought to reject deterrence as a fundamental basis for policy, at least in the long term; but the difficulty in finding an acceptable alternative has driven the bulk of the concerned public into a position of accepting deterrence and seeking a halt and reversal of

the arms race. In America the Freeze campaign, by its simplicity and comprehensiveness, has attracted the support of millions.
But the technical, and still more the political, difficulties in achieving a Freeze have dashed hopes for an early breakthrough. Meanwhile START, INF, and other negotiations have made no significant progress, and deployment has begun in Europe of the Pershing-IIs and GLCMs. The arms race speeds on and is so perceived.
Lacking success in halting and reversing the arms race, some of the more sophisticated elements among those concerned have been shifting their focus, at least partially, to asking 'How might a nuclear war actually begin?', and seeking to close off all pathways they discover. If the arms race cannot presently be halted, at least the greatest danger may be prevented, that of actual nuclear war itself.
The value of deterrence in forestalling deliberate nuclear war being implicitly conceded, two answers to this question present themselves. 'War by technical accident' is one. Known cases of false alarms in the US strategic warning systems, the now widely discussed dangers of 'launch on warning', and the hazards of the Pershings short flight time have drawn attention to risks created by weapons technology itself. There is widespread anxiety now that our machines may destroy us. Some computer may fail, or the systems may be wired to a hair-trigger. However much or little this anxiety is based on technical realities, it has itself become a psychological and social reality.
The other answer is 'war by escalation of a regional crisis'. Memories of various Middle East wars and crises, of East-West confrontations over Berlin, and above all of the Cuban Missile Crisis, remind everyone of times when nuclear warfare - despite deterrence - seemed a real danger. Wars throughout the Third World are if anything more numerous now than ever, and many possible 'ignition points' can be imagined for a dangerous superpower confrontation. Dimly the public senses, too, the analytic arguments about multiplying scenarios. There is growing public awareness, and anxiety, that some day some crisis might race out of control. Again, however much or little this anxiety is based in political and other realities, it is becoming itself a psychological and social one.
Both these answers focus on a potential East-West conflict that is not deliberate, at least not in its early stages. After the technical accident occurs, or after a regional crisis leads to superpower escalation, governments may be acting deliberately. But the ignition was not intended.

I have laid emphasis on the growing public awareness of these sorts of 'inadvertent' war because it is by no means impossible that this awareness could become a significant social force in the West. And it could result in pressures of various kinds on governments to alter their behaviour in crises and in situations that could become crises. Especially if 'classical' arms control continues to be seen for some time as fruitless or impossible, public anxiety about nuclear war could fasten on fears of 'inadvertent' war, with consequences that are not entirely predictable.

History

Interest among analysts in crisis control measures is not new. In 1960, for instance, a leading American specialist, Thomas Schelling, came to the annual Pugwash Conference (that year in Moscow) with a proposal for the two sides to agree to station observers in each other's homeland to spot city evacuations. The communications link that eventually became the Hotline was first proposed in a popular magazine article in 1960 and by a White House arms control panel in 1961.

But the establishment of the Hotline in 1963, following the Cuban Missile Crisis, seemed to satisfy the need for high speed direct communications. And the enormous increase in each side's 'national means' of gathering information provided each with many kinds of data that might otherwise have been sought by agreed joint measures. Obvious needs apparently were being met. Through the 1970s, advances on actual measures for use in a crisis were confined to simple technical improvements: converting the Hotline to satellite links (1971) and creating a small number of codes for communicating certain urgent messages by Hotline extremely quickly (1976). Meanwhile each side was making various improvements in its own capacities for command, control and communications (C^3I).

The two sides also agreed, during the détente period in the 1970s, on certain principles of behaviour in crises. The 'Prevention of Nuclear War Agreement' (1973) includes a statement that the superpowers will consult with each other in any situation carrying a higher than normal risk of nuclear war. The 'Accidents Agreement' (1971), widely regarded in the West as more significant, commits each side to the following:

- to notify the other at once in the event of an accidental or unauthorised event that could lead to a threatening nuclear detonation;
- to give notice of any missile test firings in the direction

of the other's homeland;
- to maintain and improve internal arrangements intended to prevent unauthorised or accidental nuclear use;
- and to 'act in such a way as to reduce the probability' of actions being misinterpreted should a nuclear incident occur.

Revival in the United States of analytic interest in creating additional joint measures for use in a crisis may perhaps be dated from 1981. In March of that year Senator Sam Nunn sent a query to the Strategic Air Command (SAC) about the capacity of both the USA and the USSR to cope with 'catalysts' of nuclear war more likely than deliberate attack, such as a disguised third-party attack. SAC conducted a study and concluded that both sides 'must dramatically improve' their capacity to cope with such catalysts.

Shortly thereafter Senators Nunn and Henry Jackson (later joined by Senator John Warner) proposed that the USA and USSR jointly create a 'military crisis control center'. Such a centre, perhaps located in a neutral country, would be staffed by personnel from both nations and would, among other things, monitor what are sometimes called 'extramural' nuclear weapons - those outside the arsenals of the established nuclear powers. In 1982, these Senators also co-sponsored an amendment to the 1983 defence budget authorisation bill, requiring the Defense Department to conduct a study of crisis control, including the following possibilities:

- a multinational crisis control centre to monitor extramural nuclear weapons;
- a Soviet-American forum for the exchange of information on the same subject;
- improvements in the Hotline; and
improvements in the arms control verification;
- measures to reduce the vulnerability of both sides' C^3I;
- measures to lengthen warning time of attacks.

About the same time, Senator Alan Cranston proposed that the superpowers station teams in each other's capitals to provide authoritative information in crises.

President Reagan announced, in speeches in Berlin and at the United Nations in June 1982, that the USA would propose to the Soviets some strategic 'confidence-building measures' intended to reduce the dangers of surprise attack and of war arising from uncertainty and miscalculation. In a speech on 22 November 1982 he announced three types of confidence-building measures that he had proposed in a letter to the Soviet leadership; he also directed American negotiators to discuss the three proposals in the Geneva START and INF talks. These measures were:

- advance notification by both parties of all launches of ICBMs, SLBMs, and intermediate-range missiles of the type being discussed at INF;
- mutual exchange of data on both strategic and intermediate-range forces;
- advance notification by both parties of all major military exercises worldwide, notably including strategic exercises.

On 11 April 1983, the Defense Department released its report in response to the Congressional amendment[2]. Secretary Weinberger's report pointed out that strengthening C^3I is already part of the Reagan Administration's strategic programme; that the Soviets have been carrying a similar effort; and that increasing warning time is not feasible.

The report rejected the concept of a multinational crisis control centre, partly because it would be far from the centres of decision-making in Washington and Moscow, and partly because it would add a time-consuming decision-making layer. If it included parties in addition to Americans and Soviets, it would be even more cumbersome and ineffective. The report also rejected the idea of a bilateral information exchange forum because it could be misused for gathering intelligence and disseminating disinformation. A substitute for these concepts, the report suggested, might be an agreement among the world's nations to consult in the event of a nuclear incident involving a terrorist group.

The Defense Department report not only accepted the desirability of improving the Hotline in certain respects, but proposed adding two more high-speed communications links. To the Hotline would be added a high-speed facsimile capability but not voice or video. A high-speed data link would be added from each national capital to the embassy in the opposite capital. And a Joint Military Communications Link would connect the two national military command centres with a high-speed facsimile transmission capability. This link, said the report, could be used for crisis communications not requiring the attention of the head of state, for transmitting urgent technical and military information in a crisis, for communications in a terrorist incident, and for some non-crisis functions. In its comment on the crisis control centre idea, the report said that this link might 'point the way to a bilateral mechanism linking separate crisis control bodies located in Washington and Moscow'.

Since the release of the Weinberger report, the USA and the USSR have agreed on adding the high speed facsimile capability to the Hotline. After three exchanges of technical working groups in 1983 and 1984, the two sides announced agreement in July 1984.

Meanwhile Senators Nunn and Warner co-sponsored, early in 1984, a Senate resolution, which commended the President for his confidence-building proposals and for initiating negotiations on the communications links, and urged him to pursue the possibility of negotiations for a joint crisis control centre. This resolution passed the Senate (by 82 to nil) in June 1984.

In the last year and a half, crisis control has also been commanding the attention of a significant number of analysts in the United States. A national conference of specialists, yielding a book on the subject, was held in Texas early in 1983. The Roosevelt Center for American Policy Studies created a working group, chaired by Senators Nunn and Warner, which released a report on crisis control later that year[3]. A team of specialists at Stanford University has published a booklet on the joint centre concept[4], and the Arms Control and Disarmament Agency contracted with a Harvard group for a report on crisis control as a whole[5]. Another conference, sponsored by the International Institute for Strategic Studies was held in London in April 1984. A number of other independent papers have been written, and the topic is now a common one in American arms control circles.

There have been recent indications that the highest levels of the Soviet government are taking an interest in at least some aspects of the subject. On the occasion of Vice-President Bush's visit to Moscow for the Andropov funeral, President Chernenko reportedly told Bush that there should be 'safeguards against any inadvertent use of nuclear weapons'. And on 2nd March 1984, Chernenko delivered a speech proposing that norms be formulated to guide the behaviour of nuclear powers.

Although the future of crisis control seems even more unpredictable than the future of other aspects of arms control the subject seems likely to command continuing interest, and could possibly capture tremendous interest.

Crisis Control and Confidence-building

The subject of crisis control is sufficiently amorphous that some clarifications may be helpful. For instance, measures to control crises and confidence-building measures are sometimes discussed as if they were nearly the same thing, but it is analytically useful to distinguish them.

Confidence-building measures may be most usefully defined as measures intended to increase confidence on one or both sides that actions taken by the other side, which might be misinterpreted as hostile or as preparatory to conflict, are not so intended in fact. This concept of 'confidence-building' applies to the measures agreed to in the Helsinki Final Act of 1975, to two of President Reagan's three confidence-building proposals of 1982, and to the confidence-building proposals advanced by the West in the Stockholm Talks that began in January 1984. In this meaning, confidence-building measures apply mainly to normal times. They help avoid miscalculation when nothing escalatory is actually occurring. Most of them do **not** apply or come into play when something escalatory **is** occurring, except in the sense that the indicator of confidence may be strikingly absent at a time when other intelligence indicates that something is afoot.

Crisis control measures are just the reverse. At least, the main focus of most American discussion of crisis control measures has been on the reverse situation. These measures are intended to come into play precisely when something escalatory is indeed occurring; the more critical the situation is becoming the more they should come into play. Hotlines, for instance, are reserved for acute situations. The greatest interest in crisis control centres has been sparked by the supposition that they could play some vital role, otherwise difficult or impossible to accomplish, in the midst of certain kinds of intense crises.

The distinction is helpful in the abstract, and does in fact correspond to the dominant usage of the two terms in American discourse. But the distinction is not always observed, and further ambiguity has been created by the meaning of 'crisis control' having enlarged to include some actions intended to help prevent crises.

Crisis Control and Crisis Prevention

Even a superficial examination of the question reveals that 'control' and 'prevention' can be divided only arbitrarily. Where 'prevention' leaves off and 'control' begins is mostly a matter of at what point one decided 'a real crisis' has started. In fact little crises are going on constantly at various points around the globe. The successful control of a relatively smaller crisis can be seen as the same thing as the prevention of a bigger one. The same is true at any point up the escalation ladder.

In current American usage, crisis control and crisis prevention have become combined in another way too. The crisis control measure that has caught the imagination of the officials, analysts and the informed public, far more than any other measure, is the joint crisis control centre. Although the glamorous aspect of this idea is its supposed uses in the midst of a crisis, most serious analyses of the concept have gone on to argue that it might also have significant uses in normal times, in a crisis preventative role. This possibility is suggested, for instance, in three of the best known analyses of the concept[3,4,5].

Crisis control and crisis prevention are sharply distinguished by those analysts who address 'crisis prevention' in a different sense: ways in which the USA and USSR might achieve written or unwritten understandings about 'ground rules' for their global competition, intended to keep the competition restrained and hence prevent crises. The Basic Principles Agreement of 1972 represented the first major East-West effort of this type. Crisis prevention in this sense, along with aspects of crisis management within a single government, was the topic of a Pugwash Workshop held in Geneva in December 1978 on 'Crisis Prevention and Crisis Management'. By common consent the leading American specialist on crisis prevention in this sense is Alexander George[6].

An Example of Analytic Ambiguity in a Successful Agreement

Although these various distinctions aid clarity in the analysis of the many issues that arise in this area, when theory turns to practice they tend to overlap. An example is provided by a Soviet-American agreement that many Western analysts now look to as a model for the kinds of limited but useful steps that can be taken — the Prevention of Incidents at Sea Agreement.

A series of increasingly severe and dangerous incidents between American and Soviet naval vessels, involving blocking action, 'shouldering', and in at least one case the aiming of weapons, led in 1972 to negotiations, mainly at the working level among naval officers, and an agreement that was unheralded and widely unnoticed at the time. The two sides agreed on 'rules of the road' for naval vessels at sea (later extended to civil maritime craft) intended to prevent future incidents. They also agreed to hold regular conferences to review any incidents that still occurred, to make further improvements in the procedures. In the years since, these measures have been almost completely successful in forestalling dangerous incidents, although several incidents have recurred that have posed little escalation danger.

Clearly this Agreement represents successful crisis prevention. It also can be regarded as a confidence-building measure of a kind, since it increased confidence on each side that the other did not want to seek naval incidents and would cooperate to avoid them. The aspect of the Agreement that involves ongoing procedures is cited by crisis control specialists, who assert the need for continuous, 'affirmative' action to monitor potential crises. For instance, some advocates of a joint, permanent crisis control centre suggest that such a centre could monitor and immediately resolve incidents of all kinds where the many forces of the superpowers can come in contact in all environments – sea, ground, air and space.

Conclusion

Crisis control is a complex and ambiguous subject. It is not limited to, or even centred on, technical and hardware questions. More than most aspects of arms control, it deeply involves political values, and questions of great political delicacy. Crisis control touches upon the most sensitive of all questions: how Washington and Moscow would make decisions on the threshold of a nuclear war.

Interest in developing new crisis control measures has, at least until very recently, been largely an American phenomenon. It may to some extent reflect an American cultural tendency to believe that conflicts are not thoroughly real, but can be partly or entirely cleared up through better communication and better negotiation. On the other hand, many conflicts historically **have** been exacerbated, and even pushed over the brink into war, by miscalculation, miscommunication, and misunderstandings. These can take many forms, but can be at least partially anticipated.

If the Hotline and its several improvements represent the 'first generation' of crisis control measures, the second generation is still in its infancy. A great deal of work will be required before measures can be designed whose value seems convincing. But a growing number of analysts believe that this work should be done.

The impulse towards a new generation of crisis control measures springs ultimately from two suspicions: that we may be headed towards a more dangerous world, and that it may no longer be enough for nuclear powers to maintain a passive stance toward crises. Full moral and political responsibility may demand of them more 'affirmative' action, to work together on an ongoing basis to find ways, evolving along with the technology, of reducing the risks of crisis miscalculation lurking in that technology; and in some cooperative fashion to monitor the global situation constantly for crisis dangers.

References

1. D. Frei and C. Catrina, Risks of Unintentional Nuclear War (Geneva: United Nations Publications, 1982). Also D. Frei, 'Improving Crisis Control Measures', in J. Rotblat and A. Pascolini (eds.) The Arms Race at a Time of Decision: Annals of Pugwash 1983 (London: Macmillan, 1984) pp.88-103.
2. United States Department of Defense, 'Report to the Congress by Secretary of Defense Caspar W. Weinberger on Direct Communications Links and Other Measures to Enhance Stability', 11 April 1983.
3. Roosevelt Center for American Policy Studies, 'A Nuclear Risk Reduction System' Report of the Nunn/Warner Working Group on Nuclear Risk Reduction (November 1983).
4. J.W. Lewis, and C.D. Blacker, 'Next Steps in the Creation of an Accidental Nuclear War Prevention Center'. A special Report of the Center for International Security and Arms Control, Stanford University (Palo Alto: October 1983).
5. W.L. Ury and R. Smoke, 'Beyond the Hotline: Controlling a Nuclear Crisis'. A Report to the United States Arms Control and Disarmament Agency. Nuclear Negotiation Project, Harvard Law School (January 1984).
6. A.L. George, Managing U.S.-Soviet Rivalry: Problems of Crisis Prevention (Boulder: Westview Press, 1983).

Acknowledgment

Part of the research on which this paper is based was supported by the Ploughshares Fund, and the preparation of the paper was indirectly supported by an institutional support grant to the author's institution, Peace and Common Security, by the Columbia Foundation; both foundations are located in San Francisco, California, USA.

5 Nuclear Forces and Proposals for a Nuclear Weapons Freeze

JOHN HOLDREN

Pugwash Workshops on Nuclear Forces in Europe and Their Relation to Strategic Arms Limitation have been held twice yearly in Geneva since January 1980. This paper evaluates the Tenth Workshop held on 1-2 June 1984, as well as the First Workshop on Proposals for a Nuclear Weapons Freeze which followed immediately (3-4 June).

Given the closely related topics of these two workshops and the correspondingly large overlap in the kinds of expertise appropriate for each, it made sense from a logistics standpoint to hold them one after the other with many participants in common. This arrangement turned out to have the further benefit that the gloom generated in the Tenth Nuclear Forces Workshop, which re-examined the dilemmas and dangers of the current state of the nuclear arms race in Europe and elsewhere, was able to be somewhat alleviated by the focus in the Freeze Workshop on some promising and specific measures for bringing that arms race to a halt. The logical transition between these two perspectives was provided by a discussion of the sorts of independent initiatives on the two sides needed in order to re-establish a climate in which a rather comprehensive interim freeze, as a prelude to force reductions, could be pursued with some hope of success.

The statement of the Pugwash Executive Committee (see Appendix) summarises most of the points on which there was a substantial amount of agreement among those present at the workshops (although not everyone would have agreed with everything in it). In what follows I elaborate on some of these main points and mention a few additional ones that were raised.

Several themes from the Ninth Nuclear Forces Workshop (11-12 December 1983) were extensively revisited in the Tenth: the lack of any function for nuclear weapons except to deter others from using theirs; the undesirability of either side's taking steps that could undermine the other's confidence in the adequacy of its forces for this purpose;

the substantial margin by which the extant survivable forces assure this mutual deterrent adequacy today; the room this margin provides for independent initiatives in refraining from further deployments and moving towards less aggressive doctrines and postures; and the need for such initiatives in order to help dissipate the present poisonous atmosphere of superpower relations, and to forestall dangerous developments that will become irreversible, if solutions are postponed until formal negotiations are reconstituted and completed.

Issues Concerning Deterrence

With respect to the unusability of nuclear weapons for any purpose other that deterrence, there seems to be widespread agreement. Controversy arises over two sub-questions, however: what kinds of nuclear forces and postures are needed to keep deterrence 'credible'? and is nuclear deterrence applicable against non-nuclear threats?

Concern with keeping deterrence 'credible' arises largely from the idea that threatening mutual suicide is unconvincing as a means of discouraging an adversary from actions that do not directly imperil one's national survival. Thus it is argued that the possibility of 'limited' use of nuclear weapons by an adversary required, for credible deterrence, that one have the capacity to make a correspondingly 'limited' nuclear response. This concept, if accepted in its most general form, leads directly to an endless competition for advantage in an infinitely subdividable set of categories of nuclear weaponry – it leads, in other words, to the sort of nuclear arms race we are experiencing.

The way out of this trap, it seems to me, is to recognise that: (a) the major nuclear powers already have more than sufficient diversity of nuclear forces to make their **initial** response to a limited nuclear attack a limited one at virtually any scale they choose; and (b) there is a high likelihood that any nuclear exchange, at whatever scale it **begins** will escalate to all-out nuclear war and, hence, mutual suicide. It follows that a potential attacker considering the use of nuclear weapons confronts a choice no easier than the one his nuclear attack would impose on the other side: the option of limited initial use exists, but the risk of total disaster ensuing is great. This is the essence of deterrence, and it requires no further refinements in arsenals to keep it credible. Indeed, one of the greatest present dangers is that refinements made in the name of increasing the credibility of deterrence actually are increasing the probability that nuclear war will start by mistake or misjudgment of intentions. That is, in the attempt to reduce further an already small danger - the danger that deterrence will fail through a calculated decision by one side that the other has no 'credible' options - we are increasing the already much bigger danger of nuclear war by 'accident'. The concept of 'extended deterrence' - using the possibility of use of nuclear weapons as a deterrent against non-nuclear threats such as attacks with conventional forces in Europe or Asia - poses more difficult dilemmas. Here, first of all, there is a **real** problem of credibility, both in the sense that no military advantage accrues to first use of nuclear weapons where both sides possess them in superabundance, and in the sense that the prospect of initiating mutual suicide deters first and foremost the defender in this case (rather than at least equally, as above, the potential attacker). And if, as argued above, there is already a problem of increasing the chance of accidental nuclear war while attempting (needlessly) to increase the credibility of nuclear deterrence against nuclear threats, an even greater danger of this sort is likely to result from attempts to make the fundamentally incredible proposition of **extended** deterrence seem credible. All this is in addition, of course, to the troublesome ethical and political problems associated with planning, as it were, to be the first to use nuclear weapons.

Notwithstanding all these difficulties with extended deterrence, the absence of major armed conflict in Europe for nearly forty years promotes the impression (justified or not) that it has worked - that is, that a deliberately enhanced risk that conventional war would become nuclear has made conventional war less likely. Thus the question was posed in the Tenth Workshop on Nuclear Forces - as it has been in many previous ones in this series - whether measures to decrease the chance of nuclear war in Europe will not inevitably increase the chance of non-nuclear war there. Given the extraordinary destructive power that even non-nuclear weapons have now attained, including, for example, fuel-air explosives and chemical weapons, and given also the high likelihood that any nuclear war in Europe would escalate to global scale, the question in its starkest terms becomes: must we increase the risk of the (non-nuclear) destruction of Europe in order to reduce the risk of the (nuclear) destruction of the world?

This question can only be addressed sensibly, from the Europeans' standpoint or from any other, by being more specific about relative risks and about the options being considered. How big is the chance of conventional war in Europe, and how dependent is that chance on the choices being considered? How big is the chance of nuclear war, and how does it depend on these choices? In fact, the chance of conventional war in Europe seems rather small; for, even without the prospect of escalation to the nuclear level, the risks for the initiator would be very high in relation to the potential gains. Moreover, there are no choices available, short of the abolition of nuclear weapons, that could provide complete confidence that conventional aggression would not lead eventually to nuclear war; there will always be a degree of **de facto** extended deterrence, irrespective of declared policy, as long as nuclear weapons exist. If, then, the chance of a nuclear war – say, by mistake, in a period of high tensions – is not so small, and if that chance can be appreciably reduced by the changes in doctrines and deployments associated with abandoning reliance on a **policy** of extended deterrence, there is a strong case for doing so; the gain from significantly reducing a big hazard far outweighs the loss from marginally increasing a small one.

I believe the argument just stated follows logically from discussions at the Nuclear Forces Workshop, although it was not made so explicitly there (and probably would not be accepted by all the participants). This position is reinforced, as a number of participants pointed out, by the possibility of reducing the chance of conventional conflict by restructuring conventional forces. Useful groundwork for a detailed exploration of this possibility – based on increasing conventional defensive capabilities while decreasing offensive capabilities – was laid at the Pugwash Symposium on Conventional Forces in Europe held in Vedbaek, Denmark in March 1984 (see pp.287-92).

The Margin of Safety

At the Tenth Workshop on Nuclear Forces and at previous ones in this series, there has been little argument with the proposition that both superpowers have more than enough nuclear weapons to deter each other from their use. This is not simply a matter of diversity and numbers of weapons, of course, but also a matter of other characteristics of the nuclear forces related to maintaining confidence on each side that no conceivable pre-emptive attack could deprive it of its capacity to retaliate devastatingly. There has been consensus also that neither side is even close to acquiring the capacity for a disarming first strike, although on the question of whether this situation can be counted upon to persist indefinitely there has been a wider range of opinion. A most important point of agreement, in any case, has been the undesirability of steps that move either side even slightly closer to a first-strike capability, or towards appearing to want one.

Acceptance of this important point means that a number of developments in the last fifteen years of action and reaction in the nuclear arms race are particularly to be deplored. Extensive MIRVing and increasing accuracy in land-based missiles that are themselves vulnerable are two such developments. Another is the reciprocal stationing of short-flight-time missiles close to one another's boundaries. Doctrines that look favourably on the possibility of 'decapitation' strikes against the leadership and other command-and-control elements of the other side compound the problem. The increasing possibility that one or both sides will adopt 'launch-on-warning' postures for vulnerable forces is but one of the startlingly dangerous consequences of these developments.

The imminent advent of submarine-launched ballistic missiles having, for the first time, the accuracy to destroy the most hardened military targets is a further development along these lines that was discussed at some length in both workshops. The Trident-II (D-5) missile on the U.S. side will be the first SLBM with such accuracy, but it may be presumed that a Soviet counterpart will not be far behind. Perhaps because of the simplistic idea that even a counterforce weapon is not destabilising if it is not itself vulnerable, there has been rather little controversy so far about the wisdom of deploying this new class of SLBMs. The Workshop discussions suggested, however, that such deployments would be highly unfortunate.

One obvious reason for this view is that the addition of more counterforce weapons, deployable so as to reach their targets in even less time than the 30 minutes required by land-based ICBMs, can only increase the pressures pushing both sides toward computerised launch-on-warning postures. A second and more subtle point can be appreciated by recalling the recent 'window of vulnerability' debate in the United States. The Scowcroft Commission declared this 'window' closed (for the time being) by explaining that it was not possible for US ICBMs and intercontinental bombers to be destroyed simultaneously in a counterforce strike: shooting at US ICBM silos with Soviet ICBMs accurate enough to destroy them would provide enough warning time for US bombers to get off the ground; SLBMs quick enough to catch the bombers on the ground would not be accurate enough to destroy the ICBMs. The trouble with accurate new SLBMs, then, is that they will appear to open the 'window' of vulnerability on land-based intercontinental forces that the Scowcroft Commission's simultaneity argument had slammed shut: they will be able to attack both ICBM silos and bomber fields simultaneously, with high accuracy and short warning.

No one had argued that the third leg of the triad - the

submarines - would be vulnerable in any case. But the idea that two of the three legs **might** be becoming vulnerable was enough to cause a flap that lasted a decade and led to a decision to deploy MX missiles in Minuteman silos, a move that would increase Soviet vulnerability without reducing US vulnerability one iota.

To be troubled by these issues is not to concede any real validity to the fear that either side - even **with** accurate SLBMs - would be close to having the capability for a disarming first strike. The practical difficulties of orchestrating such a strike just against land-based forces will remain overwhelming, and there is no prospect in sight that either side will acquire the capability to knock out all of the other's submarines, even **one** of which could inflict staggering retaliation. The difficulty, again, is that even moving in the general direction of a first-strike capability is dangerous and stupid, given the precedents it sets, the perceptions it engenders, the responses it stimulates. It is worth recalling, in this connection, how much of the nuclear arms race to date has been driven by each side's making worst-case assessments of the capabilities and intentions of the other - and then reacting to those assessments in one's own deployments and doctrines. Given US reactions to the increasing accuracy of MIRVed warheads on Soviet land-based ICBMs, which after all followed the US lead in these technologies, it is painful to contemplate what large-scale deployments of highly accurate, highly MIRVed SLBMs on both sides will bring.

There is perhaps a simpler way to express the fundamental liabilities of deploying weapons with first-strike characteristics: they foster the illusion of usability of nuclear weapons for more than deterrence, and they diminish the confidence of the other side in the sufficiency of its own forces for deterrent purposes. At worst, these effects can lead to an action-reaction upward spiral in which the nuclear arsenals on both sides increase without limit. At best, they shrink the 'margin of safety' - the margin by which each side can conclude it has more nuclear weapons than it needs, and which is so important to the prospects both for negotiations and for independent initiatives towards force reductions.

Independent Initiatives

The idea that independent initiatives offer more promise in the present situation than does the early resumption of formal negotiations on nuclear forces was discussed extensively at the Ninth Pugwash Workshop on Nuclear Forces based in part on Robert McNamara's list of eighteen such initiatives that could usefully be taken by NATO. This theme was developed further at both the Tenth Nuclear Forces Workshop and the Freeze Workshop.

Particular attention was given to the idea that independent initiatives hold the key to bringing an early halt to the round of nuclear-missile deployments and counter-deployments now underway in Europe. There is little reason to think that formal negotiations covering such missiles could be quickly reconstituted, or that, once resumed, they would be likely to find a solution quickly. Indeed, the Soviet official position has been that a precondition for resumption of formal negotiations is the removal of the new NATO missiles put in place since the new deployments started in December 1983, and this precondition is most unlikely to be met either by the present US administration or by a new one. On the other hand, the Soviets have also said that their responses to the NATO deployments would be strictly proportionate, which implies that a pause on the NATO side would be followed by a pause in Soviet counter-deployments. A de facto 'freeze' of this sort on European missile deployments would provide a breathing space in which informal discussions and further independent initiatives might be able to establish the basis for a longer-term approach to the problem, and at least the further damage of continuing deployments in the meantime would be avoided.

The point has emerged from many previous discussions of the Euromissile issue, both in and out of Pugwash, that the deployments on both sides have had and continue to have more political than military significance. Both sides, it seems, have been willing to take steps that reduced their own as well as their adversary's security, apparently in pursuit of compelling political rationales. On the one hand, this suggests that more attention needs to be given to changing the prevailing political 'realities' through education of the public and policy makers about the consequences being entrained in the name of political necessity today. But another implication of the primarily political nature of these deployments is that both sides have already made their main political points: NATO has shown that it is capable of carrying out an alliance decision to deploy new weapons despite strong external and internal opposition; the WTO has demonstrated that it will not let NATO have the last move. With these political demonstrations accomplished, it is hard to see what further political obstacles should now prevent a mutual pause.

Both the new generation of submarine-launched ballistic missiles and the development of enhanced anti-satellite capabilities represent additional dangers that may already be too close to head off by means of formal negotiations, especially given the poor prospects for even starting such negotiations soon. Both problems are highly amenable to the independent-initiative approach, however, because simple moratoria on testing would stop them in their tracks. Each side need only declare that it will not test either new long-range ballistic missiles or anti-satellite weapons unless and until the other side tests such weapons. Verification of such moratoria on missile flight tests is a rather simple matter for both sides. The diversity of possible anti-satellite technologies poses somewhat greater verification problems, but they do not seem insurmountable, especially in light of the substantial number of tests that would be needed for either side to develop confidence in a significantly increased ASAT capability. The importance of an early halt to ASAT development stems not only from ASAT's probable role as the initiator of an all-out arms race in space, but also from the great difficulty of limiting anti-ballistic-missile technology unless ASAT is limited as well.

The Freeze Concept

Stopping the Euromissile deployments and the testing of new ballistic missiles would be useful ingredients of a comprehensive freeze on the testing, production, and deployment of nuclear weapons, and virtually all freeze proponents would define it to include non-nuclear ABM and ASAT weapons as well. The dilemma of whether to try first and separately for some important and easily achieved parts of a freeze, or to try for the freeze in a more comprehensive form, was one of the focal points of discussions at the Workshop on Proposals for a Nuclear Weapons Freeze. The case for a comprehensive freeze is summarised in the statement from the Executive Committee (Appendix). This approach circumvents the problem of overcompartmentalisation that has plagued most arms-control negotiations in the past, and it avoids the well-established phenomenon whereby partial agreements simply redirect the arms race into uncontrolled channels.

Against this case for comprehensiveness, two points are made. First, trying for comprehensiveness adds such complexities and ambiguities to the definition of a freeze as to make a long, drawn-out process of formal negotiation inevitable. Second, the degree of common interest in terminating some aspects of the arms race is much greater than that in terminating other aspects, and this high degree of common interest is the key to getting early agreement. Both these points suggest that trying for comprehensiveness would be likely to eliminate one of the greatest attractions of the freeze concept, which is the idea of bringing an **early** halt to particularly threatening developments.

No fully satisfactory resolution of the dilemma of comprehensiveness was found in the Freeze Workshop - probably there is none to be found. Still, some bases for optimism were identified. Perhaps most importantly, emphasising that the freeze is an initial, interim measure, rather than a permanent framework for arms control, makes plain that some of the complexities - such as how to deal with non-nuclear anti-submarine and anti-aircraft capabilities - are not so important. No developments along these lines that are possible in a period of a few years could greatly affect the strategic balance. The interim emphasis also makes clear, of course, that it is not the intent to freeze permanently into place the many undesirable characteristics of present nuclear forces. The freeze must be understood as a prelude to reductions in nuclear forces, starting with the most destabilising weapons. It is simply a way of buying time for the more complicated questions associated with reductions to be worked out, while avoiding in the meantime the further progression of dangerous technological developments and new deployments - a way of keeping things from getting even worse while we strive for prescriptions to make them better.

Another basis for optimism about achieving a relatively comprehensive freeze is the extent to which the detailed negotiations necessary for such a measure already have been completed. The SALT II agreement, for example, modified only by the removal of the loopholes for new land-based and submarine-launched ballistic missiles on both sides, could serve as the core of a rather comprehensive freeze. And it has long been clear that the main technical issues relating to a comprehensive ban on the testing of nuclear explosives (CTB) were in fact worked out in the CTB negotiations adjourned in 1980 for reasons external to the testing issue. Even the concept of a cut-off of production of fissile material for weapons - often considered to be one of the more problematic elements of a comprehensive freeze - was shown in discussions in the Freeze Workshop to be closer to attainability than one might have thought, largely because of the applicability of safeguards on the relevant kinds of facilities already worked out and in place under IAEA auspices in non-nuclear-weapon-state adherents to the NPT.

Papers presented on the CTB at the Freeze Workshop served as the focus for a particularly detailed discussion on that element of a freeze. Several conclusions stand out. First, recent developments in the science of seismic verification of underground nuclear explosions are serving to increase confidence that the sort of verification network agreed in the previous CTB negotiations would suffice to detect explosions down to the range of one kiloton. Second, nuclear testing is not required to maintain an adequate level of reliability in weapons already in the stockpiles. Third, there seems to be little to be gained by clandestine testing at yields below the threshold of detection: few imaginable further developments in nuclear weaponry could make enough difference to be worth the effort needed for a clandestine programme; those that could (conceivably bomb-pumped lasers, for example) do not lend themselves to testing at the tiny yields compatible with a clandestine programme; and testing anything really new inevitably carries the risk of a higher-than-expected yield that would lead to detection.

Most of us at the Workshop would agree also, I think, that there is no good reason to settle at this point for an agreement that merely lowers the present 150-kiloton testing threshold, embodied in the unratified Threshold Test Ban Treaty and apparently being observed by both the United States and the Soviet Union. Lowering the threshold to some conservative interpretation of the level of certain detectability, say 5 kilotons, rather than agreeing on an actual comprehensive test ban, would concede too much to the rigid proponents of the view that every agreement must be 100% verifiable. It is always important to compare the risks of a small gap in verifiability with the risks of no agreement, or those of a much less restrictive one. In the case of nuclear testing, merely lowering the threshold would not conclusively accomplish any of the main aims of the comprehensive test ban. It would, however, contribute to the continuing suspicion around the world that the superpowers are simply trying to fine-tune the rules in such a way that only they will be able to play the game.

Conclusion

These two Workshops generated the usual mixture of optimism and despair: the former about what could be achieved, given a modicum of wisdom and goodwill from the leaders on both sides; the latter about the apparently poor prospects that what is possible and needed will actually be done. Still, despair and pessimism must not be allowed to predominate. As one participant emphasised, the least we should be doing in the present gloomy period, when next to nothing is happening at the official level, is to develop a compelling vision for stopping and winding down the arms race - matched by coherent, comprehensive, well thought-out proposals - to put forward when official progress again becomes possible. These workshops, I think, were steps in that direction.

THE STRATEGIC ARMS RACE

Appendix

STATEMENT OF THE PUGWASH EXECUTIVE COMMITTEE

The Tenth Pugwash Workshop on Nuclear Forces and the First Pugwash Workshop on proposals for a Nuclear-Weapons Freeze were held in Geneva, Switzerland, on 1-2 and 3-4 June 1984, respectively. Participants in the workshops comprised 42 scientists and public and military figures from 15 countries.

The purpose of the Tenth Workshop on Nuclear Forces - extending a series of meetings begun in January 1980 - was to continue the search for ways to terminate the counter-productive action-reaction sequence now underway in deployments of nuclear missiles in Europe and elsewhere, and to identify feasible steps towards limitation and reduction of nuclear forces. The aim of the Workshop on Freeze Proposals was to initiate a systematic exploration of the possibilities and problems associated with various elements of the 'nuclear freeze' approach to progress towards nuclear disarmament.

The participants in the Workshops took part as individuals, not as representatives of their governments or institutions. The present statement was prepared following the Workshops by the Pugwash Executive Committee. It should not be interpreted as a consensus of the participants, among whom a wide range of views was represented.

European and Other Nuclear Forces

The deployments and counter-deployments that began after the collapse late last year of both sets of Geneva negotiations on nuclear forces are reducing the security of everyone. A major contributing factor in this new phase of the nuclear arms race - as in previous phases - is the idea that there must be parity in every subcategory of nuclear weaponry and that every deployment requires a counter-deployment. This pernicious idea has no valid military basis, given the nature and numbers of nuclear weapons that already exist; and if it seems to derive instead from 'political realities', that only shows that those 'realities' need modification through education of the public and of policy makers.

The essence of the needed education is this: nuclear weapons should never be used. They can serve at most one purpose, which is to deter others from using theirs, and for this purpose both sides have more than enough. Neither superpower is at all likely to acquire the capacity for a disarming first strike. Nevertheless, deployments that move either side in that direction make all of us less safe: they feed mutual fear and distrust, establish dangerous precedents in capabilities and doctrines, and push both sides towards hair-trigger postures.

This syndrome represents the greatest danger in the present deployments and counter-deployments (and in others in prospect), but there are other dangers, too. The introduction of cruise missiles may lead to uncontrollable increases in the total numbers of nuclear weapons, and expansion of the arms race into space - highly destabilising in itself - also could produce almost unlimited increases in the military's diversion of economic resources from compelling human needs. The continued failure of the superpowers to stop and reverse their own nuclear arms race, moreover, is steadily eroding the barriers against the spread ofnuclear weapons to a much larger number of nations.

Our prescription for the present predicament begins with essentially the recommendations we made following the Ninth Pugwash Workshop on Nuclear Forces last December; an immediate, reciprocal pause in all nuclear deployments in Europe, including the European part of the Soviet Union; and the use of the 'cooling off' period provided by this mutual halt for further independent measures to reduce the tensions and risks associated with present force postures. Such independent measures could include; withdrawal of nuclear weapons to a distance of 100 kilometres or more from the NATO/Warsaw Treaty organisation boundary; renunciation of strategies incorporating 'decapitation' strikes directed at the leadership of the other side, as well as 'launch-on-warning'; moratoria on testing and deployment of antisatellite weapons; and cessation of other weapons tests and construction activities likely to be interpreted as threatening the ABM Treaty.

On the NATO side, movement towards a flat declaration of 'no-first-use' of nuclear weapons, which already is the stated posture of the Soviet Union, should be encouraged. NATO's recent decision to reduce its inventory of nuclear weapons in Europe by 1400 bombs and warheads between 1983 and 1988 is to be welcomed as a step in the right direction. Further reductions by independent initiatives on both sides should be sought.

It is essential for the purpose of facilitating progress on such measures - and for the broader goal of reducing the hazards of misinformation and misjudgments - that there be established a pattern of regular, private, informal meetings of political and military leaders on both sides. Pugwash intends to use its contacts to promote this possibility.

Beneficial results from such communication and from the sorts of independent initiatives mentioned above could create the conditions for eventual resumption of formal negotiations on nuclear forces. As we argued in December, moreover, the scope for independent initiatives is great. Because both sides possess nuclear weaponry far in excess of the needs of deterrence, both can afford to be flexible in taking independent steps to reduce the risks of nuclear war by mistake or unwanted escalation.

Nuclear Freeze Proposals

Achieving a first step in arms control by means of freezing the quantitative and qualitative characteristics of nuclear forces on both sides is not a new idea. Such an approach was proposed by the United States in Geneva as early as 1964; freeze resolutions have surfaced in the US Congress at least three times since 1970; and freezes in various forms have been proposed by the Soviet Union on numerous occasions starting in 1976.

Notwithstanding the long history of the freeze concept, a combination of recent developments and current conditions have made accomplishment of a nuclear freeze both more urgent than ever before and more practical. The new urgency arises from the need to stop recent and impending trends in the qualitative characteristics of nuclear weapons, which, even more than increasing numbers alone, are tending to undermine nuclear deterrence and to increase the chance of nuclear war by mistake or inadvertent escalation. This urgency was underlined by the United Nations General Assembly in passing a comprehensive nuclear-weapons-freeze resolution in late 1983.

The greater possibility of achieving a freeze has arisen from convergence of several factors: a situation of essential equivalence in the overall nuclear forces of both sides, in which differences of detail confer no meaningful advantages on one side or another; the high technical capabilities of each side for verifying the compliance of the other with a freeze agreement; the vanishingly small potential gain to either side from any clandestine activity that might escape detection; and, not least, a high degree of public concern with the risks of nuclear war, translating into growing political pressure to bring the arms race to an early halt.

The level of public concern and interest, which is crucial to the prospects for progress, recently has been further increased by global impacts of nuclear war on climate and ecosystems. The prospect that these impacts could imperil the survival even of noncombatant societies apparently is increasing pressure from the non-nuclear-weapons countries for a halt to the nuclear arms race, and this pressure is most welcome.

Most of the attraction of the nuclear freeze concept depends on its comprehensiveness - that is, on the ability to stop testing and production as well as deployment, and to do so with delivery vehicles of all types as well as with the nuclear bombs and warheads themselves. This comprehensive approach avoids two shortcomings that have plagued arms control for decades: first, the overcompartmentalisation of negotiations, producing endless disputes about the boundaries of the compartments and encouraging the unproductive pursuit of parity in every category; and, second, the channelling of the arms race into those categories of weapons that have not been covered by agreements. The importance of avoiding these pitfalls means that a comprehensive freeze should remain our goal, notwithstanding the extra complexity and potential difficulty of achieving it.

Crucial to both the desirability and achievability of a nuclear freeze are two aspects of its timing. First, as much of the freeze as possible should be put in place **as quickly as possible**, to achieve its purposes of cutting off dangerous developments and build-ups rather than allowing them to continue while negotiations drag on. Second, the freeze must be understood to be an **initial** measure, beyond which deep and stabilising reductions in nuclear forces are to be sought. This approach disposes of the objection that the status quo is much too dangerous to freeze permanently into place.

Proposing the freeze as an interim measure of, say, 2 to 3 years' duration initially, has the further merit of reducing concerns that unfrozen or clandestine activities could significantly affect the nuclear equilibrium while the freeze is in force. A period of 2-3 years is, at the same time, long enough to represent a meaningful interruption of dangerous trends and to permit meaningful progress towards longer-term solutions, while short enough to maintain the pressure on decision makers to work out these longer-term solutions promptly.

While emphasising the desirability of achieving a comprehensive freeze and moving rapidly to substantial reductions, we recognise that some aspects of a freeze may prove more difficult to accomplish than others. This consideration, combined with the special urgency of some of the particular threats a freeze seeks to abate, draws attention to the question of what components of a freeze could be achieved essentially at once, with little or no further negotiation. Obvious candidates for inclusion in this category are: a comprehensive ban on the testing of nuclear explosives; a ban on flight-tests of new land-based and sea-based ballistic missiles; and a ban on testing of antisatellite weaponry.

With respect to a comprehensive test ban (CTB) on nuclear explosions, the sorts of monitoring networks needed to verify compliance down to yields of the order of one kiloton already were agreed in the trilateral (USA-USSR-UK) CTB negotiations that ended in 1980. We believe that there would be little to be gained by clandestine testing below the detection threshold, and that adequate performance of existing stockpiles can be assured without any further nuclear testing at all. Any risks associated with small uncertainties in these respects are tiny by comparison to the benefits of a CTB. These include: first, the termination of potentially destabilising lines of development in 'third generation' nuclear weapons; second, the end of nuclear testing's contribution to the illusion that there are functions for nuclear weapons for which existing stockpiles are not adequate; and, finally, the antiproliferation benefits of an early concrete demonstration of superpower resolve to halt their own nuclear arms race.

With respect to a flight-test ban on new land-based and sea-based ballistic missiles, the motivation comes from the danger of continuing trends in increasing accuracy, particularly on submarine-launched ballistic missiles. Without testing, these trends will be stopped. The early achievability of this component of a freeze is assured because the measures needed to verify it were already agreed to exist in the SALT negotiations.

Finally, a freeze on the testing and deployment of antisatellite systems is especially urgent because, while both sides already possess such systems in rudimentary form, their development to much more threatening levels of effectiveness could be blocked by an early and easily verified testing halt. Failure to do so will open up an expensive and dangerous arms race in space that can benefit no-one, while threatening at the same time the early undermining of the ABM Treaty.

Other components of a freeze that might be achievable especially rapidly are a halt on production and deployment of additional heavy bombers, a halt on deployment of sea-launched nuclear-capable cruise missiles, and a cut-off of weapons-oriented production of plutonium and highly enriched uranium. While Pugwash plans further study of these and other aspects of a comprehensive freeze, at least one other measure can be advocated at once and without reservation: a freeze on the abusive rhetoric that - along with recent perverse developments in nuclear forces and doctrines - has been making progress towards arms reductions impossible.

6 Proposals for a Nuclear Freeze
WALTER SLOCOMBE

In writing about freeze proposals, it is appropriate that I begin - to use the British parliamentary formula - by 'declaring my interest'. I am in some sense one of those traditional arms control advocates who, while welcoming the freeze movement as mobilising almost unprecedented broad public support for arms control, nonetheless have reservations about the utility of the concept as an organising principle for a long-term, agreed structure for the US-Soviet nuclear relationship. My theme is that whatever those reservations may be, and I think they are justified, translating the concept into a plausibly definable and verifiable proposal should be directed at arranging a pause in the competition to give more focused negotiations a chance, not using the freeze concept as an organising principle for **permanent** structuring of the nuclear relationships between the superpowers.

The nuclear freeze concept has offered a rallying cry for public concern over the danger of nuclear war. Unencumbered by the baggage of technical detail, the notion of a quick and straightforward agreement to stop the testing, production, and deployment of nuclear weapons, matches well the public sense that the stakes are so great that the superpowers should forget the details and just stop.

But like other great political rallying cries - from 'power to the people' to 'get the government off our backs' - the broad public appeal of the nuclear freeze concept rests in some significant part on its very lack of specificity. Transforming 'the freeze' into a concrete programme for negotiating action, forces confrontation of questions legitimately left unmeasured at the level of politics. In conversion to a proposal, the freeze concept has to encounter that very concern with detail for which its advocates have so much criticised traditional arms control. Indeed, a freeze that seeks maximum comprehensiveness for a long period must deal with issues of detail that more focused (or more limited) agreements could safely ignore.

Problems of a Long-Term Freeze

The present difficulties in operationalising the freeze concept have to do with the following:

- **Coverage.** No matter how simple the basic concept, a concrete freeze proposal must determine exactly what systems are frozen, on the ground that they are nuclear systems, and those which are exempt from the freeze, on the ground that they are not (or not primarily) nuclear attack systems. The existence of many aircraft, ships and artillery types capable of carrying either conventional or nuclear armament makes this problem especially acute.
- **Definition.** All freeze concepts that have been put forward permit maintenance of the existing force. That is, the forces that are 'frozen' would not have to be permitted to fall into disrepair. Breakdowns could be repaired. New crews could be trained. Components that wear out could be renewed. Indeed, identical copies of existing aircraft, missiles, and the like could be constructed to replace predecessors. Permitting such force-maintenance activities is necessarily implied by viewing the freeze as a **freeze** rather than an attempt to abolish nuclear weapons by a process of enforced aging. But permitting maintenance introduces a whole new range of items that must be agreed upon. What, for example, is the distinction between a test for training purposes and a test for purposes of discovering whether a modification of an existing system works as predicted? The problem is further complicated by the possibility that some modification may occur even in a replacement, if changing production techniques make it no longer practical to build an exact copy.
- **Verification.** A freeze must establish plausible mechanisms for verifying compliance with the constraints it imposes. Some of the core activities, whose restriction seems to be inherent in a comprehensive freeze concept, are themselves very difficult to observe without thoroughgoing cooperation by the other side. This would be true, for example, with respect to the production of nuclear materials for nuclear explosives. The scale of the problem may be indicated by the fact that even with a quite extensive system of international inspection of a limited number of facilities in non-nuclear weapon states, our confidence that nuclear materials intended for peaceful purposes are not being diverted to military purposes is pretty low.
- **Defences.** Many defence systems whose mission is primar-

ily to negate the other side's nuclear attack capacity do not themselves use nuclear weapons and therefore would not, presumably, be frozen. The class of defences at issue includes, for example, many anti-aircraft systems and a variety of anti-submarine weapons. Many proposals for improved (in contrast to presently deployed) anti-ballistic missile defences would not use nuclear weapons. Indeed, as guidance and surveillance technologies improve, it may become feasible to destroy nuclear systems preemptively without using nuclear weapons. Even today there is no particular reason to believe that either side would regard tactical and theatre nuclear weapons (for example, at air bases or naval vessels) as immune from conventional attack prior to first use of nuclear weapons.

A freeze which attempted to constrain absolutely the nuclear offense while leaving unlimited conventional defensive systems (and conventional offensive systems useful for preventive attacks) is unlikely to achieve the long run objective of draining the venomous effects of the arms competition on East-West relations, much less contribute to stability. On the other hand, any attempt to extend the freeze limitations to non-nuclear defensive systems introduces a mass of new complexities.

- **Economy of negotiating effort.** No doubt there are, in theory at any rate, answers to all of these questions, and serious efforts have been made by freeze advocates to define comprehensive long-term freezes which respond to these concerns. There is, however, a principle of economy of negotiating effort involved as well. The superpowers have found it very difficult to reach agreements even on far more limited subjects, and there is nothing about the freeze concept (and certainly not about the current state of US-Soviet relations) which leads one to believe that they would find it any easier to reach agreements in the near future. It is worth bearing in mind that none of these problems is likely to arise in the abstract - each possible resolution of the myriad points of contention would entail particular impacts on particular systems of each side. Therefore, it is appropriate to ask whether the comprehensiveness of the freeze, only arguably a virtue once achieved, is not also a defect from the point of view of negotiating requirements.

An Alternative, Short-Term Freeze Concept

These generally critical observations about the problems of proposals for a long-term nuclear freeze that seeks to establish a continuing nuclear regime do not mean that no agreement which can meaningfully be called a 'freeze' would be worth trying for. All of these elements - scope, definition, verification, effect, and negotiating costs - have a time dimension. The freeze by definition would perpetuate the current situation, and recognition of the dangers of that situation makes many freeze advocates argue that the freeze is not a permanent goal, but simply an effort to prevent the situation from getting worse during negotiating about efforts to make it better in the future.

Taking the freeze as a concept of an agreed intermission in the competition, rather than an effort to preserve permanently the current relationship and the current forces, eases many of the problems outlined above. Such a focus implies agreeing on a number of temporary mutual moratoria on ongoing activities, with the clear understanding that the failure within a fixed period - say a year or so - to reach more definite agreements for the future will end the interim restrictions.

Among the obvious candidates for such moratoria are:

- a ban on testing of undeployed ballistic missiles (MX, D-5, SS-24, SS-25) whether or not 'new' by SALT II definition;
- a delay in deployment of new types of sea-launched nuclear armed cruise missiles (nuclear armed naval Tomahawk, SS-N-X-21) on the ground that they would present special verification problems;
- a halt to production and deployment of additional B-1 and Blackjack heavy bombers;
- mutual pull back of shorter range tactical nuclear weapons along the GDR-FRG border;
- suspension of weapons tests and radar construction arguably inconsistent with the ABM Treaty pending negotiations on ways to strengthen that agreement;
- a halt to ASAT tests pending negotiation of the broadest possible verifiable constraints on testing such weapons;
- cessation of nuclear explosions.

The most difficult and contentious issues need not necessarily be addressed in the initial stage. Some (for example, chemical weapon production) pose special verification problems. Others (deployment of ALCMs by both sides) entail no serious strategic instabilities. Still others (NATO's Pershing and GLCM deployments, and Soviet SS-20 deployments and recently announced counters to NATO deployments) are political issues of immense difficulty. Rather than maximum coverage, the effort should be to find programmes in their early stages when a relatively short interruption in the course towards deployment does not involve fundamental values for either side, but might avoid prematurely closing some doors before negotiations had a chance.

The freeze as a 'negotiator's pause' appeals, moreover, to what I would argue is the strongest of the reasons for the public popularity of the idea: the urgency of acting to get the arms control process back on track, not a desire to insist on a particular result.

Taking the concept of the freeze as an effort to prevent the situation from deteriorating during negotiations, eases a number of problems outlined above. With respect to scope, the agreement could be limited to well-defined current and known programmes. The elimination of the need to try to cover all possible future plans, or even everything which is currently underway, would vastly simplify both boundary condition problems and negotiations. Similarly, with respect to verification, a great deal about the activities of the two sides can now be observed with reasonably high confidence by national technical means of intelligence. The task of verification is greatly simplified if the time during which the limits will remain in effect is relatively short compared to the time necessary to undertake the quite substantial efforts necessary to develop a concealed or clandestine development programme.

Perhaps most important, the key effect of such a freeze would be the attempt to clear the air for more specific and focused negotiations on reductions, restrictions on destabilising modernisation, and rules of conduct to lower the danger of nuclear war by accident or misunderstanding. On the whole, such a focus for freeze proposals seems far more fruitful than the attempt to create a permanent regime.

7 Implications of a Comprehensive Test Ban for a Stockpile of Nuclear Weapons
CARSON MARK

Background

Ever since it was demonstrated that a supercritical assembly of fissile material could provide an explosion having a very large energy, at least two approaches to achieving such an effect have been evident to everyone. One is the so-called gun method, whereby two or more pieces, which when combined would form a supercritical assembly, are brought rapidly together without changing their shape or density. Another is the implosion method, in which high explosive is employed to reduce the volume of an assembly that is already nearly critical.

Apart from the possibility of experiencing a premature initiation of the neutron chain reaction, anyone who accumulates the necessary materials and resources in skills and techniques can use either method to build a device; and without full-scale nuclear test he can be confident that, when fired properly, his device will produce some sort of nuclear explosion.

However, without testing he will not know the size of explosion his device will provide except within wide limits. Even by employing quite elaborate calculations he will have to make so many approximations and assumptions concerning processes capable of affecting the final outcome that if, for example, his calculated answer should be 3 kilotons, all he could conclude from this would be that the actual yield would lie in some range, such as somewhere between 1 and 10 kilotons, say.

In some situations this might be quite satisfactory; but this is not the situation of those who have conducted many tests, and who have worked assiduously to develop models with improved design, and intended for specific applications. Particularly (though not only) for the implosion method, many means of improving the design beyond a first elementary version suggest themselves. These offer prospects of

A COMPREHENSIVE TEST BAN

achieving the same effect with a smaller amount of fissile material or within a smaller weight and size, or in a more rugged package, and so forth.

Generally, however, these attractive features can be gained only at the price of greater complexity and precision in the assembly process. With extensive testing experience, a confident prediction of yield may be possible on the assumption that the configuration provided by the assembly process is the same as that used as a starting condition for the calculation of the explosion. However, in the case of an assembly driven by high explosive the actual starting condition is not directly observable, and the more 'advanced' or demanding the design, the more sensitive the outcome may be to small departures from the calculated assembly behaviour. For groups already possessing a stockpile of weapons of various types there can be no practical interest in a new and improved design, no matter how attractive its novel features might seem, until its actual yield should be established so that a decision could be made as to whether it should be added to the stockpile or replace items already on hand. For this purpose full-scale test is essential.

The use of thermonuclear fuels as a component in nuclear weapons very greatly increases the dependence on the results of nuclear tests. In all such devices, whether of the hybrid type, such as the so-called 'booster' or those which might be referred to as 'H-bombs' in which a major part of the total energy is obtained from thermonuclear reactions, the thermonuclear fuel is brought to the point of ignition and subsequent burning by the energy provided by a fission explosion. The performance of this triggering fission device thus becomes a starting element in the design of the complete system. Whether the fuel burns well, or poorly, or fails to ignite at all, depends entirely on the state to which the fuel is brought by the initiating fission explosion. The behaviour of the whole system is, in turn, very strongly dependent on the burning of the thermonuclear fuel. Evidently, in this case, the important starting conditions are completely unavailable to observation without conducting a nuclear test. They are, of course, also unavailable to full observation during a nuclear test, except to the extent that the total behaviour of the system may or may not confirm that the intended state was achieved. It will be apparent that no system which depends for its behaviour on thermonuclear components, and which has a design that departs in any unexplored way from one for which the performance has been established, could be considered for application as a weapon without test.

Of the hundreds of nuclear tests which have been carried out, only a small fraction have been for the purpose of experimenting with basically new principles or radically new patterns. The great majority have been concerned with trying to achieve improvements in size, weight, cost, and so forth, or with adaptation in size, weight, shape, ruggedness, to meet the requirements of particular delivery modes or applications. If, for example, a weapon is intended to be fired from an artillery piece it must fit the gun barrel, withstand the violent acceleration imposed, and have a weight consistent with the range required. If, again, it is to be used as a depth charge from a surface ship, it would be just as important that its yield not be too large as that it be large enough. Even for persons quite familiar with the general processes of fission and fusion in interacting combinations, whenever some modification requires a change in the configuration, or amounts of the nuclear materials, or of the materials affecting the assembly process, a nuclear test is required. Not infrequently, several tests with progressive adjustments have been necessary to meet a single weapon objective. This situation is radically different from that of someone merely striving to achieve some sort of nuclear explosion.

Once the prototype of a weapon scheduled for stockpile has been successfully tested, tooling is set up for the production of replicas and the desired number of devises are built and assembled. If, for convenience in manufacture, some changes seem necessary, such as in the design of joints between mating parts, such changes are given careful attention by someone familiar with the considerations important to the design to ensure that they could not in any meaningful way affect the behaviour of the object which had been test-fired. Following the build, a continuing surveillance programme is established whereby samples of the weapons stockpiled are removed and disassembled for detailed examination of all the components - electrical, mechanical, and chemical. With an extended shelf-life as an important consideration throughout the whole design process, only rarely is some component found to be deteriorating. But if, nevertheless, that is observed, various remedies are available. Electrical components, for example, can be replaced or improved. High explosive, which is not a truly stable material, may ultimately crack or crumble. If necessary, it could be replaced; though if a new and improved formulation were to be employed a new test would probably seem necessary. Plutonium and uranium are highly reactive metals, and some corrosion could result if they should be exposed to air or water vapour or the gases which slowly evolve from high explosive. Protective coatings or sealed containers can be used to shield the sensitive metal surface from such effects, but the precautions taken might prove inadequate over long periods of time. These, of course, are among the kinds of things which the surveillance programme is designed to disclose. If gradual changes are found which cannot be restored by local refurbishing of particular items, there remains the straightforward remedy of instituting a programme whereby units are removed from the stockpile on a scheduled basis and replaced with new units built to the original specifications. The fact that such full scale replacement programmes have not been usual in connection with the nuclear stockpile, if, indeed, they have ever been called for, is a consequence of two factors. One is that most of the models built have remained free of significant signs of ageing, at least until it came time to retire them for other reasons. The other is that, in the context of an active testing programme, by the time the first signs of deterioration began to show up in a particular model, so that the need of replacement became clear, it seemed preferable to substitute a new and improved model which had already been developed and certified by testing.

Effects of a Comprehensive Test Ban (CTB) on the Stockpile

From the discussion above it will be evident that, without further nuclear testing, the means are available to maintain the weapons presently in the stockpile in operable condition for as long as may be desired, with as full assurance as we have today that they will produce the same effects under the same conditions as those for which they have been certified. Of course, the change to a regime in which testing was not allowed would carry a number of implications which, though obvious, should be recognised. Some of these are:

- Most, if not all, schemes for improving nuclear performmance, the materials employed in the nuclear components, or the configuration of the nuclear materials and of the closely interacting materials, will have to be laid aside.
- In the past, some changes in the military specifications or requirements, such as requirements for safety in handling, security, cost of manufacture or maintenance, have required some modification in nuclear design of a model already tested. Under a CTB it might or might not be possible to accommodate some such changes.
- If the development of new carriers is held to be necessary, these will have to be designed to handle existing nuclear

devices rather than tailoring a new device to meet the design features of a proposed missile, as has been customary.
- Some of the weapons in the stockpile depend for their certified behaviour on having an amount of tritium within some designated range. Tritium is radioactive, with a half-life of about 12.3 years. It will be necessary to continue to produce tritium and replenish the supply in weapons requiring it, just as is presently done.
- A meticulous surveillance programme will have to be maintained and all its requirements met, including possibly a weapon remanufacture and replacement programme. Such a programme could be quite expensive, though, except for inflation, it ought to be somewhat less expensive than the original build.
- In addition to the mechanical aspects of the surveillance programme it will be necessary that a cadre of persons be available who are knowledgeable about the detailed mode of behaviour of the devices on hand and in a position to judge whether or not any of the surveillance findings warrant concern.

It is on the assumption that the requirements of considerations such as these are fully met that it may be said that the reliability of the existing stockpile to perform as presently envisaged can be maintained indefinitely.

Effects of a CTB on Confidence in the Stockpile

This is a more complicated matter than that discussed above, since it may depend as much on what is said about the situation as on the actual state of affairs. A large part of the problem arises because of the secrecy which has always shrouded nuclear weapons, both that resulting from official policy and also that coming from the aura of mystery in which so many people incline to view things nuclear. In point of fact, although a nuclear weapon may be a very complex mechanical object it is not inherently more complex than some other technological assemblages such, say, as a modern plane or space rocket. The fact that the real requirements for maintaining a nuclear weapon in working order are understood by only a relatively small group of people does not mean that they are more deeply mysterious than those applying to these other complex systems, of which most people would suppose that they could be maintained if one put the necessary thought and effort into it. Still, doubts on this point are more easy to raise in the case of nuclear weapons, even by assertions which are not entirely relevant to the point at

A COMPREHENSIVE TEST BAN

issue. For example:

- It has been suggested that, because of the increasing recognition of hazards in the workplace associated with some of the materials used in weapons, these materials might cease to be available in commerce. Beryllium could be an instance. In such an event, remanufacture to present specifications would, it is said, become impossible and, without being able to conduct a test, the use of some new material to replace the original could not be certified. The last point is true enough; but the claim that a government able to produce and handle plutonium to meet its stockpile requirements could not manage to devise proper handling for beryllium needed for the same purpose would appear to be disingenuous. As a sort of side kick it would be interesting, after OSHA may have banned the use of beryllium because of its undesirable health effects, to read their position paper on the subject of nuclear weapons.
- It has been suggested that in the event of a CTB the government might fail to provide the funds required to support an adequate surveillance programme. This might possibly be true, with or without a CTB, but it is quite beside the point. The speculation relates to the situation in which the government has first accepted a CTB and subsequently decided that maintaining confidence in the stockpile is not particularly important; whereas the topic of discussion here is whether or not there is a way to maintain confidence.
- It has been suggested that, in spite of the best intentions, it will not be possible during a CTB to restrain weapon designers, conceivably egged on by the military, from introducing small changes or intriguing improvements to the extent that confidence will ultimately be eroded. Again, it may be true that there are irrepressible and irresponsible weapon designers, but it is bizarre to suppose that such people will be given a free hand with respect to matters of national importance.
- It would be argued that without being able to test we will be unable to improve nuclear designs to withstand some new and presently unforeseen interceptor-threat with which our weapons might sometime be confronted. One can, of course, at least imagine types of threat against which improved nuclear weapon design would be of no avail, such as something capable of vapourising or greatly perforating the materials of the carrier itself. It may also be noted that without any effect at all (and at least some effort has been expended) a nuclear warhead is able to survive some

flux levels of neutrons and X-rays and heat, and the carrier is necessarily prepared to survive the very severe conditions imposed on re-entering the atmosphere. There may, of course, be some window of vulnerability here which could be further narrowed by further work; but we are not privy to the information as to just how narrow that window may presently appear to be. In any case it is clear that there is nothing fully black or white involved here. It is a matter of degree, and is entirely speculative in nature, and would remain so even in the wake of further testing.

To come back to the more basic aspects of the matter of confidence in the context of a CTB, there are at least two points which require more serious consideration than those mentioned above. One is that of the possibility of a 'breakthrough' on the part of an adversary as a result of his clandestine evasion of the test ban. This matter is usually discussed in the format that, while we are meticulously and of necessity observing the letter and spirit of the agreement, our adversary has nothing else in mind except to evade it. A serious difficulty with the discussion on that basis is that there is no way of setting any limits to the lengths to which he might go, or to the ingenuity he might apply, or to the gains he might achieve. To avoid this difficulty, it may be useful to turn the discussion around and suppose that we are the ones who put our minds to subverting the agreement. Any strain on the imagination imposed by trying to picture our behaving in a way so foreign to our character can be relieved by assuming that the responsibility for this effort is assigned to the CIA. To avoid the extraneous difficulties which the facts of our open society and ubiquitous press might otherwise introduce, we shall take as a ground rule for this game that the only viewing means allowed are those we might be able to bring to bear on locations in Asia: remote seismographs, radiation detectors, satellite observations, and the like, plus possible defectors.

Some boundary conditions would absolutely have to be met. In particular, the effort must not be perceived by our opponent. In that case, because of the radiation detectors, the tests must be fully contained underground. Because of the seismographs, the absolute maximum yield we can allow ourselves is that of the detection threshold. For the moment we shall assume that to be one kiloton, though this limit is itself a quite uncertain thing. There have, for example, been instances in which much stronger signals have been recorded at locations remote from a particular site than at stations much closer in. Having chosen a limit, since our test device is novel (otherwise why test it?) its yield is uncertain. For this reason it seems necessary to choose the design yield maximum no larger than about three quarters of the limit yields so the actual yield will have little chance of exceeding the limit. Because of the satellites, the test site must not look like a set-up at Nevada with cables running out from the zero point to an array of instrument trailers, nor like the usual arrangements at Semipalatinsk. At the same time, in view of the novelty of the device we will want more data than usual. Since big convenient earth-moving equipment shows up like sore thumbs on reconnaisance photos, we had better cook up something like a movie set for King Solomon's Mines, with the spoils carried away in baskets. For extra assurance it has been decided to hold the shot until a heavy squall line passes near the site; but on the day, the weather service says a large front is approaching, a rash of faults shows up on some of the instrument lines. And so on.

Finally the test goes off and is completely successful. By artful dilution of some of the nuclear components the test had, of course, been carried out at reduced yield, so that an actual weapon can now be certified with a yield of at least two, and possibly three, times the yield of the test. Within a couple of years the first of these jazzy new two or three kiloton weapons can be added to the stockpile. Naturally, our opponents get some wind of this. We are not sure just how, but it may have been somebody from the Amarillo Plant, or possibly Rocky Flats, or maybe in a bar in Tijuana. At the next meeting of the CTB Control Commission our opponents act a bit huffy, though they do not appear to be terrified; and during a coffee break the head of their delegation remarks blandly to the head of our delegation: 'Son, we have thought about this, and we decided that if there ever were something we felt we really had to test it would be better to withdraw from the agreement than to mess around trying to sneak it in'.

Admittedly this is not the only possible evasion scenario; but it is the way we would undoubtedly do it. And it is probably more like the real thing than the deep, dark, massive, flawless, relentless, and imperceptible moving of mountains often attributed to our opponents. In any case, whether for us or for others, the yield of a clandestine test device would have to be chosen comfortably below some low estimate of the detection threshold; and the yield of certifiable devices available from evasion under a CTB would be limited to a rather few times the detection threshold - whatever that may be. It is, of course, possible that the low yield device certified by such a test is intended for use as a component in a high yield weapon. While that might provide reassurance and comfort to the party involved, it would not change the threat posed to others since, to be employable, the larger weapon will have to have been tested and certified for stockpile already.

It should be noted that the discussion given above applies particularly to devices having thermonuclear components. With respect to pure fission weapons in the hands of groups already having some experience with them, rather large extrapolations are confidently available without testing at high yield, provided the assembly pattern is not much changed from one proved at lower yield. This is probably not an important consideration since high yield pure fission weapons incline to be much heavier and more expensive than other options already available.

Again, on the subject of evasion, there is the matter of large-scale decoupling - the big hole. This is an American speciality, and it seems improbable that anyone else would consider it worthwhile. It is rather similar to the notion of testing on the far side of the sun. In principle, a big hole could cut the signals from some explosion down to the size of those from an explosion ten or a few tens of times smaller. There is probably nothing wrong with the theory, and it offers a perfectly delightful array of difficulties. Of course, the commotion associated with constructing a large hole, or even from preparing an existing hole for use, would provide a number of potentially observable effects. These might escape detection, or they might not; but it would certainly be a very troubling undertaking to ensure that they would. Along with these worries, everyone will have in mind the unexpected and unexplained collapse of the cavity at the Nevada test site in February, 1984. To suppose that anyone would invest the physical and nervous capital required to run a few clandestine tests in this way, presupposes a quite feverish anxiety to test, an anxiety rather inconsistent with the idea of entering into a CTB in the first place. It could be that the big hole was originally designed for the purpose of containing the CTB; and that may well end up being its only use.

The last matter we need to consider is that of the continuing availability of a sufficient cadre of knowledgeable people giving attention to the findings of the surveillance programme. This is an essential prerequisite to maintaining confidence in the operability of the stockpile. It has frequently been said that this is impossible over a period longer than a very few years. Most, if not all, of those making this claim have been more interested in finding reasons for continuing in the present pattern than in trying to devise a basis for a durable CTB.

Over the whole forty years of its existence the nuclear

weapons' activity has been in an active design effort. The fully knowledgeable and truly inventive members have constituted the 'designers'. Under a CTB it would not be possible to find out whether some novel or adventurous proposal with respect to the nuclear components had any value. Under those conditions, the challenge and excitement and satisfaction to which the successful nuclear designers had become accustomed would disappear; and the most ingenious and mobile members of the design team might be expected to move bodily, or move their attention, to some other locale. In that case we would lose the ability to resume a testing programme quickly, and with the existing momentum, should the CTB be suspended on short notice - as was the moratorium on testing in 1961. This is the sort of change which is most commonly in mind when it is said our expertise would soon degrade under a CTB.

However, the ability to resume testing promptly, which does depend on the active participation of designers, is by no means identical with the ability to maintain a sensitive and comprehending watch over the state of the stockpile. Indeed, in many high technology situations, such as that of operating modern aircraft, effective surveillance and maintenance programmes proceed with little, if any, participation by designers. It should also be recalled, in connection with the assumption that it may be urgent to be able to resume testing rapidly, that a really novel improvement which may be demonstrated by a test cannot show up in operational weapons in a time shorter than a few years.

What is essential to back up a physical surveillance programme is that there be people who follow the findings, and who have a thorough familiarity with the processes involved in determining a weapon's behaviour; they must know both what needs to go right, and what might go wrong. The habit of mind needed, and the basis for satisfaction in his work, are by no means identical with these which may typify a good designer. Though persons of the two types may be coequal in knowledge and intelligence, the more meticulous person may not play as stellar a role in the design phase of an operation. Similarly, though a CTB may mark the end of the line for the committed designer, the same does not necessarily follow for the person more suited to provide reassurance.

8 The Point Count Plan for Nuclear Arms Reduction
WILLIAM EPSTEIN AND RUSSELL LENG

Given the differences in negotiating styles and the technical problems of comparing and balancing diverse weapons systems, USA-USSR nuclear arms control negotiations are extraordinarily difficult in even the most agreeable political climate. Today's climate is anything but agreeable. The air is polluted by polemics and chilled by distrust. The START and INF talks are suspended indefinitely, and the bewildering array of new weapons developed since SALT I confound any efforts to achieve agreement on the relative threats posed by different components of each side's nuclear arsenals.

Nevertheless, the increasing sizes of these arsenals, along with new technologies of destruction that threaten to extend the arms race into space, demand that we move beyond limited arms control agreements to nuclear arms reduction to secure the survival of civilisation. President Reagan remains publicly committed to this goal, and the Administration has expressed willingness to accept 'trade-offs' of the US advantages in strategic bombers and cruise missiles for compensating Soviet reductions in ICBM's.

If trade-offs are acceptable to both sides, perhaps it is possible to achieve them without confronting the political and technical difficulties of reaching agreement on the relative destructive power of competing weapons systems. In fact, this could be done through a plan that would achieve a growing reduction in the destructive capacities of the nuclear arsenals of the superpowers while progressively moving the two sides closer to actual nuclear parity. The plan is called the 'Point Count' approach to arms reduction.

Here is how it would work. Each superpower would be allotted an arbitrary number of points, say 1000, to use in assessing the distribution of the military power of the **other side's** forces. The United States would judge the relative value of different components of the Soviet nuclear arsenal and assign portions of the 1000 points to each. The USSR would do the same for the US nuclear forces. Each side

POINT COUNT PLAN FOR ARMS REDUCTION   71

obviously would assign the most points to those components of the other's forces that it considers the most threatening.

The next step would be for each side to pass its distribution of points to the other to serve as the basis for annual percentage reductions in the remaining balance of its nuclear armaments. It is important that the reductions be on a **percentage** basis - which becomes feasible with the point-counterpoint system - because they will cut more deeply into the arms of the side with a larger arsenal. The difference between the sizes of the two nuclear arsenals would be reduced with each successive cut.

Having received the point distribution from the other side, each state would have complete discretion over which of its weapons to cut, provided the aggregate reduction met the percentage figure. Assume that the annual reduction is 10 per cent. Then, in the first year, each side would reduce its arsenal by any mix of weapons it chose where the points assigned by the other side added up to 100. The annual decisions on weapons cuts would be announced simultaneously, so that neither side would have advance notice of the other's plans. The disposal of the weapons could be verified by an international commission - a process that the Soviets have indicated in the past that they would be willing to accept in the case of actual disarmament as opposed to an arms control measure. The exercise would be repeated each year, that is, each side would redistribute the 1000 points for the remaining balance of the other's arsenal following the 10 per cent reduction, and the other would again choose which weapons to eliminate to reduce its remaining weapons by another 10 per cent. Thus, by reallocating its 1000 points each year, each side could take into account any new production or modernisation of the other side's forces.

To initiate the Point Count system, the two sides would have to agree on just five points: (1) what weapons to include - strategic and medium range weapons could be merged under this system without the complications that would obtain in negotiations; (2) the size of the annual percentage reduction; (3) the annual schedule for the exchange of point distributions, announcements of cuts, and the disposal of weapons; (4) verification of the disposal of weapons; and (5) how deep to make the cuts, that is, when to stop. (Ten years of 10 per cent cuts would reduce both arsenals to roughly 3000 warheads.) Once these decisions were reached, the plan could proceed without further negotiations. Tables 1 and 2 illustrate how the system might operate over a five year period with annual reductions of 10 per cent.

To simplify the example, the tables include only strategic weapons. Consistent with recent arms reduction talks, war-

THE STRATEGIC ARMS RACE

TABLE 1
Balanced Reductions in the United States' Strategic Nuclear Weapons

	Delivery Vehicles	Year 1 A	Year 1 B	Year 1 C	Year 2 A	Year 2 B	Year 2 C	Year 3 A	Year 3 B	Year 3 C	Year 4 A	Year 4 B	Year 4 C	Year 5 A	Year 5 B	Year 5 C	Year 6 A	Year 6 Delivery Vehicles
ICBM's																		
Minuteman III	550	1650	190	0	1650	200	0	1650	200	0	1650	230	0	1650	250	-25	1485	495
Minuteman II	450	450	50	-10	360	50	0	360	50	-30	144	20	-20	0	0	0	0	0
Titan II	45	45	10	-10	0	0	0	0	0	0	0	0	0	0	0	0	0	0
Sub-total	1045	2145	250	-20	2010	250	0	2010	250	-30	1794	250	-20	1650	250	-25	1485	495
SLBM's																		
Trident	264	2112	200	0	2112	240	0	2112	300	0	2112	300	0	2112	330	0	2112	264
Poseidon	304	3040	300	-30	2736	310	-100	1853	250	-50	1482	200	-50	1112	170	-50	785	78
Subtotal	568	5152	500	-30	4848	550	-100	3965	550	-50	3594	500	-50	3224	500	-50	2897	342
BOMBERS																		
B-52G (ALCM)	199	1592	180	0	1592	175	0	1592	175	-20	1410	210	-10	1343	250	-25	1208	151
B-52D	104	416	50	-50	0	0	0	0	0	0	0	0	0	0	0	0	0	0
F-111	60	240	20	0	240	25	0	240	25	0	240	40	-20	120	250	0	120	30
Subtotal	363	2248	250	-50	1832	200	0	1832	200	-20	1650	250	-30	1463	500	-25	1328	181
TOTAL	1976	9545	1000	-100	8690	1000	-100	7807	1000	-100	7038	1000	-100	6337	1250	-100	5710	1018

A: Number of warheads
B: Points assigned by USSR
C: Percentage cuts accepted by USA

POINT COUNT PLAN FOR ARMS REDUCTION

TABLE 2
Balanced Reductions in the Soviet Union's Strategic Nuclear Weapons by Warheads

	Delivery Vehicles	Year 1			Year 2			Year 3			Year 4			Year 5			Year 6	
		A	B	C	A	B	C	A	B	C	A	B	C	A	B	C	A	Delivery Vehicles
ICBM's																		
SS-19	360	2110	250	0	2110	270	0	2110	300	0	2110	370	-45	1854	360	-35	1674	285
SS-18	308	2752	320	0	2752	355	0	2752	400	-40	2477	380	-40	2217	410	-55	1920	215
SS-17	150	570	60	0	570	75	-75	0	0	0	0	0	0	0	0	0	0	0
SS-11, 13	610	610	70	-70	0	0	0	0	0	0	0	0	0	0	0	0	0	0
Subtotal	1428	6042	700	-70	5432	700	-75	4862	700	-40	4587	750	-85	4071	770	-90	3594	500
SLBM's																		
SS-N-20	40	400	55	0	400	55	0	400	60	0	400	50	0	400	40	0	400	40
SS-N-18	224	1120	125	0	1120	145	0	1120	165	-20	980	150	0	980	170	0	980	196
SS-N-6, 8, 17	688	688	70	-30	393	50	-25	197	30	-30	0	0	0	0	0	0	0	0
Subtotal	952	2208	250	-30	1913	250	-25	1717	250	-50	1380	200	0	1380	210	0	1380	236
BOMBERS																		
Bear	100	130	15	0	130	15	0	130	15	-5	87	15	0	87	0	0	87	67
Bison	43	43	5	0	43	5	0	43	5	0	43	10	-10	0	0	0	0	0
Backfire	100	200	30	0	200	30	0	200	30	-5	167	25	-5	134	20	-10	67	34
Subtotal	243	373	50	0	373	50	0	373	50	-10	297	50	-15	221	20	-10	154	101
TOTAL	2623	8623	1000	-100	7718	1000	-100	6952	1000	-100	6264	1000	-100	5672	1000	-100	5128	837

A: Number of warheads
B: Points assigned by USA
C: Percentage cuts accepted by USSR

heads are used as the basis for the annual 10 per cent reductions. In Table 1, for example, which shows the reductions for the United States, there is a reduction of Minuteman-II ICBM's from 450 warheads to 360 warheads after the first year. The USSR assigned 50 of their 1000 points to these weapons, and the USA assigned 10 points from its required 100 points cut to this force as well. Thus the US decision to reduce them by 10 points represents a 20 per cent (10/50) cut in the 450 warheads to 360 at the beginning of the second year. The use of warheads as the basis for the assignment of points is purely for illustrative purposes. A virtue of the system is that each party could use whatever system it wished to determine the distribution of its points.

The examples in Tables 1 and 2 also assume that each side proportionately distributed its 1000 points, first across each leg of the triads, and then within each triad. The proportions are re-adjusted each year to maintain the distribution following changes wrought by the other's arms reductions. Each side's arms reduction decisions are based roughly on the age of the weapons, retention of the initial balance among legs of the triad, and minimisation of reductions in warheads. These assumptions too are made solely to clarify the illustrations in Tables 1 and 2. Both sides would retain complete discretion over the distribution of points and weapons reductions in a real world exercise.

After five years, with annual reductions of 10 per cent on the remaining balance of weapons, the US strategic arsenal would be reduced from 9545 warheads to 5710, and the Soviet arsenal from 8623 to 5128 warheads. The initial difference of 922 warheads in the US favour would be reduced to 582. The total number of delivery vehicles would be reduced by roughly 72 per cent for the USA and by 69 per cent for the USSR.

The plan encourages the balanced distribution of points illustrated in the tables because this would lead to larger overall reductions. If the USSR, for example, assigned all 1000 points to a single weapons system, say the Minuteman-III, and continued to do so each year, the USA would be required to make an annual 10 per cent cut in the remaining balance of that weapons system - but only that system - each year. After five years the US force of Minuteman-IIIs would be reduced by 41 per cent to 974 warheads; however, all other strategic weapons, which account for 83 per cent of the total US complement of warheads, would remain untouched. Consequently, there would be only a 7 per cent overall reduction in the total US complement of warheads. Nevertheless, should one side decide that a certain class of weapons held by the other is particularly threatening, it is free to assign as many of its 1000 points to that system as it wishes.

POINT COUNT PLAN FOR ARMS REDUCTION

By allowing each of the superpowers to decide which of the other's weapons pose the greatest threat, the Point Count plan avoids endless debates over the relative capabilities of different weapons or their intended purposes. By the same token, the system of incremental cuts does not require that both sides believe that parity exists. Since the process would move the two sides towards greater parity, all that is required is that each agree that parity is desirable, a position that both sides have stated many times.

In this respect, the Point Count plan would be an ideal complement to a **nuclear weapons freeze** on testing and deployment of new weapons; its adoption could facilitate a more favourable attitude toward a freeze. In the absence of a freeze, the plan would encourage the development of less threatening deterrence systems, such as the 'Midgetman' missile, as opposed to weapons alleged to have a first strike capability, such as the MX, which would be more likely to attract a high percentage of the points assigned by the other side. Reductions in **strategic** nuclear forces have been used for the illustrations in Tables 1 and 2, but the system would work equally well in achieving gradual reductions in other types of weapons, such as INFs in Europe, or even in achieving the reductions in conventional forces discussed in the MBFR talks. In fact, the Point Count system provides the most feasible approach to arms reductions should the START and INF talks be merged, as the Soviets have proposed, and as the USA has said it is willing to consider.

Obviously, the current political climate is not conducive to any immediate breakthrough in superpower arms talks. But that makes this a good time to examine new approaches to arms reduction. Indeed, the very discussion of such a new approach to nuclear arms reductions can help improve the atmosphere. If a change for the better does occur, it will be important to have fully developed proposals in place to take advantage of any opportunities that a thaw in superpower relations may present.

President Reagan says that he wants 'real arms reductions', but he opposes a nuclear weapons freeze on the grounds that the Soviets would never agree to arms reduction once a freeze guaranteed their lead in the arms race. But the Point Count plan would progressively reduce their lead, if such a lead exists. Suppose the President were to propose the Point Count plan, preferably (but not necessarily) in conjunction with acceptance of a freeze on the development of new weapons. If the USSR were to reject the idea out of hand, the USA would lose nothing, but if they accepted the proposal, we could take a major step towards a safer world.

9 The Naval Arms Race and Arms Control
JAN PRAWITZ

Introduction

All branches of military activity have in one way or another been addressed at negotiations to halt the arms race, with one notable exception: naval activities and forces. Before World War II there were some significant arms control agreements relating to naval forces, such as the 1922 Washington Convention and the 1930 London Treaty, and there is the 1936 Montreux Convention, still in force, regulating the transit of naval vessels to and from the Black Sea. Some laws of war provisions related to naval warfare were also included in the 1907 Hague Conventions. However, only a few measures were agreed after 1945.

Among these the most important are the bilateral USA-USSR limitations on submarines carrying SLBMs in SALT I of 1972 and SALT II of 1979. Related to them is a confidence-building measure: the agreement on the Prevention of Incidents on and over the High Seas. There is also the multilateral 1972 Sea Bed Treaty.

A regional measure is the inclusion of vast sea areas of the Atlantic Ocean and the South-East Pacific into the Latin American Nuclear Weapon-Free Zone, once that treaty enters into force.

Several measures have been proposed but not yet agreed. Among them are: the Zone of Peace in the Indian Ocean; the abstention from navigating naval forces in areas that are remote from their home ports and close to coasts of other states; the establishment of 'sanctuary' areas for SLBM-submarines; and the prenotification of military exercises in sea areas.

There are some recent instances of major flag states filing reservations against the extension of arms control to the high seas by reference to 'recognised international law'. One example is the ratification by nuclear weapon states of Protocol II of the Tlatelolco Treaty. Another example, where such reservation was already instituted in the treaty text, is the Antarctic Treaty in which the provisions apply to areas south of 60°, but not to sea areas.

The Legal Setting

An important reason for the lack of interest in naval forces with regard to arms control is not lack of appreciation of their importance but rather the fact that the legal regime at sea has not been defined in a clear way. During the Third United Nations Law of the Sea Conference, there was an attempt to raise the question of limiting the military use of the high sea areas of the world, considered to belong to the common heritage of mankind. The issue was, however, considered to fall within the general mandate of the Disarmament Conference in Geneva. But the DC found it difficult to deal with naval issues before the Law of the Sea Conference had defined the legal regime of the sea.

On 10 December 1982 the new Convention on the Law of the Sea (UNCLOS) was signed at Montego Bay, Jamaica. From that date onwards, there exists a legal base for discussing arms control and disarmament at sea, and therefore there should be no excuse for not addressing arms control and disarmament issues in the maritime domain.

A few states, mainly Western major powers, did not sign in Montego Bay, not because of disagreement over security related provisions in the Convention, but because of the linkage to the regime for exploitation of the economic resources on the ocean floor.

UNCLOS is a treaty based on the tradition of the freedom on the high seas dating back to the 17th century. That regime was the opposite of arms control: arms non-control at sea. Therefore, introducing measures of arms control and disarmament at sea at the present time would, depending on the circumstances of each case, involve agreement among states to abstain from specific UNCLOS freedoms they may enjoy.

According to UNCLOS, a coastal state exercises full and exclusive jurisdiction in its **internal waters** only, that is inside a coastline perimeter, the so called base line. It has full jurisdiction in its **territorial sea** extending up to 12 miles from the base line, except over passage of ships. It has jurisdiction over the exploitation of natural resources in its **exclusive economic zone** extending up to 200 miles from the base line. It has no jurisdiction in **the high seas**.

All states have the right of **innocent passage** in the territorial sea of other coastal states, and of **transit**

passage in international straits, and are subject to almost **no military restraints** in economic zones and on high seas.

While adversary land forces in peacetime are geographically separated from each other, naval forces of different states may mix all over the sea and indeed frequently do so. On the other hand, the right of access to all parts of the sea for everyone should facilitate the procedures for verification of arms control measures applied at sea.

Some Military and Technical Considerations

The technological development of the means for naval warfare has made remarkable advances in a number of respects. This trend is, of course, dominated by the two major military blocs, but the new technology is gradually influencing the navies of smaller countries as well. Developments include radically new vessel design, such as hydrofoils and hovercrafts. New missile technology also permits small ships and fast patrol boats to carry weapons with a fire power which was earlier available only to large warships.

The main conventional weapon development relates to the capabilities of ship-to-ship and air-to-ship missiles, considerably diminishing the role of conventional naval artillery. The new technology includes missiles able to fly at both high and low altitudes, to be launched from above or under the surface, and which could finish a flight by a dive to a submerged target. Advanced guidance systems, including external satellite-assistance, permit both over-the-horizon targeting and an almost one hundred per cent hit probability. Defence systems to meet the threat of the new missiles have, of course, also been developed. New methods and aids for precise navigation permit all-weather all-time operation with ever increasing precision, including submerged navigation in areas covered by ice. The major naval powers have also acquired a considerable capability for sea transportation of troops, with an increased mobility and range of their amphibious forces.

In summary, the present naval, amphibious and sea-transportation capabilities combined, provide the major power blocs with increasing possibilities not only to outbalance each other but to project considerable military force in most parts of the world. 'Gunboat diplomacy', invasion and closing of strategic sea lanes by mines are now possible at shorter notice, with more precision, over longer distances and on a larger scale than ever before.

While this situation has increased the general risks of confrontation at sea, special risks have emerged from unintended incidents and unnecessary conflicts due to difficulty in identifying correctly objects in bad weather and illumination conditions. Such risks are particularly high in relation to submarines and ASW.

A significant dimension is added to this picture by the fact that missiles, torpedoes, depth charges and mines could be adapted to carry nuclear warheads. While the strategic nuclear weapons have attracted a great deal of attention, tactical nuclear weapons at sea have not, despite the fact that they not only outnumber the strategic ones, but are routinely carried around the world in large numbers. This important fact has been largely overlooked, partly due to the policy of the nuclear powers neither to confirm nor to deny the presence of any nuclear weapon, at any particular place at any particular time.

The build-up of naval force is not an arms race independent from global or regional arms races, but is part of them. Therefore, maritime forces should be considered in the context of the general arms race when discussing arms control and disarmament applied at sea.

It would be important to consider the functions of maritime force and make distinction between:
- **strategic nuclear** forces of nuclear weapon states;
- **blue water** forces of major military flag states being able to operate oceanwide, but which could also be assigned to local missions;
- **green water** forces for operation in coastal areas;
- **brown water** activities including amphibious infiltration, sabotage and other low level operations in coastline waters, harbours, mouths of rivers, and so on.

Arms Control and Disarmament Issues

The variety of naval forces, deployed for a variety of purposes, requires a variety of objectives to be pursued by arms control and disarmament measures in the maritime domain. The main objectives to be considered are:
- **stabilising** the strategic nuclear balance;
- **limiting** the maritime arms primarily of the military forces of the major power blocs;
- providing for a reasonable **seafront security** for well over one hundred small and medium-sized coastal states;
- **confidence-building**;
- **guaranteeing** the possibility of non-belligerent states to the unimpeded exercise of their UNCLOS rights in case of war between other states.

Negotiating arms control and disarmament in the maritime domain will have to overcome a number of difficulties:

(a) the East-West imbalance in the naval domain; (b) the conflicting security interests between a few major flag states and many small and medium-sized coastal states; (c) the relation between legal instruments of the agreements and the Law of the Sea; (d) the special technical problems related to submarines; (e) the long tradition of the freedom of the high seas, which makes the mere idea of abstaining from that freedom in favour of arms control smack of red tape.

The discussion of possible areas for arms control measures in the maritime domain after Montego Bay has just begun. It would, however, be possible to identify the following general categories of possible measures:

- Limitation of sea-born strategic nuclear weapons and the establishment of sanctuaries for SLBM-submarines. The purpose of such measures would be to promote the stability of the nuclear balance.
- Limitations of blue water forces of the major power blocs, their amphibious forces and special military transportation vessels. The purpose would be to provide a maritime contribution to an attempt to achieve a general balance between the blocs at a lower level, and to limit the capabilities for gunboat diplomacy and overseas power projection.
- Provisions for guaranteeing safe transit on the high seas for ships and aircraft of neutral and non-combatant states. The purpose would be to separate vessels of states involved in military conflict from those of states not involved.
- Confidence and security building measures, such as limitation of the cruising of warships, and of naval and amphibious manoeuvres; limited or full demilitarisation on a regional or sub-regional basis. The purpose would be to relax tension, build confidence and decrease the presence of military force regionally. A possible measure would be the multilateralisation of the bilateral USA-USSR Prevention of Incidents Agreement.
- Modernisation of the Laws of War to be applied at sea, an issue which was overlooked when the Additional Protocols to the 1949 Geneva Conventions were negotiated because of the then on-going Law of the Sea negotiations.

The long-time taboo on the inclusion of maritime forces in arms control negotiations is likely to be removed following the UNCLOS agreement. The UN General Assembly in 1983 decided to undertake a study on the subject, for discussion in 1985. At the present time states should be encouraged to include maritime factors in their arms control and disarmament policy making, taking into account the specific legal and geographical aspects.

Part II
Military Aspects of Space

10 Extent of Militarisation of Outer Space
GEOFFREY PERRY

Introduction

The two superpowers were both quick to realise the potential for military operations afforded by a presence in space. The United States were first in the field when the Atlas-B ICBM, sponsored by the USAF and ARPA, became the first communications orbit-relay experiment by re-transmitting a Christmas message from President Eisenhower in December 1958[1]. Earlier that year, the Army-ARPA's Explorer-4 had mapped the radiation shells resulting from the Argus atomic weapon detonations[2] at altitudes greater than 320 km.

The USAF had commenced work on reconnaissance from space even prior to the launch of Sputnik-1[3] and an acceleration of the programme in November 1957 led to the series of Discoverer satellites commencing in 1959 and the first successful payload-recovery from orbit of the Discoverer-13 capsule in August 1960[4].

The Soviet Union's Cosmos programme, initiated in 1962, saw the recovery of Cosmos-4 in April of that year following a three-day mission[5].

Today, the vast majority of launches of both superpowers are for military purposes, and in this paper I will attempt to show that each obtains comparable results although adopting somewhat different approaches.

In November 1961, President Kennedy placed a 'top secret' security classification on all spaceborne reconnaissance activities[6], although the well-established Discoverer programme was permitted to continue until the end of the scheduled series with Discoverer-38, launched on 27 February 1962. The Soviet response was to introduce the Cosmos label for all launches outside a few named applications satellite and scientific programmes, interplanetary and lunar flights, and programmes related to manned spaceflight.

The annual Aerospace Forecast & Inventory issue of **Aviation Week & Space Technology** (AW&ST) gives details of current and planned US military programmes[7]. This paper identifies similar Soviet programmes, where they can be seen to exist, and points to others for which there is no direct parallel.

Photographic Reconnaissance

Three optical observation programmes are listed by AW&ST. The Lockheed/USAF Big Bird satellite provides broad coverage with both radio transmission and capsule return. Launched by the Titan-3D/Agena, it flies between 250 and 160 km at 96.4° inclination. The USAF/CIA KH-11 strategic reconnaissance satellites provide broad coverage with digital image transmission. Also launched by Titan-3D/Agena, at 97° inclination, it flies higher, between 440 and 300 km. A USAF highest resolution film return satellite, flying between 350 and 130 km at 96.4° inclination is launched by Titan-3B/Agena.

The announcement that Cosmos-4 had been recovered from orbit after a flight of only three days signalled the inauguration of a continuing series of satellites within the Cosmos programme which accounts for approximately 50 per cent of all Cosmos launches. Figure 1 shows Cosmos launches by year together with a plot of those with recoverable payloads. It can be seen that the 50 per cent estimate has held over the whole lifetime of the Cosmos programme. Latterly the Soviet Union has identified some of these payloads, notably those at an inclination of 82.3°, as having Earth resources roles, but their short-wave telemetry is indistinguishable from that of some military recoverable payloads.

The Soviet analogue to the Big Bird is to be found in the fourth generation flights from which no short-wave transmissions have been recognised. Frequency-modulated transmissions on 240 MHz have been observed at both low and high data-rates. Perigee heights are generally lower than for satellites of earlier generations, normally close to 175 km but occasionally falling below 160 km, making regular boosting necessary to overcome drag and maintain orbit. Imagery is probably returned digitally from orbit, and film capsules are returned to Earth around the ninth and eighteenth days of the mission. Recovery beacon signals from these capsules take the form of a succession of Morse code signals on 19.995 MHz. These satellites are generally launched later in the day than those with 14-day missions, to ensure suitable lighting conditions over the target area throughout the flight, and perigee is relocated on the southbound pass during the latter stages of those missions exceeding four weeks. There is still some doubt as to the final stages of the mission. The Kettering Group have not identified any recovery beacon signals

MILITARISATION OF OUTER SPACE

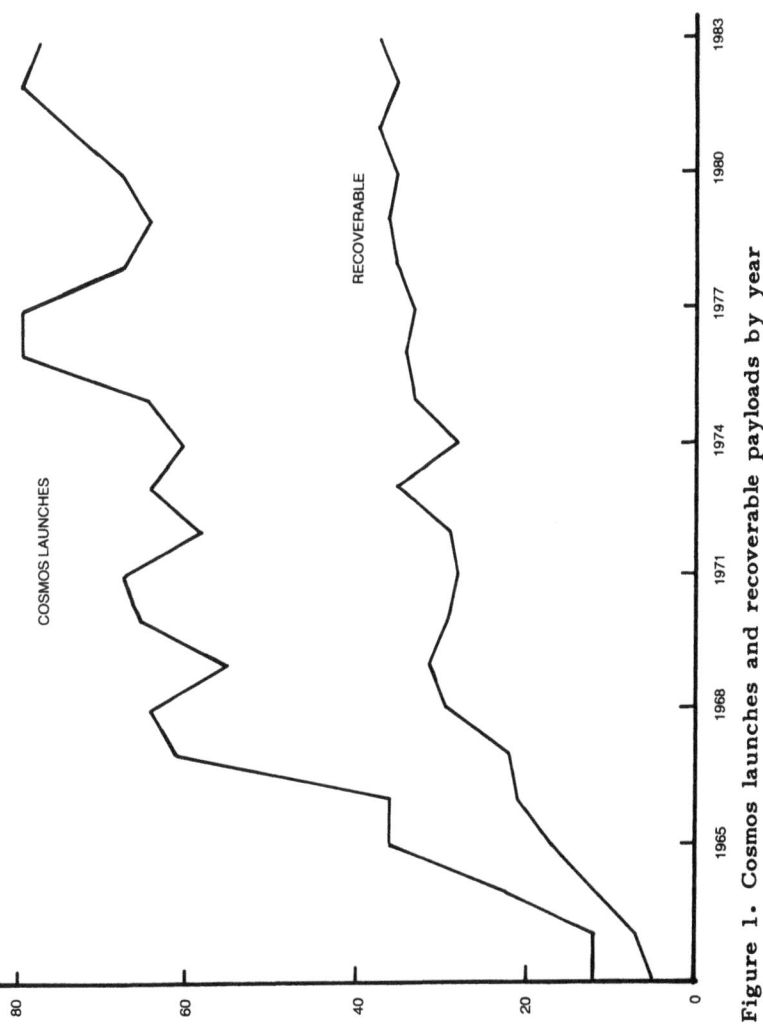

Figure 1. Cosmos launches and recoverable payloads by year

from these satellites, possibly due to the recovery time falling within the hours of darkness at the Group's locations. On the other hand, it might be presumed that these payloads are de-orbited at the end of the operational phase in the manner of Progress spacecraft.

The broad area coverage is provided by those Cosmos satellites which manoeuvre to an orbit with perigee in excess of 300 km and a period of approximately 92.3 minutes towards the end of the first day of the mission. The resulting ground-tracks produce interlaced coverage, with the tracks on even days falling mid-way between those on odd days. Superimposed on this is a general daily precession which ensures complete global coverage before recovery after fourteen days. These satellites transmit a two-tone frequency-shift-keyed (fsk) tracking beacon on the short-wave frequency of 19.989 MHz and amplitude-modulated data, on command, on 232 MHz in the VHF band. Recovery beacon signals at the end of the mission are observed as a succession of Morse code signals on 19.995 MHz.

As mentioned earlier, a further sub-set of these payloads consists of those which are designated, at launch, as having Earth resources roles. Some, but not all, are announced as reporting to the **Priroda** (Nature) Centre. These flights, at 82.3° inclination, superseded the earlier 81.3° flights which were timed to coincide with the break-up of Arctic ice along the northern seaboard of the Soviet Union. One or two, each year, manoeuvre to the high-perigee orbit and employ triple interlacing of ground-tracks. Recovery beacons observed on 19.995 MHz are occasionally the same signals as from the first generation satellites.

Some recent flights point to the possibility of the existence of an advanced reconnaissance satellite. Cosmos-1426 at 50.6° inclination out of Tyuratam, flew for 67 days before disappearing from orbit whilst its period was still sufficient to rule out natural decay. During its mission it made ten major manoeuvres, keeping the perigee continually in sunlight at a height close to 200 km[8]. Despite repeated attempts, the Kettering Group did not detect any short-wave or VHF transmissions from this satellite. The Group did not detect transmissions from Cosmos-1516 but its orbital parameters, in-flight manoeuvres, and 44-day mission, are consistent with it having been a standard fourth generation flight. If that is true then the lack of signals is of no great significance. Most recently, the flight of Cosmos-1543 has produced some uncertainty. Its 90.6 minutes, 62.8° orbit out of Plesetsk is reminiscent of the international biosatellites but no such mission was announced. Short-wave signals were not positively identified and, as yet, its role is undetermined.

Ocean Surveillance

The US Navy operates all-weather sea surveillance under its Navy Ocean Surveillance Satellite (NOSS) programme in which three spacecraft result from each Atlas-F launch. These transmit their data to the main satellite for relay to Earth. Radar, passive radio listening devices and infra-red sensors are reported to be employed.

A US Navy satellite with active radar, destined for launch by the Space Shuttle, under the Clipper Bow programme has been cancelled. The US Navy has no active radar programme.

The Soviet Union has its passive ELINT satellites, known in the West as EORSATs, flying at 65° inclinations with orbital periods maintained very precisely at 93.3 minutes. First appearing as single missions at the end of 1974, following the Cosmos-954 re-entry in January 1978, they began operating in pairs with interlaced ground-tracks. When natural decay ensues at the end of their operational phases, some have been raised to higher orbits to remove them from their replacements and it is not unknown for fragmentation to occur subsequently. Currently, only one such satellite, Cosmos-1507, is operational.

Cosmos satellites with orbital periods of 89.5 minutes at 65° inclination, but differing from recoverable photo-reconnaissance satellites in having near-circular orbits with perigees close to 250 km, first appeared in 1967. This type of satellite does not separate from the last stage of the carrier rocket on reaching orbit. After an operational phase during which micromanoeuvres maintain the circular orbit against the effects of atmospheric drag, part of the payload is separated from the final stage and is boosted into a much higher circular orbit from whence decay is of the order of several hundreds of years. It was deduced that this was a nuclear reactor device to provide power for a side-looking radar[9]. Some confirmation of this was obtained when, following a malfunction in November 1977 during the attempt to separate its nuclear reactor, Cosmos-954 re-entered the atmosphere and spread its débris across northern Canada. When the programme was resumed after an interval of two years, it was observed that two objects were being catalogued in the higher 'safe' orbit after the end of the operational phase. In a report lodged with the United Nations[10], the Soviet Union outlined precautions which could be taken to prevent radioactive débris from reaching the Earth's surface in the event of another malfunction. Such a malfunction occurred on 28 December 1982 when it proved impossible to boost the reactor-device of Cosmos-1402 into the 'safe' orbit. It was subsequently reported that the reactor's fuel core had been separated and that it would be completely vaporised during re-entry[11]. This claim was justified when the reactor shell decayed over the Indian Ocean late on 23 January and the fuel core decayed over the South Atlantic, east of Brazil, on 7 February 1983. However, to date, no more missions of this type have been mounted.

Electronic Intelligence Gathering (ELINT)

AW&ST still refers to the Thor/Agena launched second generation electromagnetic reconnaissance satellites from Lockheed/Sanders/USAF which are to be superseded by a new Hughes design (Code 711). No mention is made of the Big Bird sub-satellites which flew at 480 km for what was presumed to be radar detection and at 1450 km for inspection of antiballistic missile (ABM) radars, nor of the geosynchronous Rhyolite programme whose security was compromised in 1976[12].

The Soviet Union operates constellations of Cosmos satellites which are presumed to have ELINT functions. As transmissions from these satellites have not been intercepted, it is possible only to demonstrate systems deployed in orbital planes spaced at regular intervals around the Earth, providing the necessary global coverage.

Satellites in near-circular orbits at 550 km and 74° inclination formed a constellation of four at 45° plane-spacings from February 1971, when Cosmos-395 joined Cosmos-315, 330 and 387[13]. The constellation was maintained until the dramatic effect of increased solar activity on the atmospheric density during 1980 caused the majority of them to decay as a result of increased drag[14]. No attempt to re-establish the constellation has been made.

A heavier class of ELINT satellite with orbital parameters characteristic of the early Meteor satellites provided a constellation of six with orbital planes spaced at 60° intervals. Since 1980 the precise spacing of this constellation has degenerated and it is possible that their role is being assumed by a newer class of payload flying at inclinations of 82.5°, also with 97.6 minute periods. Some of this class are announced as having oceanographic missions but Cosmos-1300, 1328 and 1378, spaced at intervals of 45° and 90°, suggested that they were the initial members of a new constellation of four at 45° plane-spacings. However, the gap between Cosmos-1328 and Cosmos-1408, which may be considered to have replaced Cosmos-1378, was not filled until Cosmos-1536 was launched on 8 February 1984. It is not unreasonable to ask why it took so long and, also, whether the older satellites were still operational, particularly as Cosmos-

1536 could be seen to complete a new constellation of three at 60° plane-spacings with Cosmos-1445 and Cosmos-1515, which were launched during 1983.

Early Warning of Missile Launches

The Defense Support Program (DSP) satellites placed into geosynchronous orbit for TRW/Aerojet/USAF under Code 647 by the Titan-3C employ infra-red sensors to detect the launch of intercontinental ballistic missiles (ICBMs) and submarine-launched ballistic missiles (SLBMs).

The Soviet Union makes use of the semi-synchronous Molniya-type orbit for its early warning satellites. One major difference is the choice of an argument of perigee of 315° rather than the 280° of the Molniyas. This has the result of broadening the loop of the ground-track in the region of the Northern Hemisphere apogee. An initial plane-spacing of 80° evolved into a constellation of nine at 40° spacing[15]. However, there have never been nine satellites operational having stabilised daily repeating ground-tracks. The ground-tracks of Cosmos-1285 and Cosmos-1481, its replacement, were never stabilised on reaching orbit. Whereas the orbital period of Cosmos-1285 was higher than the truly semi-synchronous period, that of Cosmos-1481 was less, due to differences in launch profile. Neither were they speedily replaced. One feels that this can hardly be coincidental. A constellation of nine satellites provides some redundancy and it might be that this particular orbital slot is used to accommodate an on-orbit spare.

At the beginning of 1981, the ascending nodes of the operational satellites in the constellation were relocated from 90° W to 55° W, close to that of Cosmos-1247 which had been launched on 19 February[16]. As a result of this relocation more complete viewing of the Mid-Western United States is possible from the North Pacific loop in the ground-track and more evenly distributed coverage of the Atlantic Ocean and China is obtained from the European loop.

These satellites transmit on frequencies close to those employed by NASA's interplanetary probes and, despite their presumed military role, the Soviet Union, at NASA's request, discontinues transmissions at times of critical data reception during planetary encounters[17].

Communication, Command and Control

The largest number of programmes listed by AW&ST falls within this category. Two Defense Satellite Communications Systems (DSCS) of the Defense Communications Agency head the list.

The TRW DSCS-2 from TRW provides up to 1300 duplex voice channels with Earth-coverage and spot-beam antennae. They were launched by Titan-3C or Titan-34D/IUS. The General Electric DSCS-3, also in geosynchronous orbit, are three-axis stabilised and launched by Titan-34D or SpaceShuttle/IUS.

The Atlas/Centaur launched TRW/Navy/USAF FltSatCom satellites provide UHF communications between ships, shore-to-ship, and ship-to-aircraft. The Hughes/Navy Leasat, which will be in addition to FltSatCom, is due for a Space Shuttle launch in 1984.

The Hughes/USAF Satellite Data System (SDS) satellites are launched into Molniya-type orbits by the Titan-3B/Agena and provide UHF communications for strategic forces, communications between Satellite Control Facility ground-stations, and strategic data relay. They have also been reported as used for relaying image data from KH-11s to the United States[18].

The Soviet Union uses Molniya-1 satellites for its long-distance communications links. Early in 1976, the 32nd Molniya-1 was placed into orbit with its orbital plane precisely mid-way between two of the four standard Molniya groups. Three more launches that year completed a set of four Molniya-1 satellites positioned mid-way between the standard groups. Stephen Birkill showed that they operated only on the Asian loop of the ground-track, transmitting digital fsk signals in what is presumed to be a military mode, whereas the other four, and their accompanying Molniya-3s, carry domestic traffic on both Asian and North American loops[19].

With the introduction of Soviet communication satellites in geosynchronous orbits it is natural to presume that some military communications transponders are placed on them. No direct indication of their use has been given but Gals (Tack) satellites/transponders were planned for 1979 to establish a four-satellite constellation providing global military communications. Uplink between 7.9 and 8.4 GHz and downlink between 7.25 and 7.75 GHz are in bands officially allocated for government service but internationally accepted as military communications bands. The launch of Cosmos-1546 on 29 March 1984 into geosynchronous orbit 'to continue space exploration' rather than for communications or meteorology, opens the door for speculation as to some military role.

Tactical and theatre communications are provided by octuple launches of satéllites at 74° inclination into near-circular orbits at around 1500 km with periods close to 115 minutes. Although the orbital planes drift relative to each other due to small differences of orbital period, new launches are invariably made into the same orbital plane as that used for

MILITARISATION OF OUTER SPACE

the original launch. It is believed that a constellation of 24 such satellites forms the operational segment of a real-time tactical communications system within a given theatre of operations or a store-dump system.

A further sub-set of Cosmos satellites, having an inclination of 74° and constituting a global system with a regular replacement policy, is a constellation with orbital periods of just under 101 minutes and plane-spacings of 120°. These are thought to perform clandestine store-dump missions in a COMINT role. Beginning with Cosmos-1452 in 1983, a new constellation has been established, off-set some 10° from the older constellation.

Meteorology

The US Defense Department's Defense Meteorological Satellite Program (DMSP) obtains global meteorological information from its Block 5D-2 series of satellites, the first of which was launched by an Atlas in December 1982. The RCA satellites transmit data to USAF ground-stations which relay them to the Air Force Global Weather Center where they are processed automatically by computers.

There does not appear to be a comparable Soviet programme. The Soviet Union maintains two or three Meteor-2 satellites in near-polar orbits and currently has two Meteor-Priroda satellites in the sun-synchronous orbit. None of these send Automatic Picture Transmission (APT) continuously but there may be other transmissions of current and/or stored data which have not yet been identified.

Navigation

AW&ST identifies two programmes of navigation satellites. The Navy Navigation Satellite System using satellites built by RCA and launched by Scout into circular polar orbits at 1000 km first appeared as Transit and, later, as an improved version, as Nova. This system was declassified in 1967 and it is now estimated that 93 per cent of its utilisation is by the civilian sector.

The Defense Department's Global Positioning System (GPS) or Navstar is still in the developmental stage. Rockwell-built satellites are launched into 12-hour semi-synchronous circular orbits with three satellites spaced regularly in two orbital planes separated by 120°. The operational system is envisaged as a constellation of 18 satellites in six orbital planes at 63° inclination - a reduction from the 24 intended originally. Two signal structures are provided: a precise or P-code signal and a coarse/acquisition or C/A signal. The C/A signal provides a rapid acquisition capability for P-code high precision users and a coarse ranging signal for users who require less precise navigational accuracy. The DoD has examined a number of techniques not only to deny selectively the use of the precise signal but also to degrade the accuracy available from the C/A signal. The incorporation of an integrated operational nuclear detonation detection system (IONDS) to be carried as a secondary payload on all operational GPS satellites is another military aspect of the programme[20].

The Soviet Union developed a series of navigation satellites within the Cosmos programme but did not identify any specific payload as having a navigation function until the launch of Cosmos-1000. It has been shown that transmissions on frequencies close to 150 MHz contain time signals and positional information which is updated at three-minute intervals, together with the ephemerides of other operational satellites in the system[21]. Each satellite is given an identity number in the ranges 1-8 or 11-14. Analysis of orbital-plane spacing shows that those with identities 1-6 constitute a constellation of six at 30° plane-spacing and that, on replacement, a satellite may or may not take on identity 7 or 8. Those with identities 11-14 constitute a constellation of four at 45° plane-spacing in the opposite hemisphere. These included Cosmos-1000 and the two Cospas-equipped satellites, Cosmos-1383 and 1447. It is not unreasonable to suppose that these are part of a civilian system and that those with identities 1-8 form a military system. It is significant that the lifetimes of six military satellites up to the time at which they are replaced is considerably shorter than those of the civilian system, implying a greater need for precision in the former case.

In June 1982, the Soviet Union lodged details of an advanced navigation satellite network with the International Frequency Registration Board (IFRB) in Geneva[22]. The Global Navigation Satellite System (GLONASS) would operate on frequencies centred on 1.25 and 1.6035 GHz, close to, and having the same ratio (1.283:1) as, the US Navstar frequencies.

The first of the GLONASS tests came as a surprising triple launch at 51.6° with a plane-change to 64.8° inclination. Cosmos-1413, 1414 and 1415 were not spaced regularly round the orbit but drifted apart slowly from the common point of injection. However, Cosmos-1414 did appear to make a small in-orbit manoeuvre suggestive of some propulsion capability. The second launch in the series placed three more satellites into the same orbital plane but the third launch, at the end of 1983, put Cosmos-1519, 1520 and 1521 into a plane separated by 120° from the first six which may signal a tentative move towards an operational status.

Geodesy and Minor Military Missions

There are other continuing series of flights in the Cosmos programme for which results are never published and which, therefore, may be presumed to be military in nature. Cosmos flights in near-circular orbits close to 1200 km, with orbital periods of approximately 109 minutes, initially at 74° and later at 83° inclinations, are presumed to have a geodetic role. Flights at 1400 km with approximately 114 minute periods and others in even higher near-circular orbits might also fall within this mission category.

A sub-set of the recoverable payloads which did not manoeuvre, transmitted on 19.994 MHz and had recovery beacons, were also held to be for geodesy and mapping.

Cosmos satellites with 65.8° inclinations and periods below 95 minutes appear, at first sight, to be related to ASAT tests. Some of these, usually those with the lowest orbital periods, are never intercepted and are thought to have a calibration or diagnostic role. When fragments are catalogued, one or two at a time at irregular but somewhat lengthy intervals, it might reasonably be presumed that these 'fragments' are shed deliberately to simulate MIRV attacks, providing practice for ground-units whose duty it is to detect and/or engage such objects.

Suggestions that these satellites are used to monitor results of ASAT tests are not supported by evidence from analysis of orbital data. In the first instance when one had been in orbit before an interception occurred, Cosmos-885 was on the opposite side of the Earth from Cosmos-880 when it was intercepted by Cosmos-886.

A recent book about the Soviet Army suggests that satellites are used to verify compliance with instructions to deactivate certain radars and radio transmitters to prevent 'American spy-satellites' from obtaining intelligence over the Soviet Union[23]. It goes on to suggest that dedicated radars and radio transmissions are activated at these times in order to provide disinformation. This example is cited, not because of any implicit belief in its veracity, but to offer another possibility for a 'minor military' mission.

Anti-satellite Tests

The United States test-fired, from a McDonnell Douglas F-15 fighter, the Vought miniature vehicle anti-satellite rocket for the first time, in January 1984. Even though the launch took place outside the launch envelope, the inertial guidance system compensated for the launch error and successfully placed the rocket on the targeted point in space. Although it is intended to have the system operational by 1987[24], the DoD is prevented from testing against a target in space later this year. This is due to the Tsongas amendment[25] to the FY84 military authorisation which prohibits the testing of anti-satellite warheads against targets in space, unless the President certifies to Congress that the Administration is endeavouring in good faith to negotiate a treaty banning anti-satellite weapons in space and is willing to negotiate such a ban. Moreover, the President is required to certify that such testing is necessary to avert 'clear and irrevocable harm' to US national security.

The Soviet Union also adopted the kinetic energy or 'hot-metal kill' for its ASAT programme. Beginning in 1968, target satellites have been approached by hunter-killer satellites employing a variety of fast fly-by, co-orbit or pop-up techniques in two series of tests in the periods 1968-71 and 1976-82[26]. Initially, both target and interceptor satellites were launched by the SS-9 out of Tyuratam but, from 1971 onwards, targets have been launched by the SS-5 out of Plesetsk. By the end of the first series of tests, the Soviet Union had demonstrated the capability to intercept objects in orbits used by ELINT, meteorological, navigation, and recoverable photo-reconnaissance satellites. Although not specifically falling within the terms of reference of the SALT negotiations, the termination of testing may have been influenced to some measure by the talks.

It soon became apparent, when testing was resumed in 1976, that the new tests were no mere carbon-copies of the earlier series and that considerable development had taken place. In many cases the interceptor disappeared from orbit on the day of launch, being de-orbited over the ocean following the interception. Later tests in the series reverted to using targets in the near-circular 1000 km orbits characteristic of the Cosmos navigation satellites. One interception was made in 1980, two in 1981, and a further one in 1982.

During October and November 1981, reports appeared in AW&ST to the effect that Cosmos-1267, docked at the time to Salyut-6, was equipped with 'podded miniature attack vehicles' providing a new capability for sneak attacks on US satellites[27]. With the publication of drawings of Cosmos-1443, a similar spacecraft, in Soviet magazines[28], it seems likely that analysts mistook the fuel tanks, visible beneath the protective covering of solar cells surrounding the main section, for missiles.

Manned Spaceflight

The advent of the US Space Transportation System (STS) Space Shuttle has produced a steady flow of statements from the Soviet Union concentrating on the military aspects of its proposed usage. These are not without foundation and are based on information published in official documents and by the media. It is no secret that many of the flights listed on the Shuttle manifest are dedicated as DoD missions or carry DoD payloads.

Western analysts agree that the 3rd and 5th Salyut space stations were military in character[29]. This is largely based on their all-military crews, choice of transmission frequencies and telemetry formats, ejection of capsules, and the fact that very few pictures of the stations have been released and they have not been put on display in public exhibitions. Distinctions between civil and military experiments became less clear during the long Salyut-6 mission and the dividing line now falls within a decidedly grey area.

Other Nations and Organisations

This paper has considered similarities and differences in the military use of space by the two superpowers. Other nations and organisations have also taken advantage of the opportunities afforded by artificial satellites to develop and use space for military purposes, particularly communications.

Great Britain established the Skynet geosynchronous system with launches by the American Delta booster in 1970 and 1971. The first satellites, although using considerable British technology, were assembled by the Philco Corporation. Currently, all-British satellites, Skynet-4A and 4B, are awaiting launch by the US Space Shuttle, and two of four British astronauts in training will fly as payload specialists associated with each launch.

Although the role of satellites in influencing the outcome of the Falklands campaign has been greatly overestimated in some quarters[30], there is no doubt that the establishment of a satcom link between London and the Royal Signals mobile station at Ajax Bay was a vital factor[31].

The North Atlantic Treaty Organisation (NATO) has its own geosynchronous satellites, launched by the US Delta. Before it had this independent capability, it shared the US Interim Defense Communications Satellite Program (IDCSP)[32].

China has demonstrated the capability to launch and recover payloads from low Earth orbit and to place a communications satellite in geosynchronous orbit. They have acknowledged that they have obtained imagery of their own territory from their own satellites for Earth resources purposes and it is a small step from this to a photo-reconnaissance capability.

As early as 1973, the French Minister of Defence reported that France was studying the need for military reconnaissance satellites for the period beginning 1980-85 using Ariane as the launch vehicle[33]. Although it was reported that the project had been postponed indefinitely[34], the remote sensing Spot-1, due for launch in 1985, will have greater ground-resolution than the current Landsats – 20 m for the multispectral scanner and 10 m for black-and-white imagery. It has been suggested in some quarters that, unlike Landsat data, the greater resolution SPOT imagery may not be made freely available.

Japan has allowed its Self Defence Forces to use the Sakura-2A communications satellite[35] and may also develop a photo-reconnaissance capability. India's development of remote sensing satellites may presage such a capability[36].

Conclusion

DoD space expenditure surpassed NASA's space budget for the first time in FY82 and by FY84, at $9.9 billion was 32 per cent larger than NASA's. In fact, the DoD space budget would be even larger if NASA-funded development of the Shuttle was taken into account (DoD is expected to require two of the four authorised Space Shuttle orbiters for its operations).

Comparable figures are not available from the Soviet Union. A 1982 US Government estimate suggested that the Soviet Union spent $18 billion in 1982, or about half as much again as that spent in the United States on its space programme[37]. A 1984 DoD estimate was that 70 per cent of Soviet space systems serve a purely military role and that a further 20 per cent serve dual military/civil roles[38].

It is quite clear that both superpowers obtain, each in their individual ways, something approaching the optimum military benefit from their programmes, and that they will continue to increase their exploitation of the space environment to the utmost of their capabilities. Other nations and alliances are increasingly making use of artificial satellites to support their military programmes.

References

1. E.M. Emme, 'Aeronautics and Astronautics 1915-60', NASA, (1961) 105.
2. Ibid. p.101.
3. H.F. York, and G.A. Greb, 'Strategic Reconnaissance',

Bulletin of the Atomic Scientists, 33, No.4 (April 1977) 33-41.
4. L. Booda, 'First Capsule Recovered from Satellite', Aviation Week & Space Technology (22 August 1960) 33-35.
5. Tass in Russian for Abroad, 1232 G.M.T., 29 April 1962.
6. P.J. Klass, Secret Sentries in Space, (New York: Random House, 1971), p.108.
7. Aviation Week & Space Technology, 120, No.11, (12 March 1984) 154.
8. N.L. Johnson, The Soviet Year in Space: 1983, (Colorado Springs: Teledyne Brown Engineering, 1984), p.15.
9. G.E. Perry, 'Russian Ocean Surveillance Satellites', Royal Air Forces Qy., 18, No.1 (Spring 1978) 60-67.
10. 'Questions Relating to the Use of Nuclear Power Sources in Outer Space', USSR: working paper, U.N. General Assembly A/AC.105/C.1/WG.V/L.10 (25 January 1980).
11. O.M. Belotserkovskiy, Soviet television, 1400 G.M.T., 15 January 1983.
12. R. Lindsey, The Falcon and the Snowman, (New York: Pocket Books, 1980) pp.126-27.
13. G.E. Perry and Sarah M. Mobbs, Spaceflight, 22 (1980) 38-39.
14. G.E. Perry, 'Identification of military components within the Soviet space programme', in B. Jasani (ed.) Outer Space - A New Dimension of the Arms Race (London: Taylor & Francis, 1982) p.144.
15. G.E. Perry, 'Soviet Early Warning Satellites', J. Brit. Interplanetary Soc., 35, No.2 (1982) 72-74.
16. G.E. Perry, in B. Jasani (ed.) op.cit, pp.146-47.
17. Aviation Week & Space Technology, 113, No.18 (3 November 1980) 32.
18. Aviation Week & Space Technology, 120, No.1 (2 January 1984) 13.
19. S.J. Birkill, 'Channel Frequencies and Utilization in the Soviet Communication Satellite Systems, with Particular Reference to the Television Traffic', in Soviet Space Programs, 1976-80, Part 3, Staff Report, Committee on Commerce, Science, and Transportation, U.S. Senate, (Washington D.C.).
20. K.D. McDonald, 'Navigation satellite systems: their characteristics, potential and military applications', in B. Jasani (ed.) Outer Space - A New Dimension of the Arms Race, (London: Taylor & Francis, 1982) 179-80.
21. C.D. Wood and G.E. Perry, 'The Russian Satellite Navigation System', Phil. Trans. R. Soc. London A, 294, (1980) 307-15.
22. International Frequency Registration Board (IFRB) Circular No. 1522, Special Section No. AR11/A/3, 8 June 1982.

23. V. Suvarov, Inside the Soviet Army, (New York: Macmillan, 1982), pp.106-7.
24. 'Joint Chiefs See ASAT Capability for Soviet ABM Interceptors', Aerospace Daily, 125, No.23 (2 February 1984) 191.
25. U.S. Senate, 18 July 1983.
26. G.E. Perry, 'Russian Hunter-Killer Satellite Experiments' Royal Air Forces Qy., 17, No.4 (Winter 1977) 328-35.
27. Aviation Week & Space Technology, 115, No.17 (26 October 1981) 15, 115 No.18 (2 November 1981) 15.
28. Ogonyok, No. 40, 1 October 1983; Soviet Union, No. 2, (Moscow, 1984), pp.6-7.
29. 'Salyut - Soviet Steps toward Permanent Human Presence in Space', Office of Technology Assessment, US Congress, (Washington DC: December 1983), 21-22, 24-25.
30. R. Halloran, New York Times, 3 May 1982.
31. 'The British Army in the Falklands 1982', prepared by Director Public Relations Army (London: Ministry of Defence, 1983), p.9.
32. 'World-Wide Space Activities', Staff Report, Committee on Science and Technology, US House of Representatives, (Washington DC: September 1977), 346.
33. Aviation Week & Space Technology,(22 January 1973) 15.
34. Le Monde, 23 October 1982.
35. Kyodo Wire Service, Tokyo, 1027 GMT, 24 August 1983.
36. Marcia S. Smith, 'International Cooperation: Ensuring that Future Space Programs have their Maximum Impact on Humanity', presented at The Pontifical Academy of Sciences Meeting on the Impact of Space on Mankind (1-5 October 1984).
37. Marcia S. Smith, 'Space Activities of the United States, Soviet Union and Other Launching Countries/Organisations: 1957-1983', Congressional Research Service, US Library of Congress, Report No. 84-20 SPR (15 January 1984) 87.
38. 'Soviet Military power' Department of Defense, (Washington DC: 1984) 46.

11 Prevention of the Militarisation of Space
ALEXEI ARBATOV

The Destabilising Nature of ASAT Systems

In the context of strategic stability - to say nothing of the overall global military situation - it is difficult to determine the role of satellites in simple terms. On the one side, space systems of reconnaissance, early warning, communication, navigation and so on, contribute to stability and the retaliatory capability, and serve as the key element of national technical means (NTM) of verification of arms limitation agreements. On the other hand, space systems - especially in view of the technological achievements embodied in the latest generation of American reconnaissance, navigation and communication satellites, as well as in the light of the new strategic programmes and military doctrines of the USA - can be used for a first nuclear strike; in particular, for enhancing counterforce capability, with the objective of waging a limited and protracted nuclear war.

Accordingly, ASAT systems could theoretically endanger both the stabilising, and the destabilising, functions of satellites. However, it would be hardly possible to draw a clear-cut distinction between ASAT systems designed to destroy stabilising satellites and the systems for combating destabilising satellites.

For example, the new US F-15/ASAT system is justified by its task of combating the Soviet ocean-reconnaisance satellites (RORSAT) which could, in particular, increase the vulnerability of US aircraft carrier task forces. From the point of view of the USSR, the presence of US aircraft carriers in the proximity of the USSR's coastline - which are, as officially admitted, capable to strike, including with nuclear warheads, at Soviet naval bases and other coast facilities - represents an extremely provocative and hence destabilising situation. We do not believe the monitoring of these aircraft carriers and maintaining capability to oppose them in the event of war to be a destabilising function.

In our view, instability is related precisely to the development of the US ASAT systems for destroying the Soviet RORSAT-type and other satellites. In a broader context, the consequences of the ASAT system for the arms race and arms control, both in space and on earth, will undoubtedly be extremely negative.

In this connection, my **first** point is that regardless of the mission and role of satellites, ASAT systems are destabilising on the whole. Therefore, the banning of development of new ASAT systems and the elimination of the existing ones is a priority problem; its solution would without doubt strengthen military-political stability.

Regrettably, the US Government's position represents a clear attempt to draw such a distinction. The US satellites are regarded as fully stabilising while the Soviet ones are seen as destabilising. Therefore, the US ASAT systems are assessed as wholesome for stability, and the USA is unwilling to ban and eliminate them. Moreover, the USA intends to achieve superiority over the USSR in the field of ASAT systems.

This is the main military-political obstacle which blocks the start of constructive talks on this question. The official report of the Reagan administration to the Congress 'On US Policy on ASAT Arms Control' of 31 March 1984 says:

> No arrangements or agreements beyond those already governing military activities in outer space have been found to date that are judged to be in the overall interest of the United States and its Allies.

Role of Non-Dedicated ASAT Systems

Another view put forward not only by the official US representatives, but also shared by US specialists outside the Administration is to the effect that ASAT arms control cannot be sufficiently effective because of the existence of the so-called non-dedicated ASAT systems. They mean by this possible employment for ASAT purposes of ABM interceptors, ICBMs, and manned space ships and stations. Obviously, it is not possible to eliminate these in the framework of an ASAT agreement; these systems are the subject of other negotiations.

When and if ASAT talks begin, it seems possible to leave the existing systems mentioned above outside the framework of arms control negotiations without inviting danger. The use of such systems for ASAT purposes is extremely limited from the point of view of effectiveness and military expediency; it is also connected with employing nuclear weapons which would cause damage to friendly satellites and to the monitoring, command and communication facilities on Earth. The employment of ABM interceptors, ICBMs and MRBMs with conventional warheads would require long-term development and extensive testing which would be easy to monitor by NTMs of the two sides. This is the **second** proposition I offer for discussion.

A Freeze on Testing of ASAT Systems

The **third** point concerns the verification of the ban and the elimination of ASAT systems, the alleged impossibility of which is often used by the USA as evidence of the bad prospects for ASAT arms control. It is necessary to point out that the best method of averting the development of ASAT systems consists of freezing the tests of such systems; such a freeze could be reliably verified by the NTMs of the two sides. To verify the elimination of such a system as F-15/ASAT, after the completion of its testing, would be indeed very difficult.

Possibly, the delay by the USA to begin negotiations has precisely the objective of avoiding a freeze on testing, to complete the tests of the system and undermine the prevention of its deployment. All this is done under the pretext that the verification of such an agreement is difficult. Here, an analogy comes to mind with the reluctant position of the USA on the prohibition of MIRVs in 1968-70, which later resulted in extensive negative consequences for both sides.

The prohibition of testing and deployment of orbital ASAT weapons, both combat laser and other type stations and space mines, can be verified by the space tracking facilities available to both sides. Certain difficulties might arise in verifying the ban on space nuclear mines which could destroy satellites at distances of hundreds of kilometres, and allegedly do not require testing in space or close proximity to target satellites. But, as was mentioned earlier, the use of nuclear weapons for ASAT purposes is extremely doubtful. Nonnuclear space mines must be placed in orbits close to target satellites, facilitating the detection of violations of the agreement.

A set of agreements on the non-use of force in outer space, and from there to the Earth, as well as agreements on certain rules of deployment and movement of satellites in space, would facilitate verification of this type. A moratorium on testing or deployment of direct-ascent ASAT systems based on land, sea, and in the air, could additionally be verified by ground-, marine- and space-based electronic means.

The Need to Include All Systems

Finally, yet another US view is to leave untouched the

existing ASAT systems of both sides and agree on banning only the next generation systems, especially the ones capable of destroying satellites in high and geosynchronous orbits.

This again calls back the analogy with the SALT history. Since the mid-1970s the USA has made as absolute the balance of silo-based ICBMs, though they constituted only 30 per cent of the US strategic arsenal, but over 70 per cent of the USSR potential. The USA did not take into account the objectively existing asymmetries between the USSR and the USA and the legitimate security interests of the USSR. This approach turned out to be a big obstacle in the dialogue on the strategic arms limitation.

Likewise in the ASAT arms control area, **it would be incorrect to focus on ensuring invulnerability of geosynchronous-orbit satellites alone.** And that is my **fourth** point. The USA and its allies have stationed more than 60 per cent of their satellites in this orbit, including all the early warning satellites and nearly all communication satellites (96 per cent). On the whole, the USA has placed only 30 per cent of its satellites in low and medium orbits (below 3000 kilometres) and 70 per cent of them are in high and geosynchronous orbits. The satellites of the USSR are deployed differently. This is an objective asymmetry resulting from geographical, technological and historical factors and it must be taken into account.

An approach based on taking into account only the US interests will not result in successful negotiations. The prohibition of only ASAT systems designed for high orbits would put the USSR in an unequal position **vis-a-vis** the USA. Besides, it would be extremely difficult, particularly from the point of view of verification, to prevent the improvement efficiency of ASAT systems if certain types of them were not covered by agreements.

On the other hand, the prohibition of all new ASAT systems and the elimination of existing systems should be equally acceptable to both sides, if they are concerned only about the security of their satellites and do not seek superiority in space. This would also be the most radical solution of the problem facilitating the verification of the agreement.

The avoidance of the ASAT arms race is important not only by itself, but also as a barrier in the way of developing space strike systems for BMD defence, and for strikes at ground targets, which threatens to undermine radically the strategic stability and overall security. The matters related to developing space-based anti-missile defence systems and their limitation were reviewed in sufficient detail in a special report of 1984 by the Committee of Soviet Scientists for Peace against Nuclear Danger.

12 The ABM Problem Revisited
JACK RUINA

In the hope of a technological breakthrough, research on a variety of novel technologies for ABM has been in progress for about twenty-five years. In the last decade, both the USA and Soviet Union have intensified their efforts in the development of such technically exotic devices as high energy lasers and other directed-energy weapons for a variety of military applications - air defence, anti-satellite weapons and also ballistic missile defence.

Despite well-understood technical difficulties, the President of the United States, expressing a surprising amount of optimism about the promise of these new technologies for ballistic missile defence, embarked the country on a technology programme directed at making nuclear armed ballistic missiles 'impotent and obsolete' - a seemingly laudable goal. The cost estimate for the planned US programme is about $25 billion over the next five years. It is reasonable to assume that the equivalent Soviet programme, although proceeding with much less fanfare, will be of about the same magnitude. Given their large scale, these programmes will go well beyond modest and reasonable studies, calculations, and laboratory measurements; they will include development of large-scale experimental devices and major field tests, including tests and experiments in space.

Nevertheless, the basic goal of the US programme is to determine, within a decade, whether or not any of the proposed technologies are feasible for ABM and, if so, what form an ABM system using these technologies may have.

These intensified ABM efforts raise three basic questions in turn: the first, regarding the technical feasibility of the technologies involved; the second, regarding the ultimate costs and benefits of the programme given a realistic assessment of the limitations of systems utilising these technologies; and the third, the wisdom of the policy implied by the rhetoric associated with intensive ABM R & D efforts.

From a technical point of view, the goal of developing an

effective ballistic missile defence system (with any technology or combination of technologies proposed to date) to make nuclear weapons truly 'obsolete' is totally unrealistic - a fantasy. It is not at all clear that the technological devices and components proposed will be relevant for ballistic missile defence; they certainly have not been developed anywhere near the state required for utility in ballistic missile defence systems. Besides, all indications are that any system to be assembled using these technologies could be easily and cheaply negated by countermeasures designed for the purpose, and that the defence system itself would be extremely vulnerable to enemy attack. Finally, there are many ways to deliver nuclear weapons (cruise missiles and so on), so that even if ABM technologies and deployments could cause ballistic missiles to lose their military utility, nuclear weapons would be retained and probably would proliferate within the US and Soviet arsenals.

Therefore, despite any political rhetoric to the contrary, the issues raised by current BMD efforts really do not relate to defences that may negate the military utility of nuclear weapons, or even of ballistic missiles, but rather call for consideration of the consequences of deployment of **partial** defences and of the consequences of only intensive R & D programmes.

Three types of partial ballistic missile defences are of interest: one that is designed to destroy some fraction of nuclear weapons in a large nationwide ballistic missile attack; one that is designed to protect hardened military targets such as ICBM silos and command posts; and one that is designed to protect the nation against a limited attack, perhaps from an emerging nuclear power, or from an accidental launch. To some degree it has been and remains technically feasible to develop partial defences for one or the other of these purposes. The new, exotic technologies currently being investigated may eventually prove to be useful in such ABM systems, but concern about the consequences of deployment of partial defences are not dependent on any technological 'breakthroughs' in ABM.

The utility of partial defences has been debated for two decades and the conclusion of the national leadership of the USA and the Soviet Union is that the benefits of any defence deployments beyond those permitted by the ABM Treaty are far less than the costs and risks they entail for international security. The reasons can be summarised as follows:
1. Nationwide defences can be overcome easily and cheaply. Deployment of defences by one side is very likely to be followed by deployment of defences by the other **and** by an increase in offensive weaponry by both. Such

intensification of the nuclear arms race decreases security for all, and it is well to take steps to at least eliminate this unnecessary stimulus to the arms competition. The argument that partial defences will at least limit damage in case of a nuclear exchange is based on the unlikely premise that deployment of a defence by one side would not be followed by the opponent's build-up of his offensive weapons.

2. Defence of hardened ICBM silos and command posts may be desirable and is much less of a technical challenge than any defence of population. However, large-scale deployments of defences of hardened military sites is likely to be viewed as a first step towards nationwide ABM deployment (since the technologies involved are not that distinct) with all the consequences feared for the case of a full ABM deployment.

3. The threat of attack by an emerging nuclear power is more likely to come from weapons delivered by aircraft than by long-range ballistic missiles. An ABM system will, therefore, not decrease that threat substantially, and the fear of an accidental missile launch can be more effectively approached by addressing (and perhaps exchanging) technologies to reduce this likelihood. ABM deployment for this purpose hardly seems warranted, particularly given the complexity it adds to the strategic relationships.

Even without any decision for deployment, an intensive pursuit of ABM technologies and pre-occupation with its highly exaggerated promise inevitably make the ABM Treaty more fragile. The political rhetoric, policy directives, and so on, that go with such intensive technology pursuits deprecate the value of the ABM Treaty, creating a national sentiment hostile to or at least sceptical about the Treaty.

Most serious is that the current intensive programmes of both superpowers in ABM technology reveal a frame of mind of their top political leadership that seeks an illusory technological solution to what is basically a political problem. Nuclear weapons, by virtue of their low cost (for the superpowers) and high destructiveness, make effective defence nearly impossible. One adversary can always build more and improved offensive weapons to overcome the defensive system of the other, and all indications from the post-war nuclear age are that the first reaction to defence is an offensive build-up by an opponent. The thought that a defensive system for population defence can be made near-perfect, or that if not near-perfect it can be useful anyway given the dynamics of the arms race, is most disturbing and suggests that there may be other misconceptions as well. Whatever realistic promise ABM technologies now offer can be accomplished far more simply, far less dangerously, and far more cheaply, by simple mutual reductions in nuclear weaponry - particularly in some of the more destabilising types of weapons.

The factors that led to the ABM Treaty are still operative. Its value is as great today as ever and the USA and Soviet Union should be particularly careful not to take steps that jeopardise the Treaty. This does not preclude R & D in relevant ABM technologies, but it does preclude exaggerating the promise of these technologies and raising false hopes. It precludes, as well, overstating the benefits to be derived from partial defences while not calling attention to the high costs to international security that they entail. And it precludes expending far greater resources and soliciting far more national support for ABM technology than the technical possibilities warrant.

13 Restricting Anti-satellite Technology
BHUPENDRA JASANI

The increasing use of outer space for military purposes has played, and will continue to play, a very important and increasingly complex role in international relations, especially in arms control affairs. For example, recent advanced in ballistic missile defence (BMD) technologies, particularly some proposed space-based systems, would not only fuel the arms race on earth but even extend it to outer space. To say that the race for anti-satellite (ASAT) weapons had already started in the late 1950s would not be an exaggeration. With the deployment of the US land-based ASAT missiles and their nuclear warheads, the ASAT weapon race had already begun. The next to appear on the scene were the Soviet ASAT satellites. While they were crude weapons, they were an improvement on the US indiscriminate nuclear-tipped ASAT missiles. On 21 January 1984, the USA carried out a test of its air-launched ASAT missile which eventually will be fitted with a non-nuclear warhead. Thus, with the relative flexibility of this new ASAT system, a further impetus has been given to the arms race in this field.

When discussing arms control measures in outer space it is useful to be clear what is meant by the militarisation of this environment, so that both the cause of the arms race and the nature of the weapons are better understood. In this paper militarisation is taken to mean: (a) the use of artificial earth satellites by the military to enhance the earth-based weapon systems, and (b) the use of weapons which can be aimed at and used against such satellites.

The militarisation of outer space began only two years after the launching of Sputnik-I in 1957 when military satellites for reconnoitering the earth's surface were launched. By the end of 1983 at least 2114 military-oriented satellites had been launched. This constitutes about 75 per cent of all satellites orbited. The functions of military satellites range from navigation, communications, meteorology and geodesy to reconnaissance and anti-satellite activities (see

Figure 1).

Reconnaissance craft are probably the most important type of military satellite since not only are they primarily used for detecting, describing and pinpointing military targets but, for more than a decade now, they have been used for verifying certain arms control agreements. These satellites can be divided into four kinds: photographic, electronic, ocean surveillance and early-warning satellites. The latter have partially replaced radars that were originally deployed to give warning of a surprise attack by inter-continental ballistic missiles. The use of early-warning satellites has extended the warning time from about 15 minutes to about 30 minutes.

The importance of these satellites is emphasised by the fact that over half of all the military satellites are for reconnaissance purposes (see Figure 1). The majority of these spacecraft are photographic reconnaissance satellites. These and the other types of military satellites are becoming part of nuclear and conventional weapon systems. As advances are made in military space technology, improvements in the efficiency of weapons occur. This in turn may refine war-fighting tactics as well as give rise to new ones. Over the past two decades or so, nuclear war-fighting tactics have undergone a change from the doctrine of mutual assured destruction to those of, for example, flexible response and counterforce doctrines.

In view of the potential role of satellites in waging wars on earth, it is not surprising that they have become important military targets. Thus began the second phase of the militarisation of outer space: the development and even in some cases the deployment of ASAT weapons.

ASAT Weapons

Essentially, two types of ASAT systems have been developed: a land-based missile with a nuclear warhead aimed at satellites, and a satellite acting as a weapon by ramming its prey or exploding in its vicinity. Other variations are being considered, such as ASAT missiles launched from high-flying aircraft, or ground- or space-based high-energy beam weapons.

The US ASAT missile weapons date back to 1959 when under a programme called Bold Orion, the US Air Force began testing ASAT missiles launched from B-47 aircraft. Some four tests were conducted[1]. The first of these was successfully conducted on 19 October 1959 against the Explorer-6 satellite, launched on 7 August 1959, as a target[2]. The satellite was not damaged and it decayed by July 1961. In any

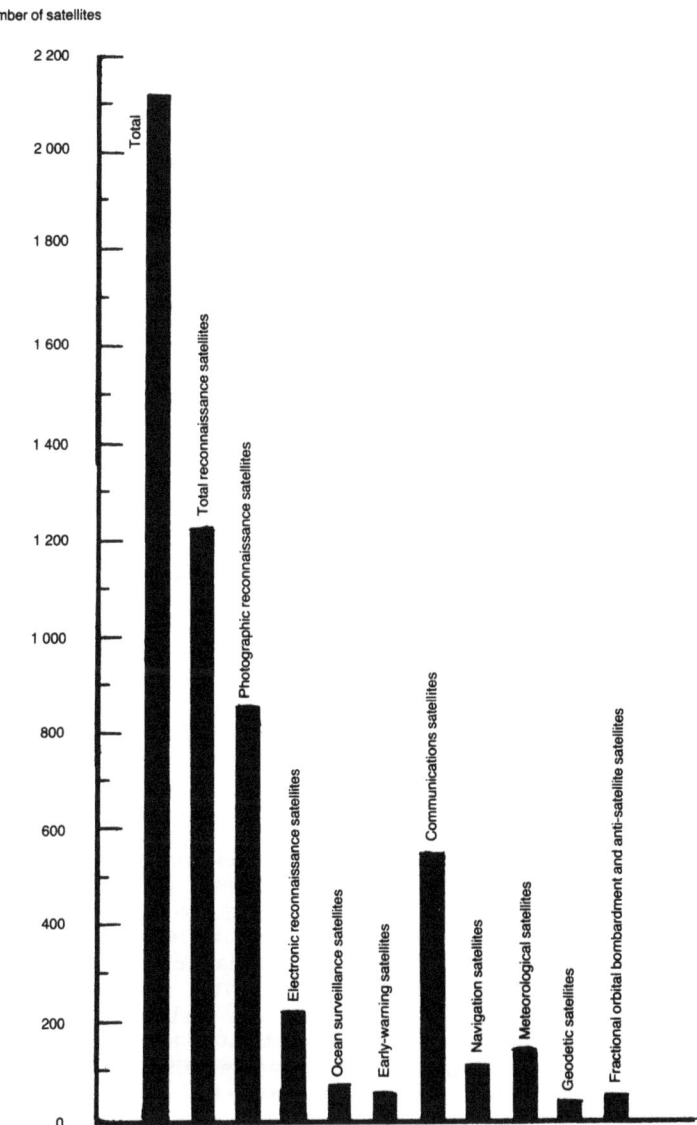

Figure 1. Number of military satellites of different types launched between 1958 and 1983

case, the early ASAT missile warheads were nuclear weapons so that a full test would not have been carried out since the EMP effects of the nuclear explosion would have certainly damaged other US satellites in the heighbourhood. The spacecraft was launched in a highly elliptical orbit with its argument of perigee at about 53° (on 26 October 1959) and a perigee height of 244 km. The satellite's apogee height was 42 200 km so that the interception must have taken place close to its perigee point[3]. This is interesting since the satellite travels with the maximum velocity at its perigee point, thus indicating the level of sophistication that must have been achieved at that time.

Under the US Department of Defense (DoD) programme called SPIN (SPace INtercept), all the three services began independently the development of ASAT weapons[4]. The US Air Force, in fact, demonstrated in 1963 an ASAT capability against satellites in low orbits. A Thor booster was launched from Johnston Island against a spent US rocket which was orbiting the earth at the time[5]. These ASAT missiles were based on Johnston and Kwajalein Islands in the Pacific Ocean. Under this Program 437, earlier systems used the Delta and Agena upper stages[4]. Some 16 tests had been carried out using the Thor system but the programme was terminated in 1976.

A second project under the US Air Force was called Program 706. This designation replaced an earlier one, SAINT (SAtellite INTerceptor), which was to demonstrate a military rendezvous with unknown or unidentified spacecraft in earth orbit. The initial launching of the SAINT was to have been made in 1962 by an Atlas-Agena-B rocket but the project was abandoned before the flight took place[6,7]. Under Program 706, however, study continued on a possible manned interceptor craft.

A third US Air Force programme was labelled Program 922, under which it is reported that a direct ascent system with terminal homing ASAT weapon was being investigated. A number of alternatives were considered which included a non-nuclear warhead. One such concept was a launch into space of a warhead containing pellets loaded with chemical explosives which would destroy a satellite in orbit[4]. This was a concept similar to that being investigated by the US Navy.

Under the US Navy ASAT programme called Early Spring, a submarine-launched missile was to have been developed. Such a missile would hover up to some 90 seconds in space waiting for its target to arrive[4]. In another concept, called Skipper, a batch of steel pellets would have been launched by a rocket in the path of a satellite. Under yet another programme, called Hi-Ho, actual testing of ASAT weapons was

ANTI-SATELLITE TECHNOLOGY 111

carried out. For example, in 1962 the Navy conducted two ASAT missile tests. As in the case of the US Air Force Bold Orion programme, the ASAT missiles were launched from an aircraft but this time from F-14 fighter planes[1]. It is interesting to note that both these tests involved the use of the Altair rocket as a second stage, just as it is used in the new US F-15 launched ASAT missiles.

The US Army was also involved in the development of ASAT weapons in the early 1960s. Under Program 505, Zeus and Nike-X missiles were based at Kwajalein Islands in the Pacific Ocean[4]. These missiles were originally developed as part of the anti-ballistic missile (ABM) system, which was operational between 1964 and 1968.

By the mid-1970s, most of these programmes were cancelled. However, the effort in ASAT weaponry was not lost altogether because some of the earlier ideas have found their way into the current US Air Force programme in which a direct-ascent system is being developed. This system is based almost entirely on well known, well proven and readily available technology. It consists of a booster with a Short-Range Attack Missile (SRAM, AGM-69, first deployed in 1972) as the first stage and a Thiokol Altair rocket as the second stage. A Miniature Homing Vehicle (MHV) with its infra-red heat-seeking homing guidance sensor (the only unproven element) is mounted on the Altair. The entire weapon is about 5.5 m long and about 0.5 m in diameter, and is mounted under the F-15 fighter aircraft. The MHV warhead weighing about 1200 kg, would be launched from an altitude of 10 to 15 km. The F-15 has a horizontal range of about 2500 km which can be increased to 7500 km if the aircraft is fuelled in air. The SRAM has a range of between 60 and 160 km. The Thiokol two-stage rocket has a range of up to about 300 km. Thus presumably the system can have a range of up to 475 km. In fact such a system was tested on 21 January 1984, but without the warhead and target. Some 12 tests are planned[8,9]. The first test carried a simulated MHV but no target was orbited. The US Air Force could not test the weapon against a target since, according to the Tsongas amendment to the FY-1984 Defense Authorization Act, the President is required, before an MHV test against a space object, to certify that the USA is endeavouring to negotiate in good faith a verifiable comprehensive ASAT treaty with the Soviet Union. Secondly, the Congress required a report on the President's arms control policy for ASAT weapons by 31 march 1984, before the Pentagon could spend funds allocated for such weapons.

On 31 March 1984, a report on the US Policy on ASAT Arms Control was presented to the US Congress. During his testimony to the House Foreign Affairs Panel, Kenneth Adelman

(Director of the US Arms Control and Disarmament Agency) said that this report indicated that 'we are endeavouring to respond to the thrust of the Tsongas Amendment by concentrating, in the ongoing studies, on the more limited arrangement that would ban or otherwise limit specific weapon systems types of activities or threats'. However, as mentioned above, there are some 12 tests of the US F-15 ASAT weapon planned for and after the initial evaluation flights of the missile; the MHV will be tested against a target satellite called 'Tomato Can'[10]. Moreover, there are indications that work has already begun on the next generation of ASAT missiles for destroying satellites in higher orbits[11].

By 1987, some 28 F-15s will be ready for use with two MHVs deployed on each aircraft. By 1989, two squadrons will be fitted for ASAT missions. The F-15s need short runways so that virtually any airport could be used to launch the ASAT weapon. Since the system is not confined to any specific launch pad on earth, the MHV can be used as a direct-ascent system against satellites in any orbital inclination.

As the F-15 system has a limited range, two other ASAT systems are being considered in order to increase the range. In one, an MHV would be launched by larger launchers from submarines. In this way the advantage of a moving launch-platform of the F-15 system would be retained and the range of the weapon would be increased to a geostationary orbit of 36 000 km. In the other system, high-energy beam weapons are thought to be useful as ASAT systems. Such weapons are attractive not only because they can deliver destructive energy with the speed of light, but also because they have a high fire-power potential per weapon. They could be switched rapidly from one target to another. The directed-energy weapons (DEW) of particular interest are high-energy lasers.

The US high-energy laser weapons. Under this programme a number of potential devices are being investigated for weapon applications by the US Air Force, Navy and the Defense Advance Research Project Agency (DARPA). The US Air Force has carried out a number of tests using its airborne laser laboratory (ALL) equipped with a 400 kW carbon dioxide gas dynamic laser[12,13,14,15]. The laser radiation wave-length is 10.6 µm.

A laser beam can damage the target essentially in two ways. For energies between 10^6 and 10^9 W/cm^2, the incident continuous laser beam melts or evaporates the solid surface. For longer pulses at low intensities, 10^6-10^7 W/cm^2, the laser produces deep narrow holes in the surface. A 10 J pulse delivered in .1 ms produces a crater of about 1 mm depth. At higher energies (considerably greater than 10^9 W/cm^2) and with shorter pulse lengths, the solid surface is not only vaporised but it is ionised, producing a high density plasma which continues to absorb the incident laser radiation. The very rapid temperature increase at the surface of the solid causes the laser-produced plasma to blow off or ablate towards the laser beam. This, in turn, drives a intense hydrodynamic shockwave into the solid, probably rupturing the target skin.

A consideration of the energies needed to damage satellites at various ranges and laser wavelengths shows that, for a continuous beam of laser light, short-wave lasers are more effective. Also, since beam target coupling strongly increases with decreasing wavelength, the need for short-wave lasers is further emphasised.

DARPA, under its Triad programme, is investigating the use of a ground-based chemical laser device to demonstrate the feasibility of a laser suitable for deployment in outer space. The most commonly used chemical reaction is between hydrogen and fluorine emitting radiation at a wavelength of 2.7 um; for deuterium and fluorine the wavelength is 3.8 um. The Triad programme consists of three elements: **Alpha**, under which the feasibility of generating infra-red chemical high-energy lasers is being investigated; **LODE** (Large Optical Demonstration Experiment), under which a large mirror 4 metres in diameter, to steer and control the laser beam, is being developed; and space-borne **Talon Gold**, under which the target acquisition tracking and precision-pointing techniques are being investigated[16].

The energy of the laser being investigated under Alpha is classified information. Even if it were of the order of 5 MW, there would be a considerable range over which the weapon could be useful. For example, at 500 km a 5 MW laser would damage the satellite's skin in one second. However, chemical lasers have a chemical-to-laser energy efficiency of at most about 250 kilojoules per kilogramme of fuel so that about 20 kg of chemical fuel would be needed. It is assumed that the conversion efficiency is 25 per cent. For a useful weapon, a range considerably greater then 100 km is needed so that large amounts of fuel would have to be transported to orbital laser platforms.

Three more advanced laser concepts are being investigated. These are the excited dimer or excimer laser, the free-electron laser, and the gamma-ray and X-ray laser. In the excimer laser (emitting radiation of 0.3 um) electrons are used to bombard inert gases, such as xenon or krypton. The resulting ions, in their excited state, react chemically to form xenon fluoride or krypton fluoride. Even at a laser energy of 200 kW, a considerable range can be obtained - of the order of 1000 km. However, existing excimer lasers suffer from low overall efficiencies (1-3 per cent) requiring multi-megawatt input power for weapon application. Moreover, there are problems of severe corrosion and maintenance of the purity of the lasing material, making such lasers unsuitable as space-based ASAT weapons.

A relatively new and, in principle, different and tunable laser type is the free electron laser (FEL). When electrons are accelerated, they radiate. Thus, if a beam of electrons is injected through a magnetic field of suitably changing direction, the electrons can be made to emit coherent radiation. For shortwave radiation, the electrons must be highly relativistic.

In principle, a wide range of frequencies may be available together with tunability. Such a device can, in principle, reach a high efficiency but needs a particle accelerator as an electron beam source.

Other potential devices which have entered the high-energy laser weapon debate are the gamma-ray and X-ray laser. These have been the subject of theoretical analyses both in the USA and USSR for more than a decade[17,18].

In contrast to optical lasers which derive their beam energy from the stimulated release of energy stored in excited atoms or molecules, the radiative energy emitted by a gamma-ray or X-ray laser originates from excited states in the shell structure of the atoms, like the excited states in the high-energy K and L shells. The pumping of X-ray lasers requires very intense radiation like that emitted from a nuclear explosion[19].

An X-ray laser can in principle be pumped by a high-intensity flash of X-rays from a conventional X-ray source. However, these are generally not intense enough to achieve the required gain, except for the possibility of optical resonances existing in the nuclei of some isotopes[20,21].

X-rays can neither be reflected by mirrors nor refracted in prisms. The normal laser technique cannot therefore be used in X-ray lasers. In addition, the lifetime of a high-energy excited state is very short compared with normal excited atomic states. These factors necessitate the use of copious radiation from a nuclear explosion as the pumping source of the X-ray laser. This means that such an X-ray laser (with wavelengths between 10^{-3} to 10^{-4} um) operates as a single laser pulse device. Its beam properties, particularly the beam divergence, therefore, are determined by the geometry of the lasing medium normally taken as long rods pumped by the nuclear explosion. It was reported in 1981 that the Lawrence Livermore Laboratory tested the concept of the X-ray pumped laser during an underground nuclear explosion[22,23]. The device apparently produced an X-ray laser pulse of 1.4 nanometer wavelength and several hundred terawatts power (this would correspond to a few hundred joules for a pulse of picosecond duration). A second test of this, the so-called 'Excalibur' laser, was also reported and more are planned[24].

There would be a number of problems even if X-ray lasers were made to work. For example, if deployed in the geostationary orbit, the radiation generated from the nuclear explosive may damage other friendly satellites in that orbit. At lower altitudes, such a weapon may also affect other satellites by its electromagnetic pulse which may be extensive enough to affect objects on the earth's surface. Above all, there are considerable implications for the arms control treaties.

Two other concepts are worth mentioning here. The idea of a laser powered directly by nuclear energy in the so-called nuclear-pumped lasers was proposed soon after the discovery of lasers[25]. The walls of a chamber containing a lasing gas are coated with ^{10}B or ^{235}U compounds; alternatively ^3He or gaseous $^{235}UF_6$ is mixed with the lasing gas. The thermal neutrons from a reactor are then allowed to interact with the gas in the chamber to produce nuclear fission products. When a high-energy fission fragment is absorbed by the lasing gas it loses its energy by inelastic collisions causing ionisation and excitation of the lasing medium. The population inversion in a lasing medium by nuclear pumping is thought to occur in several ways, but at present knowledge is limited. However, using ^3He-A gas, a laser power output of one kilowatt has been achieved at a wavelength of 1.79 um. This power output has been doubled in the Soviet Union using a ^4He-Xe mixture. The laser wavelengths in this case[26] have been 2.63 and 2.48 um.

The second concept, electromagnetic (EM) guns, is not a directed-energy weapon but it could be regarded as a hybrid between conventional weapons and more futuristic directed energy weapons. This is partly because an EM gun requires the same intense bursts of electrical energy as that needed for many types of directed-energy weapons. An EM gun simply accelerates a projectile by using electromagnetic forces rather than those produced by the expanding gases from chemical reactions. The main advantage would be considerably higher projectile velocities. Thus an EM gun would be an important intermediate step towards the possible realisation of directed-energy weapons.

Soviet ASAT weapon research may have begun as early as

1963 but rigorous testing with targets and interceptors began in 1967. Until 1970, both the targets and the interceptors were launched from Tyuratam. But since 1971 all the targets have been launched from Plesetsk and the interceptors from Tyuratam. In most cases the interceptions have been made at altitudes between some 200 and 1000 km.

The targets have been intercepted basically in three ways. In one the interceptor makes several orbital manoeuvres to achieve an eccentric orbit. The interceptor then passes close to the target at a considerable speed relative to it. Soon after the pass is made, the interceptor is exploded, presumably to test the kill mechanism for the destruction of the target.

In a second method, the interceptor makes a slower approach to the target. Both the interceptor and the target are usually launched at an orbital inclination of 65° and in the same orbital plane. In the third method, the interceptor climbs close to the target, intercepts it and then is commanded back to the earth before it has completed a full orbit. The interceptor enters the earth's atmosphere and disintegrates. In all the tests conducted so far, no target has apparently been destroyed. It has been reported that soon after the last test conducted in June 1982, the USSR launched two ICBMs, an SS-20 and an SLBM and then carried out two ABM tests. If these tests were co-ordinated with the ASAT test, then they provided, for the first time, an actual nuclear war scenario in which it was envisaged that a nuclear war was started by the destruction of a military satellite, followed by the launch of strategic missiles.

As for the Soviet directed-energy weapons, not much information is available from the USSR. However, evidence reported in the West suggests that they are also investigating the potential uses of directed-energy weapons.

The above brief discussion indicates the extent of the development and deployment of ASAT weapons. It is interesting to note that such developments continue despite the fact that since 1972 many of the military satellites have been protected by legal measures. Thus, before considering some of the new arms control proposals, it is useful to look at the extent to which existing treaties protect satellites.

Existing Legal measures

The existing legal regime of outer space consists of the 1967 Outer Space Treaty, a handful of other agreements, and a number of arms control treaties with provisions related to activities in outer space.

The 1967 Outer Space Treaty deals very inadequately with

the problem of the militarisation of outer space. The only
limitation placed on military activities in this environment
is the prohibition of the placing in orbit of nuclear weapons
or other weapons of mass destruction (Article IV.2). The
treaty thus legitimises other military uses of outer space.
Under article IV.2 of the Treaty, the Moon and other celestial bodies are demilitarised, but outer space as a whole
only partially demilitarised. Indeed, it is doubtful whether
the treaty was ever meant as an important arms control
measure[27]. The use of nuclear weapons and any other
weapons of mass destruction in or from orbit is very doubtful
from the point of view of their military effectiveness. If a
total ban on the use of outer space for military purposes had
been included in the treaty, the question of the extension of
the arms race to this environment may not have arisen today.
ASAT weapons are being developed because of the existence of
the military satellites.

With the exception of the 1963 Partial Test Ban Treaty,
other subsequent treaties have legitimised the military use
of outer space and, in fact, offer protection to the majority
of military satellites. For example, the 1972 ABM Treaty and
the SALT I and II Treaties contain pledges not to interfere
with the national technical means of verification. This means
that effectively photographic, electronic and early-warning
satellites, as well as ocean-surveillance satellites, are
protected by these treaties from destruction or interference.
The 1973 International Telecommunications Union Convention
obligates parties to the Convention to avoid harmful interference with the radio services or communications of other
parties.

Thus, only military navigation, geodetic, meteorological
and most civilian satellites are without any protection. But
when devices to detect nuclear explosions are deployed on
board the US NAVSTAR satellites, these might also be
classified under the category of national technical means of
verification and so be protected by some of the abovementioned arms control treaties.

A number of other arms control measures achieved since 1972
would also protect most of military satellites under the
verification clauses. Some new arms control measures in outer
space have been proposed both officially[28] and by nongovernmental organisations[29].

New Proposals

In 1981, the Soviet Union proposed a prohibition on objects
carrying weapons of any kind 'in orbit around the earth'
(Article 1, paragraph 1)[28]. Such a provision may be taken

to mean that direct-hit weapons are allowed. Most weapons that are deployed today and may be deployed in the near future are all launched either from earth or from within the atmosphere (such as the US F-15-launched ASAT missile). The protection of some military satellites is further emphasised in Article 3 of the proposal in which it is stated 'Each State Party undertakes not to destroy ... space objects of other States Parties if such objects were placed in orbit in strict accordance with Article 1, paragraph 1 ...'. This means that only the **weapons** placed in orbit may be destroyed. It is interesting to note here that the nature of such weapons is not made clear. As can be seen from the above technical description of some ASAT weapons, a satellite can be destroyed by another colliding with it.

A second draft treaty proposed by the Soviet Union in 1983 apparently includes prohibition of all weapons but the proposal is not without ambiguity[28]. For example, Article 1 of the proposed treaty prohibits the '... resort to the use or threat of force in outer space and the atmosphere and on the Earth through the utilization ... of space objects in orbit ...'. While this prohibits weapons which are space-based only, the Article continues, 'It is further prohibited to resort to the use or threat of force against space objects'. However, this part of the Article does not elaborate on the method by which the force or threat of force is applied. This may also be interpreted as allowing the **possession** of ASAT weapons as long as they are not space-based. Such an ambiguity is carried over in Article 2 of the proposal which deals with the prohibition on testing of ASAT weapons but only in orbit. An interesting feature of this proposal, however, is the inclusion of the limited prohibition of anti-ballistic missile weapons or ballistic missile defence systems, emphasising the dual nature of BMD and ASAT systems.

A third proposal was made by the Union of Concerned Scientists in the USA in June 1983[29]. Article I of this proposal states 'Each Party undertakes not to destroy, damage, render inoperable or change the flight trajectory of space objects of other States'. Again under this the possession of ASAT weapons is not prohibited. However, Article II, paragraph 1, prohibits deployment of weapons but only 'in orbit around the Earth'. Again an interesting feature of this Article is that it does limit the space-based BMD systems. Moreover, under paragraph 3 of this Article, 'Each Party undertakes not to test such weapons in space or against space objects'. The usefulness of such a measure may be limited since certain weapons need not be tested in space or even against space objects.

A serious problem with the above proposals is that they do not prohibit possession of ASAT weapons. A prohibition on possession of ASAT weapons is essential for two reasons. Firstly, in time of crises, a nation having such weapons may be tempted to use them leaving no time for reflection. Secondly, in the present political climate, a collision with a military satellite could arouse fears that an anti-satellite weapon had been used. It must be remembered that about eight in every ten satellites in space are military, so any collision is very likely to involve a military satellite. In fact, on three occasions in May 1980, within a period of two weeks, six satellites, five military and one civilian, were involved in near collisions[30]. All of these were in the geostationary orbit and they all belonged to the USA so that evasive actions were possible. Thus an effective ASAT treaty is essential not only because it may strengthen the ABM Treaty (since ASAT and BMD systems are similar) but also because such a measure would protect civilian satellites. Today, most of such satellites have no legal protection.

Moreover, even though the technical problems related to some of the ASAT weapons, such as laser weapons, are enormous and may not be solved in the foreseeable future, the mere proposed application of high-energy laser beams raises considerable difficulties from the point of view of arms control. For example, during the developmental phase of X-ray lasers, the 1963 Partial Test Ban Treaty (PTBT) would be jeopardised since such weapons will have to be tested. The PTBT prohibits nuclear explosions in outer space, in the atmosphere and under water. Moreover, if such weapons could be made to work then their deployment would violate the Outer Space Treaty. In any case, the development, testing and deployment of ASAT weapons would violate the spirit if not the letter of this treaty since such activities could not be regarded as peaceful ones. Perhaps the most important problem raised by modern ASAT weapons is from the point of view of a possible anti-satellite treaty. This is because some of the ASAT weapons are thought to be applicable to BMD systems also.

It is, therefore, essential that an ASAT treaty is negotiated soon. If the above-mentioned proposed treaties are taken to be the basis for negotiations, the least that could be done is to couple with the above types of treaties a commitment to no-first-use of ASAT weapons. Should the nuclear explosive-generated lasers become a reality, then the Soviet Union and the People's Republic of China have already partially made a no-first-use of ASAT weapons declaration. Such lasers are regarded as third generation nuclear weapons and both these nations have declared that they will not be the first to use nuclear weapons.

It has been argued that verifying an ASAT Treaty would be difficult[31]. Some preliminary thoughts on this are briefly considered below.

Verification

A close examination of the way in which the two big powers use different orbits for satellites performing various military missions indicates that there are distinct differences in the orbits used. In Figure 2 the number of military satellites launched by the USA and USSR is plotted as a function of their orbital inclinations. It is seen that while the USSR launches its satellites in a very narrow range of orbital inclinations (between 48° and about 100°), in the USA a much wider range of orbital inclinations has been used. There is thus some overlap between the orbital inclinations of the satellites of the two powers (for example, 57°, 63° and 98°). However, if the US satellites launched after 1966 are examined, it is found that the majority of them have orbital inclinations greater than 75°. With the exception of only a few, satellites after 1972 have been launched between 50° and 83°, and a few Meteo satellites in sun synchronous retrograde orbits (see Figure 2).

Therefore, if there were a ban on ASAT weapons, the USA would be easily alerted to possible violation on the part of the Soviet Union, since it would be rather unusual for them to launch satellites in orbits that are used by the USA. An exception to this, of course, is the geostationary orbit (GSO) where both powers orbit their satellites. However, the present Soviet ASAT system has a maximum range of about 1000 km; the GSO is at 36 000 km. Moreover, the Soviet Union uses a specific type of launcher to orbit its ASAT satellites. Therefore, a launch of an ASAT could be detected from space by observation of the launcher.

On the other hand, the US ASAT system is very different from that deployed by the USSR at present. The US system is a direct ascent system which can be launched against satellites in any orbit. While this flexibility together with the small size of the weapon increases its survivability, the verification of its ban would be very difficult to achieve using the normal space-based surveillance systems.

Verification of the ban on weapons of the more futuristic variety would not present any significant problems since, at least in the early stages, such weapons are likely to be large and therefore easily observable. However, once the US ASAT weapon is fully tested, a ban on its deployment would be very difficult to verify. Thus, if no steps are taken soon,

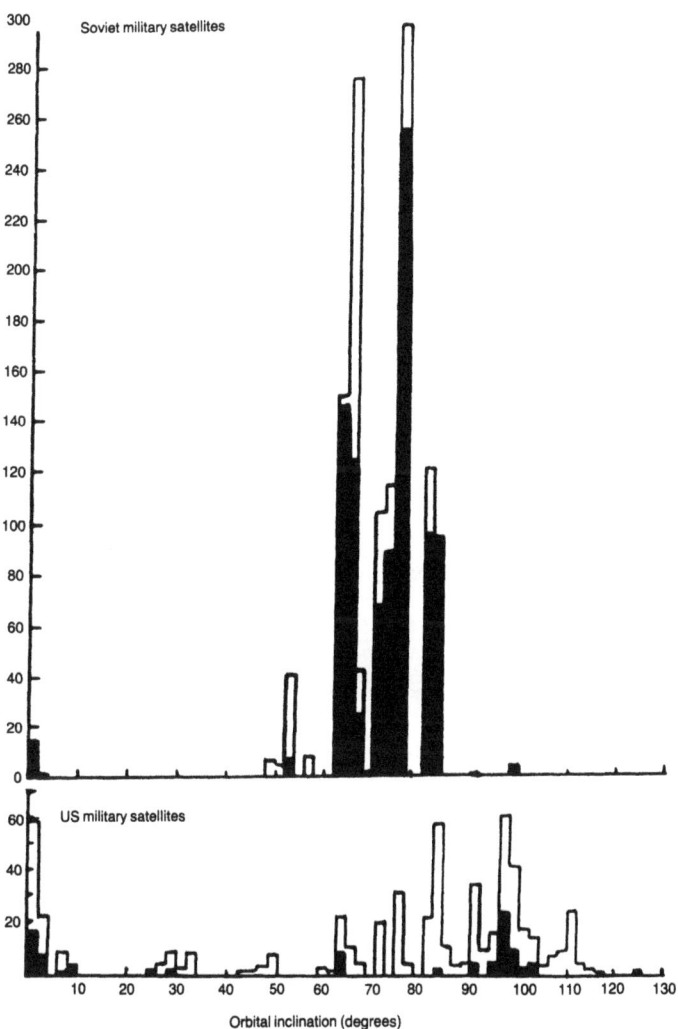

Figure 2. Number of US and Soviet military satellites as a function of their orbital inclinations:
□ satellites launched between 1958 and 1982;
■ satellites launched between 1972 and 1982.

it may be too late to achieve any meaningful arms control in space.

References

1. J. Pike, 'Anti-satellite weapons', F.A.S. Public Interest Report, 36, No.9 (November 1983).
2. P.B. Stares, 'déja vu: The ASAT Debate in Historical Context', Arms Control Today, 13, No.11 (December 1983).
3. D.G. King-Hele, H. Hiller and J.A. Pilkington, 'Revised Table of Earth satellites, Volume 1: 1957 to 1968', Royal Aircraft Establishment, Technical Report 78012, p.3 (January 1978).
4. 'SPIN', DMS Market Intelligence Report (January and August 1968).
5. 'Anti-satellite effort decision awaited', Aviation Week & Space Technology, 104, No.4 (24 January 1977) 19.
6. C.S. Sheldon, 'United States and Soviet progress in space. Summary data through 1976 and a forward look'. Congressional Research Service, Library of Congress, Report No. QB. 1C.Gen, 76-;32 SP (2 February 1976).
7. V. McGuire, 'AF hoping for cheap SAINT', Missiles and Rockets, 7, No.20 (14 November 1960) 38-40.
8. 'USAF Flight Tests Asat Weapon'. Aviation Week & Space Technology, 120, No.5 (30 January 1984) 19.
9. 'Telemetry Data shows US Anti-Satellite "Performed Well"' Defense Electronics, 16, No.2 (February 1984) 30.
10. 'Controlling Space Weapons', Hearings before the Committee on Foreign Relations, United States Senate. 98th Congress.
11. 'US DoD Developing Second-Generation ASAT Missile', Interavia Letter. No. 10458 (6 March 1984) 4.
12. 'USAF tests high-energy laser weapon', Flight-International 119, No.3744 (7 February 1981) 334.
13. 'Laser fails to destroy missile', Aviation Week and Space Technology, 114, No.23 (8 June 1981) 63.
14. 'Second laser laboratory test', Interavia Air Letter, No. 9778 (26 June 1981) 8.
15. 'Airborne laser lab downs missiles', Laser Focus/Electro-Optics, 19, No.9 (September 1983) 82.
16. 'DoD's space-based laser program--potential progress and problems', General Accounting Office, Report No. C-MASAD-82-10 (26 February 1982).
17. J.M. Douglas, 'Russian progress on the nuclear laser', Science News, 105 (5 February 1984) 8-9.
18. G.C. Baldwin and R.V. Khokhlov, 'Prospects of gamma-ray lasers', Physics Today (February 1975) 32-39
19. F. Winterberg, 'Nuclear and thermonuclear directed beam

weapons', Fusion (August 1981) 52-54.
20. 'New hope for gamma-ray lasers', Laser-Focus, 18, No.10 (October 1982) 14-15.
21. G. Chapline, and L. Wood, 'X-ray lasers', Physics Today, (June 1975) 40-48.
22. C.A. Robinson, Jr., 'Advances made on high-energy laser' Aviation Week & Space Technology, 114, No.8 (23 February. 1981) 25-27.
23. J. Hecht, 'The X-ray laser flap', Laser Focus. 17, No.5 (May 1981) 8.
24. 'Laser Wars', Foreign Report, No. 1812, pp.1-2 (23 February 1984) (London: The Economist).
25. N.W. Jalujka, 'Direct nuclear-pumped lasers', NASA Technical Paper 2091, 1983.
26. R. Gamin and J. Pike, 'Space Weapons', Bulletin of the Atomic Scientists, 40, No.5 (May 1984) 2S-11S.
27. B. Jasani and M.A. Lunderius, 'Peaceful Uses of Outer Space - Legal Fiction and Military Reality', Bulletin of Peace Proposals, 11, No.1 (March 1980) 57-70.
28. 'Soviet proposal for a draft treaty on the prohibition of the stationing of weapons of any kind in outer space', UN Document, No. A/36/192, 20 August 1981; 'Soviet proposal for a draft treaty on the prohibition of the uses of force in outer space and from space against the earth', UN Document, No. a/38/194, 23 August 1983.
29. 'A treaty limiting anti-satellite weapons', Anti-satellite Weapons: Arms Control or Arms Race? (Union of Concerned Scientists, 30 June 1983) 33-35.
30. B. Jasani, L. Perek, P. Lala, and L. Sehnal, 'Physical nature and technical attributes of the geostationary orbit', UN Report No. A/AC.105/203/Add.4 (18 May 1983).
31. Report to the Congress on UN Policy on ASAT Arms Control, 31 March 1984.

14 An International and Regional Satellite Monitoring Agency
TORLEIV ORHAUG

Introduction

Space observations have been used for military purposes since the beginning of the space age. Still, direct information about this activity is very limited. There is, however, a growing amount of indirect evidence that such observations have been of great importance for various tasks such as surveillance, crisis monitoring and treaty verification. Today only the two superpowers possess the capacity to perform extensive observation from space for military purposes. On the other hand, several other nations are now developing similar capabilities.

Parallel to the military use of space observations, a growing civilian use of similar techniques has emerged. In particular, weather satellites and other remote sensing satellites are acquiring imagery data for various applications.

Experience of using such data, as well as knowledge of methodology of processing and analysing the data, is rapidly spreading to a large number of countries. Even the knowledge how to design and build system parts and satellite systems can be found in a considerable number of countries. The monopoly of the two superpowers in the field of space technology has therefore been reduced. It should be emphasised, however, that only the superpowers possess the economical and technical background, as well as the necessary industrial infrastructure to construct the broad spectrum of civilian and military space systems.

In view of the important use of space observations as a means for various control functions, and for the creation of mutual stability and security, it is not surprising that the idea of using this technique for enhancing international stability was discussed as early as in 1961. Later, following a suggestion by the President of France, a UN study was conducted to investigate the legal, technical and financial

A SATELLITE MONITORING AGENCY

problems related to the use of satellite observations for monitoring military activities by an International Satellite Monitoring Agency (ISMA)[1].

Due to great difficulties in creating an international organisation and to special problems on the European arena it has recently been suggested that, as an intermediate step, a regional organisation (RSMA) be implemented instead of an international one[2].

This paper discusses some of the problems related to the use of satellite observations, by an international or a regional agency, for treaty verification and/or crisis monitoring.

Military Uses of Space Technology

Since the beginning of the space age in the latter part of the fifties, military support functions have gradually been developed approximately simultaneously by the two superpowers, the United States and the Soviet Union. These functions are: communications; navigation; and observations. The latter functions include: early warning; meteorology; reconnaissance; signal intelligence; ocean surveillance; geodetic satellites; and nuclear explosion detection.

In many cases, one single satellite may serve more than one function. As an example, the US NAVSTAR system will in addition to transmitters for navigation signals, also incorporate nuclear explosion detectors. Also, very often more than one satellite is needed to support one single function. In order to obtain necessary global coverage, several communication satellites are needed. The same is also true for several observation satellite systems.

The number of satellites launched may be found in international publications since every nation which launches satellites is obliged to report the launch characteristics to the UN. The direct function of the satellite is, however, not always given; this is particularly true for military satellites. Some indications can, however, be inferred from orbit and other data. According to recent estimates, approximately 3000 satellites have been launched between 1958 and 1983[2]. Of these, some 75 per cent (2020) have been used for military purposes, although some satellites are of dual use. Of the military satellites, some 50 per cent have been used for intelligence functions, such as early warning, signal intelligence, photographic reconnaissance, ocean surveillance.

The satellite systems and the functions they provide play an increasingly important military role for the superpowers and their allies. If this were not the case, these nations would have made the important technical and economic investments in their space systems. The impact may be found at different levels, namely: national prestige; intelligence functions; support for military C^3I-systems; targeting information; treaty verification; weapon navigation; alert for surprise attack; crisis management; control of military manoeuvres.

The military functions provided by space technology listed above are all 'non-aggressive' and it is generally considered that on the whole these functions are stabilising, in particular with respect to strategic war-fighting. It should be emphasised, however, that the majority of the space functions above also act as 'force multipliers' in the sense that they enhance the capability of existing weapons (nuclear and/or conventional). It is therefore no surprise that we can see now the development of systems both to combat and to protect satellite systems. Consequently, we can consider the military space technology also as a significant extension of the arms race.

Since the characteristics of the military satellites and their detailed use and incorporation in military organisations and weapon systems are classified information, it is difficult to assess the degree of dependence on such systems. It is generally considered that the superpowers are highly dependent upon their systems for peacetime use (verification, targeting, intelligence). This is probably also the case for the grey zone between war and peace (crisis monitoring, early warning). During war-fighting, the survivability of the space systems and functions does not only depend upon attacks on the satellites themselves but also upon attacks on the control and support functions (launching sites and ground stations) as well as the use of more conventional countermeasures (jamming, false signals, and so on). The question of survival of, and dependence upon, the space functions will therefore to a great extent be related to the particular war scenario.

A detailed description of existing space systems and militarisation/weaponisation of space is outside the scope of this paper. I shall instead concentrate on the role and characteristics of the observation satellites which have relevance for an SMA application.

The objective of observation satellites is to register objects and activities on, below, or above the surface of the earth. Due to several reasons (among others, the distance involved) the most effective way of gaining such information is the use of electromagnetic radiation. The following mechanisms may be involved:

- scattering/reflection from the scene of incoming natural

electromagnetic radiation (light and microwaves);
- scattering/reflection of man-made radiation (radar systems, laser systems, and the like);
- generation of natural electromagnetic radiation due to the physical temperature of the objects (so-called Planck radiation);
- generation of man-made radiation (from communication transmitters, radar transmitters, and so on).

In civilian applications, the first three methods are often labelled remote sensing (using passive or active sensors). The third method is a typical military activity conducted also from land-, sea- and air-based platforms; it is used by most nations for surveying 'radioactivity' in the surroundings (signal reconnaissance or signal intelligence).

The kind of information which may be acquired by satellite observations may be categorised in several ways. A categorisation with respect to the 'time scale' of the phenomena or activity is the following:

Non-changing data: geodetic; topographic. Timescale: very long.
Slowly changing data: construction; vegetation. Timescale: days to months.
Moderately changing data: military units at land and sea; weather. Timescale: hours to days.
Rapidly changing data: communication, radar; weather; military units; missiles, airplanes; nuclear explosions. Timescale: fraction of second to hours.

In order to acquire the data necessary to obtain information of the above activities, a large number of different sensors are in use. Many of these have been developed specially for use on satellite platforms. In most cases, the information needed is not only the particular radiation characteristics ('signature') but also the geographical location of the source of the radiation activity. Most sensors therefore are 'image forming' since they record both the electromagnetic radiation (or rather one or several of the properties of this radiation) and the angle of incidence normally given in terms of geographical coordinates on ground based on sensor and satellites parameters. The accuracy of position information depends both on the nature of the signals and on the sensors used for detection/registration. A brief categorisation with respect to geographical accuracy may be made as follows:

- kilometres or more: signal reception; weather; nuclear explosion detection; missile launch;

- hundreds of metres to kilometres: radar (SLAR-mode); weather; oceanographic parameters (microwave radiometers);
- tens of metres: electro-optical cameras; photographic cameras; radar (SAR-mode);
- metres: electro-optical cameras; photographic cameras; radar (SAR-mode); laser radar;
- decimetres: photographic cameras.

The main characteristics of sensors are: (a) resolution: ability to distinguish fine details; (b) range: ability to cover a wide range.

This can be applied to three important parameters of an imaging sensor:

(a) spectral: spectral resolution (narrowness of spectral channels); spectral range;
(b) intensity: contrast accuracy; contrast range (dynamic range);
(c) geographical: spatial (two-dimensional) resolution; area coverage.

All these parameters influence the quality of the sensor.

Many of the military interesting targets and activities are revealed by the detection of target shape and details. Therefore, high spatial resolution is needed. The spatial resolving power of an imaging sensor is determined by the following parameters: focal length; detector resolution (lines per mm for film as detector); satellite altitude; size and quality of lenses (aperture); wavelength of radiation; disturbing effects: atmospheric haze; atmospheric irregularities (turbulence); platform stability.

The actual resolution of the best cameras in military reconnaissance satellites is subject to stringent classification. For a given camera, the configuration resolving capacity can readily be calculated. The most important parameters are focal length (F), satellite altitude (H) and film characteristics (L line pairs per mm). The resolution X is then given by the formula:

$$X = H/LF$$

It is generally believed that camera and satellite technology permit focal lengths of several metres; this should give a resolution of a few decimetres. For example, for a camera at a 200 km altitude, with 4 m focal length and a film giving 200 lines pairs per mm, X = 25 cm. For resolution values as good as this, atmospheric conditions start to be important. The small-scale irregularities of the atmosphere (which give rise to star-twinkling effects) put a limit of 5 - 20 cm to the resolution. In principle, this effect could be compensated for by changing camera optics synchronously with seeing effects (so-called adaptive optics). There are reports indicating that such systems do in fact operate on board the best US reconnaissance satellites.

It should be pointed out that cameras working in the visual part of the electromagnetic spectrum are needed for detailed investigations of ground activities. Cameras working in the infra-red (IR) do not give the same ground resolution. On the other hand, such cameras are very useful for the detection of hot objects (ICBM-launches), camouflage penetration and underground activities.

The performance of satellite sensors is limited as follows:

observation repeatability: satellite orbit; satellite manoeuverability;
cloud and other atmospheric conditions: visual; IR (cloud penetration);
lighting conditions: visual (daytime); IR (daytime and nighttime); microwaves (day and night, fairly weather independent).
camouflage: non-movable targets; time delay of information.

The limitation to static targets is important. This means that the present systems are not very useful for tactical war-fighting. There are indications that the USA is developing special mosaic sensors which could make it possible to detect and track movable targets like aeroplanes and tactical missiles.

Since the photographic camera gives the best resolution, film is often used in reconnaissance satellites. This causes an appreciable time delay, since the film must be captured, developed, transported and interpreted. It is likely that real-time observations, using electro-optical cameras, are made nowadays. This development is expected to accelerate.

Camera systems are likely to perform two, somewhat different, functions: large area surveillance (using ground resolution of the order of several metres); close look reconnaissance (with resolution down to a few decimetres).

The US Big Bird satellite is believed to perform area-surveillance; the film is probably developed on board the satellite, converted to digital signals and then transmitted to ground stations. Electro-optical sensors, giving digital imagery data as output are probably also used. The US KH-11 is believed to perform close-look functions. A summary of satellite sensors and their functions is given in Table 1.

As already mentioned before, the actual ability to investi-

MILITARY ASPECTS OF SPACE

Table 1. Military Satellite Sensors[3]

Sensor	Functions	Type of Satellite
Photographic	Detection of: ABM-systems; ICBM-deploy-ment; cruise missile deployment; military facilities; troop movements	US optical reconnaissance satellites (Big Bird, KH-11), Soviet Cosmos satellites
IR	Detection of: missiles; aircrafts; cruise missiles (potential)	US and Soviet early warning satellites
Nuclear radiation detection	Detection of: nuclear explosions in the atmosphere; nuclear explosions in outer space	US Vela satellites and IONDS-systems on GPS-satellites
UV	Detection of: fluorescence from boosters; fluorescence from nose cones (during ballistic flight)	US and Soviet early-warning satellites
Electronic signal detectors	Interception of radio- and microwave transmission; radar signal detection; missile telemetry interruption	Soviet Cosmos and US ELINT satellites; US Rhyolite and Chalet satellites (in GSO)
Radar	Detection of: naval surface ships; ground-based military objects	US Seasat 1 (1978) and Soviet Cosmos ocean surveillance satellites
IR (thermal) scanners or radiometers	Night time reconnaissance. Detection of: buried structure; underground construction.	US Seasat 1

gate signal details is a complicated matter. Perception experiments regarding detection and interpretation indicate that 2-5 resolution elements are needed across a target in order to detect its presence as an object in a specific background environment. In photo-interpretation one normally defines several different levels of target interpretation. Based on a vast amount of experience in photo-interpretation, Table 2 reviews the resolution capacity needed to perform various tasks for different military-type targets. The various levels of target interpretation in Table 2 are as follows[4]:

Detection: location of class of units, object or activity of military interest;
General identification: determination of general target type;
Precise identification: discrimination within target type of known types;
Description: size/dimension, configuration layout, components-construction, count of equipment, and so on.

Symbolically, we may consider a target made of details of various sizes. In order to make an interpretation on the next high level, details describing that level must be detected. Therefore, if identification needs detection of details which are 1/5 the size of the target, approximately 5 times the resolution which suffices for detection is needed for identification.

A recent (August 1984) publication[13] shows an image, claimed to be from a US military satellite, with a resolution of 0.5-1.0 m. The best space images published are from Skylab cameras. Another method to obtain photographic products indicating the resolution obtainable from military satellites are from aerial photography. By computer degradation of such images, any resolution lower than the one of the original image may be obtained[5].

Civilian Uses of Space Technology

The civilian community uses space for several functions:

exploration of the celestial environment (astronomy);
exploration of the environment in the vicinity of the earth: magnetic fields; ionosphere;
exploration of environment on and close to the earth; observational satellites;
support functions: communication; navigation;
space manufacturing.

Table 2. Resolution (in metres) required for Interpretation Tasks

Target	Detection	General Identification	Precise Identification	Description	Analysis
Bridge	6	4.6	1.5	0.9	0.3
Communications					
Radar	3	0.9	0.3	0.15	0.04
Radio	3	1.5	0.3	0.15	0.15
Supply dump	1.5	0.6	0.3	0.03	0.03
Troop units	6	2	1.2	0.3	0.08
Airfield facilities	6	4.6	3	0.3	0.15
Rockets and artillery	0.9	0.6	0.15	0.05	0.01
Aircraft	4.6	1.5	0.9	0.15	0.03
Command and control headquarters	3	1.5	0.9	0.15	0.03
Missile sites (SSM/SAM)	3	1.5	0.6	0.3	0.08
Surface ships	7.6	4.6	0.6	0.3	0.08
Nuclear weapon components	2.4	1.5	0.3	0.03	0.01
Vehicles	1.5	0.6	0.3	0.05	0.03
Land minefields	9	6	0.9	0.03	—
Ports and harbours	30.5	15	6	3	0.3
Coasts and landing beaches	30.5	4.6	3	1.5	0.08
Railway yards and shops	30.5	15	6	1.5	0.6
Roads	9	6	1.8	0.6	0.15
Urban areas	61	30.5	3	3	0.3
Terrain	—	91	4.6	1.5	0.15
Surfaced submarines	30.5	6	1.5	0.9	0.03

Source: 'Reconnaissance Handy Book', p.125, published by McDonnel Douglas Corporation, USA.

A SATELLITE MONITORING AGENCY

For our purpose, the observational satellites are of special interest. They are as follows: geodetic; meteorological; land use; oceanographic.

The best known is the Landsat satellite programme (started in 1972 as the ERTS-programme). In this programme five satellites were launched. Landsat 1-3 carried sensors with pixel size about 80 and 45 m respectively; for Landsat 4 and 5 the size was 30 m. It should be borne in mind that the altitudes of these satellites are in the region of 700 - 900 km. If, therefore, the same camera (multi-spectral scanner) was carried by a satellite at a 200 km altitude, the corresponding pixel size for Landsat 4 and 5 would be approximately 8 metres.

Due to the coarse resolution, Landsat 1-3 can only be utilised for the detection of large features, such as land forms, lakes, roads, airports, or urban characteristics. The usefulness of observational data from these satellites is, however, partly due to the spectral information given by the multispectral sensor (Table 3). It should be emphasised that in ordinary photo-interpretation, as in direct vision, the scene is generally interpreted by the use of geometrical features, such as shape and form, texture, shadow, occlusions. The Landsat data, on the other hand, are generally analysed using spectral features. This is often rather efficient for land/water studies, vegetation studies, environmental monitoring, coarse urban studies, and so on. It should also be pointed out that one of the most important characteristics of the Landsat data is the fact that they are available in digital format. This has had a significant impact on the use of digital computers for image handling, presentation, processing and analysis.

Of special interest are the plans for future civilian satellites. Table 4 summarises some of the more relevant space sensors and their characteristics. The French SPOT satellite, scheduled for launch in 1985, is supposed to acquire monospectral data of 10 m pixel size and multispectral data of 20 m pixel size. If operated at 200 km, this sensor would produce data of 3 and 6 m pixel size respectively. Such data would already be of relevance for monitoring purposes.

Verification of Strategic Arms Development

The detailed characteristics and use of the military space systems operated by the superpowers are, as indicated earlier, not available. The same is true for the intelligence organisations making operational use of these and other data. One of the problem areas where satellite data are used, which

Table 3. Summary of Sensor Characteristics of Landsat satellites

Satellite	Sensor	Wavelength region (m)		Pixel size (m)	Times of functioning
Landsat 1,2	RBV (did not function properly)	Band 1: 2: 3:	4.7-5.7 5.8-6.8 7.0-8.3	79 79 79	Landsat 1: 22.7.1977- 6.1.1978
	MSS	Band 4: 5: 6: 7:	5-6 6-7 7-8 8-11	79 79 79 79	Landsat 2: 22.1.1975- 25.2.1982
Landsat 3	RBV		5.0-7.5	45	Landsat 3: 11.7.1978- at present standby
	MSS	Same as for Landsat 1, 2			
Landsat 4, 5	MSS	Same as for Landsat 1, 2, 3			

	TM	Band 1:
		2:
		3:
		4:
		5:
		6:
		7:
			4.2-5.2
			5.2-6.0
			6.3-6.9
			7.6-9.0
			1.55-1.75
			10.4-12.5
			2.1-2.3
				30
				30
				30
				30
				30
				120
				36
					Landsat 4:
					22.7.1983-
					MSS: still
					   func-
					   tioning
					TM: ceased
					   func-
					   tioning
					   13.2.1983
					
					Landsat 5:
					1.3.1984

Table 4. Summary of some planned civilian spaceborne sensors

Country	Satellite	Sensor	Pixel size (m)	Comments
France	SPOT	multispectral: 3 bands	ca 20 m	1985
		monospectral:	ca 10 m	
ESA	ERS-1	SAR	30 m, 100 m	1985-1986
		Radar altimeter accuracy: 10 cm		
USA	Space Shuttle	Large Format Camera	10 m	proposed
ESA	Space Shuttle - Spacelab	Metric Camera	20 m	
USA	Mapsat	3 telescopes, F = 1 m	10-60 m	proposed
USA	Stereosat	3 telescopes	15 m	proposed
Canada	Sarsat	SAR	25-30 m	proposed
Japan	MOS-1	Marine productivity studies		1986 (planned)
	ERS-1	Experimental earth sensing satellite		1990 (planned)
		Sensors in future satellites: SAR microwave altimeter high resolution optical sensors		

is subject to some insight, is the monitoring and verification of parts of the SALT agreement. It may therefore be of some interest to review some of the information sources and the corresponding technology used by the USA for this verification task[3,6,7,8].

The SALT-treaties comprise the following main agreements:

prohibition regarding construction of additional fixed land-based ICBM after 1 July 1972;
prohibition on conversion of land-based light ICBM-launchers into heavy ICBM;
limitation of SLBM;
limitation of the number of re-entry vehicles per launcher;
prohibition regarding interference with 'national technical means' for verification.

The 'national technical means' play a most significant role in the verification process. It is generally understood that these means comprise several technical methods, including satellite observations.

The objective of the treaties is to:

restrict the number of strategic weapons by satellite observations;
restrict qualitative improvements on existing strategic weapons by non-satellite observations;
restrict developments on new missile systems by satellite and non-satellite observations.

The US technical means of verification seemingly consists of ground-based, sea-based, airborne and spaceborne systems. The technical methods used are:

radars: line of sight radars, ground-based, sea-based, airborne;
OTH radars: ground-based;
IR-sensors: satellite-borne;
photographic sensors: satellite-based, sea-based;
interception of communication, radar and telemetry signals: ground-based, airborne, satellite-borne, sea-based.

These verification methods are efficient because the introduction of new missile systems, as well as most weapon systems, has to go through research, development, testing, production, and deployment phases. It is very improbable that a system could go through several or all of these stages without detection.

A SATELLITE MONITORING AGENCY

The information which might be gathered by these sensor systems is as follows:

Radars: detection of existence of missile test: determination of missile trajectory; character of re-entry vehicles; frequency of test used to infer propagation of system through the various phases test-deployment.
Early warning satellites (IR): existence of launch.
ELINT (electronic intelligence): telemetry data indicating status of test (size, payload, fuel consumption).
Photographic reconnaissance satellites: information about hardware.

This summary description indicates that the national technical means used for SALT and ABM verifications make use of many independent methods.
An important role is also played by electronic intelligence. The monitoring tasks relevant for an SMA could, of course, be different from those covered by the ABM and SALT treaties. Nevertheless, it is important to consider the tasks given to an SMA in light of the verification means which would be reasonable for use by such an organisation.

Monitoring Tasks Relevant for an SMA

The UN-study[1] discusses the relevance of an ISMA organisation for monitoring existing international arms regulation and disarmament agreements. The existing agreements for which an ISMA would give some or significant information for verification purposes are summarised in Table 5.

Of great interest is the question whether and to what extent the USA and the Soviet Union have been using their observational satellites for crisis monitoring. Since neither of them has directly admitted this type of activity, inference has to be made from studies of orbital parameters such as perigee, inclination, ground track and conduct of orbital manoeuvres. A review of such studies has been made by Santhanam[9]. Some of the Soviet and US satellites which seem to have been used for such activity are:

Sino-Soviet border conflict, 1969
   satellites: Cosmos-281, 283, 286, 289; Big Bird-19A, 26A, 39, 41A, 50A.

Indo-Pakistan crisis, 1971
   satellites: Cosmos-463, 464, 465; Big Bird-56A.

Table 5. Information obtainable from ISMA for existing agreements

Agreement	Contribution	Sensor	Resolution
Geneva Protocol 1925	Some	Advanced spectroscopic equipment	About 0.5 m
Antarctic Treaty 1959	Significant	Area surveillance Close-look SAR IR Nuclear radiation	3-5 m (optical) 0.5 m (optical)
Partial Test Ban Treaty 1963	Some	Photographic Nuclear radiation detectors	3-5 m 0.5 m
Treaty of Tlatelolco 1967	Some	Photographic	3.5 m 0.5 m
NPT Treaty 1968	Some	Photographic	3.5 m 0.5 m
Biological Convention 1972	Some	Photographic	3.5 m 0.5 m

A SATELLITE MONITORING AGENCY 139

Arab-Israeli war, 1973
satellites: Cosmos-596-600, 602

Cyprus crisis, 1974
satellites: Cosmos-666, 670; Big Bird-20A, 65A

Satellite investigations of the (possible) South African nuclear test (1977), the OTRAG rocket test in Zaire (1977), as well as the Indian nuclear test (1974), have also been reported[9].

Another important monitoring task is the continuous investigation of military manoeuvres. The control of naval activities on international waters by conventional means (ships, aircrafts) is well known. Recently, Jasani[10] has studied the (possible) Soviet investigation of the Bold Guard combat exercise (August 1982) by Cosmos-1407 and Cosmos-1402, and the (possible) US investigation of the Zapad manoeuvre (September 1981) by KH-11 (1980-10A), KH-11 (1981-85A) and NOSS-IC.

Referring to the incomplete knowledge of the use which the superpowers make of their space observation systems and the various studies cited above, the possible tasks for an SMA-organisation may be summarised as follows:

verification of existing international treaties;
verification of possible future treaties;
monitoring crisis areas;
preventing crisis situations;
settling disputes between countries;
early warning of potential armed conflicts.

The main purpose of such an organisation is therefore to act as an instrument for enhancing and building confidence among nations.

Although the principal and basic arguments for an SMA instrument are credible, it should, nevertheless, be pointed out that there are important uncertainties and obstacles. Some of the technical obstacles are:

satellite and sensor limitations: area coverage; temporal coverage; problems due to weather and protection (manoeuvring; camouflage, radio silence);
information requirement versus information availability.

With regard to crisis monitoring, an SMA could give information about dynamic changes in the strength of forces and their movements, activity of surface vessels, as well as deployment of aircraft. As an example, there are indications that the present Landsat system may detect large aircraft[11]. On the other hand, it has been argued that there is no indication that existing satellites have been a factor inhibiting the outbreak of hostilities[9]. An interesting question is to what extent an SMA-instrument with free information could affect world opinion and therefore prevent crisis, as contrasted to the present situation where only the superpowers have access to relevant satellite information from crisis areas.

Another point which should be emphasised is the fact that the superpower's acquisition of satellite information is used by an intelligence organisation in which both kinds of 'hard' data as well as 'soft' data (from conventional espionage, for example) are available. In addition, the hard data are not only acquired by photographic satellites but also from electronic reconnaissance satellites. Furthermore, it is well known that electronic intelligence plays a very important role for most nations for monitoring military activities in their surroundings. It is very unlikely that an SMA-instrument could make use of such data, for several reasons. The conduct of electronic intelligence is a complicated matter and is based upon a very detailed knowledge concerning military communications, military hardware and weapon systems, military organisations and tactics. Furthermore, for political reasons it is improbable that several nations could cooperate in an SMA with such tools.

Due to these factors it is important to study to what degree would an SMA-organisation be efficient if only sensors like photographic cameras and radar instruments were utilised.

The UN-study[1] also indicated that the ISMA-data could be used for civilian purposes, like environmental monitoring and resources management. One reason for this dual-use was cost benefit. It has recently been argued that for both political and technical reasons, the operations of satellites for civilian and peace-keeping purposes should be kept completely separated[12].

In accordance with its mandate, the UN-study[1], investigated the various implications concerning the establishment of an international SMA-organisation. The 37th United Nations General Assembly passed a resolution recommending that the proposal for the establishment of the ISMA should be considered and the study should be disseminated as a UN publication; it was adopted by 126 votes with 9 no-votes and 11 abstentions, but neither the USA nor the Soviet Union voted in favour.

It might, therefore, be both interesting and reasonable to start the implementation of the idea of a non-national SMA with an intermediate step on a regional basis, a Regional Satellite Monitoring Agency (RSMA), as suggested by Jasani[2]. In this connection, the European region might be considered for the following reasons:

high concentration of conventional and nuclear arms;
possibility of confidence-building not only between single nations but also between the two blocs;
existence of a space technology infrastructure (in the ESA and the Intercosmos organisations as well as among several of the countries within and outside these organisations).

It was emphasised earlier that the SAR-microwave sensor is essential in many monitoring tasks. This is particularly true for the European theatre since this continent is often covered by clouds. In this connection, one should mention the high level of radar technology existing in several European countries, and the significant knowledge of SAR-technology in Europe.

Conclusions

The experience during a quarter of a century of space technology has proved that the various military functions provided by this technology are among the most important application areas. Even though these applications act like force multipliers for the superpowers, they have important positive effects both in bilateral treaty verifications and as confidence-building instruments in other circumstances such as crisis monitoring.

The idea of an ISMA for general international confidence building, without the sole control of the superpowers, is based on the general understanding of the important role played by the observation satellites in the relationship between the two superpowers. For the moment there does not seem to be sufficient political support for implementing this idea within the UN framework. The implementation of an intermediate step, like an RSMA, seems both reasonable and feasible, at least from a technical viewpoint. Europe seems to be an interesting region for the implementation of such an agency.

References

1. UN, 'Study on the implications of establishing an international satellite monitoring agency', A/AC.206/14 (6 August 1981).
2. B. Jasani, 'Reconnaissance from space'. SIPRI Work-

shop on 'Measures to reduce the fear of surprise attack in Europe', (Stockholm: SIPRI, 1983).
3. B. Jasani, 'A role of satellites in verification of arms control agreement'. Working paper presented at the Pugwash Symposium on An International Agency for the Use of Satellite Observation Data for Security Purposes, (Avignon, France: April 1980).
4. B.G. Blair and G.D. Brewer, 'Verifying SALT agreements'. ACIS working paper no.19, Center for International and Strategic Affairs, University of California, Los Angeles, (January 1980) (also in W.C. Potter, 'Verification and SALT'), (Boulder, Colorado: Westview Press, 1980).
5. T. Orhaug and G. Forrsell, 'Information extraction from images'. Paper 6 in B. Jasani (ed.), 'Outer Space - a new dimension of the arms race' (London: Taylor & Francis, 1982).
6. T. Greenwood, 'Reconnaissance, surveillance and arms control'. Adelphi Papers No.88 (London: International Institute for Strategic Studies, 1972).
7. F.J. Moncrief, 'SALT verification: How we monitor the Soviet arsenal', Microwaves (September, 1979) 41-51.
8. L. Aspin, 'The verification of the SALT II agreement'. Scientific American, 240, No.2 (1979) 30-97.
9. K. Santhanam, 'Use of satellites in crisis monitoring', in B. Jasani (ed.) 'Outer space - a new dimension of the arms race', (London: Taylor & Francis, 1982).
10. B. Jasani, 'Outer Space, militarisation outpaces legal control'. Paper presented at the UNV and IISL joint symposium on 'Conditions Essential for Maintaining Outer Space for Peaceful uses'. (The Hague, 12-15 March, 1984).
11. T. Orhaug and N. Olander, 'Landsat 4 TM-data: Examples of resolution capacity'. FOA Report C 30329-E1, ISSN 0347-3708 (September 1983).
12. C. Voûte, 'Agreement and disagreement on an international satellite monitoring agency', International Journal of Remote Sensing, 5, No.2 (1984) 479-483.
13. Jane's Defence Weekly, 2, No.5 (11 August 1984).

15 A Space Policy for Peace
CAESAR VOÛTE

Some Facts and Figures

One way to look at space policy and its trends is by analysing past, present and expected future expenditure, which provides us with some highly significant figures[1].

One can observe a worldwide increase from about 22 billion US dollars in 1981 to about $35 billion in 1983. In the same period US expenditure increased by 75 per cent from about $8.5 billion to $15 billion, and the European programmes (national programmes plus those of the European Space Agency) by 30 per cent from $1100 million to $1400 million. US civilian expenditure peaked in 1968/1969 with slightly over $5000 million, when it was twice the military total at that time; it has only exceeded this level again in 1983. But current US military space expenditure is 35 per cent higher than the civilian total ($8500 million against $6300 million). Out of the USSR space expenditure for 1983, estimated at $18 billion, 70 to 75 per cent is believed to be for military purposes.

We thus see that at present two countries (USA and USSR) account for 94 per cent of space expenditure, a large proportion of which is for military purposes. Japan (at present at 1.3 per cent of world expenditure) and India (at present at 0.25 per cent) show considerable increases, whereas the European effort (ESA plus national programmes) is progressing at a much slower rate, representing in 1981 4.25 per cent of the world total and in 1983 only 3.8 per cent.

The European trend could become reversed if a suggestion by the French President were to be followed up and a European Space Community created to strengthen the European military defence power, for instance, through launching a European manned space station for surveillance purposes and defence action[2]. It could significantly contribute to the emergence of Europe as the third space power.

It would also mean that military space expenditure would

continue to grow proportionally faster than civilian expenditure, not only in the USA and USSR, but also elsewhere. Until now European space expenditure, like in Canada, India and Japan, has been mainly or almost entirely for civilian purposes.

Meanwhile, military space expenditure in the United States is increasing even more rapidly with the decision to develop and deploy new anti-satellite weaponry systems. These involve annually an additional $5 billion for Research and Development, and $90 to $95 billion by the year 2000 for deployment[3].

In the preceding paragraphs no mention has been made of the People's Republic of China, even though it is generally known that this country is actively developing space capabilities for both military and civilian purposes. However, no public sources are available which permit an estimate of the magnitude of these efforts in comparison with those of the USA, USSR, (Western) Europe, Canada, India or Japan.

Irrespective of the accuracy of the figures and percentages quoted, it is clear that funding for peaceful uses of space and space technology is increasing slowly, notwithstanding the proven or expected benefits. On the other hand, funding for military purposes is increasing very rapidly, while at the same time the debate on its usefulness for promoting security and peace is intensifying.

We are thus faced with a curious situation. On the one hand, there are high hopes that the civilian applications of space technology will contribute significantly to socio-economic development, although one hears more and more often expressions of disappointments and impatience about the slowness of the actual impact of this modern technology. On the other hand, from many sides fears are worded that the increasing militarisation of space, and in particular its weaponisation will increase instability, while great doubts are expressed about the value of space weaponisation as an approach to increase security and reduce the risks of nuclear war. Under these conditions, it seems illogical that the priority decision for the use of human and material resources should focus on applications of space technology with uncertain advantages, and not on those with proven capabilities.

Pondering on the various facts and figures, one easily gets the impression that there are two entirely different issues at stake:
- On one side, the militarisation and weaponisation of space, and also the use of space technology for surveillance, crisis management, increase of stability and promotion of peace - or, in other words, 'a Space Policy for Security and Peace';

A SPACE POLICY FOR PEACE   145

- On the other side, the use of space technology as one of the tools to promote economic and social development (including national prestige) - or, in other words, 'A Space Policy for Human Benefit'.
In reality, these two issues are intimately linked because the spin-offs of the one serve the other; because of the competition for scarce resources (human and financial); and because emphasising one reflects positively or negatively on the other in terms of confidence building or accentuating distrust.

Outer Space and Security

Much of the debate centres on two aspects:
- contributions of reconnaissance satellites to crisis management and arms-race stability;
- space-based ballistic-missile defence; feasibility, desirability, controls.

The first of these aspects has been discussed at two Pugwash Symposia in 1980 and 1982[4]; it has furthermore been the subject of an important United Nations document[5].

However, it is not my purpose to review and analyse once against the arguments for and against either the establishment of satellite systems for crisis management, or space-based or ground-based anti-satellite and ballistic-missile defence systems. It will be sufficient to refer to the abundant literature on the subject, to recent reports[6] and to the frequent exchange of opinions in the media at both sides of the Atlantic.

Nevertheless, a word of warning should be said. The debate suggests that in dealing with these two aspects, and in general with the issue of military connotation of the conquest of space, be it for the protection of mankind, the foundations for a 'space policy for peace' are being laid. This is only partially true, because such a limited policy does not solve the problems with which we are confronted. It would only be effective once agreement is reached on more far-reaching issues, which divide mankind.

An International Satellite Monitoring Agency (ISMA), in particular, cannot replace negotiated agreements on arms control or disarmament. Its establishment should rather be one of the results of such agreements, if we want an ISMA to be operational and accepted by all parties concerned.

It will therefore be useful to repeat here the summary of some statements which I elaborated elsewhere[7]:

> Militarisation of space in terms of weaponisation is no panacea for crisis management and even has destabilising

effects. The use of space technology for information gathering, crisis monitoring and treaty verification contributed to 'transparency' of world affairs, reduces the risks of coercion or violence in situations of confrontation and the occurrence of 'accidental war', but does not solve the underlying problems and causes of contention. The only long-term viable approach in defence and promotion of peace is through changing the pattern of management on the earth and providing all nations, societies and individuals optimal opportunities for development. The space age creates entirely new conditions which, if well exploited, taking into account human aspirations and the potential of the environments, can contribute significantly towards the establishment of permanent peace.

It is my firm conviction that the Pugwash Conferences on Science and World Affairs should address the risks of militarisation of space and the positive values of space policy for peace as a holistic concept. The responsibility of the scientific community goes much beyond the task of warning of dangerous developments. It includes equally the obligation to indicate alternative roads to progress by an authoritative review of the long-term benefits which can be derived from a more appropriate use of science and technology.

Limiting the discussions at Pugwash Conferences, Symposia and Workshops, and the formulation of statements to the authorities and the public to the effects of the arms race, carries with it the hazard that the scientists involved will be looked upon as 'doom-thinkers', or at least as being one-sidedly concerned with the problems of society. This reduces the weight and impact of our work.

There is a precedent with the traditional discussions at Pugwash about the Third World problematique under the title 'Security and Development', when the destabilising effects of insufficient or unbalanced development are identified as some of the causes of conflict, and where the critical (not always positive) role of science and technology is pointed out. It will be sufficient to refer to the Statement of the Pugwash Council published after the 33rd Conference in Venice in 1983[8].

In this context, there is no difference between 'North' and 'South', 'East' and 'West', the industrialised nations entering into a post-industrial period, the emerging newly industrialised nations and the technologically and economically underdeveloped countries of the Third World. All are faced with exactly the same issues when the conquest of space and its use for the benefit of humanity are concerned. When space is involved, the convergence of circumstances in all parts of the world is very apparent.

A Space Policy for Peace

The conquest of the space and the use of space technology have in common that they have basically global effects. Furthermore, there is now another dimension available to human endeavours, and even more important, to the human mind. This new dimension merits exploitation in a novel manner within the framework of a general policy, which could be described as 'A Space Policy for Peace' or perhaps even more properly as 'A Space Policy for Humanity' (where humanity stands both for 'mankind' and for an essentially humane or humanistic approach).

A major requirement is to generate an overall, coherent and consistent space policy, encompassing all scientific, technical, economic, legal, social, cultural, ethical and political aspects, including the distinct (only in appearance) issues of militarisation/defence/peacekeeping and socio-economic development. This general framework can then serve to develop in a proper perspective and in a well-equilibrated way policies at different levels and for different scientific and practical applications of space.

Governments still tend to address space policy in a fragmentary manner. Perhaps even more serious, there is still a general tendency to address matters of space policy principally from the perspective of national interests, and - as in the case of the USA, USSR and France - from the viewpoint of national prestige.

The conquest of space and the operationalisation of space technology for socio-economic purposes, by their very nature call for international cooperation. Through their global functions, and because they reach across the boundaries of nations, societies and culture, they could - and should - be used as a basic policy to promote international cooperation and international confidence-building and interdependence of nations.

While all efforts continue to try and put a halt to the increasing militarisation and weaponisation of space, we need not wait for a successful outcome of negotiations in this area. Rather we can start today, and initiatives can be taken by any group and any nation (whether large or small, industrialised or developing) to promote such a general space policy for peace and humanity. It can even be expected that - as international cooperation and interdependence develop - distrust will diminish, mutual confidence will increase, and in the long run negotiations on the more difficult issues will be facilitated.

A start of such a policy, addressing, on the one side, a broader issue in relation to advanced technology in general, and, on the other side, more limited in scope because aiming essentially at development co-operation, was recently proposed at the North-South Conference of the Parliamentary Assembly of the Council of Europe[9]. It is interesting to note that the proposal for the establishment of an international Satellite Monitoring Agency (for surveillance only) is included in these proposals.

Such an approach appears more promising than the analysis of the present situation, however true and valuable, by an author like Daniel Deudney[10]. It is certainly more advantageous - internationally seen - than the formal USA space policy[11,12].

Europe's Possible Role in an International and Regional Satellite Monitoring Agency

One important component of a space policy for peace and humanity is constituted by the proposed international satellite monitoring agency (ISMA) mentioned earlier. It is not a new proposal - the first ideas date back to the late 1950s and the 1960s, while a formal proposal was submitted to the United Nations in 1978 by Giscard d'Estaing, then President of the French Republic. Although little progress has been made thus far, it is receiving more and more attention.

In view of the great difficulties to create an international organisation, it has been suggested recently that a regional satellite monitoring agency (RSMA) could perhaps be established as an initial phase[13,14]. This would prevent a loss of momentum or a complete blocking of the original proposals, while serving simultaneously as an instrument for promoting regional stability and confidence-building. Could Europe play an effective role in this context?

Europe has been mentioned as the proper region for the establishment of an RSMA because of the special problems of the European arena. Moreover, Europe is particularly well equipped because of its strong intellectual capital and its technological and industrial potential. It has achieved a sufficient level of capability in space technology to take a credible political initiative towards the setting-up of such an agency, the European Space Agency (ESA) being the third space power in terms of exploration and peaceful uses of outer space. Another advantage is that there already exists a well-organised intergovernmental infrastructure suited for addressing technical aspects of an ISMA or an RSMA through

A SPACE POLICY FOR PEACE

ESA in Western Europe and the Interkosmos Council in Eastern Europe[15].

However, when discussing the establishment of either an ISMA or an RSMA, the mere availability of proper technological capabilities is not sufficient. More essential is a political environment suited for taking the necessary initiatives and pursuing these through adequate measures for implementation and negotiations. Such action exceeds the mandates of either ESA or the Interkosmos Council. At present the prospects are dim for fruitful discussions within the United Nations system. The lack of interest in cooperating with further studies, the opposition against such studies or the reluctance to provide voluntary contributions to the United Nations space programme among several countries having a space capability, prevent such studies from being undertaken in the immediate future by UN bodies. On the other hand, any initiative to establish an ISMA, starting either as an RSMA limited to the European region, or as an interregional or international venture outside the UN system, should have a provision for its eventual inclusion in the UN.

Under the circumstances several relevant initiatives at the European level are noteworthy. There is the suggestion by President François Mitterand[2] to create a European Space Community to strengthen the European military defence power, for instance through launching a European-manned space station for surveillance purposes and defence action, apparently as a parallel organisation to the European Economic Communities (EEC). At the EEC European Summit held in Fontainebleau on 27 June 1984, it was decided to establish a special working group to elaborate this particular proposal. During his official visit to the United Kingdom in October 1984, President Mitterand considerably played down the military aspects, stating that the main purposes for such a European manned space station would be research, the testing of industrial production possibilities, and earth observations.

There is also Recommendation 410, discussed and adopted on 20 June 1984 by the Assembly of the Western European Union (Belgium, France, Federal Republic of Germany, Italy, Luxemburg, Netherlands, United Kingdom) at its Paris meeting, referring to the military use of space in a broad way, including the establishment of an ISMA and the development of a European space strategy. This initiative, and the above-mentioned by President Mitterand, are due at least in part to the fear that Europe would be technologically lagging further behind, the USA and USSR having an almost absolute monopoly in the military use of outer space. Military use of space for defence was also discussed at the WEU Ministers Conference in Rome in October 1984.

Similar considerations are at the base of discussions held during the French-German Summit at Rambouillet on 28 May 1984. The topics included a study for the development of a joint military reconnaissance satellite as a follow-on to the French Samro programme, which was cut back in 1982 because of defence-spending constraints.

Perhaps more important, and probably more promising with regard to future negotiations with the two superpowers and with Third World countries, is the action undertaken by the Parliamentary Assembly of the Council of Europe. It submitted a special report to the Second United Nations Conference on the Exploration and Peaceful uses of Outer Space[16], supporting the ISMA proposals as a most effective instrument in contributing to efforts to reduce worldwide arms expenditure - thus making possible the shift of resources in favour of the developing countries called for in Council of Europe Resolution 747 of 12 May 1981 on global prospects - human needs and the earth's resources.

Furthermore, the Council of Europe adopted, on 24 January 1983, Resolution 789 on the future of the European space programme, Resolution 788 on the Second United Nations Conference on the Exploration and Peaceful Uses of Outer Space (noting **inter alia** concern about the increasing militarisation of space and recommending to exploit the potential of space technology as a stabilising factor in international relations, for instance through an international satellite monitoring agency) and Recommendation 957 on the proposal for an international satellite monitoring agency. The last mentioned Recommendation states explicitly that possibilities for renewed initiatives should be examined by Council of Europe member states, either individually or collectively, or in association with non-European industrialised or developing countries with a space capability.

Mention has already been made of a report submitted at the Council of Europe North-South Conference[9]. This went even further by adopting the 'Lisbon Declaration' of 11 April 1984, which stated that the Council of Europe and its members should undertake joint planning with developing countries of projects such as an international satellite monitoring agency, to ensure worldwide access to satellite-gained remote sensing information.

The Council of Europe Sub-Committee on Space Policy, Information Technology and Telecommunications is currently investigating ways and means to implement Recommendation 957 in the light of the Lisbon Declaration. It should be noted, by the way, that the Council of Europe normally looks upon

ESA (14 states, with some neutral countries as members or associate members and Canada as observer) as the main agency responsible for implementing a European space policy.

Conclusion

It is clear that there exists a divergence of opinion on the desirability and usefulness of an international or a regional satellite monitoring agency. There equally exists a divergence of opinion on whether or not such an agency should be integrated in the United Nations system, and which nation or group of nations should take the lead.

Nevertheless, there appears to be a widespread feeling that the proposals tabled thus far have been investigated in a preliminary way and that they deserve further study as an instrument for monitoring, by satellite, of compliance with arms control agreements, supplementing national means of verification.

On the other hand, there is disagreement when it comes to the functions and responsibilities to be entrusted to such a satellite monitoring agency. Some want the tasks limited to data gathering, and restricted to verification of arms control agreement; others advocate in addition assessment functions; while still others are in favour of including also responsibilities with regard to crisis management. There are also those who intend to widen the scope of a space policy for peace by mandating ISMA with both surveillance and socio-economic functions. While they, in doing so, show their understanding for the importance of socio-economic development to increase international stability, they nevertheless overlook certain technical, political and psychological factors, which could endanger the functioning of an ISMA in both ways[17].

It is, therefore, important that the various components of a comprehensive space policy be analysed with due regard to their mutual relations. In this context, further studies should be made of the several proposals for a regional system currently under consideration, as a first step towards the concept of an international regime.

References

1. G. Dondi and M. Toussant, 'The Outlook for World Space Expenditure', ESA Bulletin 37 (February 1984) 98-102.
2. F. Mitterand, Allocution prononcée par Monsieur François Mitterand, Président de la République Française à l'issue du Déjeuner offert par le Conseil des Ministres du Royaume des Pays-Bas (La Haye, Mardi 7 Février 1984).

3. C.A. Robinson, Jr., 'Panel urges Defense Technology Advances - Senior Interagency Group advises strong nuclear missile defense efforts coupled with early demonstration plans'. Aviation Week & Space Technology (17 October 1983) 16-18.
4. See 'An International Agency for the Use of Satellite Observation Data for Security Purposes' in J. Rotblat and A. Pascolini (eds.) The Arms Race at a Time of Decision (London: Macmillan 1984) pp.36-43.
5. 'The implications of establishing an international satellite monitoring agency', United Nations; 1981/1983 (New York: United Nations, 1983) E.83-IX.3.
6. Office of Technology Assessment 'Directed Energy Missile Defense in Space', (Washington, D.C.: Congress of the United States, April 1984).
7. C. Voûte, 'Peace and the challenge of space' in Brett-Crowther (ed.) Defense not Aggression (In press).
8. See J. Rotblat and A. Pascolini (eds.) The Arms Race at a Time of Decision (London: Macmillan 1984) pp.275-83.
9. H. Aarts, 'Science and Technology for Development'. Parliamentary Assembly of the Council of Europe, North-South Conference: Europe's Role (Lisbon, 9-11 April 1984). Document AS/CEC (84), 4, 1984.
10. D. Deudney, 'Unlocking Space' in Foreign Policy, 53, (Winter 1983-1984) 91-113.
11. NASA Advisory Council NAC, 'Study of the Mission of NASA'. Conducted by the NAC Task Force for the Study of the Mission of NASA. (Washington, DC: NASA 12 October 1983).
12. W. Lepkowski, 'US Space Policy Ready for Next Big Leap', Chemical & Engineering News, 62, No.8, (February 1984) 9-16.
13. T. Orhaug, 'An International and Regional Satellite Monitoring Agency', 1984. Chapter 14 of this book.
14. United Nations University UNU, Summary Report on the Tokyo Seminar on Peace, Science and Technology, (Tokyo, 15-17 April 1984), UNU UPDATE No.21, May 1984.
15. B. Jasani, 'Reconnaissance from Space: An international and Regional Satellite Monitoring Agency', the United Nations University (Tokyo, 15-17 April 1984).
16. L. Pettersson, Contribution to 'UNISPACE-82'. Committee on Science and Technology, Parliamentary Assembly of the Council of Europe. (UN Document A/CONF.101/IGO/10, July 1982).
17. C. Voûte, 'Agreement and Disagreement on an International Satellite Monitoring Agency'. International Journal for Remote Sensing, 5, No.2 (1984) pp.479-83.

Part III
Prohibition of Chemical Warfare

16 Chemical Warfare: Status of Technological Developments and Deployments

JULIAN PERRY ROBINSON

Introduction

This paper is about the present state of the technology of chemical weapons and its acquisition in different countries. It concentrates on matters thought most relevant to current discussion of chemical disarmament. In accordance with Article IX of the 1972 Biological Weapons Convention, negotiations are proceeding in the Geneva Conference on Disarmament for a complementary convention on chemical weapons.

Developments on the defensive side of chemical-warfare (CW) technology are not reviewed. This is an area where there has been rapid growth in recent years, illustrated in the wide variety of new anti-chemical protective equipments that have been and are being developed, and in the competition that is developing among their manufacturers for what has become an expanding market. English-language readers new to the subject could do well to turn first to three publications during 1983 from the Swedish National Defence Research Institute[1,2] and to the more recent review by Benz[3]. A wealth of technical detail, including accounts of some of the newer approaches to anti-chemical protection, is contained in several authoritative texts from the GDR[4]. A recent text from the FRG[5] gives much new detail on approaches to the treatment of CW-agent poisoning. Of the many publications by American specialists, a recent encyclopaedia article may be found particularly useful[6].

As a general reference work for all aspects of chemical, and biological, warfare - technical, military, political, legal and historical - the study undertaken by the Stockholm International Peace Research Institute (SIPRI)[7] during 1967 and 1973 remains useful despite its shortcomings and the passage of time. Among the more recent general books on the subject, those of Harris and Paxman[8], Frailé[9], and Murphy, Hay and Rose[10] may particularly be mentioned. The first, a popular but closely documented study by two British journalists, is strong on history; the second is by a French international lawyer; and the third, which is a polemic against CW weapons by three British scientists, illustrates something of the current political realities.

Reviews similar in scope and focus to the present one, but with greater detail, are to be found in the SIPRI Yearbooks for 1982, 1983 and 1984. Except where indicated specifically, the documentary sources for most of the information presented below are cited in those SIPRI reviews.

Chemical Weapons Technology

Let us here distinguish between **acquired** and **potential** technology: between the CW weapons that are already in the arsenals, or in an advanced state of development for them, and those that are still in the laboratories; between weapons concepts already reduced to practice, or nearly so, and concepts that exist only in the realm of possible feasibility.

It will be a major function of the projected Chemical Weapons Convention to create an effective barrier between the two categories. This function - of preventing CW-weapons development - also requires that barricades against weaponisation be placed around technologies which are being developed for applications quite unrelated to CW but which could nonetheless contribute to CW weapons - just as industrial insecticide research led directly to the G-series of nerve gases in the mid-1930s, and to the V-series in the early 1950s. People in Geneva must therefore know not only about the present state of CW-weapons technology but also about the areas of scientific inquiry from which new influences upon it may emerge. It is always conceivable that future technologies may present so great a military allure that, even in a world in which a CW-disarmament treaty is in force, pressure builds up against the barriers to the point where violation of the treaty becomes more likely than it would with existing technology. The tendency in Geneva has been, or so it seems, to belittle this danger, perhaps because CW-weapons technology is viewed as one so mature that the chances of substantial technological surprise seem small. It is indeed the case that no really major technical change has surfaced since the advent of the nerve gases. But an alternative view of the technology is that its current largely static condition is a consequence, not of maturity, but of a general low interest in developing it. Should such an interest become stimulated, the picture might well change very rapidly indeed. One way or the other, it is surely imperative that the CW treaty regime, in its control of CW technology, be constructed with sufficient strength to withstand the pressure of technical change.

The problem of secrecy makes difficult any detailed discussion. It is conceivable that what is no more than a potential technology, even an unperceived possibility, in one country, could in fact be secretly acquired technology in another. The nerve gases again illustrate the problem, in the success which Germany had in protecting Gerhard Schrader's discovery of tabun and sarin from enemy knowledge for a period of several years - a period exceeding that which it took German industry to develop the discovery to the point of large-scale provision of tabun weapons. The problem should not, however, be exaggerated. First, the danger of technological surprise is one to which military authorities are now much more sensitive than they were half a century ago - so much so, indeed, that attempts at pre-empting it have become a significant contributory factor in the overall arms race. Second, the chances of a threatening new technology emerging from secret military research seem much less than the chances of its emerging from academic and industrial research, if only because almost all past major developments in CW weaponry have originated in non-military research, which is bound to be more wide-ranging in its scope and, overall, provided with far greater scientific resources. Effective secrecy is less likely to obtain. It is a characteristic of the pharmaceutical industry, for example, that, however great the incentives may be to keep secret the particulars of a potential new commodity, this will rarely be possible for more than a year or two; a period significantly shorter than that required to weaponise any such discovery. This consideration operates in favour of an effective CW control regime. While it is perhaps possible that market economies and centrally planned ones may differ in their capacities for secrecy, the difference seems unlikely to be great in the civilian sector.

It is far beyond my competence to review the potential loci of danger. They may be conceived as lying in two main areas: in the CW agents themselves, the poisons available for weaponisation; and in the delivery means, the devices and techniques available for conveying a CW agent to its target and disseminating it in an effective form.

Acquired CW-weapons technology

(a) CW agents

The anti-personnel CW casualty agents that are important in

currently acquired CW-weapons technology are shown in Table 1, which gives some details of their origin. The potency and current stockpiling of these agents are given in Table 2.

The stockpiles in the USSR (according to official USA sources, but without Soviet confirmation) include various other CW agents, apparently on the basis, of **inter alia**, reports from Afghanistan. They include the blistering nettle-gas phosgene oxime, an unidentified incapacitant capable of causing rapid unconsciousness for an hour or more, and at least one toxin including the epoxytrichothecene **Fusarium**-mould metabolite implicated in the 'yellow rain' reports from South-East Asia. The most detailed American listings of supposed Soviet CW agents occur in: (a) Chart IV-19 of the Joint Chiefs of Staff Military Posture Statement for Fiscal year 1985; (b) the booklet, **Continuing Development of Chemical Weapons Capabilities in the USSR**, published in October 1983 by the Office of the Secretary of Defense; and (c) Defense Intelligence Agency testimony before the Warner Sub-committee of the Senate Armed Services Committee on 7 April 1983. There are inconsistencies between these three lists. The Joint Chiefs' list refers to four nerve agents and six blister agents.

One might hazard the guess that what is true for the present US CW arsenal is also true for the aggregate world CW arsenal, namely that mustard gas (in various forms) is the CW agent currently stockpiled in the largest quantity, just as it was during World War II. Although mustard gas displays neither the rapidity of action nor the singularly high ratio of casualty-rate to munition-expenditure believed characteristic of the nerve gases, it has one militarily significant property which the nerve gases lack: dosages of its vapour that are readily establishable in the field except in cold weather can produce heavy, albeit delayed, casualties amongst personnel wearing gas masks.

It is, however, the nerve gases which quite rightly dominate current assessments of the military status of chemical warfare. In terms of national security, they are the most important of all the currently stockpiled CW agents. The basic reason for this is simply that they can furnish weapons that may be competitive with modern conventional weapons in a range of tactical applications which, although not large, is not vanishingly small. It seems to be the case that the technology of conventional weaponry is now advancing towards the point where almost all of the singular offensive characteristics of CW weapons - their area-effectiveness, their search-out capacity against troops protected against machine-gun fire and high-explosive artillery, their ability to deny terrain by casualty-threatening contamination of it, and

Table 1. Origins of CW Casualty Agents reportedly stockpiled today

Agent*	Discovery Year	Type of Laboratory	Initial Large-Scale Production as CW agent Year	Country
CHOKING GAS				
Phosgene	1812	Academic	1915	Germany
BLOOD GAS				
Hydrogen cyanide	1782	Academic	1915	France
BLISTER GASES				
Mustard	1822	Academic	1917	Germany
Lewisite	1917	CW	1918	USA
Runcol	by 1931	CW	1938	UK
Nitrogen mustard	by 1935	Industrial	1938	Germany
NERVE GASES				
Tabun	1936	Industrial	1943	Germany
Sarin	1938	Industrial	1953	USA
Soman	1944	Academic	ca 1960?	USSR?
Agent VX	by 1956	CW	1961	USA
INCAPACITANT				
Agent BZ	1951	Industrial	1963	USA

*Runcol, sometimes known as Agent HT, is a reaction product comprising mustard and bis(2-chloroethylthioethyl) ether. The nitrogen mustard referred to is tris(2-chloroethyl)amine. Agent VX is O-ethyl 2-diisopropylaminoethyl methylphosphonothiolate. Agent BZ is 3-quinuclidinyl benzilate.

Table 2. Potency of CW Casualty Agents reportedly stockpiled today

Agent	Acute lethality in mice (LD-50, mg/kg)	Field dosage for 50% casualty rate* (tonnes per km^2)		Current stockpiling
		Airborne challenge	Contact effects	
Phosgene	--	21	NA	USSR
Hydrogen cyanide	2.7 (i.m.)	26	NA	USSR
Mustard	26	4	19	USA, USSR
Lewisite	1 (rat)	--	--	USSR
Runcol	--	--	--	USA
Nitrogen mustard	6.9	12	--	USSR
Tabun	0.4	2	14	USSR
Sarin	0.2	0.5	NA	USA, France, USSR
Soman	0.1	--	--	USSR
Agent VX	0.02	NA	2	USA, ? France
Agent BZ	125	0.6	NA	USA

*The figures given in this column are calculated from firing tables for prominent munitions charged with the agent concerned, or, where such tables are unavailable, from the field-test data from which firing tables are derived. For comparability, the figures are for 50 per cent casualty-rates among unprotected target populations and for a standard set of meteorological conditions (typical of a warm overcast day), variations in which could of course call for very large changes in munitions expenditure.

their impacts upon morale - can be matched by conventional weapons, including high-fragmenting and cluster munitions, fuel-air explosives, artillery-scatterable minelets and the new airfield-attack weapons. Yet conventional weapons have not entirely eclipsed the battlefield potentialities of CW, especially in regions of the world into which the new conventional-munition technologies have not yet permeated. It does, however, seem to be only the nerve gases that can confer cost-effectiveness attractions upon CW weapons. They do so - if they do so - by virtue not of any one particular property, but by virtue of a combination of them. One is their potency expressed in terms of weight of munitions required for a given effect; another is the overall aggressivity provided by their rapidity of action, their potency and their percutaneous effectiveness. All of this enables the nerve gases to be exploited by battlefield commanders without the latter having to organise and deploy their forces in a fashion radically different from that needed to support conventional battlefield tactics. From this military standpoint, use of the older types of CW weapon carried substantial opportunity costs. For the nerve gases, such costs would seem to weigh less heavily in the overall cost-effectiveness assessment.

Their benefits can, however, be almost completely negated by adversary anti-chemical protection. If that protection is good, then most of the attractions of nerve gas, considered as an element of firepower, would be lost, leaving only whatever benefits might stem from having forced the enemy to encumber himself with protective clothing and other such equipments, and to delay himself with protective procedures, such as decontamination of clothing, weapons and areas used for maintenance, supply or staging.

When there is no anti-chemical protection deployed against it, nerve gas could become a weapon of mass destruction. The lethality against unprotected people of a single tactical aircraft armed with nerve gas would be of the same order as a kiloton-range nuclear weapon. The 'collateral damage' to people outside the target area might well be substantially greater than that from the nuclear weapon. While it might take a tonne or more of nerve gas to achieve significant casualty effects against a company-sized target of troops carrying anti-chemical protection, that same quantity might well, through atmospheric diffusion, endanger lives over an area forty or more times greater.

The nerve gases, as Table 1 shows, are old technology. Those that are in the arsenals are not necessarily the optimal ones, given what is now known about them. One might doubt, for example, whether agent VX would still be the agent of choice in meeting the requirement that it was originally introduced to satisfy. Its O-cyclopentyl homologue, for example, is said to be no less stable, to be substantially more lethal and, in addition, to be refractory to oxime therapy. However, although there may now be 'better' nerve gases than there were when the present arsenals were established, they would seem to offer only a marginal increase in overall aggressivity. The more significant development is probably the realisation that G-type nerve gases of intermediate vapour pressure can pose a greater casualty threat to clothed and masked personnel than do the V-agents, despite the latter's greater percutaneous toxicity. Hence, very largely, the fact that the next new American nerve-gas weapons to emerge from the R & D process in the absence of a Chemical Weapons Convention are likely to be based neither on sarin nor on VX but on EA 5774. This is an intermediate-volatility agent (IVA) comprising, so it seems, a thickened form of soman. American practice will then mirror the American perception of Soviet practice.

Still undisclosed in the open literature is the chemical identity of EA 5365, a member of a new family of nerve gases encountered round about 1970, and which was for a time a leading candidate for the US Army's IVA requirement.

(b) Agent delivery

It is in the technology of delivering and disseminating CW agents, rather than in that of the agents themselves, that the major changes of recent years seem to have taken place.

The basic principles governing the transformation of a munition-payload of bulk CW agent into the physical state optimal for the target effects of that agent, and many of the techniques for achieving such dissemination, were developed decades ago. Agent-disseminators capable of providing the requisite clouds of aerosol or vapour (in the case of respiratory-effect agents) of the requisite medium-to-coarse liquid sprays (in the case of percutaneous-effect agents) have long been available in forms that can be used to arm virtually every type of weapons delivery system. Table 3 illustrates this with examples from the current US CW arsenal and from current Western perceptions of the Soviet CW arsenal. The latter perceptions may or may not be accurate reflections of reality. The USSR itself, in contrast to the USA, releases no information whatsoever about its CW weapons; even the very existence of Soviet CW weapons is discernible in official Soviet statements only by implication.

Most conspicuous among the more recent developments has been the adaptation to practice, in the USA, of the binary

Table 3. Current CW-capable weapon systems

Category of Weapon	Currently deployed US weapons for which lethal CW munitions are held	Corresponding weapons deployed by the Soviet Union according to Western sources
Landmine	(M23 mine)	(KhF-1 and KhF-2 mines)
Mortar	4.2-inch, M30	120 mm, M-1943 SP 240 mm, M-1976
Howitzer	105 mm, M-102 155 mm, M-114A1 and M-114A2 SP 155 mm, M-109A1 and M-109A2 SP 8-inch, M-110A1 and M-110A2	122 mm, D-30 SP 122 mm, 2S-1 152 mm, D-20 SP 152 mm, 2S-3
Long-range field gun	—	130 mm, M-46 180 mm, S-23
Multiple rocket launcher	—	SP 122 mm 40-tube, BM-21 122 mm 12-tube, M-1975 SP 220 mm, 16-tube, BM-27
Heavy artillery rocket	—	550 mm FFR, FROG-7B
Battlefield support guided missile	—	S-21 (FROG replacement) 850 mm SSM, Scud-B, SS-1c SS-23 (Scud replacement) 1100 mm SSM, Scaleboard, SS-12, SS-22 (Scaleboard replacement)
Short-range cruise	—	Shaddock/Sepal, SSN-3/SSC-1b
Intermediate-range ballistic missile	—	SS-20
Tactical strike aircraft	Several of the front-line Tac Air and Naval aircraft types can be armed with available CW munitions: - bulk-filled bombs - spraytanks	Specific Soviet aircraft other than the Mi-8, have not been publicly identified as armable with the putative stocks of: - air-to-ground rockets - bulk-filled bombs - cluster bombs - spray tanks
Attack helicopter	—	

munition' concept. Binary munitions are loaded, not with actual nerve gas, but with a separated pair of chemical reactants adapted to mix and interact to generate nerve gas only during the period immediately preceding coincidence of target and munition - while the bomb is falling, for example, or while the artillery shell is on its target trajectory. A non-binary CW munition is loaded with the purified product of the final stage of nerve-gas synthesis. A binary munition is the actual reactor within which that final stage, even earlier ones too, is conducted.

Binary technology changes the character of the techniques that would need to be applied in order to verify compliance with a ban on CW-agent production. No longer are safety measures of an exceptional stringency characteristic of plant producing fill for CW munitions. And there may be several different pairs of chemicals that could generate the same nerve gas within a binary munition.

Binary technology also offers a broadening of the range of poisons having candidacy as CW agents, for, with it, the stability of a CW agent during long-term storage is no longer of primary importance. In this regard, it is interesting to note the recent published reference[11] to a pair of binary reactants (isopropanol and O-dichloroformoximidyl methylphosphonofluoridate) that would yield a mixture of sarin and phosgene oxime.

The poison to which the present binary-munition concept was initially applied in the USA, in 1954, was agent VG, 00'-diethyl 2-NN-diethylaminoethyl phosphorothiolate. This agent is better known as amiton, a substance discovered in the agrochemical industry to which high commercial and silvicultural hopes were attached for a short time during the mid-1950s as a miticide - until, that is, the implications of its ferocious percutaneous toxicity in mammals came to be appreciated: a characteristic which precipitated the rapid development from amiton of the V-agent nerve gases. Amiton has recently appeared in the news in connection with the putative nerve-gas capability of Iraq[12]. In the US binary programme it gave way to the V-agent which later came to be standardised as CW-munition fill, namely VX. If the programme proceeds as currently planned, the first two binary munitions to enter the arsenals in quantity will disseminate VX and the other standard US nerve gas, sarin. It is expected that subsequent binary munitions will disseminate a dual-threat or intermediate volatility agent such as the EA 5774 referred to earlier. Table 4 illustrates the scope of the US binary R & D programme.

Contrary to some reports, neither US nor any other Western forces yet have militarily significant supplies of binary

STATUS OF CHEMICAL WARFARE

Table 4. Weapon systems for which nerve-gas munitions have been studied in the US binary-munition R&D programme

Weapon	Binary ammunition*
BINARY MUNITIONS NOW STANDARDISED FOR PRODUCTION	
Howitzer, 155mm	Sarin projectile
Strike aircraft (Navy and Tac Air)	500-1b VX spray bomb
BINARY MUNITIONS CURRENTLY IN DEVELOPMENT	
Multiple Launch Rocket System, 227mm SP	IVA warhead
Howitzer, 8-inch	IVA projectile
Howitzer, 155mm	IVA projectile
Joint Tactical Missile System	Warhead
- Lance battlefield-support missile	IVA warhead
- Corps Support Weapon System	IVA warhead
- Aircraft Conventional Standoff weapon	Warhead
- Terminally Guided Submunition	Warhead
Division Support Weapon System	--
Howitzer, 8-inch	Extended-range projectile
Howitzer, 155-mm	Rocket-assisted projectile
'Special Purpose Chemical Agent Dissemination System'	?
Ground Launched Cruise Missile	Warhead
Attack Drone (RPV)	--
Strike aircraft	2.75-inch rocket warhead
Strike aircraft (Tac Air)	750-1b bomb
Strike aircraft	Minelet dispenser munition
Howitzer	Minelet-cluster munition
Lightweight Portable Rocket	--
Mortar, 81-mm	--
DEVELOPMENTS CURTAILED, ABANDONED OR POSTPONED	
Pershing II guided missile	Warhead
Mortar, 4.2-inch	IVA cartridge
Howitzer, 8-inch	VX projectile
Howitzer, 8-inch	Sarin projectile
Strike aircraft (Navy)	G-agent cluster bomb
Recoilless rifle, 106-mm	--
Strike aircraft (Tac Air)	VX spray tank

* 'IVA' stands for Intermediate Volatility Agent (for example, thickened soman).

munitions available to them. Such production as has occurred
has been on a pilot scale in support of the development
programme. The new munitions cannot, on the present factory-
construction schedule, begin to enter operational inventories
until the latter part of 1985 at the earliest, and probably
not before the Autumn of 1986[13]. And although the
Congress in 1983, during the immediate aftermath of the
shooting-down of the Korean Air Lines jumbo-jet, authorised
the full-scale production funding that President Reagan had
first requested in February 1982, when he certified the
production as 'essential to the national interest', the
Congress subsequently declined, both in 1983 and in 1984,
actually to appropriate the requisite funds. Should it
reverse this position in 1985, decisions will become
necessary almost immediately on whether and where the munitions are to be deployed in Europe. Early in 1983, the US
Defense Secretary directed that a half-million binary sarin
artillery shell and 40 000 binary-VX spraybombs were to be
procured by mid-1989. That would amount to about 32 000
tonnes of ammunition, equivalent to nearly 6000 tonnes of
binary-chemical payload or some 4000 tonnes of disseminable
nerve gas.

One other development in agent-dissemination technology may
also be noted here. In view of the importance attached by
CW-weapons specialists to quick-acting dual-threat weapons –
ones that can threaten rapid casualties by both respiratory
and percutaneous challenge – not a little attention has been
paid to enhancing the penetrability of candidate CW agents
through skin and other tissue. This has led to the exploitation of various solvents, skin-transferral agents and other
adjuvants whereby effective dosages of poisons, especially
solid ones, and their time to effect, can be reduced. While
such techniques could no doubt be applied to a wide variety
of poisons, including toxins, details are available in the
open literature only as regards their application (in the
USA) to certain casualty incapacitants, a category of CW
agent that is discussed further below. An example of a
candidate CW agent taking the form of one such mixture is EA
5302, which is a solution of a psychotropic glycollate in a
cycloheptatriene that is also a powerful irritant agent.
Ternary solutions incorporating the skin-transferral agent
DMSO have also been investigated.

Potential Technology

A number of ways can be envisaged in which the current pre-
eminence of the nerve gases might be challeneged by emergent
CW technologies. None of them yet appears to cast doubt on

the wisdom of the Geneva negotiators in concentrating attention on the nerve gases in their concern with the arrangements for assuring compliance with the Chemical Weapons Convention. But certain of them may seem sufficiently plausible to require that the negotiators do not produce a treaty that is little more than a nerve-gas ban. If confidence in the regime is to persist far into the future, the treaty must be comparably forward-looking.

It is often the case that commentaries on possible CW-technology futures lay special stress on the appearance of new CW agents having a greater toxicity than that of the nerve gases, it being supposed that such agents would automatically provide more threatening weapons. This is not necessarily the case. A good many such poisons are already known. But they all appear to lack other attributes of aggressivity which the nerve gases powerfully display. Agent-toxicity is only one factor among several that determine the level of expenditure of CW munitions needed to achieve a given target effect. And an increase in agent-toxicity could carry major costs in the form of greater handling/storage hazards, and even in the form of an increase in collateral damage that was disproportionately greater than that in target damage. It might be that if the increase in toxicity were very great – two orders of magnitude, perhaps – new targetting options might be opened; battalion-sized targets, say, rather than company-sized ones. However, in order to exploit any such new options, field commanders would probably have to re-organise their forces and their tactics in a fashion that departed drastically from conventional-warfare norms. This would introduce major opportunity costs, for the forces would then become less capable of fulfilling their normal missions. One might therefore think that, given current military attitudes towards CW outside the specialist CW services, only a major shift from the present almost negative enthusiasm to something a lot more positive might make such costs tolerable. The pre-condition for such a shift would be a much closer assimilation of CW into military dostrine and capabilities than – if the situation in the West is representative – exists today.

However, were such a shift to occur, then not only might agents of greater toxicity seem attractive, but so also might agents of a **different** toxicity. Toxicity can manifest itself in forms of which only a rather small fraction is displayed in currently acquired CW-weapons technology. Once the requirement started to fade that CW munitions resemble conventional munitions as closely as possible in their effects-profiles (for therein at present lies the chief chance of closer assimilation) then other forms of toxicity might acquire more allure: chronic, as opposed to acute, effects, for the long-term debilitation of an enemy; delayed effects, for insidiousness; even effects that discriminate between races on the basis of some biochemical characteristic of ethnicity. One might think that it is in the warding-off of such hateful possibilities that the present CW negotiations have their greatest value.

It would take a fundamental alteration in military attitudes to bring about such technical changes. Another type of fundamental alteration that needs to be considered is one in the basic structure of the chemical-industrial economy. The present structure is rooted deeply in petrochemicals, meaning that CW agents derived for the most part from petrochemicals are more accessible than others; that, for example, they will cost less to produce in quantity. Should the chemical industry move away from its heavy dependence on petroleum, so too might some toxic agents at present regarded as inaccessible for CW purposes, even as laboratory curiosities only, become less costly; or conversely, current CW agents such as the nerve gases become more costly. One such incipient shift may already be evident in the opening-up of new biotechnologies. If one considers the extraordinary diversity of toxic effects displayed by oligopeptides and toxins, for example, can one doubt that this shift may not eventually generate a range of new and possibly feasible toxic-weapons concepts?

Then there are the lessons that may be learned from the Yellow Rain allegations, regardless of whether Washington's assessment of these allegations is or is not correct, and regardless of whether trichothecane-type mycotoxins really have or have not been developed and used as weapons. For there is now a sufficient body of belief in a CBW causation for the Yellow Rain phenomenon to make people take some of the implied toxic weapon concepts a lot more seriously than they had done previously.

One such concept is that of basing toxic weapons on poisons against which an enemy's anti-chemical protective devices and procedures are not designed: poisons which will not trigger his CW-agent detectors, for example, or whose toxic effects cannot be countered by deployed self-aid or other first-aid field therapies. It may be that existing precautions against this form of technological surprise (that is reliance upon those physical counter-measures - masks, protective clothing, and so on - whose efficacy is largely independent of the precise chemical nature of the challenge) are sufficient to marginalise the worth of such concepts. But the suggestion that they have nonetheless actually been reduced to practice could jolt CW institutions at present preoccupied with the nerve gases out of that preoccupation. The result could be a substantial increase in the research resources at present allocated to searches for CW agents competitive with the nerve gases. With more people exploring the vast and poorly charted terrain of toxins, say, or other toxic biotechnological-process products, who can say what new candidate agents might not appear?

A second concept that the Yellow Rain may have promoted is that of casualty-incapacitant CW weapons. It has long been appreciated - and, in mustard gas, reflected in acquired CW-weapons technology - that the toxicity of a CW agent does not necessarily have to be a lethal toxicity in order to furnish militarily useful CW weapons: a soldier will be just as much a casualty in military terms if he is incapacitated as if he is dead. It has also long been appreciated that a toxicity that is incapacitating but of low lethality may confer certain particular attractions upon CW weapons: greater political acceptability, for example, or utility in battle areas where collateral damage among non-combatants might otherwise inhibit military operations. This concept, too, has been reflected in acquired CW-weapons technology, for example in the weapons based on agents SN, BZ and PG that were once standardised for US inventories, and their candidate successor agents (such as the EA 5302 and its ilk referred to earlier) that are being considered for standardisation. But what has now acquired some prominence is the concept of incapacitating agents of intermediate lethality. These might provide weapons as capable as the nerve gases of eliciting high casualty rates, but leaving a larger fraction of the casualties to survive, not only as a burden on enemy medical capacity and logistics, but also as a demoralising influence on combat units or as a terrorising influence upon civilian populations. The more hideous the toxic effects of the agent, the greater its morale impact.

As to other conceivable stimuli of technical change, the continuous possibility must again be noted of technology-transfer from non-military into CW enterprise. Toxicity and related forms of biological activity are attributes of chemicals which have, of course, brought forth a burgeoning manufacturing industry, most conspicuous in its pesticide and pharmaceutical sectors. In the quest for new products great numbers of novel toxicants and potential drugs are synthesised. Areas of chemistry known to be rich in biologically active chemicals are systematically scanned. Just as Gerhard Schrader's march through organophosphorus structures eventually yielded the insecticides of great value that his employers were seeking (and the nerve gases), might not similar results attend a march through, say, organosilicon structures, starting from the silatranes of Mikhail Voronkov – a family that has already yielded a variety of drugs and a commercial rodenticide that is as lethal to mice as the nerve-gas soman[14]? The great majority of new chemicals which such searches disclose are useless; and among those which are rejected on safety grounds there will continue to be potential CW agents. Even among those that are not rejected and which do indeed go on to find civilian applications, there may be candidate CW agents. An area which is often overlooked in commentaries on this topic is that of veterinary drugs and mammalian-pest killers. Currently topical examples include the animal-tranquilliser fentanyl and the carbamate T3327 which is now undergoing trials in the UK as a vulpicide[15]. The concern here is not only with the emergence of possible nerve-gas competitors. It is also that this particular form of technology-transfer could accelerate the motors of CW-weapons proliferation. The existence and possibilities of amiton and paraoxon, to take a topical pair of examples, are not extraordinary.

Finally, and perhaps most important of all, there is the possibility of some new development emerging which offers the prospect of breaching or circumventing the existing primary means of protection against CW attack, namely air filters (as in respirators or collective shelters) and protective clothing. Although the technical possibilities currently known here, largely from the field of fluorine chemistry, do not appear amenable to effective weaponisation, better ones may yet be discovered. If that were to happen, the present lowly status of chemical weapons within overall military capability could alter abruptly.

Deployments

Two main kinds of public information are available about countries that have acquired CW-weapons technology: official statements about acquisition or non-acquisition; and reports of the actual use of the weapons.

Because international law prohibits use of CW weapons, their possession is legitimate only for the purpose of reprisal. States that have reserved the right to use the weapons against transgressors of the 1925 Geneva Protocol can no doubt argue that it is legitimate to keep the weapons for purposes of retaliation-in-kind as well. One might think that such policies of dissuasion would require that publicity be given by the possessors of CW weapons to the existence of their stocks. One might even think that secrecy about possession indicated disregard for the law; in other words, that such secrecy implied the existence alongside the stocks of an employment policy which did not exclude initiatory use of the weapons.

The USA is the only country whose government officially and publicly acknowledges possession of CW weapons today. The French Government has not publicly disavowed statements by US officials that France possesses stocks. The Soviet Government has made no explicit statement on the matter since 1938, when it affirmed possession; but in recent years there have been numerous statements by Soviet officials which make no sense unless it be supposed that the USSR has maintained its CW-weapons capability.

Several other governments have issued public statements to the effect that their countries do not possess CW weapons. Amongst those that did once possess militarily significant CW stockpiles are Britain and Japan. The FRG has also declared non-possession, a condition which is in any case required of it, at least until 2005, under the terms of the 1954 revised Brussels Treaty.

There have been many reports of the actual use of CW weapons in different conflicts in recent years - in at least 14 conflicts over the past seven years. Given, on the one hand, the high emotiveness of CW and, on the other, the seeming implausibility of the particular allegations in not a few of the reports, it seems likely that at least some of these allegations have been driven more by political or black-propaganda objectives than by reality. The same may be said of the various other allegations, not of actual use, but of preparedness for use. If all of these reports were true, the following countries would have to be added to the list of states that currently possess CW weapons, raising the total from three to 22: Afghanistan, Argentina, China, Cuba, Egypt, El Salvador, Ethiopia, Guatemala, India, Iran, Iraq, Israel, Libya, North Korea[16], Pakistan, the Philippines[17], South Africa, Syria and Vietnam. Of these countries, India is among those states that have issued formal statements of non-possession of CW weapons; and the government of South Africa is among those that have issued strong denials both of use and of possession.

Of the three states that are definitely known to possess CW weapons - France, the USA and the USSR - some of the stocks are deployed abroad. Whether this is true of France, in particular, is not known - though it is perhaps relevant to observe that, in the days when Britain was a possessor state, it kept supplies of CW weapons at several locations in Africa and Asia, and relied in part on CW-agent factories in certain of its then-dominions overseas (Canada and South Africa) for CW-weapons supply. As to the superpowers, the USA has officially acknowledged the existence of CW-weapons stockpiles

Table 5. The American Stockpile: rough estimates of holdings

Agent type	Pacific (Johnston Atoll)	Europe (FRG)	United States (8 locations)
MUNITIONS FILLED WITH TOXIC AGENT (short tons of munitions)			
Nerve	10 000	7 500	56 000
Mustard	2 900	0	28 000
Incapacitant	0	0	400
TOXIC AGENT HELD UNWEAPONISED IN BULK STORAGE (short tons of agent)			
Nerve	) 200	0	6 200
Mustard	)	0	12 600
Incapacitant	0	0	5

under its sole control on Johnston Atoll in the Pacific (whence they had been moved, in 1970, from Okinawa) and in West Germany. Additional overseas storage locations have been alleged, but denied by Washington. These locations, and those that have been alleged for deployments abroad of Soviet CW weapons, are as follows:

USA: FRG, Johnston Atoll, Britain, Italy, Japan, Pakistan, South Korea, Thailand

USSR: GDR, Afghanistan, Cuba, Czechoslovakia, Ethiopia, Iraq, Laos, Poland, Syria, Vietnam

Both lists look improbably long.

Particulars of current American deployments of CW weapons are given in Table 5. Total French CW-agent holdings are said to be similar in magnitude to the American stocks in FRG.

Western officials believe that the USSR is fully prepared, in terms both of current military doctrine and of deployed weapons, to use CW on a large scale. One may estimate from the numbers of CW-capable weapons in the Soviet force-structure for Europe that those weapons could deliver as much as 1000 tonnes of CW agent per day on NATO targets to a depth

STATUS OF CHEMICAL WARFARE

of several kilometres. Much the same estimate can in fact be made for NATO deployments of CW-capable weapons against the WTO, but whereas NATO is not actually supplied with the full range and requisite quantity of agent-filled munitions for that purpose, Western officials seem to assume that Soviet forces have been so supplied. Whatever solid evidence there may be for this assumption has never been publicly disclosed. What is unquestionably true, however, is that Soviet forces are lavishly equipped and trained for protection against the effects of CW weapons, their own or anyone else's.

In its 1982 White Paper, the British Defence Ministry put a figure 'in excess of 300 000 tonnes' on the size of the Soviet CW-agent stockpile (thus implying the existence of maybe three million tonnes of Soviet CW ammunition). This figure looks remarkably like the arithmetic mean of the largest and the smallest of the upper estimates that have been produced - according to Harold Brown when he was the US Defense Secretary - by different US intelligence organs, namely 30 000 short tons (smaller than the American agent stockpile) and 700 000 tons. That spread illustrates the need for caution in accepting uncritically what is written in the West about Soviet offensive CW capability.

Whatever its actual size may be, the greater part of the Soviet CW-agent stockpile is thought to be concentrated within the USSR, much of it near the Chinese border. As to the actual whereabouts of the stocks thought to be deployed abroad, the NATO Supreme Commander declined - in an interview published in **Armed Forces Journal International** in September 1983 - to confirm a 1981 report that '19 or 23 Soviet offensive chemical sites ... had been moved forward', stating only: 'We do know that they have chemical storage sites built in forward areas ... which we believe contain chemical weapons'. It is said that, of those sites, there is only one in Europe - at a Soviet airbase in the GDR - which Western officials are tolerably certain really is a CW-weapons depot.

In October 1983, the US Defense Department published an illustrated booklet which disclosed considerably more than hitherto of the official US perception of Soviet CW-weapons capabilities. While there can of course be no assurance that this perception is an accurate reflection of reality - or, indeed, that the perception presented in the booklet is a true reflection of informed opinion generally in Washington - perceptions count as much as reality in the Geneva negotiations. It is worth noting here, then, some of the features that are perceived in the Soviet CW stance which bear most heavily both upon the Geneva negotiations and upon the WTO proposal for a negotiated CW-weapon-free-zone in Europe:

- The Soviet CW-weapons capability is believed to include an emphasis on long-range (theatre-wide) systems, including warheads for missiles deployed at Army and Front levels, and perhaps even for weapons of the Strategic Rocket Forces. It will be seen from Table 3 that the USA has at the moment no ground-force weapons of greater than artillery range - though it did have such weapons prior to 1976 and will do so again, as Table 4 indicates, if the binary munitions programme proceeds unabated. There is a recent published report which traces the putative Soviet emphasis on CW guided-missile systems to 'the Politburo's 1965 ruling that one in three of Soviet missiles should carry a CW-warhead'[18].
- Apparently on the evidence of satellite imagery, open-air-field-testing of CW munitions is believed to be continuing. So is production of CW agents.
- At least some production of CW agents is believed to take place within chemical complexes that also produce civilian chemicals.
- Part of the Soviet CW-agent stockpile is believed to be held in bulk unweaponised form, as is part of the US stockpile.
- At least part of the Soviet supply of weaponised CW-agent is held at multi-purpose locations which also include non-CW munitions.

Exactly where the truth may lie in all this, I am not competent to judge.

References

1. The Swedish National Defence Research Institute. FOA orienterar om Chemical Warfare Agents, June 1983.
2. The Swedish National Defence Research Institute, Department 4. Proceedings of the International Symposium on Protection against Chemical Warfare Agents, FOA Report C40171-C2,C3, June 1983; and its Supplement, FOA Report C 40174-C2,C3, August 1983.
3. K.G. Benz, 'NBC defense - an overview, Part 1: protection equipment', International Defense Review 16(12): (1983) 1783-1790; and 'Part 2: detection and decontamination', IDR 17(2): (1984) 159-164.
4. S. Franke et al, Lehrbuch der Militärchemie (2 vols, 2nd edition, Berlin: Deutscher Militärverlag, 1977); K-H Lohs, Synthetische Gifte (4th edition, Berlin: Deutscher Militärverlag, 1974); D. Martinetz, Immobilisation, Entgiftung and Zerstörung von Chemikalien (Leipzig: VEB Deutscher Verlag fur Grundstoffindustrie, 1980); and R.

Stohr et al. Chemische Kampfstoffe und Schutz vor chemischen Kapfstoffen (Berlin: Deutscher Militärverlag, 1977).
5. R. Klimek, L. Szinicz and N. Weger, Chemische Gifte und Kampfstoffe: Wirkung und Therapie (Stuttgart: Hippokrates Verlag, 1983).
6. B.L. Harris et al. 'Chemicals in war', Kirk-Othmer Encyclopedia of Chemical Technology (3rd edition), 5, (1979) 393-416.
7. Stockholm International Peace Research Institute, The Problem of Chemical and Biological Warfare (6 vols, Stockholm: Almqvist & Wiksell, 1971-75).
8. R. Harris and J. Paxman, A Higher Form of Killing (London: Chatto and Windus, 1982).
9. R. Frailé, La Guerre Biologique et Chimique: Le Sort d'une Interdiction (Paris: Economica, 1982).
10. S. Murphy, A. Hay and S. Rose, No Fire, No Thunder (London: Pluto, 1984).
11. Klimek, Szincz and Weger, ibid (ref.5) pp.69-70.
12. I. Mather and R. McKie, 'How Iraq built a secret horror plant', The Observer (London), 11 March 1984, pp. 1,11.
13. Defense Week, 'Army abandons quest for chemical arms funds: new political tactics', 13 February 1984, p.3.
14. M.G. Voronkov, G.I. Zelchan and E.J. Lukevitz, (Silicon and Life) (Riga: Zinatne, 1971, in Russian); and M.G. Voronkov. 'Bio-organosilicon chemistry', Chemistry in Britain 9 (9), (1973) 411-15.
15. D. Brown 'Foxes poisoned in Porton Down tests', Daily Telegraph (London), 11 March 1984, p.4.
16. R. Halloran, 'US finds 14 nations now have chemical arms', New York Times, 20 May 1984, p.22.
17. K. Dalton, 'Manila investigation into napalm bombing claim', The Times (London), 26 September 1984, p.4.
18. J. Reed, 'Chemical and biological warfare', Defence, Communications and Security Review, No. 83/3, pp. 45-47.

17 Negotiations on a Chemical Weapons Ban
JOHAN LUNDIN

Introduction

The efforts to get rid of chemical weapons have gone on now for more than a century. The Brussels declarations in 1874 were the first to ask expressly for a prohibition on the use of poison as a weapon. In 1925 the so-called Geneva Protocol appeared, which prohibits the use of chemical and biological weapons. Negotiations have now been going on for more than fifteen years, to prohibit the development, production and stockpiling of chemical weapons and to prescribe for the destruction of existing stocks.

This is an example of the time frame of all disarmament efforts. In the short term perspective such a pace seems very disappointing. However, on the long term perspective, there is reason for optimism that sooner or later real disarmament measures will come. Indeed, hopeful movements towards an agreement on chemical weapons have appeared during the last two years.

While it is impossible to foresee a chemical weapons convention coming soon, there is a need to analyse the problems involved, to ask whether and how they are solvable.

History

The 1925 Geneva Protocol

As already mentioned, the use of chemical and bacteriological weapons is prohibited by the Geneva Protocol of 1925. While the Protocol itself is clear in prohibiting the use, many parties to the Protocol have nevertheless made reservations that the Protocol should rather be understood as a prohibition of a **first** use of chemical weapons. The reservations imply that some parties feel free to use chemical weapons in retaliation for their use against them or their allies. Many consider this status of the Geneva Protocol unsatisfactory. Others hold the opinion that the risk for retaliation might have had a deterring effect in many cases. An example is the situation during the Second World War, when both Germany and the Allies possessed nerve gases, the most dangerous chemical weapons, but they were not used, probably because of the perceived risk of retaliation by the other side. Where chemical weapons were used after the First World War, this was usually against adversaries without retaliation possibilities and protection, the so-called 'downhill use'. In these cases there was no deterrence. For these reasons, the need to strengthen the Geneva Protocol has been advocated by many.

Two approaches have been tried. One calls on the parties to remove their reservations so that a comprehensive prohibition of use would result. Measures to provide the Convention with some mechanisms for verifying allegations of use of chemical weapons have been adopted in the United Nations General Assembly in the last few years. The other approach taken up seriously on two occasions, is to prohibit not only the use but also the development, production and stockpiling of chemical weapons, and the destruction of those already existing. The first attempt was made in the beginning of the thirties, when the League of Nations tried to settle the problem, but without success. The other attempt started at the end of the sixties when the then Eighteen Nations Disarmament Conference (ENDC) took up the question in 1969.

The Biological Weapons Convention

The Geneva Protocol also prohibited the use of bacteriological weapons. This was farsighted at the time. When discussions started in 1968 and 1969 on a prohibition of the development and production of chemical weapons, a corresponding prohibition on bacteriological weapons was included. It was then realised that bacteria were not the only existing micro-organisms which could be utilised as biological weapons.

It turned out to be easier to agree on a convention prohibiting the development, production and stockpiling of biological weapons than on one for chemical weapons. The main reason was that biological weapons, unlike chemical weapons, are not integrated into the armed forces. Further, although being potential weapons, biological weapons were considered dangerous, not only for the attacked party but also for the attacker. Another obvious factor was that it was not considered necessary by the main powers to provide for any particular verification measures under the Biological Weapons Convention, which came into force in 1975. The prescription for the destruction of all biological weapons can be considered to be the first real disarmament treaty. The Convention also prohibits the acquisition and possession of bacteriological (biological) and toxin weapons. However, in view of the lack of verification measures and of an adequate complaints mechanism under this Convention, it is very difficult to be assured that its provisions are being complied with.

Chemical Weapons

After the Biological Weapons Convention was completed, efforts were concentrated on getting a corresponding convention on chemical weapons. Four different attempts to outline the contents of a Chemical Weapons Convention were made during the seventies by the USSR, UK, Japan and a group of neutral and non-aligned countries in the Conference of the Committee on Disarmament (CCD). But it was not until 1980 that serious multilateral negotiations started. In the meantime, during the years 1976 to 1980, the USA and USSR held bilateral negotiations on a chemical weapons convention. These resulted in some basic, but far from complete, agreements which were presented to the Committee on Disarmament (CD) in 1980. In 1982 Poland also presented a draft treaty.

In the following years, a Working Group, and later, a Committee on Chemical Weapons within the CD, has been negotiating a chemical weapons convention. Although slow, there has been notable progress, and I can state without doubt that the basic content of a convention is now outlined. It is also clearer, where there are agreements and which subjects have to be further negotiated. 1984 started on a good note with both the great powers indicating their serious will to negotiate. The USA made clear its intention to present a draft treaty, and the Soviet Union took some important substantial steps with regard to verification of destruction of stock.

Given the political will, especially of those countries which possess chemical weapons, further progress could be made. Some of the outstanding problems are described below.

Problems of Substance concerning a Chemical Weapons Convention

Prohibition of Use

The prohibition of use of chemical weapons contains one of the main problems with respect to the Convention, namely, whether or not it should contain a new - or renewed - prohibition on the use of chemical weapons in order to make up for what many consider as a deficiency of the 1925 Geneva Protocol. Several of the negotiating parties in the CD advocate a renewed, clear cut prohibition of use in the Convention. Others consider that this would create a risk that the Geneva Protocol, which by now has more than a hundred parties, might suffer and be not regarded as valid any longer. They consider that it would be sufficient to make a reference to the Protocol in the new Convention, because of the widely held view that the use of chemical weapons is prohibited by customary international law. However, there is no opposition that the Convention should contain some reference to the prohibition of use. In any case, the general view is that the Convention should provide for verification of allegations of use, but there are many complicated legal problems connected with the detailed formulation of the provisions on use in a new convention.

Military Preparations for Use

At the very start of the work on the Convention in 1969, Sweden proposed that military preparations for the use of chemical weapons should also be expressly prohibited. This proposal takes into account that the acquisition of chemical weapons in itself might not be the decisive factor for a country wishing to acquire a chemical weapons capability that could also be used against a well protected adversary. A crucial and time-consuming activity is the tactical education and training of military commanders and staff, and training of troops to use chemical weapons and to fight in a voluntarily contaminated area. Although there is some support for including this prohibition in the Convention, some delegations hold the view that it would only complicate the negotiations. Such a provision would also be difficult to verify. If the use of chemical weapons was expressly prohibited, a prohibition of military preparations for use would be a logical consequence, just as the other, already recognised, preparations, namely, development, production and stockpiling of the weapons. No particular verification measures would have to be instituted, as long as alleged use of chemical weapons could be invesitgated under the Convention.

Definition of Chemical Weapons

Another problem concerning the scope of the Convention is how should chemical weapons be defined.

A particular problem lies in what to call the toxic chemicals which actually constitute the effective load of the weapon. In the technical literature they are generally and somewhat loosely referred to as 'chemical warfare agents'.

Some of the parties negotiating the Convention hold the view that only those chemicals which are warfare agents, that is those which actually are used, have been used or possibly might be used in chemical weapons, should be covered by the Convention. Such chemicals should then preferably be denominated 'chemical warfare agents'. However, several of the chemicals which have been used as chemical warfare agents are now widely used in the chemical industry. It would certainly be inappropriate to label them as chemical warfare agents in their present peaceful use.

Further, in order to be able to define the production of a chemical warfare agent, one would also have to define and demonstrate that a suspected production is really intended for hostile military purposes. This is very difficult to do, because one could never tell with certainty that a certain production is intended for hostile purposes only. Another approach was used by the USA and the USSR in their bilateral agreement, namely, to prohibit all production of chemicals not intended for non-hostile purposes. The reason for this rather complicated approach is that it is easy to state what a non-hostile purpose is, and therefore one would have a legally correct expression to rely upon. However, this approach has a drawback in that it formally prohibits all production of chemicals, although only an extremely small part of all production would need to be prohibited. Production is allowed only as an exception from this general prohibition. However, for the practical purposes of the Convention this approach might be useful, and most delegations now seem to share the view that this approach should be chosen. Discussions are going on whether the use of the expression 'chemical warfare agent' could perhaps facilitate some problems of definitions in the Convention.

Should the Convention also cover **toxins**? The development, production and stockpiling of toxin weapons are already prohibited in the Biological Weapons Convention. The definitions agreed upon so far in the work on chemical weapons would certainly comprise toxins unless some explicit exceptions were to be made. On the other hand, that would imply a definition of toxins. This technical question was not solved in connection with the Biological Weapons Convention. It would probably be equally difficult to accomplish for the Chemical Weapons Convention. Political problems exist in this context which have made this question very sensitive.

Tear-gases also constitute difficult delimitation problems. Some negotiating states do not see them as being covered by the definitions of chemical weapons and point to their necessary civilian use. Other parties consider that the definitions used certainly also comprise tear-gases. The difficulty is not a technical but a political one. Many consider that exceptions should allow tear-gases to be used by the police, including military police, and other civilian authorities, in order to avoid, as an alternative, the use of small arms.

A similar problem is whether **herbicides** should be included under the definition of chemical weapons. Many consider that since they are used not directly against man but against plants in order to kill or defoliate them, they should not be put on the same level as other chemical weapons, which directly attack the physiological mechanisms in man. Also, it is argued, herbicides have widespread civilian uses in huge amounts and it would be unpractical to prohibit the production of any herbicides and even less practical to verify the production, and the purposes for which they are being produced. But the countries which have suffered from the use of herbicides as well as countries in geographically similar regions, perceive herbicides as effective weapons, and they find it absolutely necessary that herbicides are included under the Convention. A possible solution of this problem is to recognise that all use of toxic chemicals as chemical weapons should be covered by the Chemical Weapons Convention. Nevertheless, clear cut assumptions should be made with respect to civilian uses. This is realised in the work on the Convention, since one of its basic principles is the so-called 'general purpose criterion', which states that only such production which is intended for 'permitted purposes' should be allowed.

A technically, as well as politically, very difficult problem concerns the so-called **binary chemical weapons**. These weapons deliver a chemical warfare agent, a nerve-gas, onto the target. Production of nerve-gases will of course be prohibited under the Convention, but the problems lies in the fact that in these weapons two relatively untoxic compounds are loaded in the grenade, or bomb. They are mixed only when the warhead is on its way to the target. The question then arises how to characterise the components which form the nerve-gas, and whether to prohibit their production. This is particularly relevant to the most important ones in each set of components, namely the so-called 'key precursor'. Key precursors can also be identified in the ordinary production process of the toxic chemicals used in chemical weapons. These chemicals do not meet all criteria, especially not the toxicity criteria, which constitute part of the definition of chemical weapons, and particular criteria have to be agreed upon. While much technical work has been done to solve this problem, so far no definite solution has been reached. Although these weapons might not exist in the arsenals, production could start at short notice upon a decision to do so.

Elimination

The main problem is presently the question of the **elimination of chemical weapons** including its verification. It is not so much the destruction as such, which constitutes the problem. The main question is whether some chemicals used in weapons should be allowed to be diverted to peaceful purposes or whether they should be all destroyed. This problem will presumably be solved along purely practical lines.

Another problem concerns the **elimination of the production and weapons filling facilities**. Here, too, differences exist with respect to what really constitutes a production facility and how much of it should be destroyed. It is obvious that insofar as a production facility for chemical weapons exists together with other chemical production facilities for peaceful purposes, it would be difficult both to destroy and to verify such a destruction sufficiently well for the purpose of the Convention.

One main problem with respect to elimination both of weapons and of production facilities is to agree upon what types of **declarations** should be made regarding amounts and locations of weapons, stockpiles, and production and filling facilities. Also the time frames for such declarations, including the plans for the actual destruction, are far from being agreed.

The bilateral report of the USA and USSR states that it will take ten years from the entry into force of the Convention to destroy the chemical weapons and the production facilities in these two states. This view seems now generally accepted. The consequences with respect to the security of other states, however, should be noted.

As already mentioned, some progress has been made during the last two years with respect to solving some of the problems concerning the **verification of elimination**. However, the problems still remain to a large extent, and have to be discussed extensively.

The convergence of positions that now seems to appear, is that verification of destruction of the militarily most important and most toxic weapons, should consist of continuous on-site inspection during the destruction periods. However, there remain to be worked out many detailed regulations and procedures on how to implement such a verification system in practice.

A BAN ON CHEMICAL WEAPONS

Production of chemical weapons

With regard to the **prohibition of the production of chemical weapons** the negative approach mentioned above may be chosen. The difficulty is again to find a convenient and acceptable verification procedure for the compliance of this provision. Above all, the problem is how not to disturb the civilian chemical industry and cast doubt on its activities. The difficulties are exacerbated by the fact that some industrial chemicals which could be used as chemical weapons also have civilian uses. The so-called key precursors for binary weapons, mentioned above, constitute another problem. At least one of the components is usually a very common chemical, for example, a common industrial alcohol. The other component might be (presently or in the future) necessary for producing other compounds with a peaceful, non-hostile use. During the negotiations intricate schemes have been suggested for verification systems, which would be sufficiently effective both to detect possible violations and to deter such violations. It has never been the intention that the whole chemical industry should be subject to verification measures. On the contrary, the general opinion is that only relatively few production facilities might be of interest. This would reduce the mechanism necessary for such verification to a practical and modest scale.

In this context, it has been suggested that some chemicals which might be needed for protective purposes, or perhaps also other permitted purposes should be allowed to be produced in so-called 'small-scale production facilities', which could be easily verified. Only one such facility would be allowed for each party wishing to have one. So far all parties seem to agree that verification in this case should be made by on-site inspections. However, full agreement does not exist with regard to which substances actually should be produced in such a small-scale facility. It has been suggested, for instance, that key precursors, or at least some of them, should be produced there. Others think that this might be acceptable only with regard to actual toxic chemicals used for chemical weapons and key precursors, for protective purposes. In the view of many negotiating delegations, if the prescription were to apply also for other permitted purposes, it would impose an impossible restriction on production for research and development of new chemical products for non-hostile purposes.

Compliance

The whole question of how to monitor compliance with a convention has long been an area where basic agreements have been lacking. However, since a basic understanding now seems to be emerging that some destruction activities covered by the Convention could be verified by continuous on-site inspection, it might be easier to come to a general understanding also with respect to other mechanisms for ensuring compliance with the Convention. Some of the problems which exist in this area are whether or not **national technical means of verification,** (mainly reconnaissance satellites) should be given a particular position under the Convention; as well as how the information received by such means should be utilised under the Convention.

Another problem concerns the so-called **verification by challenge,** namely that a party, when it has reason to believe that another party is violating the convention, should have the right to ask for on-site inspection to clarify the problem. This could be regarded as a last measure to be taken in a long range of measures in order to clarify outstanding problems between parties. For a variety of reasons the complaining party, or, eventually, the Consultative Committee mentioned below may not be allowed by the other party to undertake an on-site inspection. One such reason might be that other weapons exist together with chemical weapons in the same stockpile. In such a case, the challenged party would possibly not accept having to disclose them under a chemical weapons convention. Some negotiating delegations are of the view that all requests for on-site verification, should be obligatorily met by the challenged party. Other delegations find this an unacceptable intrusion on their sovereignty. Although this is a question of delimitation rather than of questioning the sovereignty of states, the views about the circumstances under which a party would have to yield to a request for verification still seem very divergent.

The problem of verification by challenge is closely connected with the decision-power the organ to perform such activities, that is the **Consultative Committee** should have under the Convention. Would a decision be made by majority vote or would it be necessary to have consensus in all or in some cases? Will it ever be possible for the Consultative Committee to take any initiatives of its own? The same questions could be asked with respect to requests for clarification or fact-finding, other than on-site verification, directed at the Consultative Committee. It is important to mention that eventual agreements on the rules on how the Consultative Committee should function might have implications outside the Chemical Weapons Convention. Thus, the measures agreed for a chemical weapons convention, which would need to be rather extensive and elaborated, could certainly have consequences for conventions in other disarmament areas as well. For this reason, the solutions are worked out with utmost care.

Conclusion

The recent statement by President Chernenko concluded that the outcome of the negotiations on the Chemical Weapons Convention might well constitute a watershed with respect to further arms limitations and disarmament measures to be taken by the two superpowers. Thus the importance of the Chemical Weapons Convention for disarmament efforts, cannot be over-emphasised.

18 Verification of Chemical Disarmament
MAYATEN RAUTIO AND JORMA MIETTINEN

Introduction

One of the biggest obstacles in the negotiations on a Chemical Weapons Convention has been the question of verification of the implementation of the Convention. Both superpowers agree upon the need of verification, but hold widely differing opinions about the methods of verification. The United States demands very effective on-site international inspection at the production and destruction facilities and at stockpiles. Though initially hesitant, the Soviet Union has lately taken a favourable attitude towards allowing international inspectors inside its territory.

At the moment[1] the main goals of the Convention have been agreed upon but the details have not yet been worked out. It is therefore not possible to speak of the demands upon verification of the future Convention.

One suggestion has been that a specific body, the Consultative Committee, be established for verification of the implementation of the Convention. This body would be responsible for sending international inspectors at agreed intervals to verify destruction of stockpiles and closing of weapons production plants. The inspectors would be trained to collect samples from the different targets to be verified. The samples would be analysed either on the spot, in a mobile field laboratory sent to the target area, or in the central laboratory of the Consultative Committee or in any central laboratory selected by the Committee.

The central laboratories could also analyse samples collected by inspectors in the case of alleged use from a combat zone[2,3].

Challenge inspection could be another form of inspection. A State Party could be issued with a request for a challenge inspection, if concrete evidence were given supporting a suspicion of non-compliance with the Convention. Such inspections could be of undeclared stockpiles or production plants.

There is disagreement on the reasons for refusing such challenge inspections and on how often they can be requested.

Continuous presence of international inspectors has not been a favoured method during the negotiations, and measures need to be developed that require a minimum presence of inspectors. One possible way would be verification of permitted production and destruction plants by automatic analytical measuring and registering equipment, so-called black boxes, which would be handled only by international inspectors[4,5,6].

The ideal solution of the verification problem would of course be for each State Party to be able to verify implementation of compliance with the Convention by neighbouring States Parties from its own territory, but this possibility is still in the far future.

One useful method could be remote monitoring of ambient air. In this technique large volume air samples are collected, and compounds absorbed on filters of a high efficiency sampler are analysed. Such a sampler could collect air on a continuous basis.

Two parallel samples could be prepared at predetermined intervals from the absorbed compounds. The first sample would be analysed immediately and the other stored for later analysis in the event that banned agents or their degradation products were found in the first sample.

This technique might be employed to detect combat use and field tests during combat training. However, it would not be effective in the verification of development of new agents, non-production, or in destruction of existing stockpiles[7].

Verification of Prohibition of Development of New Chemical Warfare Agents

Verification of prohibition of development of new chemical weapons will be only marginally possible because no State Party would allow international inspectors into its military laboratories.

Scanning of the relevant literature has revealed laboratories developing volatile toxic compounds with no obvious civilian use. If toxic compounds (incapacitants for example) were found, a subsidiary organ of the Security Council of the United Nations, such as the future Consultative Committee, could request explanation of the reasons for developing such agents and request a challenge on-site inspection of the laboratory in question.

Verification of Non-Production of Chemical Warfare Agents

During the negotiations it has become clear that the best way to prohibit production of chemical warfare agents is to raze the existing production plants. After entry into force of the Convention the facilities must first be closed in a manner that will render them inoperative in a verifiable way. Inactivity could be verified using continuous monitoring with on-site automatic instruments and systematic international on-site inspection. The filling facilities, in particular, should be razed as they have no civilian use.

The conversion to peaceful use of the production facilities proposed by some delegations is the most unsatisfactory solution, as reconversion would be easy to do and difficult to verify[2].

The operative state of a clandestine facility producing super-toxic lethal agents might be revealed from the existtence of safety constructions, or measures such as exclusion areas, test animals and alarm devices around the facility. These are used in the event of leakages of agents and, under favourable conditions, might even be detected by satellite surveillance.

Clandestine production of considerably less toxic precursors, in civilian facilities producing chemicals such as pesticides, is much more difficult to detect since such plants can easily change their production processes. Until now, the civilian industry has not been willing to accept any international inspection that might hamper its production and endanger production secrets. On the other hand, the civilian industry in the United States has not been willing to produce precursors.

Verification of Existing Stockpiles

Verification of existing stockpiles presupposes a declaration of their location to the Consultative Committee. Although agreement has not yet been reached on verification methods, general agreement does exist about an undertaking to submit declarations on the quality and quantity of toxic agents in the stockpiles[2,3].

Satellite surveillance is not capable of detecting stockpiles hidden in rock caves. These can be revealed only upon transportation of agents to and from the caves, assuming that satellite pictures can be analysed despite the huge amount of information they contain. Declared stockpiles could be verified using automatic monitors.

Verification of Destruction of Existing Stocks of Chemical Weapons

Verification of the destruction of existing stockpiles of chemical weapons has been the subject of more extensive discussions than any other verification measure. Opinions about the required comprehensiveness of the verification are still widely divergent. The most acceptable technique would be one that relies on completely automatic analytical equipment for control of the whole destruction process, and which transfers data about the destructed agents and the destruction products formed to the central computer of the Consultative Committee.

If frequent sampling were performed at undeclared intervals, one could be sure that the destruction facility was really destroying the declared agents in declared quantities. If automatic monitors were installed in a manner rendering them tamper-free from outsiders, and the whole facility were under TV surveillance, possibilities for falsification would be minimised.

International inspectors could ensure that no falsification of analytical data was possible and that the equipment was functioning correctly. If monitors themselves could alarm the central computer about malfunctions they could be left under the control of one international inspector and service personnel. Such instruments are commercially available and used in civilian industry for process control.

Verification of Alleged Use of Chemical Warfare Agents

During the negotiations in Geneva, it has been stressed that concrete evidence must be obtained of violation of the Convention before international inspectors are sent to a combat zone. In well-documented cases inspectors would collect on-site samples for preliminary analysis in a mobile field laboratory sent to the target area. Final analyses would be performed in a central laboratory. After the report on the preliminary analyses the inspectors could collect new samples if necessary.

The most beneficial sampling places could be located with the aid of field tests, based on the chemical or enzymatic colour reactions taking place in the presence of nerve agents, mustards or such toxic gases as hydrogen cyanide or cyanogen chloride. Liquid agents could be detected by test papers. Field tests can be used to detect certain groups of agents but they cannot reveal structures of compounds unambiguously.

For juridically valid results from analyses, it is essential to use authorised sample collectors. If the central laboratory receives samples from unexploded munitions, complete analysis of the agent formulate, including solvents, stabilisers, antioxidants in addition to the agent, might reveal the origin of the munition. This would succeed especially if an undertaking was included in the Convention to send samples from all stockpiled agents to the central laboratory. Discrepancies might then be avoided in determining which State Party was responsible for using chemical weapons. This would, however, not succeed in cases where the agent was clandestinely produced in an undeclared facility.

To increase the reliability of the central laboratory, analyses could proceed in a manner adopted for tests of doping in the Olympic games. The analysts receive samples provided only with codes, and the samples include several controls spiked with known amounts of the agents suspected in the preliminary field tests. Control samples could include non-spiked 'pure' control samples as well. If analyses reveal banned agents, a parallel sample could be analysed in another central laboratory. A representative of the suspected State Party could be accorded the right to be present in the laboratory during the analysis of the latter sample, in order to eliminate any later argument about the methods used.

The Finnish Contribution

Since verification has been one of the greatest obstacles to the conclusion of a comprehensive ban on chemical weapons, the Ministry for Foreign Affairs in Finland established a project on verification of chemical disarmament in 1971. The goal of the project has been to create a verification capacity that would cover all the verification needs: verification of non-production, destruction of stockpiles, and alleged use. Because of this, Finland has been allowed to be present as observer at the sessions of the Conference on Disarmament.

Experimental work, initiated in 1973, has centred on development of the analytical techniques required for verification to meet the most exacting demands. Since 1977 the project has progressed from the production of brief annual reports to the publication of annual 'Blue Books', each one some 100-200 pages in length. All seven of the published comprehensive reports (see Table 1) have been distributed to the members of the Geneva Conference on Disarmament. The 1200 pages of the research reports contain data allowing the identification of all known agents, their precursors and degradation products.

The main laboratory of the project is in the Department of

Table 1. Structure of the Finnish Research project for CW Verification

---

General title of report series:
METHODOLOGY AND INSTRUMENTATION FOR SAMPLING AND ANALYSIS IN THE VERIFICATION OF CHEMICAL DISARMAMENT

Already published:

A. GENERAL REPORTS

    A.1 Chemical and Instrumental Verification of Organophosphorus Warfare Agents 1977

    A.2 Technical Evaluation of Selected Scientific Methods for the Verification of Chemical Disarmament 1984

B. SYSTEMATIC IDENTIFICATION OF CHEMICAL WARFARE AGENTS

    B.1 Identification of Organophosphorus Warfare Agents. An Approach for the Standardization of Techniques and Reference Data 1979

    B.2 Identification of Degradation Products of Organophosphorus Warfare Agents 1980

    B.3 Identification of Non-phosphorus Warfare Agents 1982

    B.4 Identification of Precursors of Warfare Agents, Agents, Degradation Products of Non-phosphorus Agents and Some Potential Agents 1983

C. TRACE ANALYSIS OF CHEMICAL WARFARE AGENTS

    C.1 An Approach to the Environmental Monitoring of Nerve Agents 1981

Organic Chemistry of the University of Helsinki, but scientists from several other laboratories participate in the research, for example, from the chemistry departments of the Universities of Helsinki, Oulu and Jyväskylä (see Figure 1).

The project is able to identify about 200 agents, agent homologues and their presursors, and degradation products in low concentrations from air, water and soil samples. In addition, the project is able to elucidate the structures of unknown compounds spiked in soil samples.

The elucidation task first requires separation of the agents from the sample and isolation as pure compounds by high performance liquid chromotography using enzymatic detection. Structure elucidation is performed by high resolution mass spectrometry and nuclear magnetic resonance spectrometry. With the aid of the last-mentioned method, known compounds containing phosphorus and fluorine can be identified and structures elucidated even from a mixture of several compounds. Degradation products of nerve agents and pesticides, both being derivatives of phosphoric acid, can also be distinguished from the first aqueous residue after extraction with organic solvents.

One of the future goals of the Finnish project is to determine the range of applicability of remote monitoring of ambient air for detection and identification of organic compounds. In this context, sampling techniques will be developed for simultaneous quantitations of emissions.

Detection of extremely low concentrations of agents in a heavy background will require further refinement of the high precision gas chromatographic technique developed within the project. Identification of individual agents can be made with the new tandem mass spectrometer, even without prior separation from samples. This instrument can be used to monitor banned agents from samples without prior separation.

After air analysis, priority will probably be put on the development of automatic methods for verification of destruction of stockpiled agents. This presupposes complete automation of the techniques developed within or adapted by the project.

Juridically valid results from analyses require that sample collectors be authorised by an official organisation, such as the Consultative Committee or UN Security Council. This type of sample has not yet been sent to Finland, and therefore the project has not analysed samples from combat areas. However, the techniques developed within the project are being used by several civilian analytical laboratories, for example, to detect pesticides in food and to monitor environmental pollution. The techniques are especially applicable to air analyses which require sensitive trace analysis methods.

CHEMICAL DISARMAMENT

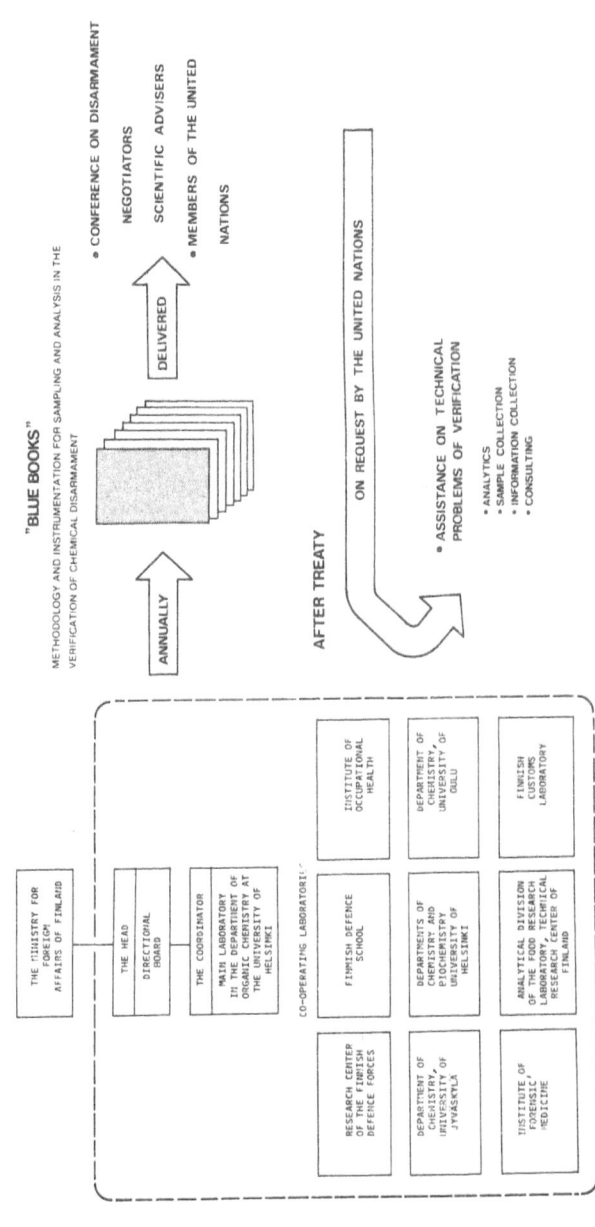

Figure 1. The working structure of the Finnish Project for Verification of Chemical Warfare Agents

The Finnish Government offers the automatic analytical methods, and data collected from agents, for use by the signatory States Parties of the future Convention and by the international Consultative Committee to be established. In this way Finland is filling the gap which exists in the production of impartial practical information about methods for analysis of chemical warfare agents.

References

1. J. Perry Robinson, 'Chemical and Biological Warfare: Developments in 1983', in SIPRI Yearbook 1984, pp.319-349.
2. Report of the Ad Hoc Working Group on Chemical Weapons to the Committee on Disarmament. Document CD/416, 22 August 1983.
3. Report of the Ad Hoc Committee on Chemical Weapons to the Conference on Disarmament. Document CD/539, 28 August 1984.
4. 'On Instrumental Monitoring of Incineration of CW Agents', submitted by Finland. Document CD/CW/WP.64, 31 January 1984.
5. 'Illustrative On-site Inspection Procedures for Verification of Chemical Weapons Stockpile Destruction', submitted by the USA. Document CD/387, 6 July 1983.
6. 'Verification of the Destruction of Chemical Weapons', submitted by the Federal Republic of Germany. Document CD/518, 17 July 1984.
7. Technical Evaluation of Selected Methods in the Verification of Chemical Disarmament. The Ministry for Foreign Affairs of Finland, 1984.

19 Chemical Weapons Verification
ESMAT EZZ

Introduction

Mutually accepted and adequate verification mechanisms which would assure compliance with the provisions of the projected Convention banning chemical weapons has been the major stumbling block to the conclusion of such a Convention. Despite the great variety of proposals presented over the years in the CCD and CD, there are still distinct differences of opinion with respect to the extent of intrusiveness which must be allowed in the process of verification, the role of international inspectors, the role and nature of what is called national verification, and whether verification should be systematic continuous, systematic non-continuous, regular, random or by challenge, or any combination of these.

The problem of verification involves political judgment which would depend on the levels of trust or mistrust between the parties to the convention, but verification is basically a technical matter.

In this paper, I discuss some of the basic aspects of verification requirements in the light of the current situation of negotiations in the Committee on Disarmament, in an attempt to elaborate on the areas of agreement, to explore the areas of difference and looking for ways to bridge the various points of view.

A paper presented by Canada, to the CD, on Verification and Control Requirements for a Chemical Arms Control Treaty, contains a list of basic activities requiring some form of monitoring and verification. These activities fall into two groups:

Activities to be undertaken and monitored:

- Declaration of existing agent and chemical weapon production facilities including specific sites.
- Declaration of existing agent and weapon stocks including

storage sites and numbers.
- Dismantling of existing production facilities.
- Destruction of existing agent and weapon stocks.

Activities to be banned and verified:

- Development of new agent weapon systems.
- Construction of new agent or weapon (means of delivery) production facilities.
- Production of chemical agents.
- Retention, stockpiling or other acquisition of chemical agents and weapons.
- Offensive military training or other activities in preparation for undertaking chemical warfare.
- Use of chemical weapons for war purposes, including dual purpose agents and binary components.

From a survey of various proposals presented to the CD, both before and after the submission of the Canadian paper, there appears to be general agreement on the activities to be undertaken or banned as mentioned above, but no general agreement has been reached on the verification mechanisms which would assure faithful compliance with the provisions of the Convention. The various aspects of this problem were extensively discussed during the 1983 summer session of the CD and its subordinate bodies but it was impossible to bridge the differences between the various points of view.

During the 1984 spring session, two important developments with respect to the verification mechanisms had occurred. First, and in my judgment a step forward, the acceptance by the Soviet Union for the first time of 'permanent presence at the special facility of the representatives of international control, as well as by a combination of systematic international verifications at the facility including also the storage of the stocks of weapons at it, with the use of instruments'. Second, the presentation by the United States of America of a Draft Convention on the prohibition of chemical weapons. Other valuable contributions during that session which dealt with verification aspects were by Sweden on 'Verification of Destruction of Stockpiles of Chemical Weapons'; by the United Kingdom on 'Verification and Compliance, the Challenge Element'; by China on 'Major Elements of a Future Convention on the Complete Prohibition and Total Destruction of Chemical Weapons'; by the Netherlands on 'Size and Structure of a Chemical Disarmament Inspectorate'; by Yugoslavia on 'National Verification Measures'; and by France on 'Elimination of Stocks and of Production Facilities'.

CHEMICAL WEAPONS VERIFICATION

These presentations reflect the state of affairs in the negotiations on the projected Chemical Weapons Convention. They contain enough elements of agreement to constitute a good basis for a meaningful and reliable verification mechanism. The areas of differences could be bridged without encroaching on the effectiveness of the process of verification.

General Considerations

Since it is impossible to verify declarations with a 100 per cent degree of certainty, the only solution is to work on a certain degree of mutual trust, and accept declarations as honest until there is reasonable doubt, in which case some sort of challenge inspection would be warranted.

If a country wanted to cheat, it would be easier and more logical to cheat on declarations, and present false data about its stocks and/or its production facilities, rather than on the destruction of the stocks and facilities. It is important to keep that in mind when discussing the adequacy of the verification mechanisms.

Some countries do not agree, and others do not favour a declaration of the site or sites of their stocks. It is reasonable to accept that any country has the right, if it so desired, to move its declared stocks to an area or areas of its choice where they can be inspected and controlled before they are moved to the destruction facility or facilities.

It is generally agreed, that the degree of intrusiveness of verification can be reduced by making use of the advancements of science and technology, but there is no substitute for on-site inspection.

The practical approach is to start with the basic elements of verification in the hope that in the process of implementation of the convention, and the development of confidence between states, any additional measures could be worked out and added to the verification régime.

Verification of Non-Production of Chemical Weapons

Non-production can be assured by the actual closure, mothballing, dismantling or destruction of the production facilities. Some countries raise the possibility of conversion of these facilities to the production of civilian products, others insist on destruction, since they do not consider conversion to be cost-effective; they are also concerned about reconversion to military purposes. Production facilities could be used for destruction of stocks and destroyed or dismantled after the end of the destruction of stocks. It is important that the declared production facilities go out of service after the entry into force of the Convention. This should be done under the supervision of international inspectors. Systematic checking of destruction or closure should be carried out at regular intervals.

The plants to be put under supervision are: (a) for production of toxic substances and their precursors; (b) for production of delivery systems specifically designed to carry chemical warfare agents; (c) filling facilities.

To make sure that no undeclared production of super-toxic chemicals or their key precursors is taking place in quantities that are relevant in the context of a chemical weapons convention, some inspection of the chemical industry would be necessary. This was dealt with in the Netherlands proposal, which suggests that it is possible to organise inspections in such a way as to avoid hampering industrial production and compromising industrial secrets. The plants to be inspected are not only those which actually produce super-toxic chemicals and their key precursors, but any plant that could produce these in relevant quantities.

Verification of Destruction of Stocks

The identity and quantity of the chemical weapons should be verified after declaration, and before and during their destruction. Visual observation, whether directly or with closed circuit television, would be enough to confirm the quantity, if certain other parameters, such as measurement of weight or volume are considered. The identification of the chemical agent requires sampling and analysis. This could be done automatically and monitored remotely, if the system of destruction is designed to incorporate such an operation. It is obvious, that in such a case, initial and random inspection of the system of analysis and monitoring would be necessary to ascertain reliability and security. The Swedish document analysed the need for continuous on-site inspection of the destruction of chemical weapons at a destruction facility, and reached the following conclusions:

- On-site inspection would be necessary during the construction of a destruction facility as well as after the termination of the destruction activities.
- If a destruction facility has been designed without taking into account special requirements for enabling verification, the continuous on-site presence of an international inspection team would be necessary.
- Such a facility can be modified to allow verification by means of a combination of monitoring equipment and

occasional on-site inspections. However, there might be a risk that impermissible activities at the facilities would remain undetected by the verification procedure.
- If the need for verification is taken into consideration when the facility is being designed, more reliable arrangements can be made. The risk of undetected impermissible activities might then be reduced to a very low level.
- If a very high degree of confidence in the verification methods is considered necessary, further technical work would be needed in order to improve the reliability of the process monitoring equipment, and to eliminate the need for continuous on-site presence of inspectors.
- Even when extensive remote monitoring is available, on-site visits are necessary during the destruction period in order to verify the functioning of the monitoring, data acquisition and data transmission equipment. Furthermore, the presence of inspectors during certain types of maintenance or repair work seems to be desirable.

The Soviet Union proposed that the effectiveness of verification, from the beginning of the destruction process to its completion, should be ensured either by the permanent presence of international inspection representatives at the special facility, or by a combination of systematic international inspections at the facility, including the associated weapons depot, by the use of instruments.

France asked that the destruction unit should, before every round of destruction, be inspected by international monitors in order to verify conformity and to install a number of sensors provided for in the procedure. The destruction process should be the subject of continuous on-site monitoring in close collaboration with the national 'safety teams'. The USA asked that the destruction procedure should permit systematic international on-site verification. On-site instruments as well as inspectors, should be used for verification. Inspectors should be present in the destruction facility continuously when it is operating.

Challenge On-Site Inspection

This issue was extensively discussed during the 1983 summer session of the CD.

The latest contribution to the subject is the United Kingdom paper, which stresses that challenge on-site inspection cannot be a substitute for routine on-site inspection, but can be an effective way to deal with instances of suspected non-compliance which would not necessarily be revealed by regular inspection of declared facilities. The regime of challenge inspection would:

- Deter evasion of obligations under the Convention by providing a means of uncovering and drawing attention to breaches of the Convention.
- Provide a means of clarifying ambiguous situations, settling disputes and, on the assumption that allegations of evasion proved unfounded, restoring confidence.
- Provide advance notice of possible breaches of the Convention, thus enabling state parties to take necessary action to ascertain the facts.

The paper suggests that the arrangements for challenge inspection should fall under the following headings:

- Machinery for carrying out challenge inspection.
- Criteria for ensuring that the inspections are objective and impartial.
- Basis for requesting challenge inspection.
- Rights and obligations of a challenged state.
- Action to be taken in the case of refusal.

The paper then discusses the machinery needed for inspection, the criteria for effective verification, and the rights and obligations of each state party.

The Netherlands paper gave examples of information which justify a request for challenge inspection: indications of use of CW; finding of traces of a banned agent in a river downstream of a chemical plant; indication of a hidden CW stockpile; evidence of existence of a large versatile chemical complex that has not been declared.

In its paper, China accepts on-site inspection by challenge and considers positive responses to requests for challenge inspection authorised by the Consultative Committee as a confidence-building measure.

The US Draft Convention requires that the party to be inspected shall, except for most exceptional reasons, provide access within 24 hours of the Panel's request for an **ad hoc** inspection. This is considered by some states to be unacceptable or asking too much.

There is no doubt that an effective challenge on-site inspection must be urgent and prompt. Timely access to the suspected site is of prime importance to ascertain facts before the challenged party has a chance to change or hide evidence. It is unfortunate that some states refuse the principle of granting an international investigating team the right to conduct an immediate on-site inspection, even in the fact of a reasonable and justified challenge.

Verification of Alleged Use

Prohibition of use of chemical weapons is to be incorporated in the projected comprehensive Convention on chemical weapons, although it is prohibited by the Geneva Protocol of 1925.

The United Nations General Assembly, at its 37th session, adopted a resolution requesting the Secretary-General with the assistance of qualified consultant experts, to devise procedures for the timely and efficient investigation of information concerning activities that may constitute a violation of the Geneva Protocol or of the relevant rules of customary international law.

The Secretary-General appointed a group of qualified consultant experts to carry out this task. Their report included criteria for decisions on the initiation of an investigation and follow-up actions and conduct of an investigation. The ideas expressed were based on the experience gained from previous investigations and could be useful in considering a verification regime of allegation of use within the context of a Convention on Chemical Weapons. The main features of the verification regime are:

- urgency and promptness of the initiation of the investigation;
- appointment of highly qualified impartial members of the investigating team;
- timely access to the area and freedom of inspection, examination of casualties, collection of samples for analysis.

20 A Chemical-Weapon-Free Zone in Europe
KARLHEINZ LOHS AND KARIN MEIER

Introduction

In the age of nuclear weapons, chemical weapons still remain a military reality. Though their actual military value remains highly controversial, it is clear that intensive efforts are being made to develop them further.

Although the development of new chemical weapons since World War II has occurred mainly in the USA, the results of basic chemical and toxicological research, indispensable for their manufacture, came primarily from Europe. This knowledge was obtained there mainly as a result of non-military research, as exemplified by the works of Schrader, Holmstedt, Tammelin, Hofmann, and others.

At present, the largest stockpiles of chemical weapons stored outside the USA are – according to US information – on a Pacific island and on the territory of the Federal Republic of Germany. Additional stockpiles of CW agents are kept by the French Army on the territory of France. There is no official information available on any other stockpiles in other European countries. (Press reports on this subject are based on uncorroborated assumptions and are therefore purely speculative in nature.) In this context, it should be mentioned that the new US Army service regulations and the operative concept of the 'AirLand Battle 86' contain provisions for the offensive deployment of chemical weapons. Given the envisaged stockpiling of new types of chemical weapons, mainly of the binary generation, a new military and political situation was created by the USA which, undoubtedly, will have repercussions on the overall strategic military concept.

This is not the place to deal with the risks and dangers to Man and his environment, emanating from chemical warfare agents. Detailed studies and analyses of current problems of chemical weapons, and scenarios of modern chemical war, have already been published, or are being prepared by SIPRI. These studies have revealed that chemical weapons pose a particularly great danger to smaller states. This applies both to their possible military use and to stockpiling in peacetime. For this reason, the initiative taken by the Palme Commission in proposing the creation of zones free from chemical weapons has become a matter of great international importance.

The government of the German Democratic Republic was the first to take up officially, and support, the proposal by the Palme Commission through its UN ambassador.

The need and the aim of an agreement to create a chemical-weapon-free zone (CWFZ) were originally derived from the awareness that heightened danger of a military confrontation would also increase the danger of chemical warfare. This danger is intensified by the deployment of chemical weapons in some countries.

This is of special importance to Europe in view of the US military doctrines which consider this continent as a potential theatre of war for chemical weapons. It is from this aspect that the proposal for the creation of a CWFZ, which was submitted by the Warsaw Pact countries to the member states of NATO on 10 January 1984, has to be viewed. The creation of such a CWFZ in Europe would substantially lessen the political and military tensions, and thereby considerably reduce the danger of chemical warfare. A chemical-weapon-free zone in Europe would be a concrete disarmament measure, and would exert a general and positive influence on other disarmament negotiations. It would also encourage the convening of a worldwide convention on banning chemical weapons and could promote its implementation. At the same time, this measure would have a strong confidence-building effect, since the withdrawal of chemical weapons from the continent would substantially reduce the danger to the civilian population of Europe.

Elements of Agreement on a CWFZ

Essentially the content of the agreement will determine its form. Therefore, priority should be given to a treaty based on international law rather than to a declaration, since only a treaty can establish the duties and rights of states. At the end of the negotiations on a CWFZ it might be appropriate to have available a document that is a combination of declaration and treaty. In this way, the intentions of the participating states could be co-ordinated as widely as possible, and the document could be approved by consensus.

The content of the declaration should be a statement on the existence, or non-existence, of chemical weapons on the territory of the state concerned. Above all, the treaty on a chemical-weapon-free zone should be orientated towards the following aims:

- no introduction (manufacture, stockpiling) of chemical weapons, and no relevant research and development;
- a gradual reduction in existing weapons culminating in the establishment of a zone free from chemical weapons;
- formulation of the basic elements of a convention to ban chemical weapons, (for example, the definition of chemical weapons and the control system).

The elements of a treaty on a CWFZ should include principles guiding the participating states in their approach and actions. There should also be a definition of the **objective of the treaty**, that is a definition of the chemical-weapon-free zone, as well as a definition of chemical weapons and, as its very core, the contractual **obligations of the states**.

In the preamble to the treaty, reference should be made to the point that the basic aims of the states coincide with those of the UN Charter. Based on the principles of equality, equivalence and equal security, it is essential to establish a correlation with the fundamental principles of international law, the sovereign equality of states, non-use of force, and peaceful co-operation.

The main articles should contain the concrete obligations of the contracting states. In this context it is important to note that the rights and duties of contracting states should remain in conformity with the UN Charter, and with other existing treaties based on international law, such as alliances.

The primary duty of states will be to ban the existence of chemical weapons on their territories and at the same time prevent such weapons from being developed, manufactured or stockpiled.

If necessary, a provision could be inserted on measures to destroy existing, but no longer transportable CW stockpiles, as well as on technical precautions for converting chemical CW agents into products for civilian use. This provision could be implemented step by step, according to a procedure laid down in the treaty.

Proceeding on the assumption that the **reduction** of chemical weapons has, as its aim, their complete elimination from the territory of the participating states, the following individual steps are envisaged:

- **renunciation** by third countries of the **stationing** of chemical weapons in states belonging to the CWFZ.

- **withdrawal** of stockpiled chemical weapons by third countries from the CWFZ;
- **cessation** of the development, especially the production, of new types and systems of chemical weapons and facilities; termination of current production by the member states of the treaty;
- **destruction** of stockpiled CW agents and related weapons according to a plan to be established. If necessary, the controlled utilisation for peaceful purposes should be allowed. This may be possible for the manufacture of the precursors of binary-weapons, and appears also to be technically practicable for several other precursors and intermediary products.

The Essential Criteria of a CWFZ

A chemical-weapon-free zone may be characterised by the following major criteria:

Territorial scope. If possible, the zone should cover the entire European continent, but to begin with the two German states might provide the nucleus for a gradually extending CWFZ. This approach by stages can be accomplished in various ways, for example by including the immediate neighbours of the two German states, and gradually extending the area.

Definition of a CWFZ. Consideration is required that it comprises a definite geographical area which is subject to the sovereignty of the states therein. The postulate of the CWFZ is that no state within the zone shall develop, manufacture, acquire from a third country, or stockpile chemical weapons, nor shall it transfer such weapons and facilities to third states, or stockpile any chemical weapons outside the CFWZ on the territory of other states in the zone.

Control. Both national and international control committees should be set up. In this context reference can be made to the system of verification, proposed in the Soviet draft on the 'Basic elements of a Convention on the Prevention, Development, Manufacture and Stockpiling of Chemical Weapons and their Destruction' submitted to the Second UN Disarmament Conference. The control system of the Treaty of Tlatelolco, which possesses its own permanent organs for monitoring, permits the states to draw up periodic and special reports, and provides for special inspections, could be considered as a model. The Treaty of Tlatelolco created a nuclear-weapon-free zone in Latin America which has been in existence since 1967. The structure of the Treaty as well as the way it came into force, provide valuable guidelines for a possible treaty on a CWFZ. In February 1984, the USSR, in the wake of the CD negotiations, declared its readiness, through its ambassador, to submit to international on-site inspections of the destruction of chemical weapons. This declaration has met with a worldwide response.

It is inadvisable to distinguish in the treaty between chemical-weapon-possessing states and other states. The duties arising from the treaty refer unrestrictedly to **all** states of the geographical region and any differentiation of states with regard to the treaty should be avoided. In this context, it is irrelevant that the shares of individual states in implementing the treaty are not the same.

It is important to emphasise the correlation between a treaty on a CWFZ and a convention on the prohibition of chemical weapons. A CWFZ should be considered as a preliminary stage for a general ban on chemical weapons. Its creation is orientated towards the prevention, containment and elimination of hotbeds of conflict, in which the use of chemical weapons is envisaged. The major difference between a treaty on a CWFZ and a convention on the prohibition of chemical weapons is in the scope of application of the documents. Whereas a treaty on a zone is a regional instrument, the intended convention has a **universal** character. The connection between the two is that the basic elements of the Convention are included in the treaty on the zone.

Another possibility worthy of consideration is a combination of weapon-free zones, for example a **nuclear-weapon-free and a chemical-weapon-free zone in Europe**. It would be equally possible to create zones under the general concept of peace zones.

However, it should be pointed out that individual or even several treaties of chemical-weapon-free zones should not replace a convention on banning chemical weapons. The ultimate aim will always be to achieve a general prohibition on chemical weapons. In this connection, reference should be made to the Soviet proposal mentioned above, which encompasses all of the complexities of the problem. Special mention should be made of the Declarations and Confidence-Building Measures and Control Provisions.

Finally, it should be recalled that after the agreement of a comprehensive ban on chemical weapons and worldwide elimination of all stockpiles, it will take some six to ten years to complete the destruction, as estimated by the experts at the CD talks in Geneva. This temporal aspect is an additional argument for the creation of zones free from chemical weapons, thus encouraging the process of disarmament.

Part IV
Problems of European Security

21 The Euromissiles: Negotiating a Way Out?
LEON SIGAL

Introduction

The arrival of new American missiles on European shores has predictably provoked a sharp Soviet reaction, likely to take both military and political forms. The NATO deployments have set in motion long-delayed Soviet weapons programmes that will soon become irreversible. These actions, and the public rhetoric accompanying them, suggest that a fundamental reassessment of American intent and Soviet-American relations may be under way in Moscow.

Seven years ago, the first signs of Soviet deployment of the new SS-20 had similar effects in the West.

Both sides' deployments add, albeit marginally, to the military threat they pose to the other side. Hence the reactions of both sides to the increased threat is understandable: their security interests are being threatened. Yet the extent of that threat is greatly exaggerated and the resulting crisis greatly exacerbated by gross misperceptions on both sides: of the other side's purpose in deploying new weapons, and of the other side's likely reaction to its own deployments. These misperceptions interfere with efforts to resolve the crisis through arms control.

Arms control efforts are further complicated by a sharp disjunction between public attitudes and expert opinion about what is negotiable and what is not. The public wants disarmament, the experts want arms control, and neither group is likely to be wholly satisfied by attainment of the other's objective. By disarmament the public means a reduction in the number of weapons and a halt in the arms race, with no further deployments and zero weapons as the goal. By arms control the experts mean reducing the likelihood that nuclear weapons will ever be used: by maintaining the nuclear and conventional balance of power in order to minimise the chances that these weapons would be used deliberately; by reducing as much as possible the incentive to use nuclear weapons first in a crisis in order to decrease the likelihood of inadvertent or accidental nuclear war; and by constraining the development of new weapons likely to jeopardise stability, however precarious, in the future. To arms controllers, reductions may be a desirable but not necessary means to these ends. As a consequence, their accomplishments are doomed to disappoint the public.

The disjunction between public and expert attitudes, as well as conflicting security interests, compounded by mutual misperceptions of those interests, affect the chances for negotiating a way out of the Euromissile crisis.

Military Rationales, Mutual Misperceptions

To recognise that nuclear weapons might be used in a war and that some are marginally better than others for that purpose is not to construct a convincing military rationale for producing and deploying additional weapons in Europe. Regardless of their political persuasion or military expertise, nearly everyone knows the consequences of nuclear war would be so catastrophic that no military rationale for nuclear weapons based solely on their contribution to fighting a war, as distinguished from deterring one, is politically sustainable; deterrence, not defence, is the military rationale for the new American missiles in Europe.

The military rationale for deploying ground-launched cruise missiles (GLCMs) and Pershing-II ballistic missiles as deterrents rests entirely on their marginal utility in preventing nuclear or conventional war in Europe. As deterrents against nuclear attack they add little to the capabilities of American, British, and French nuclear forces already in place in Europe and elsewhere. They could supplement those deterrents only if they could survive nuclear attack, but according to present plans, they will not be so postured. As deterrents against conventional attack, what the new American missiles add to existing NATO and American capabilities is open to question. Quantitatively, what difference do 572 more warheads make when the United States already has many thousands targeted on the USSR? Qualitatively, how do they add to the perceived likelihood that the alliance is prepared to initiate nuclear war in response to conventional attack?

Faced with these questions NATO developed two internal military rationales for the new weapons: to fill 'a gap in the continuum of deterrence' and to add to its capabilities for 'selective nuclear employment'. Both rationales are rooted in NATO's doctrine of flexible response, which calls for deliberate escalation to the nuclear level if necessary, and requires options so graduated that the alliance would not be forced to respond disproportionately to any level of attack or threat. This need arose in the early 1960s, when the USSR acquired sufficient nuclear forces of intercontinental range to survive an American attack and retaliate against the United States itself. Once the United States became vulnerable, the rationale goes, it could no longer deter a threat by the USSR to use its intermediate-range nuclear forces against Europe by a counter-threat to use its own intercontinental missiles against the USSR. Under conditions of mutual vulnerability, or nuclear interdependence, Soviet leaders could come to believe, no matter how incorrectly, that they might use or threaten to use their intermediate-range forces, especially missiles, against Western Europe while their intercontinental forces deterred any American response. NATO thus needed some equivalent to Soviet IRBMs, though not necessarily in equal numbers.

Both rationales assumed that for the sake of deterrence it might prove necessary for the United States to initiate nuclear war. Yet GLCMs and Pershing-IIs are American owned and cannot be used without American approval. If Soviet leaders were to conclude, however incorrectly, that their threat to strike the United States precluded an American response to their use or threatened use of IRBMs in Europe, how could GLCMs or Pershing-IIs alter that conclusion? Their location is of less consequence than the fact that they are unambiguously American, and no President contemplating their use could ignore the possibility that the USSR might respond by attacking the United States. How does the location of American missiles alter Soviet perceptions of American will to authorise American attacks on the USSR? And if their location does matter, it has distressing political connotations for Europe because it raises fears that the intention is somehow to confine nuclear war to the Continent and that the missiles are supposed to substitute for American intercontinental forces.

Both rationales that NATO invokes for deploying new missiles start with the premise that the alliance might have to initiate the use of nuclear weapons. But in contemplating first use, NATO takes upon itself a burden of risk that is best left to the other side, especially since Soviet doctrine has a strong presumption for pre-emption in a crisis once nuclear war becomes imminent and seemingly unavoidable.

An alternative rationale acknowledges the vulnerability of missiles to Soviet pre-emption but regards that vulnerability as potentially helpful in deterring conventional war in Europe. Prudent Soviet planners, uncertain whether these weapons would be used against their homeland in the course of a war in Europe, would have to try to eliminate them. If

GLCMs and Pershing-IIs could be rendered invulnerable to attack, other than nuclear, then Soviet planners would have to employ nuclear weapons for the purpose. In so doing they would also have to consider striking first at US intercontinental forces, thereby putting the United States as well as the European basing countries at risk. In this sense the new deployments would reinforce coupling of the American deterrent to European security. And by forcing Soviet leaders to consider initiating use of nuclear weapons as part of any attack on Europe - a risk they might not care to assume - European-based missiles would thus contribute to deterring the Soviet Union from starting any war.

If NATO has a case for proposed deployments on these grounds, it is largely an unstated one; alliance members barely allude to this line of reasoning when they talk about risk sharing and demonstrating resolve. The rationale is too impolitic to talk about publicly because it casts the basing countries in the unenviable role of becoming even more inviting targets for nuclear attack than they already are. Yet that very exposure is essential for extended deterrence under conditions of nuclear interdependence.

None of these internal rationales is the object of much public discussion. For the public NATO has offered another rationale with a simplicity tailored for popular consumption: that GLCMs and Pershing-IIs are needed to counter the threat posed by Soviet deployment of SS-20s. It is a political argument parading in military uniform. Politically, it may seem unacceptable for NATO to tolerate deployment of a new Soviet nuclear weapon without responding in kind. But militarily, for GLCM or Pershing-II to serve as a suitable counter to the SS-20, presumes either that both sides have comparable military strategies and thus require equivalent forces, which they do not, or that the GLCM and Pershing-II are capable of surviving an SS-20 attack and of targeting SS-20 sites in return, which they cannot.

While American strategy is preoccupied with providing for extended deterrence under conditions of nuclear interdependence, Soviet strategy shows more concern with countering possible American first use of nuclear weapons. In the event of a European crisis verging on war, Soviet doctrine puts a premium on seizing the initiative. Should nuclear war seem imminent, Soviet doctrine calls for pre-emption - 'striking first in the last resort' - and for protecting Soviet assets against enemy pre-emption[1]. Interpreting the Soviet preoccupation by their own lights, many American strategists see in it a Soviet attempt to acquire the means for deliberately launching a disarming first strike - as a threat to mutual deterrence or strategic stability instead of a precaution

against American first use. The Soviet strategy of preempting imminent nuclear attack calls for missiles that have the accuracy to destroy nuclear forces in Europe but that are themselves not vulnerable to pre-emption.
The SS-20 may not satisfy the requirements of this strategy, but it is a considerable improvement over the SS-4 and SS-5. Its longer range allowed it to be based deeper inside the USSR, out of reach of some American ICBMs as well as most GLCMs and Pershing-IIs. Its mobility and improved readiness also made it less vulnerable to attack and therefore suitable for being held in reserve as a retaliatory force. Its somewhat better accuracy and longer range made it a greater threat to all Western European nuclear installations and C^3 facilities, which are just minutes away. The fact that it was MIRVed with three warheads obviously added somewhat to Soviet target coverage but did not quadruple it as the simple calculations of some analysts suggest, since SS-4s and SS-5s were being dismantled as SS-20s were being deployed[2]. Moreover, solid fuel enabled the SS-20 to maintain higher alert rates for launching a pre-emptive strike than did the liquid-fueled SS-4s and SS-5s, which took hours to ready for launch. It is not, however, more capable of maintaining higher alert rates and achieving greater accuracy than the SS-19 ICBMs, some of which have been and remain targeted on Europe. And the long time it took for the USSR to deploy a substitute for the SS-4s and SS-5s suggests that the SS-20 might be considerably more capable of performing theatre missions because of further improvements in reliability, accuracy, and mobility.

NATO's strategy, by contrast, is to deter conventional or nuclear war in Europe, in part by threatening to strike targets in the USSR with nuclear weapons. This strategy does not require weapons capable of destroying Soviet nuclear forces, but it does call for weapons capable of surviving Soviet pre-emptive strikes. Neither the GLCM nor the Pershing-II presently satisfy that requirement. The GLCM cannot threaten the SS-20 on its own; it takes too long to arrive on target. The Pershing-II force lacks the range and numbers to threaten more than a fraction of the total SS-20 force **per se** but it does have the speed and accuracy to disrupt much of Soviet C^3. With C^3 knocked out, the USSR might be unable to mount a co-ordinated counter-attack, and the remaining missiles would be vulnerable to further American attack. But Pershing-II's accuracy, speed, and proximity poses a threat to Soviet targets that exceeds NATO's requirement for deterring conventional attack.

GLCM and Pershing-II are thus ill-matched as counters to the SS-20. Moreover, the rationale is vulnerable to Soviet rebuttal that the SS-20 is merely a modernisation of obsolescent SS-4s and SS-5s, which were first deployed in 1959 and 1961, respectively. With the retirement of these older missiles, the USSR will have fewer IRBMs targetable on Western Europe than it did a decade ago: 252 as of December 1983 compared with 649 SS-4s and SS-5s in January 1970. Even allowing that each SS-20 missile could carry up to three warheads (and some do), the number of warheads aimed at Western Europe will remain about the same as a decade ago or slightly greater. Perhaps there could be fewer if all SS-4s and SS-5s are eventually retired and some variable-range SS-11s and SS-19s are retargeted against the United States.

What is the net effect of SS-20, GLCM and Pershing-II deployments on the military balance in Europe? NATO argues that its new deployments would restore the balance. The USSR insists they would upset it. Both claims are somewhat disingenuous because both take advantage of the ambiguity in the concept of 'military balance'. A **balance of power** exists when both sides are deterred from initiating any war, not just waging nuclear war. By this standard the new missiles on both sides make little difference: the critical conditions remain the relative conventional capabilities on both sides and the risk of escalation to nuclear war between the superpowers. Some strategists identify the balance of power with an **operational balance**, the relative capabilities of the two sides for waging nuclear war and the likely outcome of such a war. Yet the outcome of nuclear war in Europe is not likely to be much affected one way or the other by the new deployments. For popular perceptions, what matters more than the military calculations of exchange ratios is a **symbolic balance** focusing on static 'bean counts' of the number of comparable weapons on each side. Yet any notion of having equal numbers on each side in Europe leaves the United States out of the equation. Because of the decoupling implications of such a Eurostrategic balance, NATO's December 1979 decision carefully avoids any numerical definition of the threat and expressly disavows matching the USSR on a warhead-for-warhead basis. Numerical equality is the stuff of political propaganda, not military strategy.

While the rhetoric excesses on both sides must be discounted as mere posturing, their effect may have been more pernicious than either would acknowledge. They seem to have inspired each side to magnify the worst in the other side's intentions. In Washington the Soviet SS-20 deployment is understood not as modernisation of obsolescent missiles and a hedge against additional targeting requirements – in the Middle East, the Persian Gulf and the Far East as well as in Western Europe – but as an attempt at neutralising Europe through nuclear blackmail. In Moscow the American missile deployments in Europe are seen not as an attempt to shore up the credibility of NATO's doctrine of first use but as part of a comprehensive effort to acquire the capability for a disarming first strike. Yet neither side's interpretation is sustainable. Sober realists in Moscow are unlikely to calculate that the SS-20 threat could lead to neutralisation of Europe and the break-up of NATO, no matter how many right-wing Westerners say so - and by their insistence, inadvertently encourage this result. Similarly, prudent minds in Washington recognise that, much as some ideologues may want to try, a disarming first strike against forces as sizable and diverse as the USSR's is simply unattainable under present technological conditions. The misperceptions may be grotesque, as in the Soviet response and the American reaction to the intrusion of the Korean airplane into Soviet airspace, but distorted as they may be, these mutual suspicions are driving both superpowers towards exaggerated threat assessments and gross over-reactions in military programmes.

The New Missiles and Stable Deterrence in Europe

Even if the new missiles on both sides do not appreciably alter the fact of mutual deterrence in Europe, war can begin in ways other than through calculated, deliberate acts of policy. It can also begin unintentionally or accidentally through the unforeseen interaction between the two sides' military precautions in a political crisis. Military stability, in short, is a function of crisis stability as well as of strategic stability, and can be adversely affected by the operational character of new weapons and plans for their potential use.

Soviet missiles have long imperiled some of NATO's nuclear forces in Europe, in particular its aircraft and artillery, although the bedrock of NATO's deterrent, at sea in submarines, remains invulnerable. Yet extending deterrence to Europe under conditions of nuclear interdependence may well call for putting some American missiles on land, where they are inherently more vulnerable at present. As long as the USSR has missiles within striking distance of Western Europe - ICBMs and SLBMs as well as missiles of shorter range - and as long as some NATO nuclear forces and C^3 remain vulnerable to attack, NATO will have some incentive to pre-empt once it perceives nuclear war to be imminent, and hence some crisis instability will persist in the European theatre.

The SS-20 adds little to the crisis instability already present as a result of Soviet SS-11 and SS-19 ICBMs and SS-4 and SS-5 IRBMs targeted on Western Europe. In one respect the SS-20 is marginally more stabilising: its mobility makes it less vulnerable to attack than the Soviet ICBMs in fixed silos or than the movable though not very mobile SS-4s and SS-5s. But because the SS-20 is solid-fueled and can be readied for launch much more quickly than SS-4s or SS-5s, it can pre-empt more quickly, thereby adding somewhat to the crisis instability in Europe already posed by Soviet ICBMs.

If the vulnerability of NATO nuclear forces to Soviet attack contributes to crisis instability in Europe, so does the vulnerability of Soviet nuclear forces to NATO's nuclear arsenal. NATO's doctrine of first use has always encouraged the Soviet doctrine of pre-emption, but until now NATO forces in Europe have not been so configured that they could strike quickly at Soviet nuclear forces and C^3 installation. The GLCM does not alter this condition: it is potentially accurate enough for this purpose, but would take so long to reach the USSR that it would give ample warning for Soviet missiles to launch. It thus does not compel Soviet pre-emption in a crisis, which in turn would compel NATO pre-emption – the vicious circle of crisis instability. Pershing-II, however, does just that. Its accuracy and short flight time pose a worrisome new threat to C^3 facilities as well as to some missile sites in the western military districts of the USSR. This, plus its own vulnerability, would make it a prime target for Soviet pre-emption once nuclear war seemed about to erupt. Both its offensive potential and its own vulnerability to Soviet attack make it destabilising in a crisis.

Arms Control and Stable Deterrence in Europe

Those who seek capabilities for fighting a nuclear war and those who demand nuclear disarmament tend to have one thing in common: they think in pre-nuclear terms and insist that what counts is mostly the numbers of weapons on each side, even though they differ on whether those numbers should go up or down. In so doing, they ignore or try to wish away nuclear interdependence. While disarmers yearn for a world in which nuclear weapons would somehow disappear altogether and, with them, all risk of nuclear war, that yearning is unlikely to be satisfied in the foreseeable future, if ever. This will have to await techniques of inspection far more comprehensive than any currently available and far more intrusive than any now politically acceptable. In the meantime, military stability remains the measure of arms control. Steps can be taken to reduce the likelihood that nuclear arsenals will be used, steps that can preserve a modicum of stability, however precarious. And the preservation of military stability may facilitate further steps towards political stability.

A stabilising outcome is possible at Geneva. Such an outcome would not eliminate instability, but it could prevent the current situation from worsening. Crisis stability, and consequently arms race stability, could be enhanced, though not assured, by an accord that holds Pershing-II deployments to a minimum well below the levels currently planned and reduces the number of SS-20s targeted on Western Europe. Unilateral acts could help, too, in particular efforts to protect the weapons on each side against attack and disengagement of shorter-range weapons.

The Present Negotiating Deadlock

Despite shifts in nuance, the premise of the formal Soviet negotiating position has remained constant since the talks opened in October 1980, namely, to deny the need for any new American missiles in Europe. Later the Soviet position underwent further refinement sharpening the political implication of its basic premise. In December 1982, President Yuri Andropov said he was willing 'to agree that the Soviet Union should retain in Europe only as many missiles as are kept there by Britain and France'. He later elaborated the offer to refer to either missiles or warheads. This position posed an implicit challenge to NATO strategy by suggesting that British and French missiles along with American aircraft were adequate to protect Europe.

In October 1983, President Andropov pledged to reduce the number of Soviet SS-20 launchers within range of Europe to 'about 140', which he said was 'appreciably fewer' than the number of British and French launchers, on the condition that no new US missiles were deployed in Europe. The reference to launchers is noteworthy, since by Soviet calculations the 64 British Polaris missiles have six warheads apiece; thus in terms of warheads, the British and French forces count as 448 and 149, respectively. The proposed reduction would thus allow approximate numerical equality in warheads. Significantly, however, Andropov indicated his readiness to dismantle all SS-20s above the ceiling, the first time either superpower has been willing to destroy any of its most modern weapons as the result of an arms control agreement, though the amount of dismantling might be reduced by any increase in British and French nuclear forces.

Not only has the Soviet position consistently sought to preclude new missile deployments on the NATO side, but it has also had one other fundamental consistency: all formal Soviet proposals would permit it to retain at least 350 warheads in place within striking range of Western Europe. This suggests roughly what Soviet targeting requirements may be. Persuading Soviet military planners to accept reductions much below that level could prove difficult, especially because new NATO deployments add to those requirements.

The zero option proposed by President Reagan was rejected because it demanded just that. The logic of the option lay in its appeal to Europe's disarmers: it held out the possibility of no new NATO deployments. The appeal was only temporary, however; once the USSR rejected the zero option, disarmers could foresee for the ceiling to go nowhere but up.

In early 1983, under intense pressure from European governments to show negotiating flexibility, the Reagan Administration abandoned the zero option and reverted to the position that NATO had endorsed in 1979: 'equality at the lowest possible level'. By taking its stand on this principle, the Administration could defer for a time the awkward choice of specifying a numerical ceiling, but it initially adopted the principle in its most extreme form - equal ceilings on land-based intermediate-range nuclear missiles globally, not just in Europe. In September, 1983, President Reagan indicated that the USA would not exercise its right to match the Soviet global total by deploying an equal number in Europe alone, and administration officials said the USA has no plans to deploy land-based missiles outside Europe. The USA did not specify a numerical ceiling until November 1983 when it proposed equal worldwide limits of 140 launchers for each side. While that particular number was the same one the USSR had proposed the preceding month, it applied to missiles within range of Europe, not globally.

A European observer has compared the negotiations in Geneva to 'a provocatively slow striptease in which the two sides in turn make seductive gestures'. But, however seductive the gestures, neither side has gone very far in the formal talks.

Sketches from the Art of the Possible

Behind the scenes, however, the two heads of delegation were informally testing proposals that could serve as the basis for eventual agreement. On 16 July 1982, in the course of a walk in the woods near Geneva, Paul Nitze and Yuri Kvitsinsky sketched the outline of a deal that would have limited each side to a maximum of 75 intermediate-range missile transporter-erector-launchers (TELs) in Europe. It would also have frozen the Soviet SS-20 force east of Novosibirsk at existing levels - about 90 launchers. This proposal would have required the USSR to dismantle its older SS-4s and SS-5s - some 248 in all as of the end of 1982 - and all its SS-20 launchers in excess of 75 within range of Western Europe. It would have allowed the United States to deploy 75 GLCM launchers, or 300 GLCMs, but no Pershing-IIs. It said nothing about British and French nuclear forces. It would also have limited medium bombers - F-111s, Backfires, Blinders, and Badgers - and shorter-range (500 to 1000 kilometres) missile systems to roughly existing levels. It would have permitted modernisation, but not MIRVing of short-range weapons, a provision that seemed to permit replacement of Pershing-I by Pershing-IB but, arguably, to preclude the USSR from improving its short-range forces in lieu of adding to its IRBMs. Finally, the proposal provided for a three-month moratorium on preparations for further deployments to permit a preliminary agreement to be turned into a treaty[3].

The walk-in-the-woods understanding, characterised as a 'joint exploratory package', in no way committed the two governments, however, and by September both had disowned their negotiators' work, first the United States in the course of a 28 September meeting between George Shultz and his Soviet counterpart, Andrei Gromyko, followed two days later by Kvitsinsky when the Geneva talks reconvened. Although Shultz gave no reason for the American rejection, it was done at the insistence of senior civilians in the Pentagon who objected to trading away the Pershing-II. The reason Kvitsinsky gave for Soviet rejection was the failure to take British and French systems into account; but at least two other considerations are likely to have mattered more to his political masters in Moscow. The first was a military concern: the limit of 225 SS-20 warheads might have impinged on Soviet targeting requirements. To add insult to injury, the understanding would have permitted the United States to have more warheads, 300 GLCMs, than the USSR. The second consideration was political: the proposal conceded NATO's right to deploy some new missiles, and did so prematurely, before allied governments had paid the full political price at home in the coin of popular discontent, demonstrations, and parliamentary restiveness. It also exposed the Soviet position on British and French missiles as something of a sham, again before potential internal differences among NATO members could be fully exploited.

Rejection by both sides left the walk-in-the-woods understanding moribund but capable of being revived by either side at any time. At the eleventh hour the USSR may have tried to do just that. On 13 November 1983, just days before a debate on the missiles was scheduled in the Bundestag, Kvitsinsky requested another private meeting with Nitze. On 'urgent instructions' from Moscow he said that if the United States were prepared to offer reductions of 572 missiles on both sides, he thought his government would find it acceptable. That would mean no cruise or Pershing-II deployments for NATO, and Soviet reductions of SS-20s to a level of 120 in Europe. The Soviet ceiling was thus no longer tied to the number of British and French missiles - a key term of the walk-in-the-woods formula. Kvitsinsky made this explicit by suggesting that those missiles could be dealt with in another forum. Nitze sought instructions to allow him to explore the Soviet approach further but was turned down. In the meantime the allies were notified, and Chancellor Helmut Kohl hinted in a television broadcast that the USSR was no longer insisting on having British and French forces taken into account in any INF agreement. This suggestion had the effect of undercutting his SPD opponents, who had been urging compromise on this Soviet demand, but public disclosure of it may have prompted the Soviet government to disown the idea.

The basic terms of trade worked out during the walk in the woods remains the only way to break the deadlock over INF: no Pershing-IIs in return for a ceiling on Soviet IRBMs below the number of SS-20s currently deployed within range of Europe, and a freeze on deployments in the Far East. But neither side has yet addressed the key issue of constraints on further modernisation. These constraints could take one of several forms: a ban on testing or deployment of new nuclear missiles, whether new models of already developed types or new types of missiles, for a limited duration, say, seven years; a ban just on new types; or a limit of one new type for each side. Any of these would effectively trade American deployment of nuclear-armed sea-launched cruise missiles for equivalent limits on Soviet land-based or sea-based nuclear cruise missiles.

With these terms of trade as a starting point, it would be possible to proceed with a discussion of other issues to be resolved in the negotiations. Some of these issues are purely technical; others are political issues in technical guise. It is the latter that this paper addresses.

The Numbers Game

Negotiations put a premium on numerical ceilings, giving them symbolic importance out of all proportion to their consequence for military stability. Numbers do matter, but not the same numbers for both sides, because each side has its own distinctive military rationale for missile deployments.

To gauge from the history of Soviet deployments, Soviet military planners have long-standing target requirements against NATO that have held fairly constant for the past two decades. These requirements were partially satisfied by targeting some of the ICBM force on Western Europe, in addition to SS-4s and SS-5s. Later, however, faced with putting their ICBM force on a diet of SALT, the increased vulnerability of their land-based missiles, and the obsolescence of the SS-4s and SS-5s, Soviet military planners chose to deploy about 225 SS-20s within range of Europe. The initial deployment plan probably called for fewer missiles, but the number may have been increased to take account of potential deployments of GLCM and Pershing-II by NATO, as well as to have a reserve for bargaining purposes in Geneva. Moreover, though all these missiles could strike Europe, at least some had their primary targets elsewhere – the Persian Gulf, the Indian ocean, and China, for instance. Because these missiles would also be covered by any ceiling on forces within range of Europe, Soviet planners may have an incentive to re-assign their targets to forces further east and to redeploy missiles there accordingly.

Unlike Soviet deployments, US deployments in Europe were not needed to satisfy specific targeting requirements; all critical targets were already adequately covered by existing US and NATO forces. Of course, additional targeting requirements can always be generated or else US central systems can be re-allocated to other targets, but target coverage is not the principal criterion for designing ceilings acceptable to NATO. Insofar as the ceiling number is dictated by NATO strategy, it should be high enough to leave some doubt about successful Soviet pre-emption – yet low enough to avoid implications of decoupling. Those parameters may not be easy to satisfy, but primarily the ceiling must satisfy political requirements. It must be high enough to accommodate the location of some missiles in all five basing countries for the purpose of risk-sharing, yet low enough to satisfy popular demands for reduced force levels on both sides. Because GLCMs are configured in flights of 4 TELs or 16 missiles, a minimum of 160 warheads would meet the first criterion; any number sufficiently below 572 to permit reduced levels in all five basing countries would satisfy the second.

Another criterion established by NATO for the ceiling number is the principle of equality in rights and limitations agreed to in its December 1979 decision. This is a political, not a military criterion; the decision expressly disavowed any need to match Soviet deployments on a one-for-one basis. Equality of rights is an easily understood principle. Any alternative would be inconsistent both with the equivalent status of the two negotiating parties under international law and with their real relationship as commensurate powers in the international system. Equality of limitations has a less compelling origin in the negotiating history of SALT: in reaction to the unequal ceilings of SALT I, the United States Senate passed the Jackson amendment stipulating equal limits in any future treaty. European sentiment may find the need for equal ceilings considerably less convincing because of decoupling concerns.

Equality of rights is readily satisfied by an agreement providing for some deployments on both sides. Equality of limitations is somewhat more complicated because of differences in the capabilities, purposes, and operational arrangements of the two sides' missile forces. It also makes a difference whether the units to be equalised are launchers, missiles, or warheads. Launchers would presumably refer to TELs in the case of these mobile systems. Since each TEL carries four GLCMs, but only one SS-20 or Pershing-II, an equal ceiling on TELs would give the United States a marginal numerical advantage. It would also give both sides an incentive to mount additional warheads on each missile. Moreover, in order to meet its targeting requirements, the USSR would likely insist on a ceiling for Europe of 100 to 150 TELs. On the assumption that Pershing-IIs were banned, this ceiling would exceed NATO's planned 116 GLCM TELs except at the lower end of the range. An equal ceiling on missiles, by contrast, would give the USSR a marginal numerical advantage: its SS-20s are MIRVed while Pershing-IIs and GLCMs are not.

Warheads, or more precisely warheads-on-launchers (excluding spare missiles and reloads), are the units of account that most closely approximate a measure of military capability. Equality in warheads-on-launchers, however, would result in a higher ceiling than desirable to satisfy popular desires for reductions, because Soviet targeting requirements are 225 to 400 warheads. A ceiling of more than 572 warheads would also permit tacit compensation for British and French nuclear forces: if an agreement were within reach, European basing countries might consider relaxing the principle of equality of limitations, either formally by accepting unequal ceilings on warheads-on-launchers, or tacitly by making it understood that NATO would not exercise its right to build up to the ceiling.

The choice of particular ceilings matters primarily for the sake of appearances. What the ceiling levels should be and whether they should be equal for the two sides will have a very marginal effect on relative capabilities, or on military stability in Europe. In the absence of radical cuts in central systems, the superpowers will retain thousands of warheads in their strategic arsenals to meet their targeting needs for European security. NATO would benefit from an agreement that provides for a ceiling on Soviet IRBMs at or below their present level and for a modest American deployment. The precise numbers are a secondary consideration. When it comes to appearances, NATO seeks equality at the lowest possible level. Yet it cannot have both equal limits and the lowest possible limits. If it wants to reach an agreement on ceilings, at some point the alliance will have to choose between the two. Opinions may differ between those who prefer to reduce Soviet and NATO deployments below their planned levels and those who insist on equality even if that means relatively higher ceilings.

Mobility and Verification

Whatever the level, once numerical ceilings are in place, verifying the count of missiles becomes critical for sustaining political support for the agreement. Verification provisions are, after all, cooperative measures for threat assessment and response. In their absence there is greater likelihood of wildly exaggerated estimates of the threat and pressure for unilateral corrective or compensatory action, which would upset the political environment if not undo the arms control regime.

It is by now an article of faith in arms control that any agreement be adequately verifiable. Like many an article of faith, however, the adequacy of verification is open to varying interpretation. In order to be adequately verifiable, an INF arms control regime must close off four possible routes for evading the numerical limits it imposes: deployment of more of an existing type of missile; deployment of new types; conversion of existing conventional or shorter-range missiles into the functional equivalents of land-based INF missiles; and deliberate concealment of additional missiles near but not on launchers until ready for use. The task is not to draft provisions proscribing each of these possibilities and then to devise means of verifying the provisions, but to regulate the activities of the two sides in ways that either permit monitoring at various stages or give neither side much incentive to evade.

Deployment of new types of missiles illustrates some of the important issues of verifying an accord on INF missiles. A new missile has to pass through five stages: research, development, testing, production, and deployment. For evasion to succeed, all five stages would have to be concealed. While research, development, and to some extent testing are difficult to monitor, testing and deployment are not. SALT II took advantage of this fact to design provisions constraining activities in these two stages in ways that facilitated monitoring by various means. Yet there is a tension between the desire for tightly drawn provisions to facilitate verification and the desire for more permissive restraints to allow military programmes to proceed unhampered. The SALT II provisions, for instance, are unusually complex because both sides wanted to permit modernisation of existing types within certain limits, as well as to allow deployment of one and only one wholly new type of ICBM. While these provisions effectively prevent either side from conducting an entire test programme – normally 20-30 test launches – for more than one new type, they do not preclude tests of improved versions of existing types – up to a maximum of 12 tests. In practice, neither side is likely to risk deploying a wholly new missile system on the basis of fewer than 12 tests.

Negotiators can draw on the experience of SALT II to modify limitations on INF missile tests. That experience suggests, for instance, that a ban on new types of INF missiles would be easier to monitor than an agreement permitting modernisation. With a ban, only a limited number of tests need be permitted to ensure missile reliability. Without a comparable ban to cover missiles of intercontinental range, however, the USSR could still upgrade its capability against Europe by modernising its central systems.

Some adjustment in the SALT approach to testing may be necessary to cover land-based INF missiles. SALT provisions on ballistic missiles, for instance, take advantage of the inherent conservatism of military organisations: because the armed services are reluctant to deploy weapons that have not been tested to maximum capability, tests usually yield data that are valid indicators of peak performance. Not so for cruise missile range: unlike a ballistic missile it may be given increased range without significantly altering any of its other flight characteristics simply by adding or changing fuel. Although the size of the missile sets ultimate limits on fuel capacity and range, range estimates based on volume alone may only be a rough approximation. The room for doubt may have little military consequence, but it could prove politically nettlesome in NATO if an INF agreement sought to limit cruise missile range. Nevertheless, the SALT provisions, cautiously applied, could be the basis for INF provisions on testing.

By comparison, to ensure verifiable ceilings on INF will require going beyond the precedents set in SALT II. This is especially so in trying to prevent deployment of additional missiles in excess of ceilings. By drawing attention to numbers, ceilings call for a precision in accounting far more demanding than that needed for military assessments. SALT II satisfied this need by means of a 'type' rule and a 'counting' rule. The former stipulates that once a launcher or silo of a given type has been used to launch a MIRVed missile, then all launchers of that type count as if they too contain MIRVed missiles. The counting rule says that a missile counts as MIRVed once it has had a flight test with MIRVs, and that it is assumed to carry the maximum number of warheads with which it was ever flight tested. Paradoxically, these rules, while necessary to meet the strict standards of verifiability demanded by treaty sceptics, occasionally result in more permissive limits - and greater levels of military threat - than might otherwise be the case. Nonetheless, similar rules of accounting will be useful for INF ceilings on warheads-on-launchers: an SS-20 TEL would count three, a GLCM TEL four, and a Pershing-II TEL one.

The fixed location and visibility to satellites of ICBM silos and construction sites for ballistic missile submarines made the task of monitoring launcher numbers relatively easy in SALT II. The mobility of INF launchers, however, makes it essential to obtain agreement on cooperative measures in addition to rules of accounting to make numerical ceilings on INF more verifiable. In framing these cooperative measures the purpose should be to facilitate detection of militarily significant breaches of numerical ceilings, not to validate or falsify counts with a precision significantly more demanding than that required for typical military assessments. Cooperative measures that interfere with operational flexibility are likely to be unacceptable, not only because of Soviet objections but also because of their reciprocal effects on NATO's standard operating procedures.

In counting mobile launchers, it is useful to distinguish among types. Freely roaming mobiles can run and hide over a wide enough area and relocate quickly enough to reduce their vulnerability to attack but do not necessarily have unlimited off-road mobility. Runway mobiles, like the MX in its multiple-protective-shelter basing mode, can move along a constrained path, a road or set of tracks, but cannot range far afield. Tethered mobiles can roam freely over a restricted area or patrol zone in the vicinity of a fixed operating base, which itself cannot be relocated rapidly or temporarily. Soviet SS-20s are loosely tethered; American GLCMs and Pershing-II are more tightly tethered because they are based in more densely settled locations and their operating practices confine them more to base. All are capable of roaming freely but not for a protracted period. All can be temporarily relocated far afield from their operating bases. Rapid relocation in a crisis, however, would strain airlift capabilities beyond existing capacity. As an aid to verification of INF launcher numbers, it will be necessary to 'fence in' all existing patrol zones and declare areas beyond those perimeters off limits to any INF missiles or launchers. The dimensions of each perimeter would depend on operating practices, but for illustrative purposes it could be a circle perhaps 80 km in diameter with its centre on the operating base. Bases would be identified in the agreement. Bases and launchers could be relocated only with prior notification through the Standing Consultative Commission.

To increase confidence in the counts of launchers at or near each operating base may require displaying all launchers on their bases outside their garages or caserns two or three times a year so that they may be monitored by reconnaissance satellites. Launchers detected in the area outside the base perimeter would constitute a violation. Because the missiles would be more vulnerable on display, such 'parades' would not be held at all bases at the same time. It may be possible to arrange them first at one geographic cluster of bases, then another, allowing enough distance between clusters and too short a time interval between parades to permit relocation of launchers. Because parades do interfere with both sides' operating practices, their intrusiveness may make them difficult to negotiate, but this difficulty may be worth the added monitoring confidence. A still more intrusive cooperative measure would be on-site inspection by sensors located at production facilities to count the missiles as they rolled out of assembly areas. Such a mechanism would have little value if additional missiles or modernisation were banned. On-site inspection in the form of visits by qualified observers to pre-designated deployment or production areas, either on a regular basis or upon request, would add little to confidence about the number of INF launchers. Indeed, visits may be harmful because they are more liable than overhead reconnaissance to generate confirmation of compliance when in fact evasion is taking place.

The mobility of land-based INF launchers thus raises difficulties for verifying ceilings but not insuperable ones. So long as effective verifiability is understood to mean a reasonable assurance that militarily significant evasion cannot succeed, the probability of deploying an appreciable number of additional INF missiles, and of testing and deploying wholly new types or substantial modifications of existing types, is acceptably low.

Reloads

Launchers of SS-20s, GLCMs, and Pershing-IIs are all capable of being reloaded within a matter of hours after initial firing. While some analysts talk of rapid reloading, they exaggerate the speed with which refire missiles can be mounted on used TELs and retargeted during a nuclear war. In addition, because the launch of a missile reveals the location of the launcher, operational plans call for the launchers to be relocated immediately after firing, which would add considerably to the time it would take to reload.

Reloads represent an additional threat to both sides, but a very marginal one compared to capabilities for initial use. The other side's missile forces are a primary target for both sides' time-urgent forces. Regardless of which side goes first, few TELs are likely to survive the initial nuclear exchange. Even if some do, and even if the TELs of the side that strikes first escape relatively unscathed, their marginal utility will have declined sharply: an initial nuclear exchange in Europe will leave few valuable targets in place. The low military regard for reloads is apparent in the case of Pershing-II. The fact that reloads would accompany Pershing-II launchers to West Germany received only cursory mention in NATO deliberations; no study seems to have been made on the need for them. When word leaked in West Germany that reloads and spare missiles (264 by one count) were scheduled for deployment there, Bonn sought and won assurances that no more than 108 missiles and 108 warheads would be deployed. The putative military value of reloads is important to keep perspective in assessing the importance of seeking constraints on them through negotiations.

Ceilings on reloads would not be verifiable with present surveillance technology because they are small enough and portable enough to be readily concealed. Any operational plan for their use in the event of war would require concealed locations away from operating bases in order to make survivability possible. Even a cooperative measure forbidding deployment of reloads off-base would add little to monitoring confidence; reloads could be concealed on bases and might be hard to distinguish from spares used for training and replacement. A ban on exercises of reloading could be unenforceable because such exercises bear considerable resemblance to removal and replacement practices in routine maintenance. Finally, on-site inspection on a challenge basis would not suffice to provide high-confidence monitoring, and insistence on such a provision would almost certainly be interpreted as an effort to block agreement.

The reload issue is likely to be exploited by those opposed to any agreement, because constraints on reloads are likely to be undevisable and unnegotiable or unverifiable. The preoccupation with numbers will also tempt those who see the NATO deployment as inadequate to exaggerate the magnitude of the reload threat. Yet it is warheads-on-launchers, not reloads, that pose the principal threat. Insistence on constraining a marginal threat might jeopardise agreement constraining the main threat. Whether to do so is a judgment best left to European governments, mindful of the need to keep their eyes upon the doughnut and not upon the hole.

Medium- and Short-Range Missiles and Artillery

INF is arbitrarily defined to include all systems capable of delivering nuclear weapons at distances of 1000 km or more. Both American and Soviet arsenals, however, also include nuclear-capable missiles and artillery with ranges of less than 1000 kilometres. Many of NATO's are located in forward positions where they are vulnerable to pre-emption or to overrunning by conventional means alone, thus contributing to crisis instability. The circumstances under which they might prove usable are hard to divine. The dual capability of many of these systems may indeed detract from NATO's conventional deterrent.

Soviet shorter-range forces pose a threat of breakout, the circumvention of INF limitations in the event of crisis. Deployed in forward locations in Eastern Europe, they would be in a position to perform some of the missions of SS-20s against many Continental targets. NATO's shorter-range weapons cannot achieve the equivalent against the USSR; only Pershing-I, moved to locations far forward, could reach the Soviet frontier, but it could not reach far enough beyond it to threaten strategic targets. NATO makes much of this geographic asymmetry. Perhaps too much. Even though NATO's shorter-range forces cannot do to the USSR what equivalent Soviet weapons can do to NATO, they can wreak some havoc in Eastern Europe. While Soviet sources acknowledge the presence of short-range nuclear-capable weapons in Eastern Europe, they deny that medium-range ones have been stationed outside Soviet territory. Nuclear warheads for even the short-range weapons are probably not generally deployed forward either. The difficulty of ascertaining the locations of the warheads may be attributable to Soviet concealment practices, but another possibility is that the USSR may be reluctant to store them where they are not wanted or are less than secure.

Nonetheless, any arms control agreement would have to take into account the marginal threat of breakout through redeployment. This agreement need not take the form of numerical ceilings - the number and variety of shorter-range systems and the difficulty of verifying their numbers would probably lend false concreteness to any ceilings. Moreover, attempts to negotiate such ceilings would only delay the withdrawal and disengagement of short-range forces, which NATO should undertake in its own security interests. Cooperative measures prohibiting exercises in forward-deployed postures are also impracticable. These systems are part of both sides' conventional capabilities, and as such, they have military value mainly within range of the battlefront. Any differences between nuclear and non-nuclear modes of exercising these systems may not be readily observable. A nuclear-free zone along the lines proposed by the Palme Commission is another possibility, but the current difficulty in ascertaining the location of Soviet nuclear warheads may be a measure of the difficulty of monitoring such a provision. The marginal threat of breakout might also be contained by a noncircumvention provision on the model of SALT II, coupled with an agreement that any additional deployment or modernisation of medium- or short-range missiles and artillery would constitute circumvention.

Geographic Scope

Thus far the discussion has focused on limiting land-based INF missiles in Europe, but the NATO position is that any limitations on INF missiles must apply worldwide. The USSR, at least in its public posture, initially maintained that the negotiations must be confined to Europe, although the Nitze-Kvitsinsky dialogues indicated Soviet willingness to broaden the geographic scope of an agreement. In October 1983 the Soviet side formally modified its position saying that it would unilaterally halt deployment of additional SS-20s in the eastern USSR upon entry into force of an agreement covering Europe and contingent on no change in the 'strategic situation' in Asia.

NATO's principal stated rationale for global limits is the threat of breakout - that the USSR, if otherwise unconstrained, could deploy as many missiles as it wanted in the far eastern USSR only to relocate them within range of Western Europe in the event of a crisis. Cooperative measures fencing in patrol zones would restrict non-crisis redeployment, but some risk would remain that in a crisis and in the absence of some combination of numerical limits and patrol zones for Soviet deployments at Novosibirsk and further east, relocation could greatly increase the numbers of SS-20s aimed at Europe. Conceivably, too, the United States would remain free to deploy additional missiles at home for relocation to Europe under similar circumstances. The breakout threat should not be exaggerated, however; the USSR already has enough missiles within range of Europe to meet its targeting requirements, so relocation would be needed only if deep cuts were negotiated in that missile force. Moreover, rapid relocation would demand diversion of most airlift capacity from other tasks, to the point of virtually exhausting present capabilities. Yet the ability to relocate rapidly some INF missiles could aggravate crisis instability possibilities already present.

To advance the NATO position, the United States has formally proposed equal ceilings at the lowest possible level on land-based INF missiles regardless of their location. Were it to seek a worldwide ceiling below the level of planned NATO deployments, the United States would be trying to cut the Soviet SS-20 force in half. In order to maintain SS-20s in the Far East, the USSR would have to reduce SS-20s in Europe to a number below that of NATO. Such a ceiling stands no chance of acceptance in Moscow. Alternatively, were the United States to seek a much higher global ceiling, one requiring at most a modest reduction in current Soviet deployments, the ceiling number would seem awkwardly high for public presentation in Europe. Were NATO to indicate its intention not to avail itself of the right to build up to the ceiling, however, this formula might tacitly compensate the USSR for British and French forces.

Even if applying a single ceiling to both Europe and the Far East turns out to be non-negotiable, there are still sound security reasons for placing some limits on Soviet far eastern deployments. One form of limit might be to ban rapid relocation, but it might prove hard to negotiate and even harder to monitor. Another might be separate ceilings for deployments beyond the range of Europe. These ceilings could be relatively permissive - indeed they would have to be in order to avoid putting the United States in the awkward position of having to withstand European pressures for agreement on behalf of Japan and China. Yet they must not worsen the threat to Japan and the rest of Asia. The path Nitze explored with Kvitsinsky provides a useful way out: an agreement to freeze existing deployments in the far eastern USSR, which would not allow the USSR to redeploy eastward any SS-20s in excess of the European ceiling. That such a provision would limit the threat in the Far East and would not fix Europe's problem at Asia's expense should be acceptable to Japan and others. That the ceilings would not apply only to Europe should be welcomed in Europe as blurring any connotation of a Eurostrategic balance.

Aircraft

The formula for geographic scope need not and should not set a precedent for aircraft. Because they are not just mobile but are readily relocatable in a way that INF missiles are

not, aircraft require ceilings that would apply worldwide.
The USA and the USSR have a variety of aircraft that could deliver nuclear weapons against targets throughout Eastern and Western Europe. The US arsenal includes 172 F-111 and 176 F-4 fighter-bombers on air bases in Europe; 68 A-6 and A-7 fighter-bombers on US carriers permanently on assignment in European waters; and 63 FB-111 fighter-bombers based in the United States that the USSR considers designated for NATO use. The USSR has 100 Backfire, 310 Badger, and 125 Blinder bombers and 550 Fencer fighter-bombers[4]. While all are classified as dual-capable, not every plane of each type may be wired for nuclear delivery or have crews trained for nuclear roles. Other classes of aircraft, Soviet Floggers, Fitters, and Fishbeds and US F-4s, for instance, also have the potential to carry nuclear bombs. Both sides also have aircraft outside the theatre that have the potential to perform nuclear missions if redeployed to Europe - US carrier aircraft and Soviet fighter-bombers based in the Far East, for example. American allies in Europe - and by some accounts, Soviet allies too - have comparable aircraft at their disposal.

Even a glance at the variety of aircraft indicates that negotiating a ceiling will be a complex endeavour. Differing estimates of ranges, capabilities, and roles and missions, and consequently differing assessments of the aircraft balance, make the terms of trade hard to calculate. A notorious example is the Soviet Backfire bomber. While estimates of Backfire's range vary, it has been the US view that these aircraft can reach targets in the continental United States, and with mid-air refuelling fly two-way missions there. The United States succeeded in SALT II in getting a commitment from the USSR in the form of a note handed over by President Brezhnev on 16 June 1979, that the USSR did 'not intend to give this airplane the capability of operating at intercontinental distances' by increasing its radius or equipping it for in-flight refuelling, and that it would not increase its production rate, then 30 planes a year. Regardless of its intercontinental potential, the Backfire is capable of nuclear attacks against the periphery as well as the heart of Western Europe, and is deployed both on land and at sea with units responsible for that mission.

For aircraft of any given type it is also hard to distinguish in practice between those in nuclear and those in non-nuclear roles for the purposes of verifying any ceiling. Externally observable design features might be added to facilitate that task, but they would not necessarily be functionally related. Differentiation on the basis of training practices would be hard to monitor. One way out might be a type rule stipulating that any aircraft type in which crews have been trained for nuclear delivery is by definition nuclear-capable and will be included in the ceiling. This method, however, could have perverse effects on NATO's conventional capability, because most nuclear-capable aircraft still have the primary mission of conventional bombing. An additional type rule would have to be applied if nuclear bombloads were to be limited, as in President Andropov's 3 May 1983 proposal. This rule might prove difficult to frame in view of the claim by both sides that many planes in the category of nuclear-capable aircraft are not presently equipped or manned for nuclear roles.

In the negotiations to-date, the two sides have stressed differences over the aircraft balance and which aircraft, if any, are to be included in any agreement. Neither side has been wholly consistent in its approach, in part because any consistency can be shown to be somewhat foolish. Soviet negotiators have wavered between making substantive arms control proposals on aircraft and scoring political debating points on 'forward-based systems', which in Soviet parlance refers to all US emplacements and aircraft in Europe. As such the phrase has the connotation, unacceptable to the United States and its allies, that only American aircraft, not Soviet, are at issue. The USSR had initially proposed limiting each side to 300 medium-range delivery vehicles, which would impose severe constraints on American land-based and carrier-based aircraft. Yet in his October 1983 interview, Andropov opened the way to a resolution of the issue, indicating Soviet readiness to 'establish for the USSR and NATO equal total levels of medium-range aircraft in a mutually acceptable quantitative range which could be substantially different from the range proposed by us previously.'

Although prepared to engage Soviet negotiators on the issue, the United States initially took the position that the principal threat to military stability in Europe comes from missiles and that inclusion of aircraft would only complicate the already difficult task of obtaining an agreement to limit that threat. Yet the US position made much of the Backfire threat to Europe. While it continued to introduce Backfire into its discussion of heavy bombers – in START rather than in INF negotiations – the United States counted Backfire in its tally of INF as well. Then in September 1983 the United States proposed equal limits on certain unspecified types of land-based aircraft.

How might the aircraft issue be resolved? One possibility is to set aircraft aside in the current stage of INF talks but state in a protocol to any agreement that they would be dealt with in a subsequent stage. However, this is almost certainly insufficient to satisfy the long-standing Soviet position that there be limits on US aircraft threatening the USSR from bases in Europe. Another possibility is to ignore aircraft in the limitations, except for a non-circumvention proviso applying specifically to medium bombers and fighter-bombers and banning any increase or modernisation of those forces. A third possibility is a ceiling.

Any ceiling would have to apply worldwide because aircraft are readily relocated. One possible ceiling would limit all nuclear-capable aircraft with a range over, say, 1000 kilometres. The ceiling number would have to be permissive enough to satisfy arguments about the incommensurability of the two sides' forces. From NATO's standpoint, short-range US aircraft based in Western Europe could not strike the USSR, but short-range Soviet aircraft using bases in Eastern Europe could reach NATO. From the Soviet standpoint, improvements or increases in allied capabilities would allow the West to circumvent any ceiling, but too high a ceiling would raise objections that it did little to constrain the threat.

Perhaps the best solution is along the lines explored by Nitze and Kvitsinsky: to single out roughly comparable aircraft on both sides and limit them. The most obvious **quid pro quo** is limits on Backfire, Blinder, and Badger on the Soviet side, in return for limits on F-111s and/or FB-111s on the American. But this would require both sides to modify their negotiating positions. A partial deal would reflect the current state of the military balance of nuclear-capable aircraft in Europe, which is generally a steady one with no significant trends and, apart from Backfire, no prospect of dramatic developments on either side.

Yet from its own strategic perspective, NATO may want to consider eliminating dual-capable aircraft altogether by converting them to purely conventional roles and missions. The rationale for this is not based primarily on arms control considerations but on the perverse consequences of dual capability for NATO's own conventional strength. Somewhat paradoxically, putting the issue of dual-capable aircraft on the negotiating table may deflect NATO from this course.

Conventional Cruise Missiles

Whether they carry nuclear or conventional warheads, GLCMs are to all outward appearances identical. Thus another way, at least in theory, of circumventing ceilings on land-based INF missiles is to deploy conventionally-armed cruise missiles (CCMs) which have the potential to be converted into their nuclear-armed look-alikes by altering their payloads.

If the objective were only to frame a verifiable arms

control agreement, the remedy for CCMs would be to ban them or else to include them in the ceiling by defining any land-based cruise missile as nuclear-capable regardless of how it was in fact armed. Yet verification is not the only objective; indeed it is not an objective in and of itself but only a means to another end, NATO's security through a reduced likelihood of nuclear war. And in the view of some, deploying CCMs would do more for this objective than banning them. Doubtless, CCMs are being oversold, but the salient fact remains that many Europeans, not only in army circles but also among experts in the anti-nuclear movement, regard them as the technological fix that will make high-confidence conventional defence of Europe possible.

Is a workable set of constraints on the breakout threat posed by CCMs conceivable? Yes, provided that the threat posed is understood to be a modest one. The incremental advantage of converting CCMs to nuclear use in a war in Europe would be marginal, because the nuclear arsenals of both sides are more than ample to blanket European targets under prevailing conditions. Three provisions in an INF agreement should suffice to reduce the breakout threat still further. One would require platforms for CCMs to be readily distinguishable from TELs carrying nuclear-armed GLCMs. These externally observable design features would not, strictly speaking, be functionally related. A second provision would prohibit CCM carriers from being exercised in a nuclear capacity. A third would ban the carriers from being collocated with nuclear GLCMs. The first provision is essential; the other two might prove beneficial.

Sea-Launched Cruise Missiles

In some ways, sea-launched cruise missiles pose problems analogous to those posed by CCMs. Some SLCMs are already deployed; others are in testing. America's nuclear-armed version is outwardly indistinguishable from some of its conventionally armed ones. And conventionally-armed SLCMs could, at least theoretically, be converted into nuclear weapons by replacing their warheads, thereby posing a threat of breakout in wartime.

There the similarities to CCMs end. The CCM problem is a minor one in military terms; the SLCM problem is not. Because of the numbers each side could deploy, to allow procurement of SLCMs to proceed unconstrained while limiting land-based INF missiles, would be to leave a loophole of some military significance that critics of any agreement would be quick to seize upon in their opposition. Yet limitations on SLCMs are hard to devise. The platforms are not designed to provide a clear basis for distinguishability, and once the missiles are deployed aboard ships or submarines, counting them becomes difficult. Finally, the military utility of nuclear SLCMs is open to more serious reservation than is that of their conventional cousins. Even so, an INF arms control regime that imposed limits on land-based missiles without constraining nuclear land-attack SLCMs could have the perverse effect of redirecting the nuclear arms competition to sea.

A ban on all SLCMs is impracticable; both sides have already deployed conventional variants and have sound security reasons for doing so. A ban on all nuclear-armed SLCMs would require the antiship versions it already has, but the ban would run into monitoring difficulties because of the indistinguishability of nuclear from conventional types. There are no externally observable differences between them, at least in the case of the US Tomahawk; if some way were found to design features differentiating them, especially for the purpose of monitoring, their effectiveness would remain in doubt. SLCMs pose much more of a verification nightmare than their land-based look-alikes, the GLCMs. It is easier to change warheads on SLCMs and to exercise them in nuclear form once they are on board ships or submarines out of view of national technical means of verification. Nuclear arming could be precluded at the point of testing, but both sides' programmes have already passed that point. On-site inspection, in the form of sensors aboard ships or attached to each SLCM, might be able to distinguish between nuclear and conventional variants, but even if such sensors were developed, getting either the Soviet or the American navy to accept them would be an arduous negotiating task, and a time-consuming one.

One possible solution may be to ban nuclear-armed SLCMs with ranges in excess of 600 km. Such a ban would minimise interference with existing deployments, but would prohibit both sides from deploying new SLCMs they have already been testing. Furthermore, such limitations might not be inviolate: SLCMs tested at ranges under 600 km might be capable of flying greater distances, though perhaps not more than one order of magnitude greater.

A ban on nuclear SLCMs under present technological conditions may be harder to verify than alternative forms of numerical constraints. Monitoring a count of nuclear SLCMs aboard any ship is very difficult because they are small enough to be stowed away without being detected. Yet the number of SLCMs could be indirectly limited in a militarily meaningful way by imposing ceilings on their platforms - ships and submarines - and on the number of nuclear SLCMs each may carry. The limits would be analogous to those imposed on ALCM carriers in SALT II. Carriers of nuclear SLCM could be made distinguishable from other ships or submarines by functionally-related observable differences in the form of uniquely configured facilities for storing and launching the missiles. But although the cannisters to hold Tomahawk are no longer than those accommodating other SLCMs and thus easily recognisable, the cannisters for the nuclear and conventional versions are identical and would have to be made distinguishable. In addition, limits could be placed on the number of torpedo tubes on submarines carrying nuclear SLCMs.

An alternative limit, but one that would interfere with both sides' programmes, would be to set upper limits on the size of torpedo tubes and lower limits on the size of nuclear SLCMs to prevent them from being fired from such tubes. Such limits would facilitate counting somewhat by forcing nuclear SLCMs to be stored and launched from unique and thus more countable containers. Monitoring might be further aided by type rules covering the classes of vessels carrying nuclear SLCMs or by severe numerical limits on such ships. Distinguishing these SLCM carriers from other ships has been made more feasible by the special procedures both superpowers have adopted for handling nuclear weapons, at least some of which may be observable.

This combination of cooperative measures and counting rules would effectively raise the chances of detection for any party trying to evade an agreement by putting nuclear SLCMs aboard ships that are barred from carrying them. Although the provisions would not entirely prevent either side from slipping additional nuclear SLCMs onto designated nuclear SLCM carriers, the military advantage of additional SLCM reloads would be marginal. If their numbers were sufficiently limited, such ships would themselves be prime targets in a war and would be unlikely to launch more than a salvo or two before they were destroyed or disabled.

The prospect of limitations could lead to a thorough consideration of the military utility of nuclear SLCMs in comparison to their conventional variants. Limitations would give both navies some incentive to economise on the number and types of ships carrying nuclear SLCMs in order to leave most of their fleets free to load up with conventional ones.

The superpowers are fast approaching the end of a strategic environment relatively free of nuclear land-attack SLCMs. The initial operating capability for the American versions was estimated to be 1984, although technical problems have caused the date to be put back. The Soviet versions will not be far behind. Rather than rushing headlong to stuff nuclear SLCMs into every available ship, the two sides could use the delay to undertake net assessments of the effects of such deployments on the superpower balance and on military stability, and to consider ways of constraining the SLCM threat by arms control. A moratorium on deployments to work out such arrangements could be mutually advantageous.

British and French Nuclear Forces

The United States is not, of course, the only member of NATO to have nuclear weapons in Europe; Great Britain and France also possess them. The USSR has insisted that these weapons be 'taken into account' in any agreement on INF, something the United States has refused to do. The phrase has at least two meanings. For the moment it seems to mean that the existence of these forces requires no new American INF missiles to be deployed in Europe. At some later date, however, the USSR may shift to demand formal numerical compensation for these forces, other limits, or the right to add to its forces once Britain and France MIRV theirs. That the Soviet position is intended primarily for political effect and not to achieve a particular negotiating result is evident. The USSR seeks limitations only on American missiles and has not attempted to draw Britain and France into negotiations, which is the only way to achieve limits on their weapons. A Tass commentator made the Soviet position unusually explicit in January 1983 when he told a French broadcast audience[5]:

> the Soviet side has not tried – nor is it trying – to discuss French and British nuclear weapons at the Soviet-American talks. The Soviet Union does not propose limiting or reducing the nuclear forces of France or Great Britain. If the USSR and the United States come to an agreement in Geneva on the reduction of nuclear weapons in Europe, not a single provision of such an agreement would impose obligations on France or Great Britain. At the same time, the USSR cannot omit from the sum total of nuclear weapons those possessed by Great Britain and France, because these are not neutral countries, but allies of America in the Atlantic pact. They are nuclear powers whose missiles are capable of reaching Soviet territory.

On 23 February 1981 President Brezhnev spoke of drawing other nuclear powers into talks 'in due time'.

In both SALT I and SALT II Soviet negotiators argued that British and French systems be taken into account. They also sought a non-transfer provision prohibiting the United States from passing on missile technology to its allies. The United States successfully resisted these demands. The USSR has taken a similar position in INF, but it was slow to tie proposed ceiling levels to the specific numbers in allied forces. The walk-in-the-woods formula also notably omitted any mention of compensation to the USSR for these forces, as did Kvitsinsky's 13 November 1983 approach. These are not the moves of negotiators who deem an issue fundamental to their security and the **sine qua non** of any settlement.

There is not much merit to granting formal compensation for British and French missiles on security grounds. Andropov's December 1982 proposal to reduce Soviet missiles in Europe to equal those of the British and French implies that British and French forces, along with some American aircraft and other nuclear forces committed to NATO, are all Europe needs to counter Soviet forces, and that any supplement to the American deterrent is unnecessary. In this light, any formal inclusion of British and French nuclear forces as part of the US ceiling, especially on a one-for-one basis, could not avoid the impression of decoupling. Moreover, when Soviet bean counters tally up what they need to counter the strategic weapons arrayed against them, the number they add in for Britain and France bears no particular relationship to the 162 missiles or 140 or 120 they propose as a ceiling. All but 18 of the French and British missiles are SLBMs on just nine submarines. These submarines cannot be attacked by SS-20s unless they are in port. Even if all other British and French nuclear forces, as well as command-and-control and other nuclear facilities, were targeted by SS-20s (and there are indications that Soviet planners intend to use ICBMs for this purpose), the number of SS-20s required would be far less than 162 or 140 or 120 - or 486, 420, or 360 if warheads rather than launchers were the unit of account. It makes no difference whether the missiles on the other side are MRVed, as the British SLBMs currently are, or MIRVed, as both British and French SLBMs will eventually be. Finally, it is only in the context of negotiating ceilings on missiles in Europe that the number of British and French weapons stand out. These numbers disappear in the rounding once the intercontinental arsenals of the superpowers are considered. Only if the superpowers were to negotiate substantial reductions in their nuclear arsenals, while Britain and France added substantially to theirs, would the Soviet demand to take those systems into account have some military validity.

At this point, however, the demand for formal compensation serves Moscow's political purpose more than its military strategy. NATO is unlikely to countenance satisfying it. Apart from the demands for formal compensation, however, NATO has no need to retain a number of INF missiles equal to the number of Soviet INF missiles within range of Europe. If European governments were prepared to accept a ceiling which, **de facto** or **de jure**, left the USSR with a few more warheads-on-launchers in Europe than the United States has, so long as the difference bore no relationship to the number of British and French warheads or launchers, the United States should have no trouble agreeing to it. There is some precedent for this approach in SALT I.

Modalities: INF Negotiations and START

That SALT II would be ratified and SALT III would follow promptly was a political premise of INF negotiations from their inception. The December 1979 decision spoke of conducting negotiations on INF 'within the framework of SALT III'. The 'III' was quietly jettisoned soon thereafter, and the term 'SALT' fell into disuse a little later, but the principle of linkage between intercontinental and intermediate-range systems remains.

In the largest sense this principle is less a commitment to formal linkage than an acknowledgement of political and military reality: negotiations to limit INF cannot be conducted wholly apart from negotiations to limit intercontinental systems. Militarily, numerical ceilings on INF are meaningless in the absence of ceilings on nuclear weapons of intercontinental range, because numerically they constitute a small proportion of the superpowers' nuclear inventories. From the perspective of both Soviet and European military planners, moreover, nuclear weapons based in Europe are just as strategic as ICBMs in their ability to put homelands at risk. To the USSR a missile is a missile, to paraphrase Robert McNamara's comment during the Cuban missile crisis, whether it is based in North Dakota or Greenham Common. And from the perspective of European politics, at least the appearance of linkage is essential to underscore coupling. In addition, informal linkage in bargaining is unavoidable; any move at one table by either side is examined for its implications at the other table. This fact of negotiating life takes on institutional embodiment in Washington, where the so-called backstopping groups, bureaucrats who draft the cables of instructions to the negotiators in Geneva, have the same composition for both INF and START. The inevitability of bargaining linkage, even if it does not take a similar institutional form in the USSR will make Soviet negotiators reluctant to conclude an agreement in one forum without at least seeing the outlines of agreement in the other take shape.

Some have proposed merging the two sets of talks in Geneva.

Formal merger would facilitate bargaining linkages between INF and START, a desired result among its proponents, many of them Europeans, who doubt that the West has the leverage to conclude an acceptable agreement in INF alone, or who do not want cruise and Pershing-II missiles even as bargaining chips. Merging the talks would also diminish the visibility of British and French systems, whose numbers stand out only in the INF context. Merger might also ease the Russians' way back to negotiating on INF.

Merger, however, would possibly make concluding an INF agreement hostage to results in START. And because the prospects of a START agreement are not much better than those for INF, merger would redirect European pressure from one forum to the other, a consequence the Reagan administration recognises and resists.

An alternative to formal merger would be to adopt a common ceiling covering both INF and intercontinental weapons. One way to construct such a ceiling would be simply to aggregate the ceilings on nuclear delivery vehicles or warheads negotiated separately in INF and START upon completion of both agreements. This combined aggregate might have some beneficial effect on perceptions: it would demonstrate coupling and would allow the British and French numbers to pale in significance. Other variants of the common ceiling resemble informal merger of the two talks in disguised form. One that has gained considerable currency on both sides of the Atlantic would allow ceilings reached in an interim INF agreement to become subceilings within an equal combined aggregate to be negotiated eventually in START. If the agreement were to allow both sides to trade in intercontinental systems for INF or vice versa, it might facilitate Soviet acceptance of some new NATO deployments at the expense of American central systems. It remains to be seen whether such an approach would be acceptable to the USSR.

Present Prospects

Even with the best of will on both sides, reaching agreement in Geneva remains an arduous task. Both sides are rapidly passing a point of no return. As Tass declared after the Bundestag voted to proceed with deployments, 'The Rubicon has been crossed'. New weapons now being installed and tested threaten to upset the precarious military stability that has prevailed between the two superpowers for two decades. Some of these steps are irreversible; others can be slowed or halted in the next two or three years. If nothing is done to reverse the present direction, the problem of how to prevent nuclear weapons from being used - inadvertently, accidentally or deliberately - will become all the more unmanageable. And the arms control measures of today - trying to preclude the most destabilising developments while holding down the numbers in a verifiable way - will no longer be able to contain instability. At that point leaders on both sides will look back on the past decade with incomprehension and ask why nothing was done to keep the nuclear predicament from becoming more awful.

References

1. M. Mackintosh - quoted by J. Erickson, in 'The Soviet View of Deterrence: a General Survey', Survival, 24 (November-December 1982) 242-51.
2. R.L. Garthoff, 'The Soviet SS-20 Decision', Survival, 25 (May-June 1983), 115 and 118 note 8.
3. See J. Newhouse, 'Arms and Allies', New Yorker (28 February 1983) 70. Also E.V. Rostow in an interview with S. Broening, 'Arms Control - After the Shock', The Sun (Baltimore, 22 February 1983).
4. IISS, The Military Balance, 1983-1984, pp.4-5, 14-15, 120-21.
5. L. Ponomarev, 'Only on the Basis of Equality and Equal Security', Radio Moscow broadcast in French to Europe, 22 January 1983.

22 Disengagement in Central Europe
SVERRE LODGAARD AND PER BERG

Threats to European Security

The global hegemonic struggle of the two superpowers is a major threat to world peace. US efforts to contain the USSR and deny it equal status, and Soviet expansion to escape encirclement and assert itself as second to none, have increased the risk of military confrontation between them.

The force levels in Europe are out of proportion to the international political tension that remains in the region. No unresolved issue could justify activation of the huge arsenals deployed in the area. However, if the global rivalry of the two major powers pushes a severe international crisis beyond its original military confines into a process of horizontal escalation, Europe may be drawn into the conflict. Simultaneous eruption of socio-political instability in some European country — by chance or because someone tries to exploit it for his own political ends — could increase the risk of war. So could the offensive character of military forces in the region, especially in Central Europe. Should deterrence threaten to break down, this would put a military premium on surprise attack and may drive the decision-makers over the nuclear threshold.

In this way, Europe might once again become the main battlefield, not for reasons of its own, but because it serves as the main area of military confrontation in the global hegemonic struggle between the superpowers.

Horizontal escalation

If the major powers begin to fight each other with their own military forces in an area where much is at stake, such as in the Persian Gulf or the Middle East, the conflict could escalate to include Europe, not necessarily because the war gets out of control, but perhaps as a deliberate act by one side or the other. Horizontal escalation — the eventual opening of a new front elsewhere, at an appreciable distance from the original war theatre - is the military element of a comprehensive US strategy of global linkage. This strategy prescribes that Soviet foreign policy advances in one area should be countered by uncompromising behaviour in another. It portrays the possibility of extending conflicts in functional scope as well as in geographic domain. The understanding between Americans and Europeans to prevent non-European conflicts from expanding to Europe seems to have been replaced by a US strategy which subordinates Europe to the requirements of its global policy of containment. At risk is détente and security in Europe[1].

It is not surprising, therefore, that the risk of horizontal escalation has become a dominant threat perception in a number of European countries. It raises, **inter alia**, the prospect of a US response (to Soviet offensives elsewhere) in northern European waters.

This is suggested by the offensive approach to sea control whereby the US Navy would move into so-called high threat areas to bottle up the Soviet northern fleet, and due to the significance of this fleet for Soviet reinforcements, to trouble spots in the Third World. Conversely, peacetime military postures are such that in a number of wartime contingencies, the Soviet Union would have a strong interest in changing the **status quo** in Northern Europe by sudden westward thrusts[2].

The recent US preoccupation with strategies of horizontal excalation presumably enhances the Soviet temptation to pre-empt where the new front is expected to be opened - especially in northern Europe where vital Soviet strategic assets are at stake.

In practice, it is therefore possible that at some stage of conflict the Soviet Union will strike first in anticipation of horizontal escalation by the USA. Whichever side is first, the opening of a new front in the north would be such a dramatic development that further escalation is likely to follow. Then, both sides may try to benefit from surprise attack where conditions seem favourable to them. This is an example of a type of situation in which a Soviet attack in Central Europe could be envisaged.

In a world where two global military powers are engaged in a struggle for hegemony, the adoption of a strategy of horizontal escalation by one is likely to stimulate the development of a similar strategy by the other. There is a strong intrinsic logic in the ongoing globalisation of superpower military doctrines. It seems prudent to assume that, by now, both sides have elaborated contingency plans for horizontal escalation in considerable detail.

Socio-political instability

In Northern Europe, there is no socio-political instability to nurture war. The area is not itself a source of conflict. This is different in Central and Southern Europe. There, socio-political systems in both alliances suffer from considerable instability. Whenever domestic upheavals occur in relative isolation, disconnected from other sources of major power tension, experience indicates that they do not constitute a threat of war between alliances. They are managed within a significant margin of bloc-to-bloc showdown. However, should a revolt occur during a crisis in superpower relations, attempts to exploit it by military measures cannot be ruled out. Or the side with which the uprising unfolds may attack first to fend off weakness - especially if its military posture is an offensive one, well suited for rapid advances into enemy territory. In Central Europe, the weaker side in this connection is the Eastern one, and the WTO maintains a force posture with distinctly offensive features. One of the lessons that history taught the Russians is: if there is another war, see to it that it is fought as far west as possible. Their concern that parts of the armed forces and populations of East European countries might turn against them if alliance warfare is waged on Eastern territories, are important constituent elements of this posture. It is not to be taken as an aggressive intent, but is evidence of the underlying instability of East-West relations.

Military instability

The propensity to open a new front in Central Europe may not depend very much on the overall force level in the area. Neither is it inextricably linked to the notion of a balance between East and West. If we assume for a moment that it is possible to distinguish between offensive capabilities and those which can only be used defensively, stability essentially depends on the relative strength of offence and defence. If both sides have offensive capabilities well in excess of the defensive capabilities of the adversary, the resulting situation would tempt the parties to strike first at times of severe crisis. To a large extent, we already have that kind of situation in Central Europe, as a heritage of Hitler's blitzkreig armies and allied forces structured to regain territory and occupy Germany[3]. Not only have Soviet forces in Eastern Europe distinct offensive features; implementation of the US AirLand Battle doctrine, and introduction of new technologies for deep strikes on enemy follow-on forces by the West will make NATO forces more offensive, too.

We may be on a track from bad to worse on this score - with a piling up of time-urgent targets that make the force relationship more unstable and, consequently, Europe more sensitive to the hegemonic struggle of the major powers. It is against this background that the rationale for constraints in forward areas of the East-West confrontation in Europe appears. Constraints on military activities and force configurations, reducing and eliminating elements which are particularly suited for offensive uses, and which produce pressures for escalation once the war has begun, may slow down the trend and ultimately reverse it. Hence the case for nuclear weapon-free zones in Europe, and regulation of conventional forces in border areas. If we are seriously concerned about military stability, we ought to encourage defensive capabilities rather than offensive ones, do our best to curtail options of surprise attack, and reduce the risk of inadvertent escalation by withdrawal of tactical nuclear weapons.

The Purpose of Disengagement in Central Europe

There are three lines of action that European states may taken in response to horizontal escalation scenarios: foreign policy initiatives to reduce the likelihood of Soviet-American armed conflict in the Third World; control of the military bases and logistic links by which European states could be drawn into these clashes; and measures to reduce the likely gains from striking first, by surprise, in Europe, including means of raising the nuclear threshold[4]. The third is usually considered exclusively within the frame of East-West confrontation in Europe. However, it can be fully understood and appreciated only when considered in the context of superpower rivalry for positions and influence world-wide.

Raising the nuclear threshold

There is widespread agreement that, in the military contingency planning for Europe, nuclear weapons are given too much emphasis. Notwithstanding the deployment of new Eurostrategic arms, measures to raise the nuclear threshold are likely to remain in great demand. NATO's withdrawal of 1000 nuclear warheads, and the announced withdrawal of another 1400 warheads in the coming five years, including atomic demolition mines and warheads for Nike Hercules air defence systems, are steps in that direction. These short range tactical nuclear weapons may have to be used at the very beginning of a conflict, to avoid being overrun, captured or destroyed by the enemy. Not only do they pose a high risk of early use, but they also tend to negate the very essence of the strategy of flexible response. For they would have to be used before NATO's ability to stop a conventional attack by conventional means had been seriously tested[5].

European security would gain from further withdrawal of tactical nuclear weapons to reduce the risk of inadvertent escalation, in particular by reducing the 'use them or lose them' dilemma. This is one main rationale for a functionally designed battlefield nuclear weapon-free zone in Central Europe, as proposed by ICDSI and others[6]. In combination with measures to enhance the credibility of Western conventional defences, preferably by agreed arms reductions and/or a transition to less offensive military postures on both sides, such withdrawal would also reduce the 'use them or get lost' (losing the battle) dilemma.

A large part of the nuclear weapons to be withdrawn from the Western part of such a zone are artillery shells for 155 mm howitzers, normally stored in a few depots, ready to be coupled during a crisis or war to guns deployed near the border. In addition there are smaller numbers of 203 mm shells and warheads for Lance missiles. The Soviet Union seems to have nuclear weapons stored in the GDR and Czechoslovakia. In addition to munitions for nuclear-capable missiles and aircraft, the nuclear weapon depots in these countries may contain nuclear shells for dual-capable 152, 203 and 240 mm artillery pieces.

Reducing the fear of surprise attack

Any proposal for nuclear disengagement has to be combined with some agreement on conventional forces and/or unilateral changes in conventional defences. In an atmosphere of East-West rapprochement, a nuclear disengagement zone might have been tied to a mutual force reduction agreement. However, in a period of high tension, an accord in Vienna must probably wait for substantial improvement of East-West relations.

For that reason, and because of the intricacies of East-West negotiations even under conditions of détente, it is argued that NATO's reliance on nuclear weapons would be more effectively facilitated by unilateral conventional rearmament. However, the new operational concepts and emerging technologies that US and NATO authorities have proposed to this end would make the alliance posture more offensive, and probably lead to countermeasures by the WTO. The US Army AirLand Battle doctrine envisages the use of ground forces for counter-attacks behind enemy lines up to some 150 km beyond the FEBA (forward edge of the battle area). ACE's

(Allied Command Europe) FOFA concept (follow-on forces attack) envisages theatre-wide targeting of massed armour and chokepoints from 25 km to more than 400 km beyond the FEBA in order to distrupt and destroy WTO reinforcing echelons. A US study entitled 'Counter Air 90' discusses the use of ballistic missiles armed with runway cratering submunitions for attacking WTO air bases[7,8]. Implementation and deployment of such concepts and technologies are likely to fall victim to the fallacy of the last step: they seem predicated on the implicit assumption that they will be the last measures to be taken on the scene, as if WTO countermeasures could be disregarded. This is quite illusory; a perceived imbalance cannot be corrected unless the opponent accepts it or is unable to counteract. If he does not, and increases his military effort **pari passu**, the imbalance is likely to persist, but at a higher level of armaments.

These proposals are objectionable also on the grounds that they would increase the number of high-value, time-urgent targets, namely, forces and weapon systems that may inflict great damage unless promptly destroyed. The possessor of deep strike technologies may have to use them at an early and possibly ambiguous phase of conflict; for instance, for ballistic missiles in the counter-air role, a decision to launch within 15-30 minutes of an impending WTO air attack has been cited[8]. They put escalatory pressure on the countries that possess them. Conversely, for the opponent it will be important to pre-empt and to deploy suitable weapons for that purpose. The result is an increase in the number of targets that the military would be prepared to attack at very short notice, with subsequent compression of decision times, and greater military premiums on surprise attack and escalation; in other words, the same kind of problems that nuclear weapons pose, and that have led to the strong demand for withdrawal of such weapons from potential combat areas. There are far too many time-urgent targets in Europe already.

However, a greater obstacle to military détente in Europe is the offensive military strategy of WTO. This strategy is incompatible with arms control objectives, in particular, with the goal of crisis stability. Generally, offensive military postures in combination with the elaboration of horizontal escalation strategies make Europe more sensitive to crises in superpower relations.

In Central Europe, the Soviet forces posture is a constant reminder of the propensity to strike first at a critical stage of conflict. It is impossible for the West, especially for the West Europeans, to accept this Soviet conception of military security. In response, NATO tried to blunt the prospect of a successful WTO attack by armament measures of its own, leading to WTO rearmament to enhance the realism of its strategy. The need to break this mechanism is greater today than ever before. The signs are that both superpowers are trying to strengthen their offensive capabilities while subordinating Europe to the requirements of their global hegemonic struggle.

There is a need, therefore, to combine nuclear disengagement with a rearrangement of conventional forces which would reduce the fear of surprise attack. Removal of nuclear and major conventional arms suitable for offensive uses a certain number of kilometres either side of the dividing line - say, 75-100 km - could be a step in that direction. Tanks, medium and heavy artillery and multiple rocket launchers, bridging equipment, and so on might be withdrawn, leaving only weapons which are unfit for offensive strikes. Within the zone, the parties may still deploy military forces the way they wish - for instance, to delay and distrupt the time schedule of the attacker and to channel him towards special points of defence where the defender has geographical advantages and strong firepower, utilising high tactical mobility for reinforcement at main axes of attack - but subject to restrictions that make them distinctly defensive.

In practice, these forces would not provide many lucrative targets for pre-emption. An attacker would, furthermore, have to move his forces through 150-200 km of more or less congested roads which may be interdicted by the defender at least for the last 75-100 km before coming into direct contact with the major forces of the opponent unless the opponent decides to enter the zone in counteraction. The logistic complications would make surprise attack more difficult, and the attrition inflicted by the forces within the zone would leave the attacker in a reduced state before encountering the major units of the defender. The defender would also have a better opportunity to deploy properly.

The fear of surprise attack would, furthermore, be reduced because a zone arrangement and associated measures would function as an early-warning system, not only by increasing the warning time: in a tense situation, violation of international agreements would be seen as an unambiguous sign of aggressive intent, speeding up decision-making on the other side. This applies to the Western alliance in particular, because it has a greater number of member states and a less monolithic structure than the WTO. Awareness of this may restrain the parties from initiating military offensives in Europe, improving the chances of crisis management.

If it can be convincingly argued that such a zone would make it easier, and not more difficult, for the West to stop a conventional attack by conventional means only, it might attract political interest on both sides.

The Modalities of a Disengagement Zone

Restrictions

Dual-capable artillery units constitute a significant part of the conventional firepower. So, how can they be removed from the zone without at the same time making conventional defence much more difficult? The question leads to another argument for extending the restrictions into the conventional field, by removing major conventional systems suitable for offensive operations.

A 20-tonne weight limit might be set for armoured vehicles, and a 100 mm calibre limit on artillery, rockets and missiles, with the exception of short-range anti-tank and anti-air missiles. With present nuclear technologies, this would exclude dual-capable artillery from the zone. In addition, there should be some limitations on the range of surface-to-air missiles, so that they cannot put the opponent's peace-time surveillance and monitoring aircraft at risk. If such aircraft are to operate along the border, air defences would have to be limited to point-defence systems of a range of 10 km or so; however, given the 'not-too-stringent' verification requirements and the capabilities of modern surveillance systems, aircraft circling just outside one's own limitation zone might do. The range restrictions could, therefore, be less severe - some 75-100 km - allowing systems below the SA-10/Patriot class.

To reinforce the non-provocative nature of the arrangement, other restrictions could be considered, such as limitations on the total number of standing troops in the zone, and maximum 'out of garrison' movement within a given time period.

Transarmament within the zone

Within the parameters set by these restrictions (and those that may be applied by the EDC and MFR talks) each party should be at liberty to rearrange its military posture according to its own doctrinal preferences. The modes of defence - both technical and operational - should be well diversified, to make enemy countermeasures difficult.

Armaments

The weight limit of 20 tonnes put on armoured vehicles,

limits the degree of protection that can be achieved. This applies in relation to discrete anti-armour weapons; near misses by indirect high explosive bombardment, as well as small arms fire, could still be protected against. Thus, there could be an important role for light armour within the zone.

To a certain extent, the limits on protection may be compensated for by a combination of fixed fortifications and fieldworks on the one hand, and reduced detectability - through dispersion, camouflage, deception - on the other. This points to the need for greatly enhanced tactical mobility with maximum utilisation of terrain features such as forests and urbanised terrain. It is a question of making virtue of necessity, both tactical (light infantry), operational (light armour) and strategic (rapid reinforcements, especially to the flanks).

The losses in firepower resulting from the withdrawal of medium and heavy artillery could be filled both from the short and the long ends of the range spectrum. Short-range precision-guided munitions (PGM) - both anti-tank and anti-air - should be proliferated throughout the force structure. It is important to develop a wide variety of types with respect to range, guidance, and kill mechanism, so as to make it more difficult for the enemy to devise appropriate countermeasures. These discrete-target PGMs might be supplemented by small-calibre multiple rocket launchers for area-coverage and rapid laying of minefields. They could, furthermore, be reinforced by heavier fire support from systems deployed outside the zone. Such weapons are presently being deployed under the general term 'deep strike'. These emerging technologies raise serious arms control implications, especially as regards crisis instability and pre-emption incentives[7,8]. However, insofar as such weapons will in fact be developed, deployed and function according to plans, the further away from the front line they are deployed the better. Deployed in the rear, they would place additional risks on the offensive options of the adversary, while alleviating associated arms control concerns. In practice, this may be another case of making as much virtue out of necessity as possible.

Organisation and operational tasks

Since the restrictions apply primarily to arms, the organisation and operational doctrine of the forces in the zone will to a large extent be determined by the armaments that are available. The force structure is likely to contain at least these three main elements:

(1) Air-mechanised forces.

This would combine VTOL (vertical take-off and landing) aircraft for attack, reconnaissance and transportation with light (air-portable) armoured vehicles. In the preliminary phase of war, their main task would be to act as a screening force, identifying main enemy axes of attack. Later, they would act as a channelling and harassment force, in constant contact with the enemy. They would inflict some attrition, and force the enemy to deploy for combat rather than in marching order, delaying and disrupting his battle plans.

(2) Light infantry.

This would be a high-quality covering force deployed in close terrain, denying the enemy easy passage through towns, villages, forest, and the like.
Organisationally, (1) and (2) may be based on multinational brigades at operational level with semi-autonomous companies as the basic tactical unit. Such reorganisation - with larger numbers of smaller sub-units - would pose severe command and control problems. Logistic streamlining and improvements in C^3 could arguably facilitate the abolishing of intermediate command levels (divisions and battalions) as well as the establishment of multinational brigades. Multinational brigades would ensure alliance risk-sharing much more realistically than the present, largely fictitious, concept of national corps sectors.
Both (1) and (2) would have the target acquisition and communications equipment necessary to call on 'deep strikes' from the rear. Their low electromagnetic signature, high mobility and dispersed mode of operations would minimise collateral friendly losses from such long-range fire support, as will the accuracies achieved by means of satellite navigation and position-fixing.

(3) Territorial militia.

Rapidly mobilisable and equipped with PGMs, squads and platoons of 'home guards' could cover virtually the entire zone, protecting against special sabotage forces, identifying and possibly containing airborne operations, as well as inflicting a certain level of attrition on the advancing ground forces. In view of present demographic trends in both alliances, any exploitation of the mobilisation potential would probably be welcome.

It should be underlined that the forces deployed within the zone are not expected to stop a major enemy attack by themselves. Rather, they should identify axes of advance; 'delay, disrupt, and destroy' advancing enemy forces, leaving them in no fit state to encounter the defender's operational reserves of heavy mechanised counter-attack units. If successful, they will serve as an 'anvil' to set the attacker up for the counter-attack of the mechanised 'hammer'[9].

C^3I

In a modern, fluid battlefield, maintenance of intact C^3 facilities is vital, both for the attacker and the defender. However, technology (such as fibre optics), distance, and peacetime preparations all serve to make this a somewhat more feasible task for the defence. The key factors are coordination and invulnerability, both pointing to the need for redundancy at all levels.

As far as intelligence is concerned, it is important to distinguish between surveillance and monitoring during peacetime, and actual target acquisition and designation during war. The first requirement could best be satisfied by satellites and manned aircraft; the latter tasks are better left to larger numbers of expendable remotely piloted vehicles.

Disengagement and Military Détente

The spirit of this proposal is not the need for a single adjustment of a rather static and reasonably well functioning European security system. Europe needs a more ambitious policy of military détente, centering on crisis stability. Therefore, the idea is not only to elaborate a disengagement scheme in its own right, but to suggest a zone arrangement that might become a step towards a more comprehensive withdrawal of nuclear arms, adoption of consistent policies of no-first-use, and conversion of conventional force postures to become unambiguously non-provocative. These are the corner-stones of a policy of military détente in Europe. They are all on the political agenda: nuclear disengagement, no-first-use and measures to reduce the fear of surprise attack, have become the main issues of European debate on military security in the 1980s. They are the **leitmotifs** of the disengagement zone suggested by us. A zone arrangement in the centre of Europe should signify a policy of military détente in embryo; it might then become as important for the trends that it sets as for the absolute significance of its provisions.

Both Western and Eastern security may gain from abolishing reliance on nuclear arms to deter or defeat a conventional attack, or to accomplish other objectives than deterring the hostile use of nuclear weapons by maintaining a credible threat of nuclear retaliation. Nuclear war-fighting can in no way be portrayed as meaningful defence. The moment NATO's first-use policy were carried into effect, it would have failed, because Europe would then be subject to destruction rather than defence. It is not surprising, therefore, that NATO has never agreed on guidelines for a follow-on action in case an initial nuclear use did not succeed in persuading the adversary to stop hostilities. Neither has the fear subsided that any use of nuclear weapons would escalate into all-out nuclear war. The credibility of the first-use doctrine is, therefore, questionable also when seen from the US end of the Alliance. The deterrent effect of a doctrine which is largely incredible, and which is likely to deter the West Europeans as much as the Soviets at the time of crisis and war, is weak. A force posture based on no-first-use of nuclear weapons and a stronger conventional defence may constitute an equally powerful deterrent, and certainly a more sensible means of defence should deterrence break down.

The credibility of NATO's conventional forces can, in principle, be enhanced in three ways: by rearmament, transarmament and disarmament. An agreement on arms reductions would be preferable. Failing that, a transition towards more effective, but clearly non-provocative, forces would be second best. The rearmament alternative - essentially more of the same plus eventually more offensive operational concepts sustained by 'emerging' technologies - is questionable not only because it is prone to the fallacy of the last step, but also because the Soviet Union may take it to mean that the United States would be more prepared to take risks in Europe. If NATO's threshold for the use of nuclear weapons is raised while the conventional forces are made more capable for offence, the Soviet Union may read this as an effort by the United States to establish greater politico-military scope of action in the event of a crisis[10]. In the past, the USSR feared that there may be circumstances in which the USA States would try to fight a limited nuclear war for limited political objectives, that is, limited to Europe. In a situation of approximate parity, not only in strategic but also in tactical warfighting capabilities, such a change may be seen as a convenient adaptation to contemporary military circumstances, serving the same political end.

The disengagement advocated by us is, therefore, a step towards greater reliance on **deterrence by defence** in the European security system. There would still be an element of **deterrence by retaliation** in it, but confined to second-strike capabilities deterring others from using nuclear means of warfare. Even on the best of assumptions, some such capability will remain for the foreseeable future - not because the other side is assumed to harbour aggressive intent, but because the parties are unwilling to **rely** on the good intent of the adversary.

Nuclear deterrence is an imperfect security arrangement. It presupposes that the actors are rational, but it does not itself breed rationality. Rather, it breeds fear, like any other military force that can be effectively used for aggression. While conventional forces can be made more or less unfit for attack into enemy territory, nuclear deterrence by retaliation means that the capability to inflict unacceptable damage on the opponent is retained. This is something the parties would have to live with, also under conditions of military détente. Mutual reassurance of non-aggressive employment plans can be given by unambiguous deployment and declaratory policies, and by arms control accords and verification techniques. The breeding of rationality, can, moreover, be enhanced by improved channels of political communication, and by interaction and cooperation in civilian sectors. Hence, the security significance of the CSCE framework as an instrument for accommodating the policies of different countries and groups of countries, and for facilitating more comprehensive and better organised East-West cooperation in economic, technological, cultural and other fields.

Disengagement and Political Change

Historical evidence strongly suggests that because of the overriding importance of nuclear weapons, both as military means and as policy instruments, political change to overcome the bloc division of Europe requires a disengagement of the nuclear powers. Disengagement of conventional forces would serve the same end[11].

In Central Europe, the desire to overcome the **status quo** is tied to the German question. Closer relations between the two states of the same nation presupposes a parallel change in the military confrontation between East and West. Denuclearisation of the two German states would be a precondition for any solution to the German problem, whether on the basis of neutrality or of a confederation between them. However, in elaborating the concept of Ostpolitik, Bonn explicitly ruled out neutrality. And the salient principle of non-singularity is applied both ways: on the one hand, the nuclear burden should be shared among the allies and not fall exclusively on the FRG; on the other hand, singling out the two Germanies for exclusive denuclearisation is also objectionable. A zone extending 300 km either side would just about cover the two German states (and part of Czechoslovakia), and is unacceptable to the FRG because it would establish a special status for Germany within NATO. A narrower zone would avoid this problem.

It is sometimes argued that for the West Germans, withdrawal of heavy mechanised forces would be an unacceptable retreat from **'Vorneverteidigung'**. However, the current elaborations of NATO doctrine towards **'Vorwärtsverteidigung'** is met with greater resistance in the FRG[12]. Construction of some light fortifications and physical obstructions has been construed as contrary to the ultimate goal of German reunification, and therefore hard to accept for the Germans. This is a question of subjective interpretation; there is nothing inherent in such fortifications and prepared obstacles to make them symbolise the division of Germany any more than the present forward deployment of nuclear and major conventional arms. In fact, there seems to be an increasing readiness in the FRG to consider a more defensive force posture, and to go for a conversion programme which 'offers the chance, on the basis of lower overall defence costs, of providing an effective defence against the assumed conventional threat to NATO by the Warsaw Pact's armoured divisions, without NATO itself constituting a conventional threat. The necessary weapon systems exist or are being developed'[13]. Of course, such a conversion would gain broader political support and yield greater security dividends if it could begin on the basis of reciprocity, within the framework of an internationally agreed disengagement zone.

Recently disengagement has become a stronger and broader European concern, because of the policies of global linkage and horizontal escalation, and the corresponding tendency to subordinate Europe to the logic of the global hegemonic struggle between the USA and the USSR. A more assertive policy to limit the damage that the state of superpower relations does to European security is needed. One strategy of damage limitation is fractionisation: where there are conflicts, they must be contained; where there is détente, it must be maintained. Limit the military and political fallout from superpower rivalry wherever possible, and pursue confidence-building and arms control where conditions for that exist. European security interests do not coincide with the operational implications and requirements of a superpower struggle for world hegemony; they would be better served by a policy of military détente anchored in a political will to decouple Europe from the logic of the hegemonic struggle, and to become less dependent on ups and downs, crises and thaws, in superpower relations.

Military disengagement is a means to that end. Proposals for the establishment of NWFZs exist for all the three subregions of Europe. The strategy of fractionisation implies that these and other measures to build confidence and security in different parts of the region should not be made contingent on one another. Indeed, there is no necessary order in which they would have to be implemented. Enhanced European control of bases and logistic facilities that may be used to reinforce military operations outside Europe, to ensure that European countries get involved only when they perceive it to be in their own interest, would serve the same purpose. Also, a more independent Europe is in a better position to mediate in Third World conflicts and reduce the risk that USA-Soviet rivalry sparks a war that may spread to Europe.

However, decoupling requires more concerted action by European states, and more cooperation across bloc boundaries. The main elements of the process of détente are still most relevant in this respect. They are: a mutual scaling down of bloc politics; a strengthening of the role of the European Community to balance the reduced American influence in Europe; and a strengthening of the CSCE process as a framework for accommodation and cooperation. The CSCE is crucial for the effort to stem policies of global linkage. It is the only institutionalist political forum for all-European cooperation. Its military branch, the CDE, can reduce Europe's sensitivity to major power conflicts by promoting constraints and major power disengagement in forward areas of the East-West confrontation.

Implementation

The alternative rearmament to unilateral implementation of a no-first-use, and enhanced conventional, non-provocative defence trade-off, may yield deterrent effects similar to the present posture, may build confidence, and lead to reciprocal changes in the East. However, the latter is far from certain. Most explorations of the modalities of non-provocative defence suffer from the same weakness as the inquiries into rearmament alternatives: due consideration has not been given to the effects on the security policies of the adversary. The force posture on the other side has been treated as a more or less constant. For the rearmament route, the assumption is probably erroneous. For a system of non-provocative defence, usually designed and recommended for unilateral implementation, it would be unfortunate if it were true.

Reduced reliance on nuclear weapons combined with a strengthening of conventional forces in a defensive mode would reduce the objective basis for Eastern anxieties that the West may try to exploit political instability in Eastern Europe by military means. A consistent policy of no-first-use and an unambiguously defensive conventional deterrent should remove that concern entirely. However, this does not necessarily translate into reciprocal changes in the WTO. The historical lessons would have to be transcended; the military and political inertia of the current offensive posture would have to be overcome; and the Soviet assessment of the political dividends of a force posture holding Western Europe under threat may be another complication. Unilateral changes of NATO policies can, no doubt, strengthen the security of Western Europe even if they are not reciprocated. But in practice, maintenance of WTO forces trained and equipped for sudden moves westwards may bring such changes to an early halt, or even cause a backlash. For in the long run, the offensive WTO posture is incompatible with a policy of military détente in Europe: military détente is a process aimed at enhanced crisis stability and a reduced political role for military factors in international affairs – and the WTO posture is objectionable on both accounts.

Some mutually agreed withdrawals and restraints may, therefore, be needed to set in motion a well sustained process of reduced reliance on nuclear arms and increased reliance on non-provocative defence. A disengagement zone along the lines suggested above would reduce the incompatibility between the force characteristics and the objectives of military détente from the very beginning. Moreover, in periods of high tension, self-imposed restraints often come under pressure; they may not then substitute for international agreements, but provide too weak a basis for continuation of time-consuming force rearrangements. Worse still, they may be dropped and tension thereby increased, at a time when restraints matter most.

There is an important distinction, however, between agreements that would enhance superpower control of their respective positions in Europe and agreements that serve to transcend the division of the region. For instance, an agreement codifying the essentials of present force postures, or an agreement accepting the deployment of new nuclear missile systems in Europe, would have legitimised and enhanced the bloc division of the region under superpower leadership. This is not only a matter of content. The political effects of military accords also depend on the way at which they are arrived. Furthermore, substance often reflects procedure. In the nature of things, superpower-to-superpower and bloc-to-bloc negotiations tend to be counter-productive from the point of view of overcoming the division of Europe and reducing its dependence on the superpowers. Thus, 15 years ago, European states deliberately tried to avoid using the alliances as instruments of East-West reconciliation.

History is already rich in proposals for disengagement in Central Europe. The arrangement suggested by us does not pretend to be a blue print for disengagement in the 1980s; rather, it tries to capture some of the specifics of the European security situation of this decade, on the basis of which **guidelines** can be elaborated for negotiations. The guidelines may be formulated by the EDC, to make them applicable in relation to constraints and major power disengagement in all border areas between NATO and the WTO[14]. However, the three subregions of Europe raise a number of different problems which require different solutions.

The negotiations may be conducted by the two German states and Czechoslovakia, in consultation with their allies, by the states that have forces in Central Europe, or by the military alliances, in that order of preference. The first option may prove unacceptable because of historical sensitivities - although the major powers would, of course, be intimately involved even if the talks were formally conducted by the three states in the area. The role of the alliances would, in any case, be limited by the involvement of the EDC in the formulation of the mandate. Also, the negotiating parties would have to report back to the EDC.

The negotiations need not be very complex. In essence, it would be a matter of reaching agreement on the restrictions to be applied and on the mechanisms to verify compliance with them. Determination of the defences to remain within the zone is a much more complex question, but this would be a matter for intra-alliance decision-making.

References:

1. M. Nincic, <u>An Expanding Vortex? Soviet-American Third World Conflicts and European Security</u>, SIPRI (London: Taylor & Francis, 1984) and P. Schlotter, 'Reflections on European Security 2000', <u>Bulletin of Peace Proposals</u>, 15, No.1 (1984).
2. S. Lodgaard and M. Thee, eds., <u>Nuclear Disengagement in</u>

Europe, SIPRI and Pugwash (London: Taylor & Francis, 1983), pp.3-49, 149-163.
3. H. Afheldt, 'The necessity, preconditions and consequences of a no-first-use policy', in F. Blackaby, J. Goldblat, and S. Lodgaard (eds), No-First-Use, SIPRI, (London: Taylor & Francis, 1984).
4. Nincic, op.cit.
5. R.S. McNamara, 'The military role of nuclear weapons: perceptions and misperceptions', Foreign Affairs, 62, No. 1 (Fall 1983).
6. 'Common Security: A programme for Disarmament', report by the Independent Commission on Disarmament and Security Issues (London: Pan Books, 1982).
7. P. Berg and G. Herolf, '"Deep strike": new technologies for conventional interdiction', SIPRI Yearbook 1984, ch.8 (London: Taylor & Francis, 1984) pp.291-318.
8. Draft Interim Report of the Sub-committee on Conventional Defence in Europe of the Military Committee of the North Atlantic Assembly (presented by Karsten Voigt, May 1984).
9. R.E. Simpkin, Antitank. An Airmechanized Response to Armored Threats in the 90s, (Oxford: Brassey's Publishers Ltd., 1982).
10. S. Tiedtke., 'Alternative military defence and Ostpolitik', Bulletin of Peace Proposals, 15, No.1 (1984).
11. M. Saeter, 'Nuclear disengagement efforts 1955-1980: politics of status quo or political change?', in S. Lodgaard and M. Thee, op.cit.
12. E. Lübkemeier, 'Vorwärtsverteidigung - keine Alternative zur Vornverteidigung', Osterreichische Militärische Zeitschrift, 21, No.4 (July-August 1983) 309-11.
13. From a motion adopted by the Federal Party Conference of the SPD, 19 May 1984.
14. J.J. Holt, 'Confidence and security in Europe: a long term view', Public Lecture at Grand Hotel, Stockholm, 8 March 1984 (available from SIPRI).

23 The Stockholm Conference on Confidence- and Security-building Measures and Disarmament in Europe

ADAM ROTFELD

Introduction

The basic questions for the Conference on Confidence- and Security-Building Measures and Disarmament in Europe (CSBM) are: what kind of function should it play, and what role can it play? It is mandated to 'reduce the risk of military confrontation in Europe'; can it do this and prevent an outbreak of war in Europe? It is designated 'to make progress in strengthening confidence and security and in achieving disarmament' and to give effect 'to the duty of States to refrain from the threat or use of force in their mutual relations'. Can it do it?

As a rule, high expectations are a source of deep disappointment. To avoid this, the Conference in Stockholm should be seen in proper perspective. The aims and scope of CSBMs are limited. Wars are caused not by incidents but by deep and vital conflicts of interests. Thus, as in the past, confidence measures in the military field will probably not play an independent role; they must be discussed in the context of the general political and military situation. Moreover, there are dangers connected with the tendency to apply a theoretical and, by definition simplistic, symmetrical model, to the complex and asymmetrical reality in Europe.

A great many conflicting opinions, disparate expectations and misunderstandings have arisen on the subject of the Stockholm Conference. They centre on the origins of the meeting, its mandate, its tasks and even its designation. This being so, it is worth starting with a recapitulation of the brief history of the Conference and the agreements reached to-date.

Designation of the Conference

In the West the Stockholm negotiations are frequently referred to as the 'Conference on Disarmament in Europe'

THE STOCKHOLM CSBM CONFERENCE 261

(CDE) or the 'European Disarmament Conference' (EDC). This corresponds to the French proposal submitted to the CSCE Madrid meeting on 9 December 1980 and seconded by the United States and other NATO countries. However, it should be remembered that a day earlier Poland tabled a proposal for a 'Conference on Military détente and Disarmament in Europe. The mandate of the Stockholm Conference, as specified in the Madrid Concluding Document, is a compromise; this is reflected in both the concrete provisions and the actual designation of the Conference which, officially, is: 'Conference on Confidence- and Security-Building Measures and Disarmament in Europe'.

History

The idea of holding special consultations between representatives of the CSCE countries on military aspects of security was put forward in 1977 by the Soviet delegation at the Belgrade CSCE meeting. It suggested that military experts discuss the following items: the conclusion by the CSCE states of a treaty renouncing first use of nuclear weapons; preparation of an agreement on non-expansion of the North Atlantic and Warsaw Treaties, that is, the non-admission of new members to either grouping; further development of the confidence-building measures envisaged in the Final Act of Helsinki (such as limiting manoeuvres to a maximum of 50-60 thousand troops) and their application to the whole Mediterranean region.
It should be noted that proposals for a no-first-use treaty and non-expansion of existing military and political groupings were first put forward by the Warsaw Treaty states in the Declaration of the Political Consultative Committee adopted at Bucharest in 1976.
Agreements on these points would have effectively eliminated the possibility of an outbreak of war in Europe, checked the further hardening of bloc divisions in Europe (chiefly in connection with the prospective accession of Spain to NATO); and helped to reduce tensions, military confrontation and the war psychosis which is an increasingly frequent accompaniment to large-scale exercises involving hundreds of thousands of troops in a zone stretching from the far north of Norway to Turkey.
The NATO countries rejected in its totality the military détente package proposed by the Soviet Union. The Concluding Document of the Belgrade meeting was largely a formal summary of the proceedings. Its substantive decisions boiled down to two elements: a) the participants 'reaffirmed the resolve of their Governments to implement fully, unilaterally, bilater-

ally and multilaterally, all the provisions of the Final Act'[1]; b) they agreed to convene the next CSCE meeting in Madrid and to hold a number of meetings of experts, to ensure the continuity of the process initiated at Helsinki. The convening of a conference of CSCE representatives on military aspects of security was left unresolved, though the view of the Warsaw Treaty states of the need for such a meeting was echoed in the final stage of Belgrade by the French delegation.

The French plan for a European Disarmament Conference, submitted to the First Special Disarmament Session of the UN General Assembly in May 1978, envisaged two stages of negotiations: the first to be devoted to confidence-building measures and the second to limitation of conventional weapons. The Conference decisions would apply to continental Europe according to the formula, 'from the Atlantic to the Urals'. The idea was to exclude discussion on limitation of nuclear weapons and naval forces from the agenda, even though both are crucial components of national security and are of crucial significance for peace in the whole of Europe. This approach received the support of France's allies in NATO.

In parallel with the French initiative, the Warsaw Treaty states put forward in May 1979 a proposal for a Conference on Military Détente and Disarmament in Europe to discuss military aspects of security in Europe without any preconditions.

Consequently, what was debated at the Madrid CSCE meeting in 1980-83 was not so much **whether** there was a need to convene a special conference devoted to military and confidence-building measures as **what ought to be the aims and terms of reference** of a meeting of this kind. For an appraisal of the Madrid Conference see M. Dobrosielski[2].

Area of Applicability of CSBMs

The provisions of the Helsinki Final Act represent the striking of a balance between the security interests of the 35 states of Europe and North America[3]. This is true of all sections of the document. This balance is also embodied in the chapter entitled 'Document on confidence-building measures and certain aspects of security and disarmament'[4]. Any change in these provisions inevitably required the specification of a new balance. This was above all the case with the territorial zone delineated in the Final Act. The point of departure for defining the zone was the formula adopted in the Helsinki Final Act with reference to notification of major manoeuvres, requiring such notification to be given when they are to take place 'on the territory, in

THE STOCKHOLM CSBM CONFERENCE

Europe, of any participating State as well as, if applicable, in the adjoining sea area and air space'[5]. However, the Final Act qualified this obligation in the case of states whose territory extends beyond Europe – which in practice means the USSR and Turkey – by saying that they need give notification of only those major manoeuvres 'which take place in an area within 250 kilometres from its frontier facing or shared with any other European participating State'[5]. One can, therefore, distinguish in the Final Act three different categories of states from the point of view of confidence-building measures in the military sphere:

- states whose territory is not covered by these measures (USA, Canada);
- states whose territory is partly covered by them (USSR, Turkey);
- other European states whose territory is entirely subject to the measures agreed on at Helsinki.

The idea put forward at Madrid by the Western states that CSBMs should be applicable to the whole European territory of the USSR ('from the Atlantic to the Urals') was found acceptable by the Soviet Union – on the understanding, however, that the Western countries made a corresponding extension in the geographical scope of these measures on their side. The trade-off expected was chiefly a matter of including sea and ocean areas (the North Atlantic) in the CSBM zone, the point being that the naval forces, particularly the American fleet, deployed in this region form an important part of the overall military balance in Europe. The military activity involved is not immaterial to the state of security in Europe and cannot be bypassed in the application of CSBMs.

In view of the West's unwillingness to accede to the Soviet demand, the USSR suggested accepting a general formula for this question at Madrid, and tackling a more specific definition of the zone at the CSBM Conference. The United States vetoed this solution and came up instead with, what it called, a 'functional' approach to the CSBM zone. Essentially, this amounted to saying that none of the clauses in the section dealing with major military manoeuvres could be held to apply to independent or combined naval and air exercises[6]. Under this approach CSBMs would be applicable only to military activity on land, and the sea areas adjoining the continent being included only in the case of operations which formed an integral part of notified military activity involving land forces. In other words, the only sea and air activity subject to the CSBM regime would be that functionally connected with land-based manoeuvres or other operations. The American rejection of the Soviet quid pro quo demand became the principal cause of the prolonged deadlock in the negotiations on the Concluding Document of the Madrid Meeting. The US representative maintained that 'Europe', while including islands in the north, such as Nova Zemlya, Spitzbergen, or Zemlya Francisca Josifa, could not possibly be thought to include the waters encircling the continent[7]. The head of the Soviet delegation counter-claimed that the CSBM zone should encompass

> the whole of Europe - continent and islands - together with adjoining sea and ocean areas of an appropriate width and air space and that part of the Atlantic which adjoins Europe. We are not raising the question of US or Canadian territory. As regards the limits of the sea or ocean areas and air space, these could be defined at the Conference itself[8].

As a textbook geographical concept, 'Europe from the Atlantic to the Urals' should not be identified with the zone in which CSBMs are to be applied. Such an approach does not square either with the provisions of the CSCE Final Act or the political and military realities which determine the security of Europe.

The delineation of the CSBM zone adopted in the Concluding Document of the Madrid Conference represents a compromise. It will, it says, 'cover the whole of Europe as well as the adjoining sea areas and air space'. The Document expressly states that 'in this context, the notion of adjoining sea area is understood to refer also to ocean areas adjoining Europe'. To avoid misunderstandings, it is worth citing the formula whose negotiation was of critical significance to the decisions taken at Madrid. The Document states[9]:

> ...As far as the adjoining sea area and air space is concerned, the measures will be applicable to the military activities of all the participating States taking place there whenever these activities affect security in Europe as well as constitute a part of activities taking place within the whole of Europe as referred to above, which they will agree to notify. The necessary specifications will be made through the negotiations on the confidence- and security-building measures at the Conference.
>
> Nothing in the definition of the zone given above will diminish obligations already undertaken under the Final Act. The confidence- and security-building measures to be agreed upon at the Conference will also be applicable in all the areas covered by any of the provisions in the Final Act relating to confidence-

THE STOCKHOLM CSBM CONFERENCE

building measures and certain aspects of security and disarmament...
It will be clear from the above statements that the CSBM zone not only does not restrict or diminish the obligations undertaken in accordance with the CSCE Final Act, but in fact presupposes their extension. For that matter, this applies not only to the zone.

Basic Assumptions of the Conference Mandate

The Madrid Concluding Document states that decisions at Stockholm are to be taken

> on the basis of equality of rights, balance and reciprocity, equal respect for the security interests of all the CSCE participating States, and of their respective obligations concerning CSBMs in Europe ... They will be of military significance and politically binding and will be provided with adequate forms of verification which correspond to their content[10].

The task of the Stockholm Conference is to give concrete shape to these general guidelines. This means the necessity to translate them into the language of practical obligations. Consequently, the prospective agreement will spring from proposals that embody the principles of equal rights, balance and reciprocity, and ensure respect for the equal security interests of all the 35 participants in the CSCE process.

A point frequently emphasised in various commentaries and interpretations of the mandate of the Stockholm Conference is that its decisions are to be politically binding and militarily significant, and backed by appropriate means of verification. However, it must be remembered that they have to acknowledge and accommodate the equality of the security interests of all the participants.

This approach was endorsed at the Preparatory Meeting, convened at the initiative of Yugoslavia, which took place in Helsinki on 25 October - 11 November 1983. Its decisions laid down the agenda, schedule and other elements of the organisation of the Stockholm Conference.

The Aim of the Conference

The mandate negotiated at Madrid and confirmed at Helsinki states explicitly that the aim of the Conference is to embark by stages on new, effective and concrete steps in the process of strengthening confidence and security and bringing about disarmament. Progress in this direction entails giving teeth to the binding principle which outlaws the use, or threat of use of force in international relations.

The Stockholm Conference should be seen, on the one hand, as an essential and integral part of the CSCE process and, on the other, as an attempt to add a new dimension to this process and its influence on the sphere of military relations. The first stage of the Stockholm Conference, which commenced on 17 January 1984, is, as was decided at Madrid, 'devoted to the negotiation and adoption of a set of mutually complementary CSBMs designed to reduce the risk of military confrontation in Europe'[11].

Behind this decision lay the assumption that progress on issues of a simpler nature would clear the way to the future tackling of more difficult and complex problems. Among these we should certainly place disarmament processes.

A different stance on this matter has been adopted by the present American administration. Sizing up the results of the Madrid Meeting, it said: 'The United States joined the Western resolve that a Conference on surprise military attack has to be carefully structured in Madrid so that it did not become a vaguely worded mandate for a disarmament in which propaganda speeches rather than constructive decisions would be the major element'[12].

The decisions negotiated at Madrid represent an effort to reconcile the standpoints and views of the states involved. That being so, it seems wrong to contend that 'the East abandoned its proposal, originally submitted by Warsaw' and 'a mandate fully acceptable to us was adopted'. A specific feature of the CSCE process, of which the Stockholm Conference is a part, is that decisions are reached on the basis of consensus, which means that in each case they must be accepted by all of the 35 participants.

The Positions of the Negotiators at Stockholm

To date the course of the Stockholm Conference, the first round of which ended on 16 March 1984, has aroused varied reactions. The proceedings at Stockholm were bound to be affected by the fact that they coincided with the deployment of new American missiles in Europe. To the socialist countries this move seems to cast doubts on the **bona fides** expected of the parties, a principle that requires desisting from any steps or action that might jeopardise the purpose of the talks.

The attendance at the Inaugural Session of the Conference by the Foreign Ministers of the Warsaw Treaty, NATO, neutral and non-aligned states, indicates that both East and West attach great political significance to the Stockholm proceedings. The keynote and common theme of the majority of the speeches, from East and West alike, were a declared will to continue the process begun at Helsinki and extend it to the sphere of military relations, as well as an emphasised awareness of the new dangers and the urgent necessity of gradual de-escalation of political and military tensions. Measures and instruments are being sought which would make it possible to recover control over a situation perilously drifting towards the catastrophe of war. What is needed here are not new words, but concrete and practical steps. In this respect the signals from the opening phase of the Stockholm Conference are not very encouraging.

Needless to say, the negotiating positions taken up at Stockholm are a reflection of the broader attitudes and diverse political philosophies which govern the approach to military aspects of security of the main actors on the European stage. The United States and its NATO allies are pressing for models which would increase the quantity and range of information relating to armed forces and their activity and the verifiability of such data. This approach is exemplified by the proposal submitted by the NATO states, in which the means of information, transparency, observation and control become an end in themselves. Their adoption in a tense situation would lead - the Warsaw Treaty States argue - to a growth of threats and war psychosis. The socialist countries want CSBMs to limit military activity and thus give more concrete shape to the principle of non-use of force. Such measures should be adequate to their purpose, which is the reinforcement of confidence and reduction of the danger of surprise attack or the outbreak of armed conflict as a result of accident or misinterpretation. This aim would be served by steps towards disengagement of armed forces in Europe, a build-down of armaments, cutbacks in military budgets and expansion of cooperation.

Without negating the need to extend the catalogue and range of the confidence-building measures envisaged by the Helsinki Final Act, the Soviet Union and its allies give priority to the conclusion of agreements of a military and political nature. 'To confine ourselves in this area to a single direction would amount to narrowing the existing possibilities', said the Soviet Foreign Minister, Andrei Gromyko. The socialist countries take the view that a serious approach to confidence and security building requires the adoption of measures which would eliminate the possibility of war breaking out in Europe. These should include:

- a no-first-use obligation by all nuclear states (the

Soviet Union unilaterally undertook such an obligation at the 2nd UNSSD);
- mutual pledges by states that they will not be the first to resort to force, that is, renunciation of the use of conventional as well as nuclear weapons (in January 1983 the Warsaw Treaty countries proposed an agreement on mutual non-use of military force and maintenance of peaceful relations; a no-first-use treaty would embrace all the 35 participants of the CSCE process: NATO, Warsaw Treaty and NN states);
- an agreement on reduction of military expenditure (a Warsaw Treaty proposal for freezing and cutting military budgets was presented to NATO on 5 March 1984);
- formation in Europe of a chemical-weapon-free zone;
- establishment of regional nuclear-free zones in Europe (for example Northern Europe and the Balkans).

The Warsaw Treaty states have also expressed their willingness to alter - as the West has suggested - some of the parameters relating to the measures agreed upon in the CSCE Final Act. Specifically, this concerns prior notification of planned manoeuvres, major troop movements and transfers of forces. The socialist countries have also recommended lowering the ceiling of exercises to a limited number of troops (say 40-50 thousand). They also favour prior notification of major air and naval exercises in the waters and air space surrounding Europe. They believe that such a broad political approach to confidence- and security-building measures would make for a genuine reduction of military confrontation. The Polish delegation stressed in its opening statement that it would be a good thing if the negotiated measures were put into practice in international life as rapidly as possible. This would produce a climate for embarking on increasingly ambitious tasks. A detailed proposal submitted by Romania contains some of the elements recommended by the Warsaw Treaty states, plus some of those suggested by the neutral and non-aligned countries.

In contrast with the politico-military approach of the Warsaw Treaty states, the NATO countries proposed measures of a technical and military nature divided into three categories: measures of information; measures designed to enhance stability; observation and verification measures.

Specifically, the proposals call for: 1) annual exchange of information 'on the structure of the ground forces and land-based air forces in the zone of application for agreed CSBMs'; 2) exchange of annual plans for various kinds of military activities in the zone; 3) detailed notification of out-of-garrison land activities, mobilisation and amphibious activities and appropriate methods of verification including the invitation of observers; 4) observation of certain military activities ('to invite observers from all other participating States to all pre-notified activities and to alert activities'); 5) compliance and verification by 'national technical means' and 'monitoring of compliance'; and 6) development of means of communication.

Such a purely technical approach to confidence and security building did not meet with the understanding of the socialist countries.

The neutral and non-aligned states presented a proposal which does not reflect the concept of a compromise document, but reflects their own expectations and rather resembles the NATO position. They suggest extending the CBMs specified in the Final Act and the introduction of a number of qualitatively new measures which to a large extent overlap with the expectations of the NATO group. It is only in the explanatory section that attention is drawn to the need to subordinate these operative measures to the broader concept of non-use of force, and elements of restraint, such as limitation of the size of major manoeuvres, are recommended and treated as preliminary steps towards tackling the problem of disarmament at the second stage. These are, however, general declarations which are not the essence of the proposal.

The course of the three initial rounds of the Stockholm Conference (17 January - 12 October 1984) was a reflection of the state of East-West relations following the stationing of the first American missiles in Western Europe. The NATO states sought a technical debate and were anxious to avoid political assessments of the new situation. The socialist countries, on the other hand, regarded the Conference as an opportunity to explore the CSBM concept in a broader politico-military context. These differences spring from the dissimilar perceptions by the East and West of the aims and tasks of the Stockholm Conference. For the NATO delegates it is a meeting of experts whose job is to discuss detailed technical problems. The socialist countries see it as a forum which ought to attack the key issues involved in reducing military confrontation in Europe.

The participants of the Stockholm Conference are confronted by a dilemma: to make a routine search for the lowest common denominator in the development of technico-military measures alone; or to face up to the challenge of the times and look for long-term solutions which would give Europe a sense of genuine stability and security commensurate with the dangers at the end of the 20th and beginning of the 21st century.

CSBMs should be seen in their proper perspective. They form

part of a larger whole. They will fulfil the hopes attached to them if they are made a fundamental element in the construction of a system of joint security for the whole of Europe. In the present conditions of interdependence, mutual restraint, compliance with the principles of reciprocity and equality, and accommodation of the security interests of others, they offer a chance of reducing the role of the military factor in security systems of nations.

Assessments and Prospects

The positions presented in Stockholm by 35 representatives of states-participants in the CSCE, as well as the opinions voiced at different seminars, symposia and other meetings with participants from East and West, boil down to two lines of thinking: one, traditional; two, military-technological and politico-military.

Among advocates of the first line one can include all those, who in the process of confidence and security building ascribe a major role to measures aimed at increased openness and predictability. Such measures, in their substance, are reduced to information, notification, observation and verification. CBMs are to reflect the military situation and not aim at influencing or shaping it.

This way of thinking was dominant 10 years ago in Geneva and Helsinki. It also found its reflection in the CSCE Final Act. On the basis of experience accumulated since 1975 - quite apart from the modest scope of such measures - one may state that they have no bearing on military relations in Europe. They have not curbed military activity to any extent nor have they had any effect on easing military confrontation in East-West relations. Most likely, this state of affairs would have not been changed by other proposed parameters concerning notification. For example, more detailed and earlier information provided on the manoeuvres 'Central Enterprise 84' or 'Distant Hammer 84' would have had no impact on the objective or scope of these exercises. At the present tense situation, characterised by mutual suspicion and growing lack of trust, an 'invitation to these manoeuvres' might have been interpreted as an attempted demonstration of power. This does not mean that the passive function of such CSBMs, as exchange of information, mutual notification, observation and verification, cannot influence favourably the development of East-West relations, or the proper perception of military activity and the elimination of the threats stemming from misunderstanding and erroneous assessments. There is a danger, however, that excessive stress put on this function of CSBMs may lead to effects contrary to the ones looked for: a war psychosis and enhanced sense of threat, which in the tense atmosphere would step up rather than scale down the level of military confrontation. Moreover, it might divert attention from the need to modify the present military situation and shape new politico-military relations in Europe.

Against this background, the second line of thinking gains in importance, since it approaches confidence-building measures in a wider, political and military context. According to J.J. Holst[13], the Stockholm Conference creates a framework for negotiations and dialogue 'about concrete measures which would contribute in short term towards the construction of a more secure political order in Europe'. In the long run it gives the chance to shape a new situation in Europe, which will be characterised by 'greater equity and stability'. Such an approach is warranted by the mandate of the Stockholm Conference as agreed in Madrid.

It is worth remembering that the objective of the Stockholm Conference is to 'undertake, in stages, new effective and concrete actions designed to make progress in strengthening confidence and security and in achieving disarmament, so as to give effect and express to the duty to States to refrain from the threat or use of force in their mutual relations' (paragraph 1 of the Stockholm Conference mandate).

There is no doubt that these objectives cannot be reached only, or exclusively, through an agreement on measures mainly serving the purpose of openness and predictability. Such measures, as J.J. Holst writes[13] 'should be designed to enhance security by providing mechanisms for mutual reassurance'. He correctly proceeds from the assumption that contradictions and conflicts between East and West are not 'only or even primarily, the result of misperception and misunderstanding of cognitive dissconance'. No-one is questioning the fact that the existing mechanisms of national security, or security within the framework of existing alliances, are not conducive to mutual reassurance. 'Security in the nuclear age is also common security with the unavoidable corollary that states must exercise mutual restraint'[13].

By their very nature, measures of information designed to enhance stability, as well as observation and verification measures, have an impact mainly on perception of military activity; above all, they have a bearing, in the psychological sphere, on the explanation of intentions guiding the other partner in developing his military activity.

The passive function of such measures consists in registering facts; it is assumed that they do not have any bearing on the scope, nature, integrity or frequency of military activity. At the groundwork of such a concept of CSBMs there often lies the erroneous conviction that confidentiality of military information is dictated by aggressive designs. However, numerous examples from the past and present illustrate that military secrets are often the weapon of the weaker side, which in this way hides loopholes and shortcomings in its defensive system. On the other hand, wide information on increased military activity, such as programmes of intensified armaments, data on introduction of new types and systems of weapons, and various demonstrations of military power, may lead to the exertion of political and military pressure on a specific state or group of states, to weaken the resolve and capacity of their defence by showing a real or simulated superiority. In other words it may lead to the attainment of intended political goals indirectly by means of military power, but without resorting to its direct use. In the present conditions this relates primarily to nuclear weapons.

Limiting the development of CSBMs to this passive function may contribute to further militarisation of international relations rather than to an increased sense of security among states.

Since the adoption of the CSCE Final Act, the attention of negotiators, researchers and public opinion has been focused on the following postulates:

- adoption of an obligation by nuclear weapon states on non-first use;
- conclusion of an agreement on mutual non-use of military force and on maintaining peaceful relations;
- adoption of an obligation not to increase and to reduce military expenditures (percentage-wise or in absolute figures);
- establishment of a chemical-weapon-free zone in Europe;
- establishment of nuclear-weapon-free zones in different parts of Europe;
- establishment of other limited armaments zones; at present, for example, attention is focused on a draft proposal for the establishment of a battlefield nuclear weapon-free corridor along the borders between NATO and Warsaw Treaty states;
- limitation of military activities to a specified size, frequency and location; this refers, in particular, to big manoeuvres held independently, or to a number of exercises organised concurrently, the size and scope of which make it difficult to differentiate them from a concentration of troops for war preparations;
- other limitations in the military sphere, such as a ban

on using 'live ammunition' during exercises; limitations pertaining to the movement of troops, in particular movement of large numbers of manpower and equipment.

Measures belonging to the constraint category have an important common feature in that they introduce changes to military posture or to military behaviour, and thus limit the possibility of war, without decreasing material stocks necessary to ensure security of states within the framework of the existing balance of forces.

Criticism of the proposed measures of constraint boils down to the claim that these proposals are of a 'declaratory and propaganda' nature. This refers especially to the adoption of obligations on the non-first-use of nuclear weapons, and on the conclusion of an agreement on the non-use of military force. With regard to the latter, it has been argued for years that there is no need to conclude a new agreement on the ban of using force, because the UN Charter provides for such a ban in terms of international law, and because this ban has been reiterated both in the UN Declaration concerning the principles of international law, as well as in the Declaration on the principles of CSCE. Non-use of force is also expressed in numerous bi- and multilateral political and legal acts. The conclusion of a new agreement, according to the critics, would not strengthen, but weaken the effectiveness of a ban on the use of force.

These arguments are more of a tactical, than substantial nature. Such doubts were not raised when, for example, the FRG came up with a proposal on the renunciation of the use of force with regard to its Eastern neighbours.

The adoption of an obligation, on a reciprocal basis and in a contractual form, on non-use of military force against each other (both nuclear and conventional) by all states participating in the CSCE would stabilise the situation in Europe and increase the feeling of security among all the participants in such agreement. The treaty might include a number of obligations that would meet the critical reservations to this proposal. This is why it is necessary to undertake multilateral consultations, which would discuss the general idea of such a treaty and its specific elements.

A decision on this matter would imply a limitation on armaments. CSBMs are not a substitute for disarmament, but they may greatly facilitate it. This can come true if participants in the negotiations approach them as an element of a long-term process within a system designed not to bring momentary benefits to anyone, but common and equai security for all.

So far, the 1984 Stockholm Conference has not been a forum for dialogue and negotiation but the rostrum for monologues, albeit without polemics and confrontations. Nevertheless, there are some signals of the readiness of the two great powers to initiate businesslike talks on the issues discussed. The outcome of the first stage of the conference (before the CSCE Vienna Meeting in the autumn 1986) may combine three different expectations: a) an agreement about the mutual renunciation of the use of force, which will contribute to a code of behaviour of the CSCE countries in their military relations in the nuclear age; b) a commitment on specific confidence-and-security-building measures, more substantial than the set of CBMs adopted in the Helsinki Final Act but more limited than those proposed by the NATO countries; c) some measures of constraint, such as diminishing of military activity, limitation of number and ceiling of manoeuvres, as postulated by the group of the neutral and non-aligned countries.

The Stockholm Conference should be viewed in the broader political perspective of East-West relations. CSBMs will be of marginal significance - if not counterproductive - unless integrated with positive changes in the mutual political relations of all major partners involved in the process initiated in Helsinki.

References

1. A.D. Rotfeld, 'From Helsinki to Madrid', CSCE Documents 1973-1983, (Warsaw 1983) p.214.
2. M. Dobrosielski, 'Non-Military Aspects of European Security', in J. Rotblat and A. Pascolini (eds), The Arms Race at a Time of Decision', (London: Macmillan 1984), pp.164-70.
3. 'From Helsinki to Madrid', op.cit., p.24.
4. Ibid, p.124.
5. Ibid, p.126.
6. Ibid, p.34.
7. Remarks by M.N. Kampelman, Informal Heads of Delegation Meeting, CSCE, Madrid, 11 November 1981.
8. Quoted from my own notes.
9. 'From Helsinki to Madrid', op.cit., pp.284-6.
10. Ibid, p.285.
11. Ibid, p.284.
12. An Assessment of the Madrid CSCE Follow-up Meeting, Department of State Bulletin (September 1983).
13. J.J. Holst, 'Confidence and Security in Europe: A Long term View'. Lecture given under the auspices of SIPRI, Stockholm (8 March 1984).

24 Confidence-building by Hardware Measures
ALBRECHT VON MÜLLER

The Idea of Benign Defence and its Philosophical Roots

This paper is not on confidence-building measures in general. It outlines a specific approach that aims at building down the structural capabilities for attack.

I should emphasise that I do not see any contradiction or mutual incompatibility between the traditional approach to confidence building by software measures, and to confidence building by hardware measures advocated here. I believe that in the long run all substantial confidence building must come down to changes in the force structures - otherwise it will not be substantial, that is robust confidence building.

Before we dig in the technicalities of politically feasible transitions towards a more defensive posture, I want to raise somewhat theoretical and philosophical points relating to the idea of benign defence.

What do we mean when we speak of 'benign defence'? One of the first associations might be that 'benign' is the opposite of 'malign'. In a second thought, we might become aware that both words are used for classifying tumours.

Both associations are on the right track: all sorts of preparations for destruction (as even pure defence always is) can be considered as tumours in the bodies of our societies. Nevertheless, there is a crucial distinction: there are tumours which are programmed to grow inexorably until the whole host organism is taken over and dies. In this sense a 'malign defence' is one in which one's own defensive measures threaten the other side aggressively, thus closing the vicious circle of the arms race. On the other hand, there are so-called 'benign tumours', which also do not have a useful function for the host organism, but which are at least contained or containable. Translated into the sphere of military policy, this means defensive arsenals which do not threaten the other side aggressively, thus avoiding the vicious circle of the arms race.

275

The theoretical context from which the concept of 'benign defence' stems is the philosophy of Immanuel Kant, who has a unique position in the history of Western philosophy, not only because he is responsible for a breakthrough in epistemology, but also because he was the first and only philosopher to analyse the structural prerequisites of peace and stable international relations.

If we seek advice on how to establish peaceful relations in Western philosophical thinking, we end up by being frustrated and ashamed. For example, Fichte and Hegel consider war to be some sort of physical exercise for nations. We are not better off if we go back to mediaeval philosophy or the ancient Greeks. Trying the other direction, the late 19th century, proves to be a disaster, also. Almost all other ideas, like justice, power, happiness, have attracted much more interest and consideration than the idea of peace.

Only Immanuel Kant is an exception. His essay 'On Eternal Peace' has an almost unique position in trying to analyse the structural prerequisites of peace systematically. One of Kant's central ideas is that regular armies (**miles perpetuus**) must be abolished in the long run, because they continuously threaten all their neighbours with the ability to attack. Such a threat, according to Kant, inevitably leads to a destabilising military build-up, in which a point will come when a short, pre-emptive war with a chance to win becomes more attractive than the continuation of the resources-devouring arms race.

Translating these ideas to our epoch, one might say that for the foreseeable future it is not realistic to abolish all military defence preparations. Given the technological level of the late 20th century this implies the existence of regular armies. Nevertheless, Kant's argument concerning offensive options being the reason for a destabilising arms race is correct. There is no chance to end the arms race and to establish peaceful and stable international relations as long as we do not decouple defence capabilities and offensive options.

Fortunately, the technological progress of the 20th century, especially in the field of micro-electronics and data processing, seems to have made defence technically feasible, thus offering a chance to fulfil the basic prerequisites of peace, as outlined in the philosophy of Immanuel Kant.

The Impact of Micro-Electronics and Data-Processing on the Relations between Attacker and Defender

Technological progress is obviously ambivalent, and destabilising developments are often triggered. ABM-systems, ASW or, as an historical example, the introduction of MIRV-technology, are proof of the destabilising effects resulting from technological progress.

On the other hand, technological progress also offers a chance for stabilisation or - especially in the field of conventional defence - a transition to structural defensivity.

An enormous responsibility falls on the shoulders of political decision makers: from the broad spectrum of technologically feasible options they have to choose those which guarantee military efficiency, crisis stability and arms control, all at the same time. Until now, the awareness of this task has been very deficient - both in the Warsaw Pact and in NATO. Therefore, it is one of the main goals of the following arguments to show how and why micro-electronic and data-processing can be utilised for the integrated optimisation of conventional defence in Europe.

It is important to be aware of the structural asymmetries existing in the relation between attacker and defender. Each of them has a specific structural advantage and a specific structural disadvantage.

- The advantage of the attacker is that he is free to define a focal point of his attack, in time as well as in space. He has the momentum of surprise on his side.
- On the other hand, the attacker has a structural disadvantage, too: he has to move his forces forward into foreign hostile territory. Therefore, he must not only withstand the defender's fire power but sustain this movement while being enormously exposed, and forced to put all his assets on mobile platforms and protect them by heavy armour.

The opposite conditions characterise the task of the defender.

- He has the structural advantage of being able to fight from well-known and extensively prepared territory, without the **a priori** necessity to move his own forces.
- On the other hand, the defender has the disadvantage that he must provide space- and time-covering defence capabilities and rapidly compensate for force concentration on the side of the attacker.

It is interesting to assess the fundamental effects which micro-electronics and data-processing will have on these asymmetric relations between attacker and defender.

It has been a long tradition to identify the basic components of military action as 'fire', 'movement', 'protection' and 'reconnaissance'.

In relation to 'movement' or 'manoeuvre', progress has been made since World War II, but this was only by a factor of 2 or 3 and definitively not by an order of magnitude.

The same is true for 'protection'. Here, too, there has been significant progress - for example the development of the so-called 'active armour' in Germany and Israel - but again these improvements range far below a factor of 10.

What has changed in the sense of a major technological breakthrough are the factors 'fire' (the allocation of fire power) and 'reconnaissance', where the improvements are between a factor of 10 and 1000.

If we compare these technological trends with the fundamental characteristics of the relations between attacker and defender, we see that the attacker's disadvantage, the necessity to move, did not shrink dramatically. The same applies for the advantage of the attacker if the chances of a surprise attack and rapid territorial gains still depend on forward movement, on the mobility of his platforms, mainly of the tanks and airplanes.

A very different situation, however, has arisen for the defender. His structural disadvantage, the necessity to provide space- and time-covering defence capabilities, has been dramatically affected by improvements in reconnaissance and ability to allocate fire without own manoeuvres. When the defender had to concentrate his own tanks in order to provide the fire power necessary to stop a tank attack, he lost his specific advantage. But nowadays, due to all sorts of intelligence, ammunition and rocket-technologies with intelligence submunitions, the defender need no longer move in order to concentrate fire power. He has a good chance to exploit fully his structural advantage of not being forced to move and expose his assets.

At the same time, microelectronics and data-processing techniques have dramatically improved the quality of passive ammunition or mines. The sensors of modern mines cover an area of 15 000 m^2! And there are active mines, that follow a stochastic pattern of movements, thus again stretching the defended area. There are also helicopter mines which force attacking helicopters to fly at a height of at least 500 m, thus providing an almost ideal target for all sorts of PGMs. The same goes for remotely piloted vehicles (RPV), be it in the form of reconnaissance-drones or attack-drones.

The significance of this progress for the defender is that due to the need to provide time- and space-covering defence capabilities, his main problem is information, reconnaissance, and rapid allocation of fire power. And these are exactly the areas in which micro-electronics and data-processing can help. This is why, at least in the realm of conventional defence, there is a long-term trend to favour the defender.

All these new technologies could of course be used for offensive purposes also; every single weapon system is more or less ambivalent. But that is beside the point. Of interest to us are the overall characteristics of the defensive arsenals, and on that level of aggregation one can distinguish precisely between offensive orientation, ambiguity, or emphasis on defence.

Micro-electronics and data-processing do not necessarily strengthen the defender. Used in the wrong way, one can end up with enormous offensive capabilities, high bonuses for pre-emption and a seriously deteriorated crisis situation. The AirLand-battle concept is an obvious example of such an offensive orientation. Generally speaking, all defence concepts that seek 'deep interdiction' - or 'deep attack' - capabilities are destabilising because they can be misused offensively and because they all put enormous emphasis on 'time-critical' weapon systems.

It is our task as scientific advisers to the political decision-makers to stress the danger of technological destabilisation and to provide evidence, that there is a realistic way to establish stable and peaceful relations, leading to an end to the arms race, by using micro-electronics and data-processing to create highly efficient but clearly defensive forces.

The Integrated Defence Model

In order to convince the politicians, we have to come up with concrete proposals that not only technologically, but also politically and financially are feasible. Such proposals depend very much on the specific situation in a given country. In what follows I am outlining the proposals we made to our government in the FRG. They are of general interest since they concern the development of NATO's conventional forces.

Our defence should be organised in four zones. The first zone would be directly at the border, the so-called **fire-belt**, characterised by an enormous concentrations of fire power but with no troops of our own. The fire power would come from artillery rockets, attack drones and all sorts of passive ammunition (intelligent mines, communicating minefields, autonomous manoeuvred mines, helicopter mines). The fire-belt has a depth of only 5 km, but an attrition rate

of up to 50 per cent seems to be realistic according to our first assessments and simulations.
Directly at the back of the fire-belt, there would be a second zone, the so-called **network defence zone**. This is between 25 and 50 km in depth and filled with light infantry techno-commandos, who confront the intruder with precise fire power from a non-detectable opponent. There are no targets for the intruder's artillery, no traditional battlefield but a dense field of well-directed fire power, fully exploiting the advantages of guerilla-warfare and enhanced by the most advanced technologies (third generation PGMs, mortars with intelligent submunition, intelligent mines and a variety of cost effective light infantry battlefield gimmicks). Scenario analysis and battlefield simulations show that even a very concentrated attack by heavy armoured forces would break down after having gone through 10-15 km in such an environment of destructiveness.

In case some formations of the intruder should overcome the hook-zone, they would have gained nothing but enter the third zone, the so-called **manoeuvre zone**. Here heavy armoured forces are located in decentralised patterns that can block and destroy any residual intruders. These forces have the function of an 'internal rapid deployment force'; they are normally dispersed so as not to offer targets, and are prepared and trained for quick manoeuvres.

The rest of the territory is then covered by a fourth zone, the so-called **rear defence zone**, a network of local, partially mobile defence units. Their task is to prevent airlanded operations, and to sabotage and support the fighting zones logistically. In general this zone is not of major importance. The emphasis in the integrated defence model (IDM) lies on the first three zones and their functional synergisms.

Without going into too much detail, I would like to present the main arguments for this specific mixture of components. The purpose of the fire-belt is to exploit the options for precise fire power concentration over longer distances, up to about 50 km. Technically, longer distances may be feasible, but this would be less cost effective, and might be destabilising because of the possibility of offensive misuse.

A second function of the fire-belt is to protect the light infantry of the second zone. A weak point of light infantry concepts is that the first techno-commandos in such network defence have almost no chance of survival; this is highly demotivating and unacceptable for humane reasons. On the other hand, light infantry components are of high military efficiency, cost-effectiveness, and obviously non-offensive. Therefore, we need those components, but we also need to protect them effectively.

A third component, the heavy armoured forces, is the only offensive component in this model. There are several reasons for this. First of all, because they exist, and there is no chance to abolish them immediately; fiscal feasibility requires the use of these investments for at least the next 20 years. As a second argument, it is important to realise the complementarity of light infantry and heavy armoured forces. Together they confront the intruder with a complex threat and deny cheap counter-optimisations. For these reasons we may have to accept the existence of heavy armoured components even in the long run. An additional argument is that they are necessary for throwing out enemy forces from one's own territory. Light infantry is not suitable for these tasks. The options for counter offense are needed not on the strategic level, but on the tactical or operational level.

Thus, the IDM still includes offensive components, but they are integrated in functional interdependencies that clearly prevent large-scale offensive misuse.

The IDM is a transition model. It has to be seen in the context of the other proposals for the development of NATO's conventional defence. It is the opposite of the AirLand-battle concept and less offensive than the existing NATO posture. It is a first step towards a new paradigm of security policy in arms control that might be labelled 'benign defence'.

The Pro's and Con's of IDM

The following arguments are not intended to cover the whole spectrum of relevant aspects for the assessment and evaluation of a security policy proposal. However, at least four main topics are so crucial that they cannot be neglected, even in a short review paper. These four aspects are: the conventional strength of NATO and the task to demilitarise nuclear weapons; the problem of crisis stability; the arms-control aspects and the task to prevent technological destabilisation; and the question of political feasibility as it concerns the alliance as such, the domestic democratic consensus, the fiscal-feasibility and the interactions with civil economy.

The Effects upon Conventional Strength and the Demilitarization of Nuclear Weapons

There is a broad consensus in NATO that the deployment of

nuclear weapons in order to compensate for conventional insufficiencies is the wrong policy; hardly anybody disagrees with the goal of strengthening NATO's conventional defence. The question is how to achieve it. Most of the proposals are either destabilising, or too expensive, or disastrous for arms control.

Generally speaking, most of the proposals advanced until now, have focused on one of these topics, neglecting the others. But given the tensions already existing within the alliance, such an approach is a prescription for disaster. Therefore, it is most important to come up with a proposal that strengthens the conventional defence of NATO but at the same time improves crisis stability and the chances for arms control. The IDM was elaborated and optimised exactly for such a multidimensional set of goals.

Assessing the immediate effects of IDM on conventional strength and the demilitarisation of nuclear weapons, it is clear that the ability to defend even against an all-out conventional attack by the Warsaw Pact is much better than with the existing forces. The existing 'all-armour/all-purpose' concept is quite effective as long as it is possible to avoid regional breakthroughs. But with an overwhelming regional superiority, all the defender's disadvantages become relevant, and it is very likely that, after three to five days of intensive conventional fighting, NATO would reach the point where it has to decide either to give up or to resort to nuclear weapons.

With a fully implemented IDM, the situation changes quite a lot. Several problems are building up for the attacker. Normally it should be in his interest to advance very quickly, but the quicker he moves, the more damage the spectrum of passive ammunition will cause him. There is no chance whatsoever for the intruder to break through the first and second zones within a few hours. The primary impetus will inevitably be stopped already in the first zone and the attack of the first echelon will break down definitely in the second zone. This sort of mobility-kill has a synergetic effect with the efficiency of artillery rockets: as soon as quick manoeuvres are no longer possible the attacking formations are perfect targets for cost-effective indirect fire. Thus the IDM opens the chance for improving significantly the conventional defence capabilities of NATO, without a considerable increase in defence spending.

Apart from raising the nuclear threshold there is one more effect concerning the all-over deterrence that should at least be mentioned. Introducing IDM constitutes a sort of 'Conditional Conventional Retaliation Capability' (CCRC). It has been argued that the ability just to defend against an attack is not deterring enough and that NATO should have the ability to cause serious damage on the territory of the attacker and even to make territorial gains. This may be an argument in the logic of deterrence credibility. But at the same time those offensive capabilities would be a complete disaster for all arms-control efforts and the goal of crisis stability. Therefore, unconditional offense capabilities are incompatible with Western security interests; they are not even a goal, given the pure defensive orientation of the Western alliance. With CCRC the option for offense would not exist normally, but would depend upon an unsuccessful attack of the other side. An offensive capability would only exist after such an event.

A simplified model is as follows:

Let us assume there is a situation where A has an 'all-armour/all purpose' military concept and, say, 100 tanks. His opponent, B, has an IDM concept, that is only 50 tanks and the rest of his resources invested in a highly efficient fire belt and hook zone.

If A now tries to attack, he runs the risk that he will lose some 70-80 per cent of his tanks in zones 1 and 2 of the defender. Then - and only then - will B have superiority. He still has his 50 tanks and can now execute a limited strategic offence.

The important point of CCRC is, that the destabilising arms race accelerating effects of offensive options - which normally mean superiority - are clearly avoided. The functional complexity of the defence system allows for a reduction of offence-capable devices, and guarantees a structural non-attack capability, as long as the offender has not lost relevant parts of his arsenals, which can only happen if he is trying to attack.

Generally speaking, one can say that the IDM, by establishing a CCRC, fulfils the demands even for a conventional retaliation capability, without the destabilising effects that normally occur in this concept. Therefore, even from the point of view of pure political deterrence, the IDM reduces that burden of nuclear weapons, thus opening the way for a strategy in which nuclear weapons are purely political, and minimum deterrence is sufficient.

Effects on Crisis Stability

One of the main goals of IDM is to improve crisis stability. The crucial factors for crisis stability can be summarised as follows:

- magnitude of the bonus for pre-emption;
- dynamics of military necessities in a political crisis;
- vertical escalation dynamics;
- horizontal escalation dynamics;
- structural aptness of force structures for defence and/or offensive purposes;
- synchronous and diachronous robustness for the whole spectrum of crisis scenarios.

All these factors are crucial for crisis stability and were integratedly optimised in developing IDM. Crisis stability will be improved even if only one side implements IDM. A mutual transition towards IDM, would lead to a maximum of crisis stability, making a conventional war in Europe much less likely.

Effects on Arms Control and Avoidance of Technological Destabilisation

The third criterion in developing IDM was the chance for arms control and the task to avoid technological destabilisation. The old paradigm of arms control: 'First Parity, then Reductions' was a flop. The reason is that, due to the ambivalence of our military arsenals and the margins of insecurity in the assessment of the capabilities and intentions of the opponent, there is no point at which both sides could be secure at the same time. The only logically consistent strategy is to decouple defensive and offensive options, thus providing a structural defensiveness. Nobody can expect the leaders of the Western or the Eastern countries to rely completely on peaceful declarations by the other side. Substantial confidence-building must therefore have its roots in the characteristics of the hardware.

For these reasons it is very likely that the new paradigm of 'benign defence' would be a more effective leitmotiv for the arms control process than the old paradigm of parity. In any case it will be a revitalising stimulus for the arms control process, and therefore one should consider implementing it already in the second or third rounds at the Stockholm CSBM Conference.

As far as the threat of technological destabilisation is concerned, which is relevant not only in the nuclear sphere but also for conventional weapons, the only chance to prevent it are substantial arms control agreements.

Political Feasibility

A fourth topic of major concern is the political feasibility of a defence model. Here we can identify at least four issues: the chances of a domestic consensus; the chances of a consensus among the Western allies; the compatibility with demographic changes; and fiscal feasibility (including positive or negative interactions for the development of civil economy).

With regard to domestic consensus, IDM should have a good chance, due to the fact that it is a viable compromise between the NATO-traditionalists (who are mainly concerned about the threat of Soviet expansionism) and the camp of the critics (who are mainly concerned about the arms race as an auto-catalytic process). IDM offers the chance to rebuild a stable, bipartisan consensus on security policy which should be highly attractive for political decision-makers.

As far as a consensus in NATO is concerned, there will probably be no problems in the Benelux countries. The consent of Britain and France will depend on whether they consider IDM to be a strengthening or weakening of the German bulwark.

Whether the USA will endorse such a proposal depends very much whether or not it has any intention to exert political pressure in Europe with military means. If it does, it cannot agree on definitely defensive force structures in Europe. If it does not, there should be no problem. Even in the first case it should be the vital interest of all Europeans to deny such adventurous phantasies by structural dispositions of the conventional defence arsenals in Europe.

IDM should be feasible also in relation to demographic developments. The intensive utilisation of micro-electronics and data-processing should allow a reduction in manpower of about 10-20 per cent.

Finally, with regards to the economic implications of IDM, an annual net growth of 2 per cent for the defence budget could be sufficient. In addition, the emphasis on micro-electronics and data-processing is a major economic modernisation stimulus. For that reason alone, IDM should be highly attractive, especially for the political decision-makers in Europe.

To summarise, the political feasibility of IDM ought to be attainable.

Questions to be Answered

The idea of a transition to a 'structural defensiveness' has to be considered both from the Eastern and from the Western points of view. Several questions have to be answered. With regard to the Eastern countries, it would be important to know:

- Is IDM perceived as improving crisis stability and reducing the offensive threats that NATO forces pose on the WTO?
- Is the philosophy of 'benign defense' considered to be a new and hopeful paradigm for the arms-control process?
- Would it be possible for WTO forces to shift the emphasis away from heavy armoured forces and offense-capable logistics, towards specialisation on defence; and if so, what would be a realistic pace for the mutual transition process?

With regard to the Western countries, the important questions are:

- Can IDM be considered a balanced optimisation of the three factors 'military efficiency', 'crisis stability' and 'arms control'?
- Would a transition to IDM in the FRG be compatible with the interests of the other members of the Atlantic Alliance?
- What might be the next concrete steps towards implementtation, if the benign defence approach is considered a useful new paradigm for security policy and arms control?

25 Conventional Forces in Europe – Report from Pugwash Symposium, Vedbaek, Denmark

ANDERS BOSERUP

There has been a growing awareness in recent years that the problems of conventional disarmament deserve greater attention, both in their own right and because they have a direct bearing on the prospects for nuclear disarmament.

The need to reduce the role of nuclear weapons in Europe is today generally recognised. Most important is the question of no-first-use, and all discussions of 'tactical' nuclear weapons, of 'theatre' nuclear forces, of nuclear weapon-free zones, and so on, seem to bring us back to it. It is clear, however, that as long as the West continues to perceive that there is a significant imbalance at the level of conventional forces in Europe, there is little prospect that Western reliance on possible first-use of nuclear weapons will be given up. This suggests that in order to halt the nuclear arms race and reduce the risk of nuclear war, a new basis for security has to be found at the level of **conventional** forces.

Another reason for the growing interest in developments at the level of conventional forces derives from current NATO plans to utilise recent advances in conventional weapons technology to improve capabilities for deep interdiction by conventional means. The ostensible purpose is to provide a substitute for reliance on nuclear weapons so as to raise the nuclear threshold. There is considerable concern, however, that a deep interdiction capability will simply increase instability by encouraging pre-emption and escalation in war. In the end, when the Soviet Union has acquired a similar capability, this could actually increase rather than reduce Western reliance on the threat of nuclear escalation. In any case the implications of the new weapons need to be analysed very carefully if short-term considerations of military expediency are not to override the wider aims of long-term stability and security.

If used differently, these same technologies, which could lead us into a new arms build-up that would only enhance vulnerability and instability, might instead present us with a unique opportunity for disentangling ourselves from the present arms race in Europe. This is because these technologies, particularly the target-seeking precision-guided munitions, generally tend to favour defensive over offensive operations. If it were possible to establish a 'balance of forces' in Europe where both sides had enough strength to defend themselves but insufficient forces to mount an attack it would of course greatly enhance stability and security. It is obvious in fact, that unless the balance can be shifted away from offence-capable towards more exclusively defence-capable forces there is simply no way of achieving security for both sides at the same time. Nor do I see any other way which would make it possible for both sides simultaneously to give up the option of first-use of nuclear weapons and to relegate nuclear weapons to the limited role of deterring nuclear attack.

If we fail to see the risk of increased instability and the opportunity for creating a much more stable military situation which are inherent in the present technological trends, the risks may well materialise and the opportunities will certainly be missed. That is why it is so important at the present juncture to pause and reflect on the wider implications of the new technologies and to open a dialogue between East and West on the problems and prospects before us.

This was the background for convening the Symposium on Conventional Forces in Europe. The central theme in three days of intensive discussions was the **desirability** of relying more or less exclusively on strictly defensive, non-provocative forces and the **feasibility** of various ways of setting up such forces. As noted, greater emphasis on forces specialised for defence would have several advantages. Perceptions of security would not depend upon the achievement of an exact balance of forces and each state or alliance would be able to protect its security without impairing that of others. With less sensitivity to perceived imbalances, disarmament, whether by unilateral initiatives or through negotiated agreements, would not be as inordinately difficult as it is today. If forces were deliberately designed to reduce or minimise offensive capabilities this would promote crisis stability, enhance mutual confidence and provide a basis for genuine and robust détente.

In several respects the new possibilities opened up by developments in sensor- and guidance-technologies should favour the defence rather than the offence. It is becoming increasingly clear that it ought to be possible to design forces specialised in defence and incapable of offensive action which are much more effective in a defence role than are the forces presently available, designed as they are to be capable of both offensive and defensive operations. Precision-guided munitions increase the vulnerability of the classical weapons platforms - ships, aircraft and armoured vehicles - which are indispensable in an attack, and they put a high premium on dispersion and concealment which only the defence can exploit effectively.

Paradoxically, however, this implies that these new types of high technology weapons could pose a threat to a defence force built on the classical pattern and relying on concentrations of armour, on vulnerable supply-routes and so forth. That is the reason why plans to use the new technology in different 'deep-strike' roles causes considerable concern and could be highly destabilising, making the present defence preparations on one side or on both sides very vulnerable.

Whether the increased vulnerability of the classical weapons platforms implied by the new technologies will actually promote stability, détente and disarmament, or whether it will only enhance instability, promote fears and fuel the arms race, therefore depends entirely on the military and political context in which the new weapons are deployed. Combined with substantial armoured follow-on forces they could enhance offensive capabilities. Combined with a dispersed, infantry-based defence system they could not.

On the basis of the papers submitted to the Symposium, a variety of models and ideas for non-provocative (or less provocative) defence arrangements were discussed. These covered the full range, from the most ambitious - descriptions of forces entirely different from those existing at present and equipped and deployed in such a way that they would be wholly incapable of offensive action, to more pragmatic and evolutionary proposals - dealing with such issues as deployment and training patterns and the substitution of infantry for armour in certain tactical roles, proposals which would not imply very radical changes in force structures but which would nevertheless lead in the same direction of enhanced stability through greater specialisation in strictly defensive roles.

In my opinion we need analyses of both kinds. The more ambitious models are mainly tools for thinking. They bring out very clearly the basic principles on which defence systems must be based to ensure that they are truly non-threatening and stabilising. The more evolutionary proposals, on the other hand, help to chart first steps that might usefully be taken here and now. Despite differences in the evaluation of a number of concrete issues it was interesting to see at the Symposium that military professionals and civilian analysts were in considerable agreement on the basic principles which ought to be pursued and on means which might lead in the right direction.

The discussions also showed that non-provocative defence has to be placed from the outset in the context of disarmament and détente to mark it off very clearly from projects whose primary purpose is simply to achieve greater military strength. Otherwise, steps to enhance defensive capabilities are likely to be perceived by the other side not in the perspective of stability through an excess of defensive strength, but in a balance-of-force perspective, as nothing but a continuation of the arms race. Indeed, even the most unambiguously defensive forces could be perceived as potentially threatening since they might release other forces which could be used for offensive action.

I was myself surprised to see how deeply the idea of sustaining peace through a balance of terror has left its mark on our thinking, even with regard to conventional forces. Many regard the ability to launch a counter-offensive or to conduct reprisals as an important, indeed a necessary part of the total capability to dissuade attack, as if it were only the material destruction suffered, not the wider political implications of an aggression ending in failure, which could hold back an attacker. Thus, if one side were to adopt a truly impregnable, and strictly defensive military posture, this would limit the ability of both sides to conduct a successful counter-offensive: one side would not have the forces required, and the other side would not be able to penetrate the defences of the opponent. Consequently, it was pointed out, a strictly defensive posture might be regarded as detrimental to their security by both sides. I am not personally convinced by this argument. Nevertheless, it serves to underline that purely military measures cannot stand alone. Alterations in force structures in the direction of a strictly defensive posture have to be inserted in a wider political process if they are to assume their full significance and contribute effectively to détente and confidence building.

I should also stress, as a matter of course, that the various proposals for strong 'defensive defences' which have been put forward are not meant to constitute a long-term basis for European security. The aim is not to set up vast permanent military establishments but to find a way out of the arms race, to alleviate some of the fears which contribute to its perpetuation and to pave the way for substantial disarmament. But in order to unwind the arms race, one has to go through a phase in which states are able to defend themselves but unable to pose a threat to others. The proposed defence forces should be seen as such interim arrangements, designed to alleviate the fears and meet the security requirements of states as they perceive them today, but doing so in ways which will facilitate disarmament in the next round.

My own conclusion from the Symposium is that there is an obvious need to continue the dialogue which was begun there. I am, therefore, very pleased that the Pugwash Council has decided to go ahead with the establishment of a study group which will pursue, on a more long-term basis and in an East-West context, the issues we considered in Vedbaek.

How we are going to go about it is not, I believe, totally clear yet. We are envisaging an ongoing series of meetings at which we may discuss basic concepts and approaches to security in Europe as they relate to the forces and their structure. As I see it, the core of such discussions must be the idea of moving towards greater reliance on forces specialised for defence. This is so because it is the only possible way in which stability in the full sense of the word can be achieved, stability such that there is no fear of attack, no incentive (and perhaps also no means) for escalation and pre-emption in a crisis, and no military justification for further arms build-up. Such stability can **only** be achieved if the defensive capabilities on both sides are substantially in excess of the offensive capability of the other side. And **only** when such stability is achieved is it likely that the forces in favour of effective disarmament will prevail over the fears and suspicions which have led us instead to seek a caricature of security in a race to keep abreast in a competitive build-up of means of intimidation. **Only** on the basis of that kind of stability do I see a real prospect for eliminating nuclear weapons from the European 'theatre'; removing them from the stage and deleting them from the script.

There are many important subjects which could be taken up in the context of an East-West study group on conventional forces in Europe. We need to look much more carefully at various suggestions and approaches for shifting the emphasis towards more strictly defensive postures, examining their technical and political feasibility as well as the opportunities, and the risks they imply both in military terms and in political terms. We also need to consider in greater detail the various 'deep-strike' projects which are being developed in the West and which utilise the emerging technologies for purposes which, however defensive in intent, tend to be offensive in capability. This could be extended into a broader exploration of the systems and components on each side that are perceived as most dangerous and destabilising, and of what could be done about them. Yet another subject is the idea of disengagement zones. As has been stressed in other papers, a zone concept combining nuclear withdrawal with disengagement and restructuring of conventional forces might be particularly promising as a step towards security and stability in Europe.

In Vedbaek, of course, we could have no more than a preliminary examination of these complex, but vital and urgent issues. Much of our discussion focused on the fundamental conceptual questions of deterrence, defence, crisis-stability and so forth. And I think we were right in starting there. If we are to have a political impact, we must develop new concepts of security, based on ideas that are simple and convincing, and on approaches that are bold but also sound. Then we must design practical means to implement those ideas, means which will look credible not only to us civilians, but also to military professionals whose job it is to be cautious and who will not let themselves be carried away by concepts that look good only on paper. Finally, and most importantly insofar as the specific contribution of Pugwash is concerned, we must elaborate and refine these concepts and means in a continuing dialogue between East and West, since the aim is precisely to develop approaches that can be the basis not for unilateral but for **common** security.

Concern for conceptual clarity, attention to military expertise, and dialogue across the East-West divide, these were the three considerations that guided us at the Vedbaek Symposium. I think that they should also form the basis for our future work.

Part V
Security of Developing Countries

26 Emergence of Military Industries in the South and Their Longer Term Implications
MIGUEL WIONCZEK

Introduction

A very recent study of the global patterns of, and the prospects for, military spending, elaborated by a group of researchers headed by Wassily Leontief, one of the fathers of econometrics and Nobel Laureate, ends with an almost self-evident conclusion to the effect that[1]:

> If all regions of the world were to reduce their military purchases and if moreover the rich regions transfer part of the resulting 'savings' to the poorest of the less developed regions in the form of developmental assistance, this transfer of income would result in increased worldwide levels of production, trade and consumption.

The same study warns, however, that:

> But even with a massive rise in economic aid as well as the reduction in their own military spending, the 'gap' in economic well-being between the recipient regions and the others would be barely narrowed. Only if the transfers of resources just described are accompanied by changes in the **structures** of the poor economies might the economic prospects for the future of the poor less-developed regions appear less gloomy[2].

These quotations sum up the findings of the growing literature on economics of disarmament, that is, the reconversion of military expenditures to peaceful uses, the subject which has attracted lately attention of many international agencies and concerned political writers and social scientists. Unfortunately, these findings fall on the deaf ears of policy-makers in the real world, not only the industrial North but in many underdeveloped countries of the South. In the midst of the global economic crisis, comparable only with the depression of the thirties, worldwide military spending represents one of the few 'dynamic' sectors both in the North and the South.

According to one of the most detailed surveys of the global expenditure on arms and related equipment, world spending on these 'consumer goods' rose some 10 per cent in real terms between 1981 and 1982, inspite of the fact that most countries suffered a sharp decline in national income as well as cuts in practically all public sectors, including social services[3].

Paradoxically, the literature on the economics of armaments race itself stays very much behind that on the economics of disarmament. Moreover, very little is known about the forceful entry into the conventional but highly technologically sophisticated arms production and the international arms trade by a group of the more developed among the less developed countries, a group known in international economic parlance as the NICs (the newly industrialising countries). Some even less developed countries are joining or are about to join this group.

Since it is not the purpose of this paper to take up the subject of the economics of the armaments race in the North, I will limit myself to politics and economics of the emergence and the growth of military industries in the NICs. The sources of information are direct but reliable: the most prestigious newspapers and wide circulation journals of the Western industrial countries. Inspite of these limitations it is pertinent to mention that the general thinness of the literature on the economics of the armament race in the industrially advanced countries, and the absence of references to the armaments race both in the North and in the South in global surveys of the world economy, independently from their origin, reflect the combination of many factors.

The key ones are perhaps six:

1. The broadly extended view that the worldwide armaments race is mainly a political and technological phenomenon, that exceeds the terms of reference of global (or for that matter, regional and national) economic and industries surveys.
2. The extremely high level of political sensitivity in many parts in respect to the so-called 'national security' matters, however defined, and the belief prevailing everywhere that the armaments race is both inevitable and uncontrollable.
3. The limited access of economy experts to, and the understanding of, the disaggregated information about armaments production and expenditure of the arms spenders.

MILITARY INDUSTRIES IN THE SOUTH

4. The alleged difficulties of finding reliable quantitative data and the real difficulties to analyse national and regional policy-making processes with respect to management of military industries, military technology transfers and the modes of domestic arms procurement and international arms trade.
5. The limited worldwide supply of highly-trained social scientists with reasonably good technological background capable of treating the subject of politics, economics and technological aspects of armaments race in an intra-disciplinary fashion.
6. The ascendancy in the economic profession of the 'rococo' econometrics, namely, superficially impressive quantitative theoretical model-building, divorced from political and institutional economics, that is, from real life issues. (The term 'rococo' econometrics is an adaptation of the expression 'rococo' mathematics, coined by John von Neumann in the forties. He used it to describe sterile exercises in mathematical analysis which were not adding anything new or relevant to the solution of important gaps in the science of mathematics.)

The scarcity of knowledge about the recent emergence, the functioning, and the international implications of military industries in some NICs - and even in the developing countries which do not qualify for the entrance into this category - can hardly be explained by these six factors only. Some others must be added. First, all of those newcomers are far away from research centres on the economics of armaments and disarmament, functioning in the industrial North and within the United Nations system. Second, they are the very recent entrants in the armaments game. Thirdly, their relative weight in the global arms production, expenditure and international trade is still relatively small. The participation of NICs in 'arms transfer' to the South, an expression covering the arms jointly purchased abroad by the 'final consumer', 'free' military aid, and barter of arms for other goods and services, has been estimated at close to 4 per cent of the global arms transfers in 1982[4].

Since total arms transfers to the South in that year were estimated at $50 billion, the very conservative estimates of the South-South arms transfers put them at a minimum of $2 billion. While relatively small, it is a not insignificant figure under any circumstance. Moreover, one should be aware that although all NICs (except Mexico) and some other less developed countries count with the domestic production of increasingly sophisticated military equipment, the number of the countries which are at the same time arms producers and exporters does not, as yet, exceed six to eight in the South.

Misinformation about the Role of the South

Neither global nor country-by-country figures on military industry production in the South and the intra-South arms transfers are available from such standard and largely reliable sources as the SIPRI Yearbooks and the annual surveys on world military and social expenditures, published respectively by non-governmental research centres in the USA and UK[5].

These and other similar sources assume that the South continues to be the importer of military equipment produced in the advanced countries of the East and the West. For the first time some doubts in that respect arise, albeit indirectly, in the 1983 SIPRI Yearbook. Its analysis of the North-South arms trade notes that while from 1963-67 to 1968-72 the value of arms exports to the less developed countries doubled and it doubled again in the period 1973-77, from that last period to 1978-1982 the increase was down to 50 per cent. According to the same source: 'The main reason for this flattening out is probably the world recession, and the budget constraints it has brought about with it; there is also the possibility of a certain market saturation'[4].

There is no doubt some truth in the SIPRI diagnosis of the reasons for the recent deceleration of military equipment purchases by the South in the North. Considering that the prices of modern conventional weaponry are increasing steeply all the time, one would rejoice in the news that the acquisition of military equipment by the less developed countries shows such a socially healthy trend. There is growing evidence, not yet recorded and analysed however, that under the world crisis conditions what is also taking place is the military equipment import substitution in the South, and the entry of new producers from the NICs group into Southern arms markets.

It is part and parcel of the worldwide phenomenon, related to the so-called arms modernisation and the patterns of military procurement, as well as to inflation. A recent survey of defence industries in the industrial countries summarises this situation as follows:

> Defence costs are spiralling so high that even the super-powers and a few oil-rich countries are investing in the qualitative improvement of weapons, rather than in larger inventories. Countries are spending more on defence, but in general are getting less for it, say industry analysts[6].

According to numerous and frequent articles and reports, published during 1983 in such prestigious newspapers with worldwide coverage like **The New York Times, Washington Post, The Wall Street Journal** and **Financial Times**, the list of the countries in the South, which become both military equipment producers and exporters to other parts of the South, increases rapidly[7]. Leaving aside Israel and South Africa (mentioned in these press reports as well, although neither of the two can be considered as part of the South or as a developing country), such a list is headed by Brazil, Singapore, China and both Koreas. The corresponding roster of buyers in the South, or arms produced by the South, is even larger. It includes Chile, Argentina (until the autumn of 1983), Central American republics, Iran, Iraq, Thailand, Malaysia and Nigeria, among others.

In most cases, the South military equipment exporters, as well as importers, are extremely reluctant for 'security reasons' to release any information on arms production and sales abroad. Nevertheless, Brazil and Singapore have been such big 'success stories' in the past few years in challenging in the Southern markets the armament industries of the North's advanced countries, that a considerable amount of information on these two NICs' military industry's domestic and external performance is now available.

The South's Success Stories in the Armament Industry

Brazil began making its own light weapons in 1954. But it remained a net arms importer, mainly from the USA, until the mid-seventies. The abrogation of the military cooperation treaty with the USA in 1977 gave the local weapons industry its chance. Today, the Brazilian military industry complex is made up of some 350 companies employing one hundred thousand people, closely linked to the armed forces. Among the ten largest Brazilian weapons manufacturers some are state-controlled like Embraer, specialising in military aircraft, others are private like Engesa, claiming to be the largest manufacturer of wheeled armoured vehicles in the West, and Avibras, making a wide range of rockets, missiles and simpler air bombs.

In less than ten years, starting from scratch, Brazil has moved into fifth or sixth place in the non-socialist world as a weapons manufacturer. It is estimated that Brazil sells abroad about 1000 armoured cars and armoured fighting vehicles annually in arms-for-oil transactions in the Middle East and Africa. Its three biggest sellers are the amphibious Urutu, the Cascavel (an armoured car) and the Jaracca (a light reconnaissance vehicle). Its 1983 sales of arms are expected to exceed $2 billion and its largest single client is presently Iraq. Until now the Brazilians have successfully avoided - except in the most recent case of impounding, under pressure from the USA, Libyan shipments by air of arms to Central America - any political entanglements over their 'free-for-all' and 'no questions asked' policy towards arms sales for cash. A shroud of secrecy veils Brazil's foreign arms deals so much so that the statistics are not even recorded by the Government's foreign trade department. It is known, however, that arms exports from Brazil are closely overseen by Imbel, the official arms production coordinating agency[8].

The second 'success' is that of **Singapore**, called the 'Switzerland of South-East Asia', whose military industry was set up in the mid-1960s by the Defence Ministry. Chartered Industries of Singapore, a company owned by the Ministry of Defence through a holding company established with technical assistance from the USA and Israel, started with the production of minor 'mass consumption' automatic weapons, especially assault rifles SAR-80 and light machine guns, Ultimex 100, which are cheaper than European models and the US standard automatic rifle M-16. The respective actual production capacity of SAR-80 and Ultimex 100, is 6000-8000 and 24 000-30 000 units per year. More than half of the output is destined for exports. Moreover, Chartered Industries' thirteen subsidiaries and three associated companies also produce small arms ammunition and medium calibre ammunition for anti-aircraft and aircraft cannons. In addition, the industry manufactures grenades, anti-personnel and anti-tank mines, mortar bombs and 500-lb bombs for jet aircraft.

In 1982, several Chartered Industries subsidiaries in the aerospace field were brought under one corporation, Singapore Aircraft Industries. It can and does maintain overhaul and repair of aircraft (like the Lockheed C-130 Hercules) and jet fighters (like A-4 Skyhawks) for the US air force in the Far East. It can overhaul half a dozen types of engines, including Pratt and Whitney, Rolls Royce and General Electric, as well as aircraft-related components like propellers, landing gear, and radio, navigational and instrument systems. Finally, the company can also manufacture external fuel tanks and bomb racks, and offers servicing of avionics and defence and marine electronics.

A third arm of Singapore's military industry covers the naval sector, in which the prominent company, also under the Ministry of Defence, is Singapore Shipbuilding and Engineering. This is capable of building quite large vessels, and has recently completed for the Singapore Navy a dozen Swift class inshore patrol boats of an Australian design.

MILITARY INDUSTRIES IN THE SOUTH

Chartered Industries of Singapore, brought in June 1983 under the single umbrella of a new company, the Singapore Technology Corporation, has recently declared its technological independence in all these fields. As reported directly from that minuscule country: 'So successful is Singapore that where it once produced arms under licence for the USA (first for the use in the IndoChina covert operations after the US defeat in Vietnam), the tables could soon be turned, with the United States manufacturing Singaporean-designed arms under licence'[9].

The Singapore military industry has ambitious plans for the future. It plans to enter shortly into manufacturing a new basic jet trainer under Italian or Spanish licences. As another direct source reports, the Western military equipment companies which have provided Chartered Industries of Singapore so far with the most modern technologies, make a veritable 'Who's Who' of the world armaments industry. In a parallel way, the Singapore military industry complex makes a continuous search in the scientific and defence literature for new ideas, new processes and new developments it can use[10]. A considerable amount of relevant information is available from these sources free of charge as long as the domestic capacity for adaptation exists.

The steady build-up of domestic military technology capability does not limit itself to Brazil and Singapore. Egypt was reported in August 1983 to have developed its own version of a Soviet-made, shoulder-fired anti-aircraft missile, the SAM-7. The Egyptian copy was successfully tested and went into production early in 1984[11]. No other Middle East country has a substantial arms industry. The Egyptian military industry's capability represents in a way the heritage of the decision taken in the early seventies by the Arab League to chose that country as the site for a regional programme to make weapons, with financing provided by the Gulf States after the 1983 OPEC increase in oil prices. Although the Gulf countries pulled out of the programme after Egypt signed the peace treaty with Israel, the build-up of the Egyptian military industry continued. The country now assembles the French-FRG Alpha jet trainers and manufactures some Alpha parts for inclusion in European-assembled planes. The Egyptian arms industry refurbishes USSR-built weaponry and assembles some Western weapons under licence.

China - under its military modernisation programme, begun in 1980, which is expected to involve the expenditure of the equivalent of $41 billion over the present decade, covered partly by exports of military goods to Pakistan, Iran, Egypt and Romania, among others - is developing the Shenyang F-12, an all-weather interceptor modelled on the

Soviet Mig 23. Chinese present exports include Shenyang F-6, a derivative of the Mig-19[12]. Moreover, the country is practically self-sufficient in respect of the wide range of standard military equipment, including tanks and cannons. Experts in international arms trade and arms transfers consider China as the world's eighth most important arms exporter.

More military industries will appear in the South during the eighties. One country which is definitely bent upon achieving some degree of independence in this field is Saudi Arabia, the largest military equipment importer in the world. It plans to start its own arms industry the same way as Brazil, Argentina, Singapore, Republic of Korea and Egypt did in the seventies. The first step consists of forcing foreign military equipment producers and exporters in the industrial countries to set up local plants to build under licence parts of some weapon systems originally imported fully assembled. Discussions to that effect are underway between the Saudis and two major US producers of military aircraft. A pilot programme in local production might emerge from Saudi Arabia's negotiations for manufacturing certain parts of electronic equipment for a sophisticated systems of military command and control. According to the US parties directly involved in the negotiations in Riyadh, the next step could consist in the large co-production contracts which are likely to come with future purchases of fighter planes by Saudi Arabia[13]. Its arguments include the need to obtain advanced technology to diversify its economy and to create jobs. Other Saudi arguments are of commercial and political nature: the potentially large markets in Saudi Arabia's smaller Arab allies in the Gulf Cooperation Council; the regional political prestige arising from the availability of an advanced military industry in the Middle East; and demoting the high-profile role of foreigners and foreign suppliers (particularly the USA), in sensitive sectors of Saudi Arabia's affairs. Although the country lacks trained local industrial workers, its cadres of military technicians have been steadily growing through training programmes in the USA, run by the major aircraft companies and primarily directed towards military aircraft maintenance. Assuming the constant access to most modern military technology, assured by the steady flow of new generations of weapons of all sorts, these trained abroad local technical cadres may become the backbone of the future Saudi Arabian military industry.

Long-term Implications

The current international literature on industrialisation and

economic development correctly puts emphasis on a number of
key factors which industrial and economic planners in the
NICs and other reasonably large developing countries must
consider if their industrialisation programmes are to succeed
even partially.

First, no industrialisation programme worthy of that name
can be translated into reality in the absence of some sort of
overall longer-term economic strategy. Second, whether one
likes it or not, the role of the State in industrialisation
processes under the conditions of an even relative underdevelopment is of key importance. Third, the construction of
haphazard industrial projects, however ambitious, but not
related to the available infrastructure and the already
existing stock of industries, does not add up to industrialisation. Fourth, given the present speed of technological
advancement, no across-the-board industrialisation is within
the reach of even a large country which is well-endowed with
natural resources. Fifth, the choice of industries within a
limited number of sectors must, in the longer run, aim at the
vertical integration of the industries in question. Sixth,
since there is no single industrialisation model for all
underdeveloped countries, the debate about whether one should
start from the bottom (heavy industries) or from the top
(light final consumption goods industries) is a sterile
exercise in face of the need to use with reasonable
efficiency the available industrial projects, however modest,
through establishing all sorts of interlinkages and closing
the inter- and intra-industrial gaps. Seventh, the inflexible
import substitution industrial strategy runs into very
serious difficulties even in the most advanced industrialised
underdeveloped countries. Eighth, the speed of industrialisation depends to a great extent upon four major factors; the
constant expansion of the domestic market; the access to
export markets; the technological capability and the inflow
of new technologies; and the quality of local management
skills, both in the public and the private sector.

This brief list of major issues and factors involved in the
industrialisation process gives an idea how difficult its
implementation is for most of the underdeveloped countries.
The recent emergence and progress of military industries in a
growing number of NICs, and even the not-NICs, strongly,
suggests that while the task is difficult it is far from
impossible. The worldwide arms industry is both competitive
and technologically highly dynamic, and involves not only the
availability of highly skilled technical personnel, but the
ability of continuous 'learning by doing' and control of the
quality of the final product, the art of industrial management and the knowledge of foreign markets. In each of the

cases described here the patterns of the development of the military industrial complex are practically the same.

At the beginning arms are imported fully designed, produced and assembled in the industrial countries of the North. Next, the capacity for maintenance of military 'consumer durables' of foreign origin is established, most probably because of security considerations and because of a risk that the interruption at some point of the additional inflow of identical or similar military equipment may endanger 'national security' requirements. The maintenance activities which provide the stimulus to technological training lead to the discovery that some parts of, or accessories to, foreign-produced, even highly sophisticated equipment, might be produced at home at much lower cost if only their quality control could be assured. After having copied foreign designs successfully, and having passed through construction of prototypes and their testing under local conditions, the question arises (the same which arose two decades ago in the automobile and pharmaceutical industries in many underdeveloped countries): why must certain military goods be fully assembled abroad? At this stage, proposals are made to foreign governments and/or arms producers to provide locally-produced parts for foreign assembly units. Sometimes such proposals are presented as a condition for future purchasing contracts. Next comes the interest for transferring some assembly activities to the arms importing countries, whose degree of information about international arms and technology markets and the negotiating capacity of the new arms deals are surprisingly much better than in the non-military trade transactions.

It is worth stressing that all these activities involve a considerable degree of industrial organisation and management, which, in most cases, is provided jointly by the local military establishments and private entrepreneurs. When the local production of military goods under foreign licences or co-production arrangements start, little if anything is left to improvisation and random decisions. Given the extremely high degree of the intra-military industry specialisation on the worldwide scale, product lines are chosen according to well-defined domestic market needs, export prospects and technological capability. Consequently, the newly emerging military industries in the South are as reliable and businesslike as the same industries in the North. Moreover, they are tough competitors not only in terms of quality but in terms of prices. Brazil, Singapore, China and the Republic of Korea can undersell any long-established arms exporter from the industrial North and their military industrial enterprises not only earn hard currencies but make profits as well, unless purely political considerations advise export subsidies.

Conclusion

The stage-by-stage expansion approach, described above, adopted by the newly emerging military industries in the South, if followed by other industrial branches related to social and not 'security' needs on a national and regional scale, would, without any doubt, contribute considerably to the economic and social welfare of many underdeveloped countries. The success of these military industries strongly suggests that the obstacles for industrialisation in the South - except in the two scores of the extremely poor in natural and human resources small countries - are not reflecting a state of nature but are man-made. If a developing country can produce in competition with the industrial North not only small 'mass consumption' military hardware such as light machine guns, but also armoured cars, tanks, cannons, land-to-air missiles and eventually military jet aircraft, it could easily produce a wide range of capital, intermediate and final consumer goods for peaceful purposes. Paraphrasing the Leontief remarks quoted earlier, the **worldwide** re-allocation of financial and physical resources from military spending to peaceful-oriented production would result in increased global levels of production, trade and consumption, but only if the subsequent transfer of resources to the underdeveloped world were accompanied by changes in the structures of the so-called poor economies. The success of the new military industries in the South, based upon the efficient misallocation of resources for wrong social uses, is the example of a wrong solution of the structural problems entailing an additional threat to world security. This example might, however, offer the promise to the South, by demonstrating that its industrialisation process is not impossible and might be worth pursuing if directed towards socially-positive objectives within the framework of South-South cooperation.

References

1. W. Leontief and F. Duchin, Military Spending, Facts and Figures Worldwide Implications and Future Outlook (New York-Oxford: Oxford University Press, 1983) p.66.
2. Ibid.
3. International Institute for Strategic Studies, The Military Balance, 1983-1984 (London: September 1983).
4. SIPRI (Stockholm International Peace Research Institute)

The Arms Race and the Arms Control 1983 (London-New York: Taylor & Francis, 1983).
5. R, Sivard, 'World Military and Social Expenditures', Institute for World Order, Leesburg, Va. and 'The Military Balance', The International Institute for Strategic Studies, London.
6. Financial Times Survey of Defence Industries, Financial Times (10 October 1983).
7. D. Middleton, 'Smaller nations crack arms market', The New York Times (28 August 1983).
8. A. Whitley, 'Curtain parts on Brazil arms trade', Financial Times (1 June 1983).
9. D. Lee, 'Singapore is quietly pursuing role as an independent arms producer', International Herald Tribune (Hong Kong edition) (16 December 1983).
10. C. Sherwell, 'Singapore builds up defence industry in economic strategy', Financial Times (London) (30 November 1983).
11. 'Egypt copies Soviet missile', The New York Times (19 August 1983).
12. D. Hiro, 'As the Gulf war enters the fourth year, Iran plays a Chinese card', The Wall Street Journal, New York (22 September 1983).
13. J. Fitchett, 'Saudis said to envision own weapons industry', International Herald Tribune, Paris edition, (17-18 December 1983).

27 The Rise of Militarism: Effects on Third World Countries
UBIRATAN D'AMBROSIO

Introduction

Much of the effort for the promotion of confidence measures would have a better chance of success if the societal texture of the modern world were understood. A better comprehension of the historical factors which combine to generate the Western mode of thought would certainly help in understanding the tensions and internal conflicts which result from the body of values, knowledge and technology. Of particular interest are the aspects of militarisation of society, because the build-up of the structure of social organisation, control and priorities can be **basically** modelled on the structures and values which are typical of the armed forces. In the analysis of the underlying philosophy of social stratification, the motives of industrial and technological development, and the goals of world order, I shall place emphasis on the philosophical, practical and technological bases of social and political organisations. I hope this will lead to some practical possibilities of a better conduct of our way to the future.

Much of my argument relies on the sociological and cultural framework upon which the so-called Western civilisation is built. On the other hand, I have to recognise some bias resulting from my perspective as a citizen of a Third World country, bitter but, at the same time, eager for change. I cannot refrain from acknowledging the major achievement of the superpowers and their subsidiaries (NATO and Warsaw Pact countries), the remarkable success in the last 40 years, that practically none of the citizens of one group were killed by the other, and the fact that these countries have, by and large, managed to avoid war, probably the longest period of effective peace in modern history. But I cannot avoid noticing that this was paid for by the flesh and blood of Third World countries. Never have so many Third World people died in the name of alleviating tensions in the North. It is as if Third World blood and flesh was vampirised by a Western industrial Dracula!

While transforming the Third World into the battleground for the warring appetites of the developed powers, it is inevitable that the terror and blood flooding therein will spill over their own peaceful and prosperous gardens. Technological advance and sophistication in nuclear weaponry indicates the possibility that, in the near future, nuclear terrorism will reach the heart of the tension centres in the developed countries. The tenuous separation between nuclear terrorism and nuclear retaliation endangers the cherished equilibrium. All this is plain madness and the price is unbearable for those who are paying it now.

The Rise of Militarism

As already stated, militarism has grown as the essential form of societal organisation of mankind. It is part of the cultural evolution of mankind according to the so-called rationalistic mode of thought, which characterises Western civilisation. If we look at the neo-Darwinist explanation of the phenomenon culture, we see a model of the evolution of man as a cultural species, leading to the concept of **Homo Hierarchicus**, which is the societal counterpart of **Homo Sapiens**. In our cultural mode, which we may call the **Western mode of thought**, rationalism and its brain children, science and modern technology, represent the subordination of sensual stimuli for action to rationalised ones, whose metabehaviour is regulated by basic and fundamental laws of thought which underly logic systems.

Thus, a rational mode of thought leads naturally from the concept of creativity to a man-environment relationship, that demands adequate societal organisation. The set of norms which frame and regulate social behaviour and social relationships to conform to this structural, rationalised, and formalised mode of thought, calls for a hierarchisation of knowledge, organisation, property and production, behaviour and decision. The fitness of the species to this hierarchisation is what I called **Homo Hierarchicus**. In socio-biological terms, it is explained as the ultimate search of the species for someone to take the decision in the evolutionary cultural behaviour, similar to the appearance of **Homo Sapiens**.

Examples which illustrate this claim are encountered in the religious structures of the Judeo-Christian (Judeo-Greco-Roman) pattern which developed in parallel and syntonically with Western science and its consequences: forms of property and production; conceptualisations of normal and abnormal, and the mechanisms of correction; and concepts of individual and collective rights. All together they constitute the threads into which the main fabric of a modern, univerally adopted society, is interwoven.

The forms of property and production claim a structured ownership of goods, which resulted from a controlled holding power of collective essentials for production. In the agricultural field, land is property, water is property, and even the seeds, which are produced and result from initial expropriation of production, are property. **Ownership** of this is regulated by highly structured logical norms and rules which invariably call for a hierarchisation of ownership.

The normal and abnormal conceptualisation calls, unavoidably, for mechanisms of correction. Again, such mechanisms, like medicine, legislation, punishment and penalties are structured on the pattern of a hierarchy of normal behaviour. Someone examines behaviour, according to some laws and rules, and applies the correctives. Or prevents it by directing future behaviour and misbehaviour. This has been labelled **education**, in its broadest sense; it is unequivocally patterned on a hierarchised model.

The concepts of individual and collective rights encounter their realisation in the organisational frame of society called **politics**. Again, through a highly hierarchised system, representation and governance, legitimacy of individual behaviour according to a collective superstructure and equilibrium of several different behaviours, are hierarchised to lead to the concepts of nations, states and, ideally, to an international stately order. Concepts such as national security and national interest are thus created, and become paradigms. Mankind has been searching for this for centuries and has, increasingly, called for a reinforcement of the universality of the concepts mentioned above: property and production, normality and abnormality, and individual and collective behaviour. Eventually, this has encountered in the Western mode of thought its full realisation: its branches are based on the principles of Science and Religion and brought into practice by **militarisation**.

Militarisation of society seems to be the organisation **par excellence** to carry out the overall project of changing **homo sapiens** into **homo hierarchicus**, under the clearly identified aegis of Western civilisation. Subtle alternative models, labelled according to some variants (for example, socialistic, capitalistic, and so on) are minor variations of the basic texture of the concepts of **production and property, normal and abnormal, and individual and collective**. All the variants call for a hierarchic, militaristic organisation to achieve particular goals.

As long as mankind works and behaves according to these basic concepts, hierarchisation of the species appears the only suitable organisation model, and militarisation fits ideally for the realisation of this model. Militarism is thus in intimate relationship with Western civilisation. To understand it better we have to look into its symbiosis with the evolution of modern science. In a paper at the 1982 Pugwash Conference, I discussed the increasing role of the military establishment in modern society even when the presence of military is not directly seen in governmental and political decision levels, as well as a pushing force behind industrial development. I call this **stratocratisation** of society through control of the means of communication and information, rooted on the underlying concept of national security.

Militarised Development

I shall now touch on some issues related to the development of the arms industry in Third World countries, with specific reference to Brazil. Indeed, in Brazil, plagued by economic problems in the last decade, the arms industry has been the most efficient and successful enterprise ever taken up by the country. From being almost non-existent in the 1960s, the flourishing military-industrial Brazilian enterprise is responsible for a substantial share in the country's economy (for more detail see the paper by Wionczek in this volume pp. 295-306).

From the Brazilian experience, we observe that its arms industry is:
- the only flourishing economic enterprise in the country, with a steady increase in volume and quality;
- the only viable example of a successful developmental effort;
- the most successful example of Brazilian generated technology, that is, appropriate, or native, technology, developed in civilian academic and research institutions by Brazilian scientists, and taken to the productive phase by private enterprise with national resources. In other words, it is the most successful example of R&D jointly carried out by academic and private enterprise.

Brazilians are proud and fascinated by this successful enterprise and the efficiency of military organisation, and gain confidence from our capability to compete successfully with developed and industrialised nations. All this is led by an inspired, well educated and nationalistic sector of our society, most of them self-made men, from very humble and even poor families, who through an unequivocally democratic admission system, based exclusively on fitness and competence, join the superbly efficient, absolutely free, military academy at the age of 15. These 200 or 300 highly selected individuals, regardless of social or economic origin, are trained to become the highly nationalistic, well trained, very motivated and ideologically monolithic core of the Brazilian military establishment. This example **par excellence** of **homo hierarchicus** meets a society, in which the only match - far less efficient, less capable and internally disrupted social group - might be the religious establishment. Inevitably, military control, or at its democratic best, supervision and general guidance, is ready to 'help' society to return to its path whenever disturbing forces from inside or outside interfere with the order and progress of the state.

Returning to the considerations on the industrial-military establishment, it is surprising that a country dependent on advanced technology, which is a large importer of equipment and with no arms tradition, as is the case of Brazil, has succeeded in the short period of 15 years to achieve the results mentioned. This fact calls for a revision of a number of concepts and commonly held assumptions about science and technology in developing countries, and about the relationships between academics and the political sectors of society.

The military-industrial complex of a national political project for technological development has some characteristics which can be summarised as follows:
- establishment of a long-term joint action;
- respecting the ownership of the means of production;
- legitimising the endeavour in the eyes of the rest of society through a national ideology.

This seems to have been, in very broad terms, the model so successfully adopted in the conquest of what is now Latin America by the Spaniards in the sixteenth century.

In the Brazilian example, these three steps were taken by the scientific and technological establishment collaborating with the productive sectors, under the aegis of the state, which subscribed to the ideology of a nationalistic 'big power' destiny. This ideology, formulated after the end of the Second World War, went through stages of preparing high level civilian manpower in symbiotic ideology with the military élite. High level structures were created, such as the Instituto Tecnologico de Aeronautica de Sao José dos Campos and the Escola Superior de Guerra, which take in carefully selected civilians and military. This symbiotic ideological build-up culminated with the (also symbiotic)

civilian military coup of 1964. Elements of counter-insurgence, encouraged by the deterioration of USA-Brazil relations, were determining factors in the success of this enterprise.
It is around certain ideological concepts that successful enterprises, like the one exemplified by the Brazilian build-up of an industrial-military complex, flourish. They give the military establishment a strong hold on all aspects of society, even though the military presence goes unnoticed in everyday life. This is what I call stratocratisation of society. Examples abound even in the non-militaristic democracies of both the Western and the Eastern blocs.

Some Discussion Issues

A few issues result from the above considerations:

- what are the social costs of military expenditure?
- what are the economic costs of military expenditure?
- what are the contradictions and specificities of arms transfer versus indigenous production?
- how to implement measures on both national and international mechanisms for: (a) reporting; (b) limitation controls; (c) reduction measures; (d) taxation.

It is also desirable to analyse, in a deeper way, long-term non-quantifiable aspects of militarism, such as:

- concepts of national and individual security;
- psychological aspects of the arms race;
- public opinion and education, going deeper into understanding the acceptance and passivity by the public;
- social pressures related to the military-industrial complex, such as economic, bureaucratic, psychological, scientific, moral;
- the economic and social consequences of disarmament, such as governmental decisions with respect to security, both national and individual, and the sharing of responsibilities, at both international and national levels.

Finally, I cannot refrain from mentioning the general and broad topic of the overall and universal financial crisis as related to the military situation. Malthusian approaches to the survival of mankind tend to bring some practical (and even moral) justification for a permanent state of tension, with the inevitability of periodic large-scale exterminations. These issues, not unrelated to the main theme of this paper, need further development.

28 Arms Control and Crisis 'Management': Feasibility and Complexities in the Third World
ESSAM GALAL

Arms control in the context of East-West relationship is usually understood to imply a voluntary or mutually agreed limitation of arms acquisition amenable to verification; it is usually assumed to enhance stability.

Crisis management in the same context usually implies voluntary or mutually coordinated non-military measures to restrain the development, acuteness, severity or scope of confrontations.

In the context of the Third World arms **control** needs to reflect a more complex relationship between opponents, receivers and suppliers. With increasing frequency opponents manifest a duality of purpose as claimants and proxies. Foreign aid, boycots and bans, both military and economic, are another dimension of the complexity of **control** in the context of the Third World. A decisive **control** had a more devastating effect in the case of the special client states, Israel and South Africa. Final **control** when all the lock-gates miraculously seep, has been amply demonstrated by a series of astounding major power military incursions; they were invariably claimed to be the ultimate **control**.

Procedures and Mechanisms

As a reflection of this multiplicity of participants and functions, the arms-races in the Third World cannot realistically be subject to the same procedures and mechanisms that, in the past, produced a modicum of feasibility in East-West confrontation.

First: It cannot always be targeted towards stabilisation of the **status quo**. The **status quo** in the Middle East, South Africa, Central America and Afghanistan inherently represents a profound imbalance, imposed and sustained through arms superiority. Any mutually acceptable arms control arrangements would imply a mutually tolerable shift from the **status quo**. Thus **linkages** with political accommodation must be mutually acknowledged by all parties in the context of arms **control** in the Third World. The implication of such linkage has to be accepted not only by the parties, but also by their sponsors.

Second: Mechanisms of bilateral negotiations and verification are rarely feasible in the Third World. They are not feasible in strategic crisis areas because of the multiplicity of participants and purposes. They are rarely feasible even in the occasionally endogenic Third World conflicts because of the inherent geophysical, technical and political instabilities. International mechanisms and approaches have been consistently overridden by the entrenched influences of major powers in strategic areas and even outside it where endogenous conflicts are miraculously transformed into strategic.

However, regional mechanisms and approaches have rarely succeeded without international cooperation, but this is available only when regional organisations succeed in filling the power vacuum in their regions.

There are many political, economic, constraints on the road to effective regional organisations. This applies to the North, although obviously more so to the South. Indeed, the special characteristics of arms control are not a peculiarity of the Third World. As the Stanford Arms Control Group concluded:

> The European example shows the enormous political complexity of regional arms control negotiations. Strategic arms negotiations were relatively separable from politics, since these arms relate primarily to other strategic arms in a technical dialectic that becomes detached from actual conflict. The regional arms are, however, often protecting broad security and political interests. Thus arms control negotiations could come in Europe only in conjunction with a serious new flexibility in the political and security areas[1].

On the other hand, there are two significant differences between Europe and Third World regions. One is that stability at both the national and regional levels differs vastly. The second difference relates to the integral relationship that exists between the European countries of East and West. In the light of these differences, the area of contention at inter-group, inter-state and inter-camp levels are far more delineated and stable.

Mounting Risks

There are some reasons why the North mày eventually find it beneficial to change its negative attitude towards the participation of the South in control and management.

With the upgrading of the qualitative arms race in the Third World, the ferocity and scope of military confrontation may get easily out of control. States are upgraded beyond calculation, and proxy agents call the tune despite being paid. As the states are upgraded so is the commitment of the sponsors.

A progressive network of direct major powers military involvement or intervention is unfolding in Central America, the Middle East, the Indian Ocean, Africa, South Asia, which evoke a reflex response from the other side.

The 1980s may be said to be witnessing the beginning of the logical reversal of the role of proxies. Sometimes it is not apparent who is the piper and who is calling the tune.

The chaos resulting from the military extension of the central area of direct confrontation to the unstable periphery of the Third World has several destabilising manifestations on East-West relations:

- it involves some of the most unstable crisis-prone areas of the Third World;
- it has a built-in momentum of its own that can culminate in absurd events, like the 'Grenada Victory';
- it eventually locks the superpowers in irrational or untenable positions, such as: placating and aiding nuclear capabilities for Israel and South Africa; USA-Israel 'strategic' partnership; protecting apartheid and Namibian occupation; perpetual military support for the Afghanistan regime and the brutal and corrupt military dictatorships in Central America, South Asia and Africa.
- it has negative feed-back effects on the nuclear strategic arms race in a situation which by the very nature of its evolution is growing more and more unstable.

Third World Dilemmas

It is simplistic to explain the growing strategic involvement of the Third World in terms of neo-imperialistic designs and ambitions.

There are 62 new states with inhabitants of less than one million, and 36 of them have fewer than two hundred thousand. They often lack the physical means, human and material, to

abide by the rules of the current international security game. Their very non-participation underlines the irrelevance and inadequacy of these rules as far as they are concerned.
Size is only one dimension of the inadequacy. Even the larger Third World states have security problems arising from internal socio-economic or technical strains, inherited border disputes, meagre political, institutional and managerial resources. Militarisation rarely, if ever, offers a constructive answer to these inadequacies. But it has, however, the attraction of seeming the most feasible, final and, to its sponsors, the most profitable alternative.
Within the existing rules of the game, these growing pains are recognised only insofar as they offer or deny advantages or opportunities to dominant regional and global security systems. This is hardly a comfort.

If Third World countries are to be persuaded to participate in any comprehensive disarmament programme the international community must find creative ways of responding to their security concerns...In short, current concepts of peacekeeping possess little capacity to deter, cannot be invoked to prevent armed conflict, and therefore provide no alternative to the perceived need of Third World countries to build up independent military capabilities... Their sense of vulnerability will continue to increase, and with it their purchases of conventional arms and the heightened risks of conflict that such arms build-ups produce[2].

It is thus apparent that the notion of arms control as an instrument of crisis management in the Third World will be a realistic approach only in the - as yet unachievable - framework of major politico-military national, regional and international adjustments.

Verification

The arms trade and military expenditure have their ramifications in the Third World and no assessment of arms control feasibility is complete without taking them into consideration.

- We know little about what is really happening. '...our knowledge of Third World military expenditure is threadbare...Many countries do not distinguish between internal and external security in their budgets' (Blackaby and Ohlsen[3]), apart from the discrepancies between actual expenditure and budgeted figures.

ARMS CONTROL IN THE THIRD WORLD   317

- It is often difficult to establish whether military aid received by some countries is included or not. It may be also of interest here to recall that aid is often linked to crisis. Even the origin of supply appears to be uncertain since different estimates are quoted for the share of the USA and USSR in world exports.
- Arms transfers are not the only contribution by suppliers. The USA has major weapons produced under licences in 61 cases outside its territory; and the USSR has 10 (Landgren-Bäckström[4]).
- Another complicating factor in the arms control field in the Third World is the nature of arms transfer. The Stanford Group[1] gives illustrations of this complexity. The US arms sales in 1978 totalled $4-5 billion. 'Those sales, however, were only part of a much more elaborate program of military assistance totalling somewhere in the $10-12 billion range during the fiscal year 1974'. The difference seems to cover arms gifts, training, advisers, and so on. Little is known about these categories of transfer of military capability. Even the US programmes are difficult to analyse accurately because of extremely confusing budgetary presentation. Other nations have similar programmes. These include not only the Soviet Union, its allies, and former colonial powers, but is effectively supplemented by intermediate suppliers. Such arrangements are not responsive to arms control management in the framework of a crisis.

Profits and Motives

Arms trade represents a substantial economic resource contributing to the expenditure of arms development of supplier countries. Some variations in customers' shares may be tolerable, but the growth of the total volume is an essential manifestiation of the increasing global race. Moreover, arms supply is a very effective leverage for attaining economic and political advantages in Third World markets. It even seems to justify supplying to actively opposed sides in the same conflict, as the USA is practising in the Middle East. The increasing competition from Europe, which now exceeds one-fifth of supplies to the Third World, is a manifestation of these realities. The contribution of Third World countries to arms supplies add another dimension to the complexity of arms control in crisis management.

Shifts in strategic doctrines of the superpowers play a crucial role in arms supply to crisis areas. The Reagan doctrine of supremacy of strategic interests over national aspirations resulted in a 30 per cent increase in security assistance in 1982, mostly to the Middle East. The reflex response of the USSR helped to put Libya to the top of the Third World importers, and Syria to the fourth place.

Clearly, these doctrines are not automatically or directly reversed by crisis development in a particular location or multiplicity of locations, as is seen in Central America and South Africa. In fact, crisis development in peripheral locations seems to exacerbate the aggressive aspect of strategic doctrines, as Afghanistan has demonstrated.

Prospects

Within the limits of the current global security system, and balance-imbalance of terror, the prospects of arms control in a Third World crisis look very slim indeed. With almost 150 wars since the 1950s, no significant development on international or regional levels has improved the prospects. Past international practice and experience since the Second World War are not conducive to optimism. Supplier restrictions seem to have been, and still are, a more effective way of achieving further strategic gains than as an instrument of arms control.

These restrictions serve to advance the military and political goals of the supplier rather than restrain aggression, limit conflicts or deny military means to both sides. One-sided restriction or embargo inevitably invites a counter move by the other camp to neutralise its potential gains. The Middle East arms supply is a blatant example of the catastrophic outcome of the arms supplier manipulations of arms **control, balance, restrictions** and **management**. Even catastrophic failures do not teach. Since the Malta proposal of 1965 to the UN General Assembly on Arms Transfer Registration was defeated, no other effort has achieved any result; this is another illustration of the complexity of the control issue in the Third World. 'This lack of progress can be explained in large part by the lack of consensus on the desirability of arms control in particular regions and the nearly prohibitive difficulties of world-wide conventional force limitations.'[1]

Since 1976 world-wide limitation prospects have receded even further. And there is no consensus on upgrading regional arms build-up. There is more and more insistence on limitations on the other side. By no stretch of the imagination can this be considered the type of control that can contribute to crisis management. In fact, current approaches and practices make **control** a very effective instrument of crisis reverse-management.

References

1. International Arms Control The Stanford Arms Control Group, J.H. Barton, L. Werter (eds) (Stanford Press, 1976).
2. Common Security : A Programme for Disarmament. Report by the Independent Commission on Disarmament and Security Issues (London: Pan Books, 1982), pp. 126-9.
3. F. Blackaby and T. Ohlsen, 'Military Expenditure and the Arms Trade: Problems of Data', Bulletin of Peace Proposals, 13, No.4 (1982) 291-308.
4. S. Landgren-Bäckström, 'Global Arms Trade', Bulletin of Peace Proposals, 13, No.3 (1982) 201-10.

29 Regional Conflicts and Their Linkage to Strategic Confrontation
KRISHNASWAMI SUBRAHMANYAM

Arms trade with developing nations has become an important instrument of great power intervention. There has been a general tendency in Western literature to lump together the arms flow into developing countries; this covers up the essential significance of the arms trade as an instrument of interventionism. Nearly half of the arms flow to the developing world goes to certain oil-producing countries, and a quarter to developing countries with a relatively high GNP (about $700 per capita). The majority of the developing countries, which include some of the larger ones, like India and Pakistan, account for only 2.8 per cent of global military spending. Developing countries which import the bulk of the arms are those that borrow their threat perceptions from the military blocs. In other words, the increase in the arms flow and military spending of these developing countries is a secondary impact of the central arms race.

Most of the developing countries which incur such large military expenditures and import arms have not got the necessary administrative infrastructures to develop their own independent threat perceptions or to evaluate the equipment they import. They have difficulties in absorbing the sophisticated equipment in their armed forces. As has been shown in some of the recent wars in the developing world, the armed forces of these countries cannot even use the imported equipment effectively in war. One could say justifiably that the arms sales to these countries have followed the same strategy as that adopted by certain multinationals to sell canned milk food for babies in the developing world: mothers were told that powdered milk was better for the babies than their own natural milk. The military personnel from developing countries which go in for heavy imports of armaments receive their training in the military establishments of the industrialised world and are influenced by them. In many cases, where the rulers suffer from a sense of insecurity, they feel that such extensive and intensive military relationships will extend to them the implicit guarantee and protection of the powerful industrial power in terms of their personal and dynastic security. This appears to be the implication of the declaration that an Iran will not be allowed to happen in Saudi Arabia.

When military establishments of the developed world do not realise that increased and more sophisticated arsenals to not result in increased security, how could one expect the military establishments in the developing world to be wiser? They too opt for the use of weapons to display their power both domestically and **vis-à-vis** their neighbours. This is part of the knowledge and values they acquire when they attend training establishments in the developed countries. The Third World armaments culture is a reflection of the armaments culture that dominates the industrialised world. At a recent count it was found that 56 countries (nearly all of them in the developing world) are either ruled or dominated by the military. In this situation, it is unrealistic to expect the Third World to escape being influenced by the military culture of the industrialised world.

Arms transfers to the developing world take place for a number of reasons, depending upon the supplier. While the motivation may be commercial, as in the case of France, UK, and FRG, for the two superpowers arms transfers are part of their pursuit of strategic advantage and influence in various parts of the world, in the two-person zero-sum game called the Cold War. Arms transfers result in siphoning off petrodollars; provide highly-paid jobs to a large number of personnel of the supplier countries in the recipient country; enable a large military presence to be established in strategic areas; give access to strategic locations and advantageous points where monitoring and surveillance posts could be established; enable facilities to be developed for contingent military use and transit. Above all, they provide a stranglehold on the régimes concerned.

The arms flow into a particular developing country creates a sense of insecurity in neighbours of the recipient country, and this becomes a convenient leverage for the same or a rival supplier country to push in arms to the neighbours. The impressive statistics published on arms transfers to, and military expenditure in, the Third World do not give this aspect of the story. It is easy to disclaim that arms are not being thrust on unwilling recipients, but this is like saying that drug receivers and users are to blame, not the drug pushers. Yet society in the industrialised world considers the drug pusher to be the greater menace, and the drug receiver and user the victims. It is easier to tackle the arms transfer on the supply side, where only a few countries are involved, than on the demand side, where there is many times that number.

96 per cent of the arms supplies for the developing world emanates from the developed world. No extended war in the developing world could be fought without the support from the industrialised world. The Iran-Iraq War is fought on a ship-to-front basis, as and when supplies are received; the re-supplies have been so regulated that neither side can emerge a winner, and the battle line will not shift very far either way. There can be few protracted wars in the Third World without direct or indirect support from industrial nations to the belligerents. The security problems of the Third World cannot, therefore, be compartmentalised and dealt with separately from those of the developed world. Could the issues of Afghanistan, Vietnam, and Central American be separated and dealt with as exclusive Third World issues? Can Namibia or the Arab-Israeli issue be considered outside a global framework?

So long as the industrialised nations continue to produce more sophisticated weaponry and continue to pursue a policy of interventionism how could the developing nations afford not to get weapons for themselves? If Sweden and Switzerland, which have not fought wars for well over a century, cannot do away with weapons, how will nations which were under colonial occupation until a few decades ago, and who still face threats of intervention, dispense with arms imports? Will it contribute to 'common security' if there is to be an increasing weapon gap between the interventionist nations and their potential victims? This fear of intervention is not a hypothetical one, like the Soviet threat to Western Europe which has been talked about for 38 years without materialising. Apart from centuries of colonial occupation, the developing world has seen Vietnam, Cambodia, Dominica, Guatemala, threats of invasion to Cuba, and now Afghanistan and threats to various Central American states. There is a Rapid Deployment Force dedicated to intervention, and there is a French intervention force too.

In the last three decades, it was becoming increasingly clear that interventionist wars were expensive, and with the political consciousness of the peoples of the developing world aroused, it was very costly to occupy forcibly a territory. But the development of smart weapons may change this. It may become possible for an intervening power to inflict severe damage on a developing nation without its having to incur commensurate costs. While occupation may continue to be costly, punishing interventions may not be. This is a looming risk for developing countries posed by the new sophisticated accurate guided weaponry likely to be deployed in the future.

The interventionism of the industrialised nations arises out of two reasons. The linkage thesis as the origin of interventionism is widely recognised. The second reason is the anxiety of some leading industrialised nations about continued access to certain important minerals. The Annual Posture Statement of the US Joint Chiefs of Staff has emphasised this aspect more than once. On this account, the Persian Gulf has been declared an area of vital interest to the USA, which will be defended with force if necessary. The attitude towards the South African racist regime and even decolonisation of Namibia are strongly influenced by this consideration. G. Pauker of the Rand Corporation writes:

> There is a non-negligible chance that mankind is entering into a period of increased social instability and faces the possibility of a breakdown of global order as a result of sharpening confrontation between the Third World and the industrial democracies ... If a harsh international environment were to develop in the 1980's additional military capabilities might be required besides the forces directly dedicated to Soviet and other well understood contingencies.

This appears to be the rationale underlying the Rapid Deployment Force.

If some of these aspects are taken into account, it is apparent that Third World security issues cannot be isolated from the Cold War between the two superpowers. This was understood by the leaders of the non-aligned world even as détente was being developed in Europe. The Algiers summit declaration of September 1973 said:

> In a world which is already divided into the rich, poor countries, it would be dangerous to widen this division by restricting peace to the rich regions in the world while condemning the rest of mankind to insecurity and the domination of the most powerful. Peace is indivisible: it should not mean simply shifting confrontation from one area to another, nor should it mean reconciling ourselves to the existence of tensions in some areas while striving to remove them from others. Peace will remain precarious unless the interests of other countries are taken into consideration.

At the subsequent summit in Colombo in August 1976 the summit declaration pointed out: 'Détente, as proclaimed in official declarations, does not seem, however, to have reduced the struggle for influence which is going on in all continents or to have extinguished the hot beds of tensions'.

Détente and SALT II came to grief not on account of any happening in the developed world. The former National Security Adviser, Brzezinski, said; 'SALT lies buried in the sands of the Ogaden'. It could be argued that the calling off of the Indian Ocean talks and the conventional arms transfer talks in 1978 hailed the beginning of the second Cold War. The revival of the Cold War was justified on the grounds that one superpower was not behaving responsibly in the Third World areas, and this justification was reiterated last June before the US Senate by the Secretary of State. It would appear that when SALT I was agreed upon and the Helsinki Final Act was concluded, there was an expectation that as a **quid pro quo** for the concession of parity in nuclear arsenal to the Soviet Union and stabilising the post-World War II frontiers and settlement in Europe, the USSR would cooperate in maintaining the **status quo** in the rest of the world. This perspective was obviously based on an assumption that the entire international system was a bipolar zero-sum game.

This is a questionable perspective; while there is no doubt considerable interventionism in the Third World by the superpowers, not all developments there can be or are being controlled by either or both superpowers. Presumably, those who are still conditioned by the memories of European domination over the entire world, and subscribe to the bipolar perspective of the international system, tend to view any setback to themselves as a gain for the adversary that should be countered and neutralised. The active support by South Africa, Zaire, China and the USA of UNITA brought Cubans into Angola. The attempt by the Shah of Iran and Saudi Arabia to wean away Sardar Daud of Afghanistan from the traditional links with the Soviet Union, and that of Saudi Arabia in respect of Rubayya Ali of South Yemen, resulted in coups in those countries which eliminated the two leaders. A similar attempt in respect of Somalia and the consequent Somali invasion of Ogaden resulted in Cubans in Ethiopia with Soviet equipment. The Soviet intervention in Afghanistan followed the above developments and the decisions to station a US carrier task force in the Indian Ocean, to raise a Rapid Deployment Force there, and to break off Indian Ocean and conventional arms transfer talks. This action-reaction phenomenon in the Third World between the two superpowers cannot be tackled except as part of global détente between the two superpowers and the military blocs they lead.

With the international community conferring legitimacy on nuclear weapons and prestige on nuclear-weapons powers, the arsenals understandably became the stock currency of international transactions. With the signing of the Helsinki accord certain ground rules developed in Europe on superpower confrontation, and consequently, it shifted to the non-aligned areas of the world. It was not possible to fight wars with nuclear weapons; but they had to be used as an international currency of power. Once détente came about, nuclear weapons could not be used as the stock currency of international transactions in Europe. The only way they could still be so used was to test the efficiency of the deterrent effect of the nuclear arsenal in confrontations in the Third World, especially to freeze the **status quo** to one's own advantage. This logically led to the linkage thesis. So long as the international community confers legitimacy and prestige on the nuclear weapons this was inevitable.

The conclusion is inescapable that great-power interventionism in the Third World, the insecurity of the Third World countries, and the use of nuclear weapons as the currency of international transactions, are interlinked. The Third World nations are likely to be subject to various kinds of turbulence for quite some time to come. They have started on their nation-building and societal consolidation processes after retardation by colonialism for two to three centuries. These processes will be accompanied by a significant amount of internal violence. Transborder ethnic insurgencies may not take any note of international decisions.

The international system is today much too complicated to be managed by any one or a group of nations, however powerful they may be. The concepts and perceptions espoused by the major powers of the world are totally out of date. The present international situation is historically unprecedented. Yet there is a futile attempt to conduct international relations on the 19th century European hegemonic model. The insurgents in black Africa or Central America could not care less about the linkage thesis or the credibility of great nuclear arsenals. The consciousness of people in the developing world has risen to a level where it is no longer cost-effective to use military force to subdue them, as could be done in the colonial era. A nuclear war cannot be fought to determine the relative ranking between the superpowers or the degree of effectiveness of deterrence of one's arsenal.

The developing world consists of two categories of nations. The first category are those which do not have large enough populations to ensure their own security. The second are those which have adequate populations. Physical intervention and occupation of the latter, in the light of the political consciousness already developed, would not be cost-effective even for the great powers having the required military capability. And while countries with inadequate populations could be militarily subdued at a minimal cost, the impact it will have in the region as a whole will make such action politically counter-productive.

Unfortunately there is no adequate understanding about the decreasing cost-effectiveness of the use of force as an aggressive instrument of policy both in the developed and developing world. The leaderships in the latter borrow the perceptions of the former. An analysis of intervention operations by the industrialised world would highlight that very few of them were cost effective. The colonial powers lost all colonial wars; in the post-1945 era no sovereign state has lost its sovereignty. Only in three instances has one country been able to occupy a neighbouring territory and replace the régime therein - Bangladesh, Uganda and Kampuchea; in all three genocidal tyrants were replaced and the local population welcomed the external forces as liberators. In the West Bank of Jordan/Palestine, Afghanistan, Western Sahara and Namibia the occupations are costly to the occupier. Even Grenada would not appear to be a politically cost-effective occupation. Very few of the interstate wars resulted in significant alterations of boundaries.

While this happens to be the reality, the image projected by the industrialised world - with its dominance over the intellectual sphere and military thought - is different. They spend well over 80 per cent of the world's military expenditure and yet there have been very few instances of major violence in their part of the world. The high defence expenditure and the nuclear deterrence doctrine are thought to be justified as having preserved peace. It is difficult to decide whether peace in the industrialised world is due to a realisation about cost ineffectiveness of the use of force as a policy instrument, or to the effectiveness of deterrence. It could be argued that it is cost ineffective because all nations are armed. These projections have a powerful impact on the leaderships of the developing world.

The developing world does not lack leaders who are often tempted to take advantage of a current weakness of a neighbour, and the allegedly predictable behaviour of the two strategic alliances locked in an adversary relationship and enegaged in a cold war. The Indo-Pakistan war of 1965, the current Iran-Iraq War, the Somali-Ethiopian war of 1977-78; the Israeli invasion of Lebanon in 1982, South African incursions into Angola and Mozambique, fall into this pattern. In all these cases the support of one of the superpowers was taken for granted by the local leadership in launching the attack on the neighbour. Whether that assumption turned out to be right or wrong is immaterial. In some cases it did turn out to be a fatal miscalculation. But the decision to initiate the hostilities was apparently based on a particular expectation of superpower behaviour.

While one can trace such linkages between conflicts in the developing world and the superpower confrontation in a majority of cases, not all conflicts in the developing world are caused by such linkages with superpowers. The India-Pakistan war of 1947-48 over Kashmir, Indonesian-Malaysian confrontation in the sixties, the war in Western Sahara, to a large extent the war in Chad, and some of the border conflicts in South America, are purely local conflicts. Such conflicts may happen in the future, but once the two superpowers decide to keep off, and other industrialised powers will not initiate resupply operations, they are not likely to escalate though they may continue to simmer for some time.

The developing world will continue to have a certain amount of inter and intra state conflicts during the period of their evolution into stable nation states, just as the nations of the industrialised world went through in their history. The risks to international peace and security are likely to be enhanced by the linkages between the conflicts in the developing world and the two blocs in the industrialised world. The doctrine of non-alignment attempts to attenuate the impact of these linkages. It has not been entirely successful in its efforts to prevent the developing world being sucked into the vortex of East-West confrontation. However, the movement's contribution has been significant in eroding various military pacts which represented the institutionalised security linkages between the two central strategic military blocs and developing nations. More than that, its major role has been to challenge the conventional wisdom on international relations propounded in the industrialised world that politics among nations is a struggle for power, including military power. In the nuclear era politics among nations cannot be treated as a struggle for military power since such a confrontationist approach carries the risk of nuclear annihilation. Therefore, the non-aligned maintain that the approach to international relations should be a cooperative competition among nations with emphasis on cooperation. So long as the confrontationist approach to international relations persists and the world is dominated by a political culture in which nuclear weapons are used as a legitimate currency of power in international politics, it will be difficult to delink the regional conflicts from the central strategic confrontation.

30 Impact of the Global Arms Race on Prospects for Development
ISHFAQ AHMAD

Introduction

Among the 150-odd countries that make up our World, there are two superpowers, twenty or so powerful states (by military outlay, industrial might, population and so on) and the rest may be classed as small states which belong predominantly, but not exclusively, to the Third World. The build-up of fighting capability is going on among these countries at various levels, for diverse reasons and with different impacts on development. Foremost is the arms race between the USA and USSR which have an estimated combined nuclear arsenal equivalent to about four tons of TNT for each inhabitant of the Earth. The frightening aspect of this over-kill capacity is the unabated quest for qualitative and quantitative superiority. Indeed, the two superpowers account for about 80 per cent of the world expenditure on military research and development, 50 per cent of the global military spending, and over 70 per cent of armament production and exports. Next to these are the powerful states which include some of the major industrialised countries like West Germany, France and a few large developing countries like China and India. Their contribution to global armament, though small compared to the two giants, does nonetheless cause significant perturbations on the international scene; it corresponds to roughly 30 per cent of the world military expenditure and 25 per cent of arms exports. Finally, there are over 130 small states whose combined share in the world's military spending is only 20 per cent, and in military production hardly 5 per cent. In the diversion of the world's resources away from productive endeavour, these states play a minor role, but their military activities can and do lead to destabilisations at national and regional levels. If armament is indeed undesirable from the point of view of development – as I hope to show in this paper – we must try to understand why nations arm themselves and what internal forces and external fears contribute to the war psychosis.

Security Perceptions of Big Powers

The armament of a state is primarily linked with its perceptions of security, a concept which means different things to different people. The minimal definition of security would probably be that given by Walter Lipmann: 'A nation is secure to the extent to which it is not in danger of having to sacrifice its core values if it wishes to avoid war and is able, if challenged, to maintain them by victory in such a war'.

In this context, core values would encompass territorial integrity, cultural identity and political independence. As a nation acquires greater power, its security 'needs' expand far beyond this minimal definition. To begin with, it wants not just friendly but compliant neighbours (Sri Lanka, Lebanon, Afghanistan, Central America). Next, it cherishes a dominant and domineering role in regional affairs (Southern Africa, South Asia). Finally, it tries to prop up favoured regimes in distant lands (Taiwan, Cuba), and is infuriated by loss of face (Vietnam War, Cuban missile crisis). These political aspirations are reinforced by the vested interests of the growing and increasingly powerful military-industrial establishment. As a result, the country finds itself in an uncontrolled armament spiral.

A manifestation of this spiralling effect is the unbelievable development and deployment of weapons of mass destruction by the two giant adversaries. Deterrence has been achieved by mutually assured destruction (MAD), but the madness still continues with the ludicrous aim of amassing armaments of decreasing usability. The reason is that the superpowers have now attained an almost knife-edge balance of terror; and the moment the balance is **perceived** to be tipping ever so slightly in favour of one party, the other one over-reacts, and so the game goes on. Indeed, their arms race has gathered such a momentum - and almost a logic of its own - that it seems impossible to halt it without serious economic consequences for both of them. However, as concluded in a recent study by Wassily Leontief, 'virtually all economies are able to increase total output and per capita consumption as they progressively reduce their military spending ...' Thus, even though the process of disarmament must of necessity be gradual, it has got to be started in the self-interest of the superpowers as well as in the overall interest of the world at large.

The next category of powers, after the USA and USSR, are countries, like the United Kingdom and France, which have been colonial powers in such recent past that they are still suffering from the hangover of that bygone era. They have not yet come to terms with the fact that they have been displaced as principal actors from the world stage. It is perhaps partly an act of self-expression that some of them have chosen to develop their own nuclear arsenals even though their resources are much smaller than those of the superpowers. More importantly, they have sought to make armaments a significant part of their economic activity. Sale of arms, open and clandestine, is a brisk business in such countries. They have consequently captured a substantial share of the arms exports market, mostly to the Third World. For these nations too, the 'beating of their swords into ploughshares' would be a slow and gradual process, for economic reasons.

Finally, we have the aspiring entrants to the big power club: states which have acquired enough military muscle to intimidate their neighbours with a view to expanding their sphere of influence. Examples may be found in Southern Africa, Middle East and South Asia. Their common characteristics are intolerance and belligerence directed mainly towards smaller and weaker countries on their periphery. These aspiring mini-supers, with their ill-concealed hegemonist designs, pose an immediate threat to the security of the smaller states in their respective regions.

Security Concerns of Small States

Let us now consider the security concerns, which are the principal motive of armaments of the most numerous group of countries, that is, the 130-odd small states, mostly at the lower stages of development. How can these Lilliputians of the globe save themselves from being trampled upon by giants - especially neighbouring giants? How can they avoid being the theatres for proxy wars by world or regional powers? These and related questions are of particular relevance to the security of the small states of Asia, Africa and Latin America, although those in Europe are not entirely free from these concerns.

The dangers in the Third World are greater and have a much lower ignition point than in Europe for several reasons. First, most inhabitants of the developing countries are experiencing for the first time a consciousness of their national identities, just as the European nations experienced during and after the Napoleonic Wars. Second, this very nascent consciousness makes the people more sensitive to status disparities and therefore less satisfied with the **status quo**, both inside and outside the national boundaries. Third, state boundaries themselves look artificial in the euphoric mood and broader outlook following the lifting of the colonial yoke.

However, given their limited war capability, the small states have mostly been following a policy of defence rather than offence. The goal of a state is not the pursuit of power but the preservation of whatever assets it possesses. The problems of these states have been: first, how to avoid, mitigate or postpone conflicts; and second, how to resist superior force once a conflict has developed. The two problems relate respectively to the spheres of diplomacy and military strategy - the two main instruments of foreign policy.

In the sphere of diplomacy, the concepts of non-alignment, zones of peace, nuclear-free zones, regional and bilateral treaties and alliances - supported by an active and informed foreign policy - all play significant roles in protecting the security of small states. They should, therefore, be encouraged as worthwhile endeavours in the pursuit of peace. But their limitations should also be clearly understood and recognised. It happens only too often that, at the moment of truth, a small state finds itself alone. An independent, though possibly limited, war capability and adequate armament are essential for safeguarding security on such occasions. Other important components of security assurance are technological and economic strength, coupled with equitable distribution and social justice. One must not lose sight of the elementary dictum that just as secure peace provides the right environment for socio-economic development, development is vital for the security of a small state in present-day realities.

Development and Disarmament

Over the last eight decades the world population has increased by a factor of 3, from about 1.6 billion to over 4.5 billion - an unprecedented increase in the history of mankind. In spite of this population explosion, if one considers the per capita availabilities, Man is today better fed, better clothed, provided with better education and healthcare facilities, and is drawing greater benefits from the world's natural resources than has been possible in any previous era in the history of mankind. Yet all is not well; these averages simply mask the bitter, hard facts of life. There still exist large disparities among different groups of human beings; in fact, these disparities are much more accentuated today than ever before. On the one hand, extreme affluence is enjoyed by a small fraction of the world population. On the other hand, the vast majority is struggling for mere survival, with millions of people living in abject poverty and facing starvation. Similarly, looking at one side of the coin, we see some 150 states, large and small, freed from colonial rule. But, if we look at the other face of the coin, we find many of these very states being prey to neo-colonialism, hegemony and superpower domination. The technological revolution of the current century has certainly given Homo Sapiens a high degree of control over the natural resources of the earth, the power to extract energy from the heart of the atom, and the capability to reach the heavenly bodies. But the same technological revolution has armed Man with such destructive capacities as to endanger the very existence of his own species on the earth. Thus, in spite of the progress over the past several decades, the world has certainly not taken any significant strides forward along the path of sustainable universal peace and human welfare.

Socio-Economic Development

The present global economic production is around 18 trillion US dollars. Of this, more than three quarters is in the developed countries, which comprise less than one quarter of the world population. The developing countries, with about three quarters of the world population, account for a mere one quarter of the global GNP. The average per capita GNP in developing countries is thus lower by a factor of about 10 than that in developed countries. Averaging on such a large scale tells only half the story. If we compare the poorest and the richest groups of countries, each comprising one fifth of the world population, the disparity in average per capita income turns out to be alarmingly large: a difference by a factor of nearly 50. Further, there are large uneven distributions of income within the individual countries, both developed and developing, with the richest 20 per cent of the population commanding a 40-60 per cent share of the national income, and the poorest 20 per cent getting hardly 2-6 per cent. As a result, hundreds of millions people in the developing countries - and a few million in the developed countries as well - exist in conditions of such acute poverty that we can at best label them as destitutes. Another disturbing element is that, although during the last two decades the average per capita GNP in the world has nearly doubled in real terms, the relative disparity in per capita income between the developed and the developing countries has remained practically unchanged, while the absolute number of destitutes has in fact increased.

The slow pace of economic development in the developing countries is essentially due to the fact that they have not yet shared the fruits of the industrial revolution; their economies still depend heavily on production of primary commodities based on agriculture and mining. In 1980, the share of developing countries in the global manufacturing output was hardly 10 per cent. Although agriculture is the mainstay for most developing countries, their total agricultural output is still less than that in the industrialised countries. Indeed the present per capita agricultural production in developing countries is only a quarter of that in developed countries. During the last three decades, when the per capita agricultural and food production in the developed countries has improved at a rate of about 1 per cent per annum, in the developing countries it remained practically stagnant. Approximately 45 per cent of the developing world population now lives in countries where the average daily caloric intake is below the norms recommended by FAO. It is estimated that some 500 million people in the world are still malnourished, while millions of lives have been claimed in recent years by recurring famines in parts of Africa and Asia.

With respect to education and health-care facilities, too, there exist large disparities among different groups of world population. At present only 32 per cent of the adult population in Africa and 38 per cent in South Asia are literate, as compared with 99 per cent in the industrialised countries and 75-80 per cent in Latin America and the Far East. The situation is not likely to change significantly in the coming decades, since hardly 30-40 per cent of the school-age children in the African and South Asian countries are now getting formal schooling. The quality of education in the developing countries as a whole is also much poorer than that in the industrialised countries.

Although the World Health Organization has played a commendable role in helping to eradicate major epidemics in all parts of the world, particularly in the backward areas, disease and human suffering are still rampant in a number of developing countries, due to poor hygiene and lack of proper medical facilities combined with poor nutrition.

The high infant mortality rates (70-150 per 1000 live births) and relatively short life expectancies (45-60 years) prevalent in the developing countries, as compared with the corresponding figures (10-25 and 70-75) for the industrialised countries, are a clear manifestation of the health-care deficiencies in the developing world.

The above facts and figures provide a measure of some of the socio-economic disparities that exist today between the haves and have-nots. Another aspect which may have profound implications for the future growth of developing countries concerns the depletion of the finite natural resources of the earth and the degradation of the global environment. The large scale industrial activity during the last few decades has given rise to concern about the rapid depletion of fossil fuels and several important minerals, as well as about the degradation of the global environment resulting from excessive release of carbon dioxide, industrial chemicals and other effluents into the atmosphere. The world's annual consumption of oil and natural gas now amounts to 4.5 billion tonnes of oil equivalent (TOE) whereas the proven global reserves are only 150 billion TOE, equivalent to a mere 33 years of supply even at the present rate of consumption. It is generally believed that the cheap global resources of conventional oil and gas, including those yet to be discovered, will be nearly exhausted by the turn of the century and that the world will then have to turn to more expensive and difficult-to-mine reserves of tar sand and shale oil, use expensive technologies of solar energy conversion and coal liquefaction or gasification, and resort to large scale use of nuclear power.

Looking at the present pattern of fossil fuel resource distribution and consumption we find that the industrialised countries possess about 65 per cent of the proven world reserves, contribute 62 per cent to the global production and are responsible for 80 per cent of the present day world consumption. Of about 2 billion TOE of oil and gas now produced per year by the developing countries, only one third is used by these countries themselves (including the oil-importing countries), and the rest is exported to the industrialised countries. Thus, a large transfer of an important but rapidly depleting natural resource is taking place from the developing to the developed countries, without a proportionate real transfer in the reverse direction, of technological skills and know-how which are equally important factors of production. It is undisputable that the developing countries – which now have only about 1/40th to 1/5th as much per capita consumption of energy as the developed countries – will themselves require increasingly large inputs of energy in the coming decades to support their socio-economic development programmes. However, unlike the developed countries, which went through the process of rapid economic development in an era of abundant cheap energy, they will have an up-hill task of seeking development in an environment of global energy scarcity and rising energy prices. Miserable as will be the plight of the energy resource-deficient developing countries, even the OPEC countries will find their so-called vast resources exhausted, when still ill-equipped to make use of alternative advanced technologies for nuclear power generation or large scale solar energy utilisation. Whatever is true for energy resources, applies equally to other exhaustible natural resources.

The likely impacts of large scale environmental pollution are of global concern as they will affect both the developed and the developing countries alike. Although most of such pollution has so far been caused by activities in the industrialised world, the contribution by the developing countries is now also becoming significant and will increase with their industrialisation. Unless means are found to check the sources of such pollution and necessary steps taken well in time, the adverse impacts of environmental degradation will not only diminish the prospects of economic development in the developing countries but have a devastating effect on the economies of the industrialised countries as well.

Arms Build-Up

Since World War II none of the major powers has been engaged in direct war with another, yet the world military expenditure has continued to increase in alarming proportions; during the past three decades it increased by a factor of about 3 in real terms, and is still rising. The present expenditure on arms build-up and maintenance of armed forces worldwide amounts to about $800 billion, equivalent to about 5 per cent of the global production, or to the combined GNP of all African and South Asian countries. This translates into approximately $175 per person per year now being spent globally on war preparedness, a figure which is comparable to the average per capita GNP of the less fortunate half of the world population. More than 5 per cent of the world industrial output goes to the military sector, which is also responsible for 5-6 per cent of the global consumption of oil and a much higher percentage of other important minerals.

An estimated half a million scientists and engineers are now engaged in military R&D. Thus, the global R&D effort aimed at refinement of armaments and development of still deadlier weapons is depriving the civilian sector of some 20 per cent of the world's scientists and engineers. At the same time about 25 per cent of the financial resources ($ 150 billion in 1980) allocated to R&D effort worldwide are being channelled into military R&D programmes. The world military effort is also responsible for using up the services, directly or indirectly, of about 50 million physically fit persons in their most productive years: some 25 million people are serving as regular armed forces, 10 million correspond to paramilitary personnel, and another 15 million are employed in meeting the demand of military goods and services. Ironically, the number of personnel in the regular and paramilitary forces exceeds the total number of teachers, medical doctors and nursing staff worldwide.

What is the outcome of all this huge investment in global military effort? The world is getting armed, tooth and nail, with increasingly more sophisticated equipment of greater devastating capabilities. The stockpile of nuclear weapons amounts to an equivalent of about 16 billion tons of TNT, but the nuclear forces account for only about 20 per cent of all resources devoted to armaments worldwide.

The arms race is a global phenomenon: both the developed and developing countries are involved in it, each group diverting about 5 per cent of its GNP towards expenditure on armed forces. However, the contribution of the developing countries to the arms build-up is miniscule compared to that by the industrialised countries. Although the developing countries account for about 25 per cent of the global military spending, their share is hardly 8 per cent in global military production, 3 per cent in international export of military hardware and practically zero in military R&D.

Implications of Disarmament for Development

The fact that the countries with heavy military expenditure are generally the ones that have attained a high level of socio-economic development, may tempt one to conclude that there is a direct correlation between military outlay and socio-economic development, that military activities have very large spin-offs for the civilian sector, and that increased military effort helps to mobilise financial, technological, human and other resources. If this were true, why talk about disarmament? Should we not simply encourage the developing countries to boost their military capability so that their socio-economic development programmes may benefit from an intensified military effort?

Before showing the fallacy of this approach, one needs to point out that the existing disparity between the developed and the developing countries is not just a recent creation; it is the net result of over two hundred years of colonial subjugation of the developing countries by a handful of present-day developed countries who indiscriminately exploited both the human and material resources of their colonies to their own advantage. It was in fact through their military strength that the colonial powers maintained their grip on the colonies; the large military expenditure was helpful in building up their own economies at the expense of the colonies. Ironically, the possible use of military power by the developed countries to keep control over economically and strategically important natural resources in the developing countries, is not ruled out even in today's situation. The formation of the Rapid Deployment Force by the USA is a case in point.

At this stage one needs to be reminded of the meaning of the term development in the global perspective. It implies an improvement in the quality of life for all mankind, in a way that would significantly reduce the socio-economic disparities between haves and have-nots within a reasonable time-frame, and allow the use of limited natural resources of the earth in a sustainable and environmentally benign manner. Although development is a broad term that encompasses many facets of socio-economic changes, not mere economic growth, the latter is still the single most important factor on which the progress of almost every aspect of the development process depends.

Recalling the huge financial and man-power expenditure for military purposes, the question arises: does such a large diversion of resources by the developed countries have any adverse effect on their economies? A comparison of the military expenditure as a percentage of the GNP in various industrialised countries with the annual rate of growth in their manufacturing productivity during the period 1960-1980 shows that large military outlays in countries such as the USA, UK and France, as compared with Japan, Denmark and Italy, are having a marked negative effect on their economic growth. This is exactly what one would expect in view of the fact that military expenditure is a consumptive and not a productive use of resources; it drains away the material, technological and human resources that could otherwise be used for productive economic activities and human welfare.

It is sometimes argued that the developing countries spend as large a fraction of their GNP on military activities as the industrialised countries, and that if only the former would cut down their own military expenditures it would go a long way to bridge the socio-economic gap between the two. This line of argument overlooks the point that the security needs of the developing countries are qualitatively different from those of the developed countries. As discussed earlier, most of the developing countries are small in size, have only recently become free of colonial rule, are inflicted with border disputes arising from artificially created boundaries by the departing colonial rulers, and are faced with internal power struggles, and ethnic problems. As such, they need to have viable military establishments not only to protect their recently won independence and ensure territorial integrity but also to safeguard against internal disruptions. Even so, the military expenditure of **most** of the developing countries is quite modest; it amounts to only 1.5 per cent of the GNP for Latin American countries and 3 per cent of the GNP for groups of countries in South Asia and Africa. The overall military expenditure of the developing countries, however, amounts to about 5 per cent of the GNP, due to relatively higher levels of spendings on military activities by countries in the Middle East (12 per cent of GNP) and the Far East (6 per cent of GNP), the two regions which have experienced several armed conflicts during the last three decades. Since the Middle East countries in general are not short of funds, their socio-economic development programmes are not being adversely affected by the relatively high military expenditure which, in a way, is also necessary for protecting their valuable petroleum reserves.

Since all the military R&D effort, and over 90 per cent of the major arms production capability, are concentrated in industrialised countries, the only significant resource consumption on military effort by the developing countries is in the form of financial allocations and employment of personnel in armed forces and allied services. If the developing countries were to reduce their military effort to one half, it would save about $100 billion, equivalent to 2.5 per cent of their combined GNP, plus about 15 million personnel, equivalent to 1.5 per cent of their total labour force, for channelling into economic development and social welfare programmes. At present the developing countries are spending about 25 per cent of their GNP in productive investments resulting in an average economic growth of about 4 per cent per annum. Thus, a 50 per cent reduction in military effort could at best help to increase their average economic growth rate from 4 to 4.5 per cent per annum. This nominal improvement, important though it is, would fall much short of what is required for meeting the objectives of the New International Economic Order. However, a similar reduction in military effort by the developed countries could be of considerably more significance both for their own socio-economic development and that of the developing countries, provided the saved resources are used judiciously. It would not only save about $300 billion and 10 million useful labour force, but also release an equivalent of 10-15 per cent of both the world's R&D scientists and worldwide expenditure on R&D for diversion to the civilian sector. The increased civilian R&D effort in the industrialised countries could then go a long way to overcome the present recession in these countries, apart from being helpful in solving the global problems of food shortage, resource scarcity, environmental pollution, disease control and so on. At the same time, even if one half of the funds saved by the industrialised countries through reduction in military expenditure were used by them to help the developing countries, this would amount to about $150 billion, or five times the Official Development Assistance now being provided by the OECD countries. In pure economic terms such an enhanced financial support could help to raise the investment potential of the low income and lower middle-income developing countries (total population: 3 billion) by about 50 per cent, thereby bringing about a proportionate increase in their annual economic growth rates.

However, the saving from reduced defence outlays would not become automatically available for development of the South. It would require a degree of enlightened self-interest on the part of the North to foresee that improved economic performance of the South will stimulate demand in the North and significantly improve the latter's employment situation and domestic production. A stable South would also be less likely to get involved in East-West politics, and a more durable détente would thereby become possible.

At present there are many socio-economic development programmes in the world, which are not able to make much headway due to shortage of funds and non-availability of suitably qualified manpower. A reduction in global military effort would go a long way to improve the quality of life on the globe, provide alternatives to rapidly depleting finite resources, apart from reducing the prospects of self-annihilation.

Conclusion

The foregoing discussion emphasised the two basic realities in the present-day world. First, that the worldwide military expenditure is escalating at an alarming rate. Second, that the gap between the haves and have-nots is showing no signs of being closed. Among the have-nots, the plight of the forty or so countries designated as 'least developed' is particularly disturbing. Between 1970 and 1980, their real per capita GDP increased at an annual average of only 0.6 per cent, compared with the average of 3.3 per cent for all developing countries. During the same period, their food production per capita **declined** by 0.9 per cent per year. The infant mortality rate is 147 per 1000 births, 13 times higher than the corresponding average for western industrialised countries. The literacy rate at age 15 is 27 per cent, almost half the average for all developing countries. Given these appalling disparities, it would be difficult indeed to imagine a more divided family than that of Man.

While there is no direct causal connection between the two evils: escalating military expenditure and continuing deprivation, there is undoubtedly a common background to them. While there are socio-economic inequalities in virtually all groupings, whether regional, national, or ethnic, they are exacerbated by the existing economic order, indeed, by every economic activity that takes place in this context: trade, aid, loans, transfers. Much of the development assistance reverts back to the donor countries, and even then such assistance is being reduced. For instance, the International Development Association will disburse only $9 billion over the next three years, compared with $12 billion during the last such period, to the 40 low-income countries.

There is an obvious need for new international initiatives on both the material and the spiritual planes. There must be a realisation that concentration of wealth beyond reason does not really benefit those who have it, while being against the interest of those deprived. This realisation must then consciously lead to positive action such as inculcation of moral values and implementation of social justice together with new initiatives in respect of the International Economic Order designed to make the world move towards a more equitable distribution of goods and services. Bold action is called for in diverting global resources away from the wasteful, and potentially destructive, expenditure on armaments, towards investive uses and welfare activities related to nutrition, hygiene, health, housing and education. In this context, it ought to be borne in mind that, for countries at the lower rungs of the development ladder, defence and development are not alternate choices but are vitally interlinked. One can achieve adequate defence capacity as well as economic development only by eliminating luxury consumption of the elite and by promoting egalitarianism.

While the world as a whole must move towards disarmament, the initiative to divert resources away from armament into development must be taken by the superpowers because they have the bulk of global resources at their command, and their present policies are in conflict with the interests of the peaceful survival of mankind. Being in the position of undisputed leadership of the world, they can make a substantial contribution towards making it a safer and saner place to live in.

Part VI
Scientists, Public Opinion and the Arms Race

31 Public Opinion and Arms Control
BERNARD FELD

Public sentiment, in favour of immediate and effective nuclear arms control arrangements between the so-called superpowers, has never been as intense or as vocal as it has become during this past year or so. In Western Europe, an already strong popular movement, aimed at a denuclearised Europe, is rapidly gathering support from movements that were previously primarily concerned with such 'fringe' issues as environmental degradation, nuclear reactor siting, acid rain and so on. Even in France, that bastion of nuclear power advocacy, strong concerns are being expressed in academic and intellectual circles, about the current linkages between nuclear power - especially in the **laissez-fair** atmosphere of a competitive, commercial set of enterprises - and the proliferation of nuclear weapons into parts of the world thus far free of them. Some of the smaller nations of Western Europe, for example, Holland, Denmark, currently have powerful political forces agitating for a refusal to accept NATO nuclear deployments on their territories, a decision that has also been taken by Norway, otherwise a staunch NATO adherent. More and more, one has the impression that the old addage, which could be applied to arms control as well as to the weather: 'Everybody talks about the weather (read arms control) but nobody does anything about it!', now no longer holds on the issue of denuclearisation of Europe. Even in Eastern Europe, where this was formerly considered an issue too sensitive for open public discussion, there is a large and growing popular denuclearisation movement.

The recent round of reciprocated deployments of intermediate-range nuclear-tipped missiles (the SS-20 on the Soviet side, and the Pershing and ground-launched cruise missile by NATO) has served mainly to heighten the awareness of the average European, of both East and West, that a breakdown of Soviet-American relations with resort to force by either side would in all probability lead to the total destruction of Central Europe, a consequence that hardly accords with the concept of 'protection'. The situation is frequently compared to that of the peak period of the US 'defence' of Vietnam when spokesmen of the military often explained massive bombings of villages as having been undertaken for the purpose of 'saving' them - a probable consequence of the nuclear defence of Europe whose apocalyptic character has not escaped the notice of the average European city dweller. Indeed, so rapidly is the European 'denuclearisation' movement growing, that many serious observers believe it is only a matter of time - and not much time, at that - before European public opinion will force the governments of all the NATO countries to refuse to accommodate any new (and possibly old) nuclear missile deployments on their territories. In these circumstances, the relevant question may well become whether there is still sufficient incentive for the Soviets to agree to a negotiated European denuclearisation, hopefully extending from the Urals to the Atlantic, rather than allowing themselves to be gratuitously awarded (with perhaps a bit of prodding from pro-Soviet West European groups) a politically imposed European denuclearisation from the Rhine to the Atlantic. Although a superficial first view may indicate that the latter result is much more in the interests of the Soviet Union, this conclusion is arguable when considerations of long-term political and military stability are taken into account. Thus, for example, a greatly reduced feeling of security in West Germany could easily lead to a strengthening of those elements insisting on much greater remilitarisation of the FRG and even of forces to which the Soviets attach the characterisation 'revanchist'. In any case, it is increasingly clear that Europe will not much longer be content with the role of pawn in a Soviet-American 'end game'.

But it is not only in Europe that the seeds of nuclear discontent are germinating. Despite official denigration and disparagement, the 'freeze' movement in the United States has been greeted with widespread public acceptance. All over the country, movements have sprung up spontaneously, aimed at achieving a slowdown, if not a cessation, of the nuclear arms build-up. Even though the argument has been strongly put forward by the hard-line adherents of the President's 'negotiate through strength' policy - that a freeze would leave the United States at a military disadvantage **vis à vis** the Soviet Union, even in the unlikely circumstance that they would follow the US lead in a verifiable fashion - a substantial majority of the American people, according to most polls, seem willing to take the chance. In fact, most people would go along with George Kennan's thesis that if, suddenly, with no warning and no expectation of reciprocation, the USA were to destroy 50 per cent of all its nuclear arms and delivery systems, it would not have any significant impact on the actual (as contrasted to the psychological) state of the military confrontation between the superpowers. On the psychological side, it can be persuasively argued that the impacts would be mainly positive, and might even trigger a set of reciprocated reductions that would leave both sides in a state of reduced armaments and enhanced security.

On the other hand, with any political success, there is likely to arise a serious danger that the 'movement' may be pre-empted and taken over by the fantastically well-heeled, expert media-manipulators working for the current administration. One can already see the beginnings of such an attempted takeover in the somewhat gimmicky 'build-down' proposals of the Administration, which are widely interpreted (especially by the Soviet Union) as a means of substituting far more effective, technically modern weapons for relatively obsolete ones - that were, in any case, slated for retirement - and obtaining arms control credentials in the process.

Manipulated or not, however, the American yearning for an end to the nightmare of the present nuclear confrontation - with its already thousandfold overkill potential and its tendencies to keep breaking out in ever more virulent and dangerous directions as a result of technological innovations - cannot indefinitely be deflected by media hocus-pocus like 'star wars', laser beam 'death rays', and other grade-B Hollywood scripts. We cannot have it both ways, that is, that the Russians are twelve feet tall and can produce miraculous new weapons from under their top hats, without even having to test them, while, at the same time, asserting that old-reliable American technological knowhow will keep us 'number one'. Sometime we have got to come back to the real world. Eventually - sooner, it is to be hoped, rather than later - we shall be forced to return to the negotiating table, with a view not only to halting the present insane race in nuclear armaments, but also to reducing the current obscene numbers to a level that will no longer threaten the survival of our species should anything go wrong. Meanwhile, of course, we must stop acting as though these were usable weapons, which we are prepared to launch against the 'enemy' if he should overstep some vague boundary line - and also stop deploying them in accident- or miscalculation-prone modes of delivery.

But this need to remove the nuclear 'Damoclean Sword' from over our heads may now have become secondary to an even greater danger - also exacerbated by the Soviet-American foot-dragging in the arms control negotiations. We and the Russians have lived with nuclear overkill for almost four decades and, despite occasional tendencies of unthinking politicians to make stupid statements, neither of us is likely deliberately to unleash nuclear war except under the most exceptional - amost unimaginable - crisis situation. And our 'hotline' system - although it could use and should receive updating in terms of the most modern communications technology - is designed to prevent accidental or unintended nuclear launchings. But there are many other nations in the world, some already 'nuclear' (at least six in number). Unfortunately, international attempts at preventing the spread of nuclear weapons are in grave danger of falling victim to the disillusionment of the non-nuclear majority of nations, 118 of which have agreed, **via** the Nuclear Non-Proliferation Treaty of 1968, to forgo the acquisition or production of nuclear weapons. Article VI of this Treaty obligates the nuclear weapon states '... to pursue negotiations in good faith on effective measures relating to cessation of the nuclear arms race at an early date and to nuclear disarmament ...' The breakdown of nuclear arms control negotiations is generally taken as **prima facie** evidence of the failure of the superpowers to live up to their end of this obligation, as well as their obligation under Article IV, to help the non-nuclear states in '...the further development of the applications of nuclear energy for peaceful purposes...'. The legitimacy of complaints on this score are, however, far less clear in view of the universal failure of nuclear energy to live up to its earlier announced prospects. Furthermore, the majority of nations have still not faced up squarely to the problems relating to the connections between nuclear power and nuclear weapons technologies. These circumstances have, in the view of many, absolved the non-nuclear states from theirs. It remains to be seen whether, during the next decade or so, the score-or-more nations now capable of nuclear weapons acquisition will continue to recognise the overriding advantage - to them as well as to the rest of the world - of maintaining, and even strengthening and spreading, the integrity of the non-proliferation regime.

Towards this end, it is essential that an extended and effective educational campaign be carried on in both the nuclear and non-nuclear nations, and most especially in the nations of the so-called 'Third World', to convince public opinion in all countries of the absolute counter-utility of nuclear weapons. This will, of course, be exceedingly difficult, since it runs completely counter to the previous practices, and apparent convictions, of the so-called great powers. In this regard, perhaps the most effective immediate step that could be taken by the nuclear weapons states (short, of course, of extensive and effective nuclear disarmament with international verification which, I assume, these nations are not quite ready to adopt in any very short timescale) would be the universal adoption by them of a 'nuclear no-first-use' policy – that is, a declaration that no adherent to the agreement would be the first to introduce a nuclear weapon into **any** conflict situation. Declarative (and therefore strictly speaking unenforceable) as such a simple policy statement would be, it would nevertheless have a very great impact towards convincing the rest of the world that the nuclear powers are prepared to 'deligitimise' these weapons – to place them in the same category as chemical and biological weapons, weapons which are no longer regarded by many nations as 'usable', not even in retaliation for their use against them. Such delegitimisation may be regarded as the first step (a necessary though not yet sufficient condition) towards their eventual total elimination from all national arsenals – which must remain the urgent, ultimate goal of the worldwide nuclear disarmament movement.

As long as people regard nuclear weapons as a 'necessary evil', such weapons will remain with us. It is only when we arrive at a universal public acceptance of the fact that their very existence – and the fact that they are being stockpiled in the 'arsenals' of many countries, with military establishments being trained for their use – represents a universal and unacceptable danger to all of mankind, and when nations adopt a corresponding commitment to their total elimination, only then, can we be confident that we are on the road towards a safer and saner world.

32 Terminology of Nuclear Issues
HANNES ALFVÉN

At every discussion about what Herbert York has called the race to oblivion, we are reminded that we form a group of dissidents fighting a very strong establishment. This means that we should learn from the general studies which have been made concerning the fight between a dissident group and an establishment. It has been pointed out that the dissidents usually commit some mistakes, the first one being that they accept the terminology of the establishment. This often consists of euphemisms which are designed so as to hide the realities and give maximum advantage to the establishment. This means that unless we pay attention to semantics, we are fighting an uphill battle. Therefore, I think we should try to introduce a new vocabulary which is honest and tells the facts as they are. I will make here some suggestions how such a vocabulary may be formulated.

When discussing the consequences of a nuclear war, we usually speak about a 'nuclear catastrophe' or a 'nuclear holocaust'. 'Catastrophe' may make you think of a collision between a bus and a train - which no doubt is a catastrophe, but is not what we mean. 'Holocaust' is associated with much worse events, but still not comparable to what we are facing. The American philosopher, John Somerville, has coined the word 'omnicide' (suicide - genocide - omnicide), the murder of everybody. I think that this is an adequate word.

Similarly, 'nuclear arms' gives you an impression that we are talking about something similar to old-fashioned arms. At the back of their minds, people may associate them with brave knights who fight in shining armour. But the criminal pressing of a button, which will kill millions if not billions of **civilians**, including women and children, or rather torturing them to death, has nothing to do with heroism. I think that 'annihilators' gives a more precise definition of what we are speaking about (unless someone can find a better term).

The term 'realistic policy' is used in an inappropriate

way. People sitting in soft chairs at peace conferences are very anxious to discuss only 'realistic policies'; by this they mean a policy which the nuclear establishment can accept. They are proud if they succeed in delaying the deployment of a new type of annihilators by some months or perhaps a year. This sort of 'realistic policy' has been tried for decades and may have led to some small steps forward, but during that time there have been big strides backwards, carrying us towards omnicide. Instead, a **'realistic policy' must be a policy by which we can avoid omnicide.** No policy can be called realistic unless it leads to avoiding omnicide; to stopping and reversing the nuclear arms race.

Next we should discuss the use of the term 'expert'. Hitherto, the only people who were supposed to be competent to discuss the **race to omnicide** were those who knew the detailed structure of bombs and missiles. The very successful movement started by the medical people shows that this is not correct. The physicians call the omnicide **the last epidemic** for which there is no medical help. They are more **expert** than anyone who knows the technical details of the annihilators. Also, the demonstrators who oppose the deployment of annihilators, in Germany, Italy, the Netherlands or England, understand what is going on, even if they do not know all the details. In reality they are much better experts than those who deploy the annihilators.

There is another class of misleading terminology. Reagan conducts a propaganda of hatred against the 'Russians' and the 'communists', but he has never clarified what he means by 'Russian' and 'communists'. Of the population of the Soviet Union, the ethnic Russians are a minority; similarly, less than 10 per cent of the population are members of the communist party. The non-Russians in the Soviet Union are in part people who are being oppressed by the Russians. Why should Reagan murder them? More precisely, if he launches his annihilators, he will very likely kill Sakharov; **but** it is most unlikely that he will kill Chernenko and the Politburo, who will be just as well protected as Reagan and his friends. Similarly, we should ask Chernenko whether he has told the people in the Soviet Union that **his** annihilators will kill more workers than capitalists in Germany, and whether he seriously wants to destroy the country of Karl Marx.

England and France pretend that they represent European culture, but their precautionary measures are meant to murder more people than anyone has done since Genghis Khan and Tamberlaine. Has Mrs. Thatcher explained that Tamberlaine's roads marked by pyramids of human skulls are next to nothing compared with the misery which one of her Tridents will cause? Has Mitterand compared the nuclear aspects of the 'culture française' with the culture of Genghis Khan?

We must always remember that omnicide is the most hideous crime against humanity - worse than the sum of all the deadly sins which have been committed during the thousands of years of human history. Also, the **threat** of omnicide is a crime. The politicians say that the annihilators are produced not to be used but just to be a threat. Is this meant seriously? There are two ways to interpret this: either they really plan to commit omnicide, or it is a bluff. It should be made clear **which** it is.

Further, we must state that already the manufacturing of the annihilators and the deployment of them, as well as research to construct them, are similar crimes. The manufacture of plutonium in the so-called 'peaceful' nuclear reactors and the mining of uranium fall in the same category; as does the activity of IAEA.

The Earth is too small a planet to accommodate both plutonium and life. One of the two, plutonium or life, has to go underground - be buried for ever.

Two thousand five hundred years ago, Confucius was concerned about the chaotic conditions in China. When asked what to do, he answered that the most important thing was 'the rectification of the words', to restore the correct meaning of words. We have much to learn from Confucius.

33 Scientists and Public Opinion
SERGEI KAPITZA

The basis for the scientists' responsibility to influence public opinion comes from their professional knowledge. For ages this knowledge has been transferred to society through the educational system, for example, in schools and universities. Education is still the traditional and the main channel, not only for influencing public opinion, but also for forming and, in a very basic way, determining the way people think and act. One may assume that as the arms race is a long-term phenomenon, it will demand a long and systematic effort in educating the public on these matters. Thus, in considering the influence of scientists on these general socio-scientific issues, more attention needs to be given to basic education on these subjects than is usually done, by getting down to the fundamental values that govern the attitude and behaviour of people.

At the more emotionally charged level of current politics, scientists have a more direct duty in lending their expertise on these problems. Here we may note that a new pattern of a more systematised and organised way of studying these issues is being developed. Problems on the medical consequences of a nuclear war have been recently reported in detail in a WHO document[1]. The scientific problems of space-based missile defence have been presented in a detailed report by a panel of the Union of Concerned Scientists[2]. In the Soviet Union a study of the same problem was examined by a group of experts brought together by the Committee of Soviet Scientists for the Prevention of Nuclear War. These reports are mainly circulated as reprints to the scientific community, to experts and advisers to governments, and so on.

It is a paradox that there is no international journal devoted to reporting research papers on the scientific aspects of the arms race. The systematic effort of **Scientific American** and the **Bulletin of the Atomic Scientists** in treating these problems is certainly very important, but these publications do not usually present original work but an exposition of the results for the non-specialist and the uninformed reader in general. It should be pointed out that in the Soviet Union an effort is being made to get articles of a similar type to be published in journals like **Priroda** (Nature) and **Vestnik** (Courier) of the Academy of Sciences. In this way a much broader audience is reached than in the case of specialised scientific journals and reports.

At present, there seems to be a real need to report research on the scientific aspects of the arms race and consideration should be given to setting up and maintaining proper channels of communication, including perhaps an international journal on these subjects.

The necessity to develop and to provide an organisational national framework for mobilising the scientific effort has been recently recognised in the Soviet Union by setting up in 1983 the afore-mentioned Committee of Soviet Scientists for the Prevention of Nuclear War, consisting of 25 scientists and chaired by Academician E.P. Velikhov. One of its main purposes is to facilitate studies on the scientific aspects of the arms race, and to publish and disseminate material on these subjects. For example, at present a collection of papers on the global climatic consequences of a nuclear war is in preparation. Having no research facilities of its own, the Committee helped to bring together the necessary expertise from different organisations for the extensive and interdisciplinary research these complicated problems demand; such problems can hardly be fully treated by the individual scientist, however important his original contribution may be. For example, in the case of the 'Nuclear Winter', it was the crucial contribution of Crutzen[3] that led to the extensive, and as yet incomplete, studies of the global consequences of a large nuclear war.

Next we should consider the way in which these studies may be further disseminated so as to have their full potential delivered to society. As already mentioned, the popularisation of these studies in well-known popular science journals like **Scientific American, Priroda, La Recherche,** is an important step in a sequence of events that should follow.

One fact worthy of emphasis is that a whole system of publications and TV programmes aimed at the popularisation of science, has emerged. Moreover, not only has the scale of this effort changed in the last decades, but also the scope of the problems treated. In the not too distant past, popularisation of science was considered to be a minor activity, compared, say, with the educational process, or the entertainment industry. With the emergence of science as a dynamic and major factor of our economic and cultural development, the effort to disseminate the message of science more widely, has grown. We witness a marked proliferation of popular science magazines, museums of science and technology, and special TV programmes that have become an important and regular part of TV broadcasting. It is through these channels that the message of science is finally delivered to the public; this is the main instrument by which public opinion is determined.

In this realm, an exciting avenue for presenting to the public the results of research and the attitudes of scientists can be provided by TV link-ups. In these, the audience is exposed both to the exchange of opinion and to the body of world science in treating major socio-scientific issues, especially those connected with the arms race. A powerful example on Soviet TV was set by the discussion moderated by Drs. Chazov and Lown in June 1982 on the medical aspects of a nuclear war. Even more impressive was the live transmission by satellite of a discussion on the nuclear winter between scientists in Moscow and Washington, following the October 1983 Washington Conference.

On the other hand, it is also important to develop an exchange of points of view on the more positive aspects of science following from its progress. One cannot but note that the recent exercises in what can be called scientific eschatology, lead to a rather hopeless future. Presented with the full power of the mass media, this image of our future may help in evading a nuclear war, but at a cost of demoralising the public. There is an important social demand for generating a message of hope by the scientific community. Years ago a crude message of some optimism was provided by science fiction, but today this has lost much of its impact. Perhaps the world scientific community should now try to provide some insight into the future and thus generate hope. This need was recognised by the founders of the 'Club of Rome' and some other international bodies. Following on this, due concern should be given not only to the grave issues of the arms race, but also to the other truly global issues facing us all.

In recognising the sequence of events by which the primary scientific message is transferred to the realm of social consciousness and - hopefully - behaviour and further action, the responsibility of the scientific community can be fully exercised. We should not try to cut through and bypass the steps mentioned; it is by properly ascertaining their importance that the full impact of the scientific community may finally lead to a reasonable and just solution to the problem posed to mankind by the arms race.

References

1. World Health Organization, 'Effects of Nuclear War on Health and Health Services', Report of the International Committee of Experts in Medical Sciences and Public Health to implement Resolution WHA34.38 (Geneva, 1984).
2. Report by the Union of Concerned Scientists, 'Space-based Missile Defense' (March, 1984).
3. P.J. Crutzen and J.W. Birks, 'The Atmosphere After a Nuclear War: Twilight at Noon', in Jeannie Peterson (ed.) The Aftermath (New York: Pantheon Books, 1983) pp.73-96.

34 Scientists and Public Opinion – Differences between East and West

SVEN HELLMAN

The goals for Pugwash, as expressed in the Proceedings of the Warsaw Conference in 1982, include some principles about the responsibility of scientists:

> The Pugwash Movement is an expression of the awareness of the social and moral duty of scientists to prevent and overcome the actual and potential harmful effects of scientific and technological innovations...In addition to influencing governments by the transmission of the results of the debates, Pugwash should also aim at educating the scientific community and making an impact on public opinion by means of special types of meetings and by publications[1].

At the same Conference, a Working Group, after discussing the responsibility of scientists, recommended to scientists throughout the world that they:

1. Consider it to be a major personal responsibility to help bring about solutions to the pressing problems of mankind.
2. Form links with the medical and health professions to alert the public to the danger of nuclear war.
3. Study all aspects of the arms race, including the technical, social, political, economical, and psychological aspects.
4. Facilitate the participation of concerned scientists of all disciplines in relevant international conferences, especially those of the United Nations organizations.
5. Address wide audiences directly as well as through the mass media to provide the public with factual information concerning the arms race and its consequences.
6. Assist Peace Organizations by providing them with professional scientific knowledge.
7. Encourage scientific Academies, institutions, and journals to devote a reasonable part of their effort and attention

356   SCIENTISTS, PUBLIC OPINION AND THE ARMS RACE

to studies of problems relevant to peace and disarmament.
8. Promote education about disarmament, world peace, and international understanding and encourage the inclusion of these issues in the curricula of schools and universities[2].

These principles and recommendations signify a real expansion of the traditional role of Pugwash which has been to influence governments in an informal way by using personal relations. In this paper I want to comment on what this may mean in reality and what problems may be expected.

The Problem

The antagonism and deep mistrust between NATO and the Warsaw Pact countries and the continuous arms race have many concurrent reasons.

- The two blocs represent different economic and social systems and the two superpowers aim at increasing their global influence. This is the basic reason for their mutual suspicions.
- The military resources each bloc is building up in order to improve its own security create at the same time fears within the other bloc of offensive capabilities and intentions.
- The military efforts consume resources, which could otherwise have been used for other urgent purposes. In order to build up support within their own population for military efforts, governments tend to describe the adversary as malevolent, aggressive and militarily superior, while their own efforts are declared to promote peace and security. The military establishments and the defence industries have a self-interest in contributing to this propaganda. The world is thus described in black and white - a very gloomy picture.

On the other hand, none of the two blocs seems to be contemplating a deliberate war in Europe. The consequences of a major nuclear war will be so disastrous, not only for the adversaries but also for the whole of mankind, that they are quite out of proportion to any political goal. Even a limited war, carries the obvious risk that it will escalate to a major nuclear war. Consequently, the military forces cannot be intended for fighting and winning a war in Europe but only for deterring aggression from the adversary. But deterrence could be achieved by much smaller resources on both sides. It has been said that a twentieth of the present nuclear forces would be sufficient for a stable deterrence.

Even if nobody wants a war in Europe, it could be the result of horizontal and vertical escalation of an initially limited conflict. Contributing factors could be misjudgements, shortage of time, vulnerable military resources and limited influence on the actions of the allies. Many initiatives to reduce the probability of a war in Europe have been discussed, for example confidence-building measures, no-first-use of nuclear weapons, improved hotline, reduced vulnerability of the nuclear forces and of the command and control system.

However, as a consequence of the deep mutual antagonism and mistrust, all efforts to halt and reverse the arms race and reduce the probability of war have achieved no, or very minimal, results. On the contrary, the ongoing arms race both contributed to a further deepening of the antagonism and to increase the probability of a nuclear war. Negotiation initiatives from one side have mostly been seen by the other side as efforts to get unilateral advantages, and the difficulties about verification seemed to be quite unsurmountable.

The problems now seem to be:

- how to overcome the deep antagonism and mistrust between East and West which is preventing progress in arms control efforts?
- how to find and formulate arms control proposals which are effective and politically acceptable?
- how to put increased pressure on governments around the world, particularly the governments of the USA and the USSR, to intensify their common efforts for arms control and mutual confidence?

What Scientists Could Do

Based on their professional skills and contacts, scientists could contribute to solving the problems in the following ways:

- make politicians and the general public aware of the disastrous consequences of a major nuclear war, thereby forestalling all plans and preparations for fighting and winning a nuclear war;
- provide governments with arms control proposals and produce scientific documentation as to why particular proposals are useful and of benefit to both sides;
- produce scientific documentation about the overall military balance in order to counteract propaganda figures from the East as well as the West, and also to get rid of the simple

numbers game;
- provide an informal channel of communication between East and West and thus build up confidence;
- produce scientific documentation about destabilising and other negative effects of proposed new weapons systems, in order to forestall them being deployed;
- try to arouse the scientific community all over the world to make them aware of the present dangerous situation;
- make scientific expertise and results available to the public, and thus provide leadership for grass-root peace movements.

How to Influence Government and Public Opinion in the East and the West

In these efforts, scientists could choose between two different strategies which, in my view, could not easily be combined.

The first aims at influencing governments directly by making use of organisational, professional and personal contacts. In a non-public way scientists could promote some types of action and help governments to influence public opinion.

The second is aimed at influencing public opinion by making scientific expertise available to the public, thus providing some leadership. Public opinion is then expected to put pressure on governments and thus influence their decisions.

With regard to the first strategy: in the East members of scientific academies enjoy a high status, have a real influence on government policies, and are permitted to have scientific contacts with the West. This means that scientists from the East and the West could meet and have free and frank exchanges of ideas even on highly controversial issues if the discussions are informal and not open to the general public. Each participant could go home and work for the acceptance of the findings of the discussions. This is the traditional way of working within Pugwash and it has also been adopted by the Physicians for the Prevention of Nuclear War. A good recent example of East-West cooperation is the study of climatic consequences of nuclear war. More scientific contacts of this type are needed. May they not be further reduced by present East-West tensions!

The second strategy meets with difficulties because of the quite different conditions for working with public opinion in the West and the East. In the West, people have a legal right to found new political parties, free labour unions and grass roots movements. In fact, public opinion organised in such ways has had an influence on recent government decisions in the NATO countries. Here scientists have a real role in providing the public with factual information.

But in the East, similar organisations will be forbidden, or at least persecuted if they criticise their own government. Western contacts are risky for such so-called disident organisations and will furthe compromise them. On the other hand, government supported peace organisations could be forums for debate and could influence public opinion.

Thus, in the East, scientists are left with the possibility of cooperating with the official, peace movements authorised by the government. This means, in my view, that in the East there appears to be not much difference between the first and second strategy.

My conclusion is that efforts to influence grass roots movements in order to put pressure on governments will work only in the West. Do we really want to exercise such one-sided influence? I think that we should, because there cannot be anything negative in a better educated public opinion. However, Pugwash should primarily stick to its traditional role of frank and non-public discussions combined with informal contacts with governments.

References:

1. Proceedings of the 32nd Pugwash Conference on Science and World Affairs, Warsaw, 1982, p.77.
2. Ibid, p.46.

35 Role of Universities in the Campaign to Suffocate the Nuclear Arms Race
ERIC TOLLEFSON

Scientists, engineers and other technologists invented and developed the nuclear bomb. Despite the horrendous consequences of its use at Hiroshima and Nagasaki, these groups have continued to develop the technology so that in the event of a major nuclear conflict, the effects might destroy life as we know it on this planet.

Sidney Lens[1] describes forces which 'drive the arms race to levels where considerations of deterrence are rendered all but irrelevant'. He goes on to say:

Among the most important of these forces is the technological imperative – the relentless drive among scientists and engineers to develop even more sinister forms of weaponry. E.P. Taylor has called the process addictive. Driven by intellectual curiosity or by career ambitions, the weapons designers try to anticipate what the state of their art will be in five or ten or twenty years, pressing always for new breakthroughs in deadly destructiveness.

Instead of developing the stable deterrence which the strategists claim to be seeking, Lens says that rampant weapons technology development creates instead an unstable deterrence which enhances the prospect of war. To slow down or stop the arms race, the development of new forms of weaponry must be slowed or halted. How might steps in this direction be taken?

Recognising that the seeds from which new implements of war spring lie in the minds of scientists, engineers and technologists in laboratories in universities, in industries and in the military establishments, we as a scientific peer group might appeal to them to reconsider what they are doing and how they are making the world in which we live increasingly dangerous. It is not likely that they would consider such an appeal seriously because many of them have been doing this kind of research for decades for various personal reasons. We must realise that such work is a challenge, that it provides a good living for them and that were they to give up their jobs, they may have difficulty finding others. They will argue that the politicians and the military are the responsible parties and that they, as scientists, engineers and technologists, are merely doing a job.

Since the first atomic bombs were dropped in August 1945, the politicians and the military, despite the awesome results of these bombings, have gone on to deploy more nuclear weapons of greater power and of higher accuracy, to the point that it becomes insanity to think of using these weapons on a major scale. And yet the leaders of the superpowers accept the situation and continue the arms race at an increasing rate. Arms control negotiators from these powers have spent years at conference tables, making little if any progress. The millions of people on either side of these confrontations sit back seemingly powerless, while the governments of the superpowers and of many other countries spend hundreds of billions of dollars per annum on arms, giving little thought to the needs of millions of starving people around the world.

We cannot go on building more weapons without increasing the risk of a disaster of the greatest magnitude. Each weapon system added to the stockpiles on either side adds to the probability that it will initiate a major conflict either intentional or through: a malfunction of equipment; an erroneous communication; instability on the part of those in positions of command of armed forces; weapons finding their way into the hands of irresponsible terrorists; or bad judgment by a government or military leader in a stress-laden crisis situation. As the number of weapon systems increases, so does the probability that a disaster might take place by chance. A major nuclear encounter would destroy military and other targets as well as hundreds of millions of people. Only in the past few months have people become aware of what might be described as another dimension of such an encounter, the 'nuclear winter'. Knowledge of these effects serves to intensify the need to prevent such a disaster from occurring.

Knowing the grim consequences of a major nuclear conflict, why have the politicians on both sides gone along with the military and funded the massive build-up of armaments to the point that they themselves would probably be destroyed if a major nuclear war took place. Certainly the politicians have the power to put the brakes on the nuclear race by reducing funding for military purposes and by coming to terms around the conference table. The political will to do so, however, is lacking. It would appear that the politicians are either misinformed by their advisers, or ill-informed about the facts relating to a major nuclear conflict, or are under pressure from the military, industry and weaponry experts to keep pursuing the arms race. Lord Zuckerman, as quoted by Mark Oliphant[2], put considerable emphasis on the last of these possibilities. Otherwise, as normal human beings, surely they would be desperately seeking ways to reduce the probability of such a disaster which would destroy them, their familities and the future of the human race.

In 1978, Prime Minister Trudeau of Canada put before the First United Nations Special Session on Disarmament (UNSSOD I) a strategy of suffocation to halt the nuclear arms race. The main elements of it include: a comprehensive text ban; a halt to the flight testing of all new strategic delivery vehicles; a cessation in the production of fissionable materials for weapons purposes; and a limitation and eventual reduction on spending by the military for new strategic weapons systems. Trudeau spoke before UNSSOD II in 1982 on the topic 'Technological Momentum: The Fuel that Feeds the Nuclear Arms Race' and again presented this approach to arms control but also stating that it was never meant to be applied unilaterally. The proposal was a good one but without the support and political will of the major powers, it did not get off the ground. Within a few months, Canadians were faced with the prospect of allowing the cruise missile delivery vehicle to be tested in their far north. There were protest marches and a public opinion poll indicating that more people were against testing the vehicle than in favour. Nevertheless, ironically, Canada is now involved with the United States in flight-testing of the unarmed missile. Had the political will at higher levels of government been sufficiently strong, the cruise may not have been tested. One has the strong impression that had the public protest been somewhat stronger, the government would have had to yield and to say 'no' to the tests. Clearly, education of the public can play a very important role in the arms control process.

The Flow of Power

When one analyses the situation in a country such as Canada one sees in simple terms a power structure such as the one depicted in the diagram at the end of the paper. The educational institutes and advisory groups are shown as part of this structure although their real power is debatable.

Once a democratic government has been elected, the politicians tend to forget the people who elected them until the time for the next election rolls around. The politicians are supposedly trying to carry out the will of the people who elected them but on matters relating to defence and the arms race, this has not been followed because the people have had relatively little input. Events of the past three years particularly accompanied by major increases in defence budgets around the world have changed the attitudes of many people about the military and its objectives.

In the past the Government, through the Department of National Defence, has worked with the military leaders to produce a defence programme. The military leaders want their forces to be strong for to be otherwise would make their role less important. To supply the weapons and materials required by the armed forces, the DND calls upon industry to provide what is needed. Industry is generally only too happy to cooperate because such opportunities provide jobs and make profits. The government gains advice on the amount it should spend from advisors in the military establishments, from NORAD, NATO and various experts. At the same time, industry and the military lobby the government to urge it to spend more on defence.

The people who pay the taxes to support these expenditures have in the past had virtually no input into the process, except at election times when issues relating to the budget and the country's role in international defence systems may become part of the political discussion. For the most part the citizens have known very little about the requirements for military forces; thus the politicians could make decisions about defence and international obligations without appreciable concern for the wishes of the people. If changes are to come about, then there must be the political will. In a democracy the political will comes from what the politicans think that the people who elected them want. To change government attitudes on these matters, the people must be made aware of the facts, to enable them to develop their points of view and then make the politicans aware of what they think and want. The political will of the politicians should reflect this interaction. In a non-democratic system, an informed public can still put pressure on government in many ways to make it reconsider its spending on military versus the material and social needs of the people.

Changing the Way in Which the People and Politicians Think

How can the thinking of the politicians be changed so that they will see the folly of the present arms race? One answer would seem to be through education of the people most likely to enter politics, as well as of those most likely to be in advisory positions to the government. A recent article by Baxter and Tausig[3] describes what has been happening in Canadian universities in the past three years. Prior to the 1980s there was but one peace research group at a university

in Canada, the Canadian Peace Research and Education
Association at Brandon University started in 1966. In January
1981 a national organisation, Science for Peace, was started
at the University of Toronto. This organisation has chapters
at the Universities of Toronto, British Columbia, New
Brunswick and Waterloo. Soon afterwards, in 1981, the McGill
Study Group for Peace and Disarmament was formed. In the
past few months a group called the University Nuclear
Disarmament Organisation (Alberta) was formed at the
University of Alberta, and the Peace and Conflict Resolution
Study Group at the University of Calgary became active.

Other organisations with ties to the university system have
also sprung up. These include Physicians for Social Responsibility, Veterans for Multilateral Nuclear Disarmament,
Psychologists for Peace, and Lawyers for Social Responsibility. In addition, there are several other organisations
which have been established including Operation Dismantle,
Project Ploughshares, Voice of Women, Parliamentarians for
World Order, and The Peace Research Institute Dundas. These
latter groups are seeking to educate the public and are
calling upon interested academics in the universities and
colleges as resource leaders for discussion groups.

With the above organisations in place, the time is approaching when there will be action, in addition to protest
marches in which people carry placards calling for sanity in
control of the nuclear arms race and holding meetings to
educate the members of the groups. Politicians are being
bombarded with letters and telephone calls regarding their
stand on nuclear disarmament issues, their support of the
less developed countries and the role which Canada is playing
in peace making at the United Nations. The process will be
democratic but will be more vigorous than it has been in the
past. It is evident that many people are becoming much more
knowledgeable about what is happening in world affairs. Mr.
Trudeau's recent visit to several world leaders to discuss
peace making is thought in part to have been a response to
pressures brought to bear on him by church leaders, the peace
movement and the Canadian Pugwash Group.

The World Disarmament Campaign

A seminar held in Caracas, Venezuela in October 1983, organised by the United Nations Department for Disarmament Affairs
in cooperation with UNESCO dealt with the role of the educational community in promoting United Nations' objectives in
the field of arms limitations and disarmament[4]. Participants considered the educational community as a key constituent in the World Disarmament Campaign. The need was expressed

for universities to integrate disarmament questions into existing courses as well as establishing disarmament education as a distinct field of study as described in the Final Document of UNESCO's World Congress on Disarmament Education. The need for appropriate resources for such courses was also expressed and it was agreed that United Nations information materials were suitable for the World Disarmament Campaign based on 'legitimacy, comparability and credibility'.

A publication entitled 'World Disarmament Campaign - Disarmament Week' by the United Nations[5] describes in brief, specific proposals for inclusion in the campaign. The availability in an unhindered way of a range of relevant materials provided by governments and recognised institutes could form the basic materials upon which courses in the field of arms control and disarmament might be based.

Activating the Universities Towards the Peace Effort

As a first step it is proposed that Pugwash requests the Secretary-General of the United Nations that, as a part of the World Disarmament Campaign, he write to presidents (or the equivalent) of universities around the world encouraging them to provide courses on disarmament and arms control, so that students of all nations be made aware of the facts of the arms race and its effects, particularly on the less developed countries. The United Nations Secretary-General could request that the universities consider their policies with respect to the support of research related to the arms race, and that every effort be made to slow or halt such activities by peer group pressure on a moral basis and by appropriate adjustments to funding of such research.

References

1. S. Lens, 'Reflections - The Deterrence Myth', The Progressive. Madison. 2.
2. M. Oliphant, 'Comment on the Social Responsibilities of Scientists', in J. Rotblat (ed), Scientists, The Arms Race and Disarmament (London: Taylor & Francis, 1982) p.193.
3. H. Baxter and C. Tausig, 'The Role of Our Universities in the Nuclear Age', CAUT Bulletin, April 1984.
4. Disarmament Newsletter, 'World Disarmament Campaign Focuses on the Educational Community', United Nations.
5. Fact Sheet No. 24, 'World Disarmament Campaign Disarmament Week', United Nations.

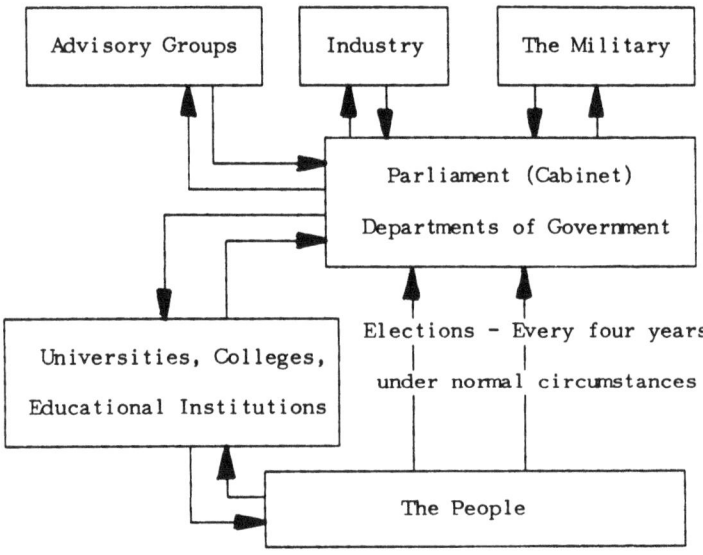

Power Structure in Canada

36 Pugwash and the Scientific Community
PATRICIA LINDOP

Historical Background

In discussions on the ways Pugwash should exert its influence two targets are usually specified; decision makers and public opinion. A third target, the scientific community, appears to have been forgotten, although it figured prominently in the early Pugwash history. The vital decisions about the direction Pugwash should take were made at the first meeting of the Continuing Committee in 1957. Even before that meeting a canvass of scientists in the UK and USA, about the type of conference to be convened, has shown that the majority:

> ...preferred small meetings of two types: (a) meetings to discuss immediate political problems, and primarily directed at influencing governments; and (b) meetings to study the social implications of scientific progress, and aimed at clarifying the thinking of scientists themselves. Some scientists were also in favour of a third type, i.e., larger meetings, to deal with general problems and to issue resolutions directed to the world at large[1].

The Vienna Declaration of 1958, which was endorsed by thousands of scientists, and is regarded as the tenet of the Pugwash Movement, was largely an appeal to the scientific community:

> We believe it to be a responsibility of scientists in all countries to contribute to the education of the peoples by spreading among them a wide understanding of the dangers and potentialities offered by the unprecedented growth of science. We appeal to our colleagues everywhere to contribute to this effort, both through enlightenment of adult populations, and through education

of the coming generations. In particular, education should stress improvement of all forms of human relations and should eliminate any glorification of war and violence.

Scientists are, because of their special knowledge, well equipped for early awareness of the danger and the promise arising from scientific discoveries. Hence, they have a special competence and a special responsibility in relation to the most pressing problems of our times[2].

Although this appeal to scientists has lost none of its validity, little attention was paid to this aspect in the subsequent years. At some Annual Conferences, usually the Quinquennial ones, topics such as 'the responsibility of scientists' or 'science and society' were taken up in Working Groups, but these issues were thought to be less pressing than the main preoccupation of Pugwash with the nuclear arms race. Anyhow, no action seems to have been taken on the recommendations from these Working Groups.

The only recent occasion when the role of scientists was discussed at length was the Pugwash Symposium in Ajaccio, organised jointly with UNESCO, in February 1982. The theme of the Symposium was 'Scientists, the Arms Race and Disarmament', and the papers were subsequently published in a book under that title[3]. The conclusions reached are of particular importance, as they link two basic aspects of Pugwash: scientists and the avoidance of nuclear war. They are also of direct relevance to this paper, in which the emphasis is on the role of scientists in arms control and disarmament, although the arguments and suggestions apply also to the other areas of Pugwash activities.

Educating Scientists

The basic assumption is that scientists do have a social responsibility for their work. In a detailed and incisive analysis, Professor John Ziman discussed the various arguments which have been used to excuse social irresponsibility, and demolished them one by one. He concluded:

> There is great public concern about many of the effects of science upon society and upon humanity as a whole. Out of this concern there now flows the demand that scientists **must** be more careful, and **must** be more responsible, in what they do, for it could bring us all to disaster. Of all conceivable disasters that might overwhelm mankind, nuclear war is far and away the most likely and terrible. Unwittingly perhaps, the scientists made such a disaster possible: inexorably perhaps, they

PUGWASH AND THE SCIENTIFIC COMMUNITY

are driven into activities that make such a disaster ever more threatening. But whether or not they should be individually blamed for what they have collectively done for the world, not one of them can now cast off a personal responsibility to think about these matters and to act to make this disaster a little less probable[4].

The recommendations of the Ajaccio Symposium advise scientists on the dangers of the nuclear arms race and how to act to avert them. In particular, they contain the following list of 12 specific tasks for scientists.

- maintain contact between scientists from different social and economic systems, drawing on the common interests and values of the international scientific community, and explore through such contacts all possibilities of resolving conflicts and fostering progress towards disarmament;
- study the technological aspects of the arms race so as to be able to offer expert advice on these matters to decision makers and the general public;
- support efforts to limit and eventually stop the nuclear arms race, in particular, to conclude without delay a Comprehensive Test-Ban Treaty;
- monitor destabilising developments in the arms race and warn the public about them;
- contribute to the ongoing research on the economic consequences of disarmament so as to be able to allay fears about unemployment and to find alternative opportunities for the utilisation of resources and manpower at present employed on military projects;
- participate in national and international meetings of scientists to debate and seek means of disseminating the findings of the studies mentioned above;
- encourage the setting up of an international committee of scientists to analyse the consequnces of the nuclear arms race and report their conclusions;
- address lay audiences and mass media and provide them with factual information about the dangers and likely outcome of a nuclear war;
- use their influence in scientific academies and institutions to induce them to devote some of their activities and budgets to the above issues;
- urge editors of scientific journals to provide space for discussions on those issues;
- promote disarmament education and, in particular, the inclusion of disarmament-related issues in the curricula of schools and universities;

- seek the effective implementation of the UNESCO recommendation on the status of scientific researchers.

Laudable as these sentiments are, they are likely to remain paper recommendations unless steps are taken to trigger them into action. It is not enough to issue an appeal and leave it at that, in the hope that somebody will react to it. The most effective way to secure a positive response to a call for action is to initiate that action. Thus, the follow-up of the Ajaccio recommendations is for Pugwash to take the initiative in implementing them.

If the scientific community is to fulfil the role prescribed in the Ajaccio document in relation to the arms race, the first step must be to educate the scientists, to supply them with appropriate information, thus enabling them to discuss these issues with authority.

One way of achieving this is by addressing scientists participating in the meetings which learned and professional societies organise periodically at national or regional levels. These meetings are usually strictly professional, but an effort should be made to secure a formal or informal niche for a discussion of topics related to the social responsibility of scientists, preferably relevant to the given discipline.

A second way would be for Pugwash to organise - at national or local levels, for example, at University centres - seminars, workshops and study groups on a number of technological and political aspects of the arms race. The teachers at these seminars would come mainly from the Pugwash ranks, but it would be desirable to invite people from outside, either to supplement technical expertise or to expose the 'students' to different, often contrary views. This is important not only to enliven the study but also to sharpen the intellect and force the audience to seek answers to criticism and defend their views.

While the main aim of these seminars would be education, that is, to generate a scientific community knowledgeable in problems of arms control and disarmament, it is likely that some of the 'students' will become sufficiently interested to want to pursue the subject further. Pugwash should be prepared for this by planning advanced seminars and encouraging them to join the Pugwash Movement.

Another probable outcome is that a number of scientists would be willing to become speakers at large public meetings aiming at influencing public opinion. For this purpose, Pugwash should organise special schools of speakers on a variety of relevant topics.

All these actions are intended to be additional to, not in

place of, the other activities of the Pugwash Movement which aim at influencing decision makers and public opinion.

The implementation of this additional task would obviously require a considerable extra effort and - in the first instance - more people to carry it out. Before discussing the problem of recruiting new Pugwashites, we need to examine the type of scientist we would like to bring in; this in turn is related to the main item on the Pugwash agenda, the avoidance of nuclear war.

Arms Control and Disarmament

The most blatant case of social irresponsibility of scientists is the crucial role they play in furthering the arms race. The Ajaccio document refers to this role as being contrary to the traditional calling of science. It implores those who are employed in the military R&D establishments to ponder on the social implications of their work. This suggests that the educational effort discussed in the previous section should be extended to scientists engaged in military research. But whether we should attempt to bring them into Pugwash needs careful consideration.

Pugwash is not a political party and has no political platform. On the other hand, it is not a purely academic study, a kind of Oxford Union in which issues are debated more for the sake of the art of scholarly disputation than to seek solutions to real problems. Pugwash has a goal which is both humane and pragmatic; the goal is peace in the world, with the avoidance of nuclear war as the most urgent objective. Within this framework fairly divergent views are expressed in the Pugwash forum, but it is difficult to imagine the advocacy in Pugwash of measures that would explicitly aggravate the nuclear arms race. Scientists propagating such views do not find a sympathetic audience in Pugwash and soon come to the conclusion that there is no place for them in our meetings. This may be one reason why well over a half of all Pugwash participants attended only one meeting.

Even without overtly negative approaches - and with the best of intentions - we may fall into the trap of recommending policies which might have an effect contrary to that expected. A classical example of this was recently described by Freeman Dyson[5]. He recalls that after the first Soviet test of the atom bomb in 1949, Robert Oppenheimer advocated the development of tactical nuclear weapons. One of his reasons was to stop in this way the development of the hydrogen bomb which was then strongly pushed by Edward Teller. Oppenheimer's proposal was accepted, but so was Teller's; the US government decided to develop both, the tactical weapons and the H-bomb.

A parallel to this may happen at the present time in our pursuit of a no-first-use policy. To make its acceptance easier it is suggested that there should be an increase in conventional weapons. If we are not careful we may end up with having a larger conventional force without a reduction in nuclear forces. A somewhat similar risk is contained in the current emphasis on defensive strategies. Defence is viewed as more desirable than offence, but sometimes defensive measures may aggravate the offensive potential. In the case of nuclear weapons this was recognised by Pugwash in the 1960s, in its strong opposition to anti-ballistic missiles. This applies also to the current 'star wars' project to develop space weapons for defence purposes, another of Teller's bright ideas. But even the call for a purely defensive strategy in conventional arms may end up with the development of sophisticated defensive weapons and the retention of offensive arsenals. The only way to achieve a peaceful world is by devising means to reduce existing armaments without substituting them for others, even if the latter seem less harmful. We need real disarmament rather than arms control.

Amateurs and Professionals

What type of scientist is, therefore, most desirable to carry out the Pugwash tasks? The ideas about this appear to have undergone a change in the recent years.

At the beginning, Pugwash consisted of scientists, predominantly from the natural sciences, who were top rate in their profession but amateurs in many matters discussed in Pugwash. As a result of participating in our meetings some of them became sufficiently informed to rank almost as experts. In addition, some genuine experts, that is people who professionally dealt with the topics discussed by us, were brought in, usually to Symposia and Workshops. These people were not always scientists; they included politicians, diplomats and high-ranking military officers (mostly retired). The resulting professional air of debates in the Symposia and Workshops contrasted sharply with the superficial treatment of topics and the generality that characterised the discussions in most Working Groups at the Annual Conferences. This has led to the notion that the real work of Pugwash is done in the Symposia and Workshops. The Annual Conferences begun to be derided as a waste of time, and there were even proposals that they should be abolished, or at least be held less frequently.

It is to the credit of the Pugwash Council that it resisted these propositions, which would have transformed the nature

PUGWASH AND THE SCIENTIFIC COMMUNITY 373

of the Movement and detached it from its initial objectives. Symposia and Workshops, in the framework of a wider programme of activities, are an important, indeed a vital component, but if they were the only, or even the dominant element, Pugwash would soon become isolated from the scientific community and be seen as an even more esoteric club than reputed.

Moreover, specialised meetings tend to become inbred and myopic. By concentrating on a narrow issue and tackling it in depth - admirable if it is a part of a more general scheme - they tend to lose sight of wider perspectives; the issue under debate, such as a complex formula for arms control, becomes an end in itself.

The way to overcome the valid criticism of the level of debate at the Annual Conferences is not by abolishing them but by raising standards. A good start towards this is the commissioning of papers on each topic of the agenda, and the request to participants to familiarise themselves with the subject of their Working Group well in advance of the Conference.

In my opinion this is the proper way to proceed. There is a wide range between complete amateurism and complete professionalism. We should aim at a normal distribution, in which extremes occur with a low frequency. The participation of a small number of people who spend 100 per cent of their time on Pugwash-like activities is highly desirable. But the great majority should be working scientists, who spend only a fraction of their time on Pugwash matters. However, this fraction must be such as to allow proper preparation and ensure competence in the debates. Pugwash should remain a movement of amateurs, but as was succinctly described at the 1972 Conference in Oxford 'Pugwash ... is no place for unprepared amateurism, however well-intentioned'[6].

Numbers and Eminence

By the nature of its activities Pugwash is destined to be a small movement numerically, but not many of us realise how tiny a fraction of the scientific community it is. In 1982, after 25 years of existence, the total number of persons who took part in any type of Pugwash activity (conferences, symposia, workshops and study groups)[7] added up to about 2000. When compared with the number of scientists and engineers in the world (about four million), the enrolment in Pugwash comes out to be only 0.05 per cent of the total potential. Even more importantly, there is no sign of an increasing trend in the involvement of scientists in Pugwash.

It should be noted that the above statistics refer to

participants in international Pugwash meetings only. National Groups carry out activities in which other scientists take part. There is not enough information about the number of the latter but it is not likely to change the total by more than a factor of two.

Numbers are of course not everything. One can advance sound arguments for the thesis that quality is more important than quantity; that a few influential scientists can achieve much more than a multitude of average standard. Certainly, we must not relax our efforts to increase the number of eminent scientists. But numbers and eminence need not necessarily be conflicting requirements; there may even be a positive correlation between them: a cause which appeals to a large number of persons is likely to bring in also a larger number of top people.

The main reason Pugwash needs more scientists was given earlier, namely, to enable us to increase our influence on the scientific community by the educational process. But there is also the need to help in the formation and influencing public opinion on issues advocated by Pugwash. As stated in the guidelines adopted in Warsaw, Pugwash should aim at making an impact on public opinion by educating the public in matters of concern to Pugwash[8]. The process of education implies the existence of teachers; making an impact on public opinion requires enough knowledgeable people to take part (as individuals) in public debates, to inject and defend the views on which there is a consensus in Pugwash.

At present there are simply not enough scientists who can speak up in public with authority on the vital issues of nuclear arms control and disarmament; to intervene when blatantly wrong policies are promulgated. As a result, the scientific community has made little impact on the public debate and the formulation of policies on these issues. This is certainly true in the UK, but it is probably also true in other countries, with the exception perhaps of the USA where other groups of scientists, not directly associated with Pugwash, play the role described above.

There is another issue related to public intervention by groups of scientists. The prime requirement of competence has already been stressed. But apart from the objectivity customary in science, political objectivity is also of major importance. For example, selection of material in such a way that only one side come out to be the good guys, or condemnation of only one side when both sides are at fault, is eventually counter-productive and leads to a loss of credibility which reflects on all scientists, including Pugwashites. Inactivity by Pugwash may result in scientists - otherwise sympathetic to us - joining other groups which may pursue their aim less objectively.

How to Enlarge Pugwash

Having argued for the need of more scientists in Pugwash, the question is how can this be achieved?

The main difficulty here arises from the limited scope of Pugwash activities, that is the frequency of meetings and their size. Unless there is a radical change in both of these aspects, one cannot expect a substantial increase in the number of scientists participating in international activities. The chief limiting factor is financial but other elements also contribute.

These limitations apply to a much lesser degree to Pugwash activities at the national level. However, our task of recruiting scientists for work at the national level is made much more difficult if we cannot dangle the carrot of participation in international meetings. The characteristic feature of Pugwash being contacts between East and West, participation in meetings where such contacts occur is the main attraction. Although there is plenty of scope for Pugwash-like activities at national levels, it is far from being a substitute for attending an international conference or symposium.

Some improvement can be achieved by a larger turnover of participants, for example, having two-thirds of newcomers at each Conference instead of one-third as at present. Another step would be to convene more symposia and workshops every year − funds permitting − combined with a larger turnover in them. But we cannot expect a significant change from these measures.

In the search for other solutions several possibilities come to mind, although they are only poor substitutes.

One is to initiate an international discussion by the method usually employed by scientists: on paper. Pugwash should encourage scientists to write papers on topics of interest, and ensure their international circulation by means of a Pugwash Journal. This would be complementary to the Annals of Pugwash, which contain papers presented at international meetings. A link between the proposed Journal and the Annals could be established, for example, by printing in the Journal comments on papers in the Annals, and conversely, ideas originating in the Journal being taken up and developed at international meetings.

A second possibility relates to a suggestion made earlier, namely to make use of **international** scientific conferences in which often many thousands of scientists meet. Pugwash should try to obtain permission from the organisers to have a plenary session, or at least one of the parallel sessions, devoted to a discussion on a subject of Pugwash concern. The programmes of such conferences are usually very tight, and the chances of such permission being granted are therefore not too good, but it is worth trying.

A third possibility is to organise regional meetings. These would generally not meet the criterion of East-West contacts, but they would enable scientists from several countries to discuss relevant problems. In most cases such meetings would be much cheaper to convene and therefore could be held more frequently.

Another possibility is to organise visits of individual scientists from the East to participate in Pugwash national meetings in the West, and **vice versa**, thus contributing to the international debate. Such visits do occur sporadically at present, but it may be worth putting this on a regular basis.

These suggestions, if implemented, would help to bring more scientists into Pugwash and subsequently to increase our positive input into the scientific community.

References

1. J. Rotblat, Scientists in the Quest for Peace: A History of the Pugwash Conferences (MIT Press, 1972) p.7.
2. Ibid, p.156.
3. Scientists, the Arms Race and Disarmament, J. Rotblat (ed.) (London: Taylor & Francis, 1982).
4. J. Ziman, 'Basic Principles' in Scientists, the Arms Race and Disarmament, ibid, 161-78.
5. F.J. Dyson 'Weapons and Hope' (New York: Harper & Row, 1984), 135-47.
6. Proceedings of the 22nd Pugwash Conference, Oxford, 1972, p.48.
7. J. Rotblat, The Fifth Pugwash Quinquennium, 1977-1982, (Pugwash Council, 1982) p.16.
8. Proceedings of the 32nd Pugwash Conference, Warsaw, 1982, pp.77-81.

Appendix
Statement from Pugwash Council
'1984 and Beyond: Science, Security and Public Opinion'

The 34th Pugwash Conference on Science and World Affairs met in Björkliden, Sweden, on 9-14 July 1984. The participants comprised 135 scientists, other scholars, and public figures - as well as 13 students - from 40 countries and 6 international organisations.

The Conference was organised by the Swedish Pugwash Group with most helpful support from the Swedish Government, the City of Kiruna, the Royal Swedish Academy of Science, the Volvo Corporation, and the Swedish Division of IBM Corporation, to whom we express our sincere appreciation.

The opening session of the Conference was addressed by Ambassador Maj-Britt Theorin, and a message of welcome and encouragement from the Prime Minister Olof Palme was conveyed. Other public sessions in the course of the meeting were addressed by (among others) Defence Minister Anders Thunborg and Minister of Culture Bengt Göransson.

The Conference took place at a time of rising tensions in international relations and seemingly poor prospects for halting and reducing the worldwide build-up of nuclear and conventional weapons. At such times - with official East-West and, in many respects, North-South relations at a dangerous low point - the Pugwash approach of building understanding and seeking solutions through off-the-record discussions among influential scientists and public figures takes on increased importance.

The participants at Pugwash Conferences take part as individuals and not as representatives of their governments or institutions. The following statement on the topics treated at the Conference was prepared by the Pugwash Council and should not be interpreted as a consensus of all the participants, among whom a wide range of views was represented.

Strategic and Other Nuclear Weapons

Deployments of new nuclear weapons now being carried out by

both the United States and Soviet Union - in Europe and elsewhere - are undermining perceptions of the adequacy of deterrent forces and eroding the possibilities for reversing the nuclear arms race. As a result, these deployments are reducing the security of everyone.

Even more than by the sheer numbers of nuclear weapons, we are threatened by certain qualitative characteristics of the weapons now being deployed or soon to be deployed. These dangerous characteristics include various combinations of high accuracy, multiple warheads on each missile, short flight times, and ease of concealment from verification measures.

The most threatening trends could and should be stopped by a freeze on deployments and a ban of flight testing of new land-based and sea-launched ballistic and cruise missiles of medium and long range. Most parts of this prescription would pose little difficulty with respect to verification. As for the more difficult parts, it must be kept in mind that the dangers of actions small enough to escape detection cannot compare to the dangers of unrestrained competition in these weapons.

Another component of a 'freeze' that is both urgently needed and easily achieved in principle is a comprehensive ban on the testing of nuclear explosives (CTB). A successful conclusion to the trilateral CTB negotiations, which were broken off in 1980 and still have not been resumed, would provide a badly needed demonstration that the nuclear-weapon-states intend to honour their obligations under the Non-Proliferation Treaty (NPT). Without such demonstrations, the NPT surely will come under intense pressure at the Review Conference scheduled for 1985. A CTB also would dispose of the dangerous illusion that the performance of nuclear weapons needs to be improved by further testing and that the existing arsenals are not adequate.

The fact is that both the United States and the Soviet Union have nuclear forces far in excess of those needed to guarantee devastating retaliation if attacked. Since nuclear weapons other than for this purpose only add to the danger of their being used, it follows that the differences of detail in the two arsenals have no practical importance; there is essential equivalence between the two sides. Indeed, the large margins by which the arsenals on both sides exceed the needs of deterrence should be recognised as providing room for large mutual force reductions on both sides, following a freeze, and for **independent initiatives** towards freezing and reducing nuclear forces as a prelude and incentive to formal negotiations.

A situation particularly suited to independent initiatives

is the presence of large numbers of 'battlefield' nuclear weapons in Europe. These weapons endanger their possessors as much as they endanger the other side, both because their short range means they would be exploded in many cases on the territory of the country being 'defended', and because their vulnerability creates a risk of hasty decisions about whether to 'use them or lose them'. Thus, their unilateral withdrawal is worthwhile whether or not the other side has the good sense to reciprocate. It may also be hoped that independent withdrawals of these weapons would provide an all-important beginning of nuclear-forces reductions that would spread to the longer-range categories of nuclear weapons.

The possibilities for halting and reversing the nuclear arms race will not become practical realities without an improved climate of East-West relations and a degree of political will to reduce the threats associated with the world's nuclear arsenals. A start on the needed improved climate requires yet another form of 'freeze' - a halt to provocative rhetoric. Increasing political will for arms reductions is partly a matter of better education of leaders and publics, a process in which scientists could be more useful in ways discussed below.

Efforts to reduce East-West tension in general and to reverse the arms race should be supplemented by new and improved measures for avoiding or terminating sequences of events that otherwise might lead to nuclear war among the major powers without any of them intending it. Possible scenarios for such 'inadvertent' nuclear war include technical and human error, 'third party' nuclear detonations, and regional crisis, or war, drawing in the major powers.

Besides improving their own command, control, communication, and intelligence capabilities, the major powers could act jointly to reduce dangers of this kind in several ways: agree on a code of political conduct aimed at the avoidance of nuclear war; improve emergency communication links between national leaders; and initiate regular, private, informal meetings between the high civilian and military leaders on each side who would be responsible for crisis management. Improved communications and better relations more generally could lead eventually to the establishment of jointly operated crisis-control centres, a desirable development.

European Security

Many of the measures mentioned under the preceding heading, including especially the freeze on missile deployments as a prelude to reductions, and independent withdrawals of battlefield nuclear weapons, are particularly germane as early steps towards increased security in Europe. Much more must also be done, but finding prescriptions likely to work quickly is difficult.

Adoption of a policy of 'no first use' of nuclear weapons by NATO, to match the stated policy of the Soviet Union, is desirable. Such policies should be accompanied by visible adjustments in force postures, but care must be taken that the resulting changes do not produce an intensified arms race in offensive conventional weaponry. The possibilities for a military balance in Europe based on defensively oriented conventional forces, at lower levels than today's, appear promising and should be pursued further.

The problem of medium-range nuclear forces in Europe could, in principle, be solved by independent reciprocal measures, and this would be the fastest and hence most desirable approach. In practice, however, barring a drastic reduction in mistrust on both sides, a complete solution may well require new formal negotiations. Such negotiations would face great difficulties if they kept 'theatre' and intercontinental weapons separate, as in the two sets of negotiations that collapsed at the end of last year; but bringing all these weapons into a single negotiation would create new problems to replace the ones solved.

Whatever the approach to this particular problem, a general reduction of tensions and increased willingness to be flexible in pursuit of common security are pre-requisites for success. Besides unilateral confidence-building measures (CBM), such as renunciations of provocative doctrines - for example, 'decapitation' and 'launch-on-warning' - and pullback of forces, the Stockholm Conference offers the only immediately available prospect of negotiating CBM to contribute to improving the climate. These negotiations should be encouraged and accelerated, as part of a wider commitment to reviving the policy of détente in Europe.

A degree of success in confidence building and the revival of détente could then lead rather quickly to such desirable achievements as nuclear-weapon-free zones in the nordic subregion and in the Balkans. Substantial progress in creating both the analytical and political support for these two nuclear-free zones has already been made.

Military Aspects of Space

Military and civilian space programmes are often connected and constitute an activity of growing interest to most industrial nations. Present reconnaissance satellite operations by the USA and USSR have an essential stabilising function in the world's strategic confrontation. The anti-satellite weapons under development by the USA and USSR endanger space activities and are a new, major step in the arms race. The negotiation of a treaty to ban these weapons should have high priority.

As an immediate step, a moratorium on the development and testing of dedicated anti-satellite weapons, established by independent initiatives, is essential in order not to exacerbate the verification of any future treaty on the subject. Although existing technology provides limited ASAT capability, this need not be a serious obstacle to an ASAT treaty.

Ballistic-missile defence (BMD) of populations using new technologies ('star wars'), is technically infeasible, especially in the light of probable counter-measures. Pursuit of these BMD technologies will increase the danger of nuclear war by threatening the existing arms-control régime, including especially the ABM treaty, by provoking further build-ups of offensive nuclear weapons of all types, and by the crisis-instability characteristics of leaky BMD.

It should be noted that a treaty banning anti-satellite weapons would strengthen the existing prohibition on the development of space-based BMD systems.

An international agency for monitoring, by satellite, of compliance with arms control agreements, supplementing national means of verification, has been investigated in a preliminary way and deserves further study. This study would include, but would not be limited to, international means for verification of the ASAT treaty recommended above.

Chemical Warfare (CW)

Significant progress towards a Chemical Weapons Convention has been made in the past three years in talks going on within the Geneva Disarmament Conference. These multilateral talks could usefully be supplemented at this point by a resumption of the bilateral USA-USSR talks that took place from 1977 to 1980. Emphasis should be given in the CW talks to careful construction of the mandate for the Consultative Committee that will oversee implementation and compliance of a CW Convention.

Given the timescale for completion of negotiations on the CW Convention (probably 3 years or more) and for the subsequent destruction of CW stockpiles (perhaps 8-10 years), there has been interest in establishing more quickly a zone free of chemical weapons in central Europe and perhaps other such zones elsewhere. The further pursuit of this useful idea is to be encouraged.

Current alarmist journalism on the chemical-biological-weapons implications of recombinant DNA techniques is poorly based scientifically and may lead to an unjustified erosion of confidence in the 1972 Biological Weapons Convention, which bans all types of biological and toxin weapons whatever their method of production.

As confidence-building measures in connection with this Convention, consideration should be given to establishing an international register of high-containment microbiological laboratories (those designed to prevent the escape of dangerous microbes) and a programme of immunological monitoring for biological warfare agents of personnel working in such laboratories.

Allegations of the use of chemical-biological weapons in Afghanistan and South-East Asia have received much publicity. While not all elements of this controversy have been fully clarified, detailed evidence presented at this Conference (and published in the recent scientific literature) established that environmental samples of 'Yellow Rain' - which have been claimed to be the residue of CBW weapons - are the dried excrement of honey-bees.

The particular difficulties of verifying compliance with the 1925 Geneva Protocol banning the use of CB weapons has been highlighted by the recent use of chemical weapons in the Iran-Iraq war. This episode illustrates with disturbing clarity the growing danger that, in the absence of the projected Chemical Weapons Convention, the weapons will proliferate throughout the world.

Security and Development

Nearly all of the approximately 150 armed conflicts since 1945 have taken place in the developing parts of the world, and most of these could not have grown to the scale they did, or have been sustained, without weapons - and in many cases military personnel - supplied by the industrialised countries. Today, such arms transfers are helping to maintain destructive conflicts in Iran-Iraq, Lebanon, Central America, South-East Asia, Southern Africa, and elsewhere. External arms supplies are in fact the dominant source of the arms build-up in the Third World, and they are a significant contribution to the insecurity there.

Arms transfers from developed to developing countries often are motivated by strategic and political as well as financial considerations, and they may lead to supplier influence over the recipient in a variety of ways. Increasing transfers of weapons and devices ostensibly for maintenance of 'law and order' are being used in some developing regions for oppression, suppression of dissidents, and torture.

More detailed study of the economic impact on developing countries, of their spending on imported and domestic weaponry is needed, but the conclusion is irresistible that some of the effects are economically detrimental. The vast economic resources devoted to the military in industrial nations also inevitably reduce the flow of such resources from North to South, inhibiting development prospects.

Many of the conflicts in the Third World have had their origin in local causes such as religious, ethnic, linguistic, and border problems - strongly influenced in many cases by the larger geopolitical environment. The diversity and complexity of developing world societies and of their relations with the developed world - combined with the difficulties associated with the political, social, and economic transition from colonial to independent nation-state status - are among the reasons that few simple solutions for the foregoing problems present themselves. Approaches to arms control and crisis avoidance worked out in the developed world often are simply not transferable to developing regions.

Therefore, a mechanism which takes account of the security needs of the Third World, first and foremost, has to be evolved if Third World crises are to be contained effectively. For such a mechanism to be evolved, the attitude of the developed world must change. Developed and developing countries must participate together in arms control and crisis management on an equal basis wherever their interests overlap. Such an approach is more likely to succeed in Central America, the Middle East, Southern Africa, and so on, than the present one-sided approach dominated by developed-country strategic and military interests.

Among other avenues that merit further study, we mention: the establishment of a mechanism to develop criteria for the control of the international arms trade; the encouragement of regional agreements on non-aggression and cooperation in all aspects of development; development of proposals for mechanisms for UN sanctions against those who fail to comply with agreements designed to avoid conflicts; exploration of possibilities for early warning of potential conflicts and the more effective application of crisis-avoidance techniques (including informal meetings of scientists and other influential persons from the affected areas); and the design and implementation of methods for collecting and making public accurate information on the sources of weapons in developing-country conflicts.

Our discussions on security and development will be continued and expanded at next year's Pugwash conference, to be held at the University of Campinas, Brazil in July 1985.

Public Opinion and Arms Control

The disturbing state of East-West relations and the nuclear threat associated with it have aroused the public in many countries and at many levels. The Pugwash Conferences were established 27 years ago with the inter-related purposes of fostering public and decision-maker understanding of the dangers of nuclear war and seeking ways to reduce those dangers; and Pugwash scientists, collectively and individually, have contributed positively to the increased state of public awareness of these problems that now prevails.

Recognising the importance of an informed and aroused public - as both a generator of the political will for arms reductions and, in a longer time perspective, as the pool from which informed and committed leaders must materialise - the Pugwash Council proposes to encourage an intensification of the collective and individual efforts of Pugwash participants in public education (including support for organisations of young scientists). Among the kinds of efforts we believe have been and will continue to be effective are the following: promotion and improvement of regular courses and special lectures on the arms race, arms control and disarmament, international security, and the consequences of nuclear war, in colleges and universities; the preparation of background materials on these topics for science museum exhibits, presentations on television programmes popularising science, and features in popular science magazines; the organisation of workshops and seminars at international, national, and local levels and improved contacts with and provision of information to the major media. The proclamation by the United Nations of 1986 as a Year of Peace should provide the framework for increased activity in these directions throughout the world.

* * *

The Pugwash Council

Chairman: Prof. M. Nalecz (Poland). Members: Acad. A. Balevski (Bulgaria), Mr. E. Bauer (France), Prof. F. Calogero (Italy), Prof. B. Feld (USA), Mr. S. Freier (Israel), Prof. J. Freymond (Switzerland), Dr. E. Galal (Egypt), Prof. H. Glubrecht (FRG), Professor L. Goma (Zambia), Prof. J. Holdren (USA), Prof. E. Leibnitz (GDR), Prof. Patricia Lindop (UK), Acad. M. Markov (USSR), Prof. G. Menon (India), Prof. J. Miettinen (Finland), Acad. O. Reutov (USSR), Dr. M. Roche (Venezuela), Prof. J. Rotblat (UK), Prof. J. Ruina (USA), Dr. H. Scoville, Jr. (USA), Prof. T. Toyoda (Japan), Prof. V. Trukhanovsky (USSR), Dr. M. Wionczek (Mexico).

Prof. Dorothy Hodgkin is President of Pugwash and Dr. M. Kaplan is Secretary-General.

Index

INDEX

A-6 & A-7 fighter bombers, 231
Accidents Agreement, 32
Advanced guidance systems, 78
Aerospace Forecast & Inventory, 83
Aircraft issues, 230-33, 251
Alpha programme, 113
Andropov, President, 35, 217
Antarctic Treaty, 77
Anti-aircraft systems, 57
Anti-ballistic missile (ABM) systems, 8, 9, 17, 47, 57, 103-6
  basic questions affecting, 103
  new technologies, 103, 104
  partial defences, 104
  R&D efforts, 103-4, 106
Anti-ballistic Missile Treaty (1972), 3, 5, 20, 26, 51, 54, 58, 106, 119
Anti-satellite Treaty, 111, 119, 120
Anti-satellite weapons, 5, 7-9, 12, 47, 54, 58, 93-4, 108
  arms control area, 102
  arms race avoidance, 102
  detabilising nature of, 99-100
  development of, 110, 380
  freeze on testing, 101
  new proposals, 117-20
  prohibition of, 102
  role of non-dedicated, 100-11
  space-based, 118
  technology restrictions, 107-23
  verification, 120
Anti-submarine weapons, 57
Arab-Israeli war, 139
Argus atomic weapons detonations, 83

Armament industry, 299-302
Armoured vehicles, 249
Arms control, 4, 18-27, 32, 35
Arms trade, 295-306, 317, 320
Arms transfer, 317, 318, 321
Artillery firepower, 250
Assembly of the Western European Union, 149
Aviation Week & Space Technology (AW & ST), 83

B-1 bomber, 58
Backfire bomber, 231-33
Bacteriological weapons, 177
Badger bomber, 231, 233
Balance of power, 209, 214, 288, 290
Ballistic missile defence (BMD) technologies, 107, 381
Basic Principles Agreement (1972), 37
Beam weapons, 9-10
Benign defence, 275-6, 281, 284
Beryllium, 65
Big Bird satellite, 84, 129, 139
Big hole effects, 68
Biological warfare, 155
Biological Weapons Convention, 155, 177-8, 180
Birkill, Stephen, 90
Black Sea, 76
Blackjack heavy bomber, 58
Blinder bomber, 231, 233
Bold Orion programme, 108, 111
Boost-phase intercept, 6
Brazil, 299-300, 310-12
Brezhnev, President, 237
Brown, Harold, 173
Brussels Treaty, 171
Bush, Vice-President, 35

Bulletin of the Atomic
  Scientists, 351

Camera optics, 129
Camera resolution, 128,
  129, 131
Canada, 362-4
Central America, 318
Chartered Industries of
  Singapore, 300, 301
Chazov, Evgeni, 353
Chemical-weapon-free-zone,
  202-6
Chemical weapons, 23, 42,
  58, 155-75
  acquired technology, 156-
  66
  activities to be banned
  and verified, 196-7
  agent delivery, 162-6
  agent identification,
  192,
  American deployments of,
  172
  anti-personnel casualty
  agents, 157-62
  ban negotiations, 176-85
  binary munitions, 164,
  181
  challenge inspection,
  186, 199-200
  clandestine production,
  188
  compliance monitoring,
  183-5
  definition of, 179-82
  development of new, 202
  elimination of, 182
  Finnish project on dis-
  armament verification,
  190-94
  international inspect-
  ors, 187
  military preparations
  for use, 179
  NATO deployments of, 173
  non-possession of, 171
  permitted use of, 170,
  183
  possession of, 171
  potential technology,
  156, 166-70
  production of, 183
  prohibition of use, 178-
  9, 201, 206
  protection against, 155,
  161, 168, 170
  remote monitoring, 187,
  192
  research resources, 169
  Soviet deployments of,
  172-4
  stockpiles of, 202

Chemical weapons (contd.)
  super-toxic lethal
  agents, 188
  toxic compounds, 187
  toxicity, 167
  verification activities,
  182, 184, 186-201
Chemical Weapons Conven-
  tion, 156, 162, 167, 178-
  86, 201, 206, 381
Chernenko, President, 35,
  185, 349
China, 95, 301
CIA, 66
Clipper Bow programme, 87
Club of Rome, 353
Cold War, 321, 323, 324
COMINT, 91
Command, control & communi-
  cations (C^3) systems,
  10-11, 32, 34, 89-91,
  213, 215, 216, 252
Committee of Soviet Scientists for the Prevention
  of Nuclear War, 102, 351,
  352
Committee on Chemical
  Weapons, 178
Committee on Disarmament
  (CD), 178, 196
Comprehensive test ban
  (CTB), 48, 49, 54, 60-9,
  378
Conditional Conventional
  Retaliation Capability
  (CCRC), 282-3
Conference on Confidence-
  and Security-Building
  Measures and Disarmament
  in Europe (CSBM), 16, 27,
  36, 259-74
  area of applicability,
  262-5
  assessments and prospects
  270-74
  basic assumptions of
  mandate, 265
  designation of, 260-1
  origins of, 261-2
  positions of negotiators,
  266-70
Conference of the
  Committee on Disarmament
  (CCD), 178
Confidence-building
  measures, 16, 27, 28, 33,
  35-6, 64, 275-86, 307,
  380
Consultative Committee,
  184, 186-9, 192, 194,
  200
Convention of Chemical
  Weapons, see Chemical
  Weapons Convention

Convention on the Law of
  the Sea (UNCLOS), 77, 80
Conventional forces, 248,
  253, 287-92
Conventional war, see Non-
  nuclear war
Conventional weapons, 8,
  42, 52, 57, 249, 287
Cosmos satellite pro-
  gramme, 83-94, 139
Council of Europe, 150
Counterforce weapons, 44
Cranston, Alan, 33
Crisis control measures,
  28-39, 139, 215-17,
  283-4, 313-19
Cruise missiles, 51, 58,
  70, 233-7, 256
  see also Ground-launched
  cruise missiles (GLCMs)
Cuban Missile Crisis, 31,
  32, 239
Cyprus crisis, 139

Data-processing, 276-9
Decapitation strikes, 44
Defence against ballistic
  missiles (DABM), 5
Defense Advance Research
  Project Agency (DARPA),
  112, 113
Defense Meterological Sat-
  ellite Program (DMSP)
  91
Defense Satellite Communi-
  cations Systems (DSCS),
  89-90
Defense Support Program
  (DSP) satellites, 89
Denuclearisation movement,
  344
Department of National
  Defence, 363
D'Estaing, President
  Giscard, 148
Detonations of unknown
  origin, 30
Deudney, Daniel, 148
Development prospects,
  328-40
  and disarmament, 331-2,
  336-9
  and security, 382-3
Directed-energy weapons
  (DEW), 6, 7, 9-10, 112-
  14, 116, 119
Dirks, Leslie, 12
Disarmament Conference, 77
Disarmament economies,
  295-6
Disarming first strike, 45
Discoverer satellites, 83
Disengagement, see Military
  disengagement

Dyson, Freeman, 371

Early warning satellites,
  89, 110
East-West relations, 245,
  246, 274, 291, 292, 313,
  315, 339, 355-9
Economic development,
  332-5
Educational needs, 363
Eighteen Nations Disarm-
  ament Conference (ENDC),
  177
Eisenhower, President, 83
Electromagnetic (EM) guns,
  115
Electromagnetic pulse
  (EMP), 11
Electromagnetic radiation,
  126, 127
Electronic intelligence
  gathering (ELINT) satel-
  lite, 87-9, 140
Energy supplies, 334
Environmental pollution,
  335
EORSATs, 87
Epoxytrichothecene, 158
Egypt, 301
Escalation concept, 18-27
Europe, 22-3, 215-16,
  209-59, 287-92, 379
European Economic Communi-
  ty (EEC), 149
European Space Agency
  (ESA), 149-50
European Space Community,
  143
Everndon, J, 11
Experts and expertise,
  349, 363, 372

F-4 fighter-bomber, 231
F-14 fighter aircraft, 111
F-15/ASAT system, 99, 101,
  111, 112
F-111 bomber, 231, 233
Falklands campaign, 95
FB-111 fighter-bomber,
  231, 233
Fencer fighter-bomber, 231
Financial crisis, 323
Finnish chemical weapons
  disarmament
  verification, 190-4
First-strike capability,
  43, 45
First Pugwash Workshop on
  Proposals for a Nuclear
  Weapons Freeze, 40, 46,
  47, 50
Fissile material, 60, 61
Fletcher Commission, 5
Flight-tests, 53, 54

FltSatCom satellites, 90
Fossil fuels, 334
France, 202, 237-9, 262, 343, 349
Fuel-air explosives, 42
Fuel resources, 334

Gals (Tack) satellites/transponders, 90
Geneva Protocol, 176-7, 179
Geodesy, 93
George, Alexander, 37
Geostationary orbit (GSO), 120
Geosynchronous satellites, 95
German Democratic Republic, 203
German Federal Republic (FRG), 202
Global Navigation Satellite System (GLONASS), 92
Global Positioning System (GPS), 91
GNP, 332, 335-8
Governments, how to influence, 358-9
Grand accounting exercise, 23-5
Gromyko, Andrei, 219
Ground-launched cruise missiles (GLCMs), 31, 58, 210-14, 216, 219, 221, 222, 225, 226, 235
Gun method, 60
Gunboat diplomacy, 78

Hague Conventions, 76
H-bombs, 61
Health-care deficiencies, 333
Helsinki Final Act 1975, 36, 262, 324
Herbicides, 181
Hi-Ho programme, 110
Holst, J.J., 271
Homo Hierarchicus, 308
Homo Sapiens, 308
Horizontal escalation, 242-3
Hotline, 32-5, 38, 346
Hydrogen-atom beams, 6

Implosion method, 60
Independent initiatives, 45-7
India, 139
Indian Ocean, 76
Indo-Pakistan crisis, 137
Infant mortality rates, 333
In-flight refuelling, 231
Integrated defence model, 279-86

Integrated operational nuclear detonation detection system (IONDS), 92
Intercontinental ballistic missiles (ICBMs), 4, 24, 44, 45, 70, 89, 116, 213, 215, 216, 221, 225, 239
Interkosmos Council, 149
Intermediate-range ballistic missiles (IRBMs), 211, 214, 216, 219, 220
Intermediate-range nuclear forces (INF), 224, 226, 229, 230, 239-40
International Development Association, 340
International Economic Order, 340
International Institute for Strategic Studies, 35
International Satellite Monitoring Agency (ISMA), 125, 137, 140, 141, 145, 149-51
International Telecommunications Union Convention, 117
Iran-Iraq war, 21, 322

Jackson, Henry, 33
Japan, 96
Joint Military Communications Link, 34

Kant, Immanuel, 276
Kennan, George, 344
Kennedy, President, 83
Kettering Group, 84-6
KH-11 strategic reconnaissance satellites, 84, 90, 129, 139
Kinetic-energy kill vehicles, 6
Kohl, Chancellor Helmut, 220
Krypton fluoride, 113
Kvitsinsky, Yuri, 218-220, 229, 233

Landsat satellite programme, 133, 134, 140
Large-scale decoupling, 68
Laser beams, 112-14, 119
  see Directed-energy weapons
Latin Amercia, 205
Latin American Nuclear-Weapon-Free Zone, 76
Launch-on-warning postures, 44
Lens, Sidney, 360
Leontief, Wassily, 295

INDEX

Libya, 318
Life expectancies, 333
Light infantry, 251
Lisbon Declaration, 150
LODE (Large Optical Demonstration Experiment), 113
London Treaty, 76
Long-range bombers, 24
Lown, Bernard, 353

McNamara, Robert, 45, 239
Manned spaceflight, 95
Marietta, Martin, 5
Marx, Karl, 349
Medium-range missiles, 228-9
Meteorology, 91
Micro-electronics, 276-9
Middle East, 318, 338
Midgetman, 75
Militarism rise of, 307-12
Military assistance programmes, 317
Military détente, 247, 252-4
Military disengagement, 245-58, 292
Military expenditure, 295-306, 312, 316, 320, 328, 335-7, 339, 363
Military industries, 295-306, 317, 320
Military instability, 244-5
Military procurement patterns, 298
Military R&D programmes, 335-6
Military rationales, 210-15
Military-strategic concepts, 16, 17
Miniature Homing Vehicle (MHV), 111
Minuteman, 45
Minuteman-III, 4
Missile mobility and verification, 223-6
Missile reloading, 226-8
Mitterand, President, 149
Montreux Convention, 76
Multiple independently targetable re-entry vehicles (MIRVs), 5, 44, 45, 213, 219, 222, 225
Mustard gas, 158
Mutual and balanced force reduction (MBFR), 27
Mutually assured destruction (MAD), 329
MX missiles, 45, 75

Namibia, 323
NASA, 89, 96
National technical means, 136

Naval arms race, 76-80
Navigation satellites, 8-9, 91-3
NAVSTAR satellites, 91, 117, 125
Navy Ocean Surveillance Satellite (NOSS) programme, 87
Nerve gases, 157, 158, 161, 162, 164-7, 181
Neutral particle beam (NPB) weapons, 6, 9, 10
Nevada test site, 68
Newly industrialising countries (NICs), 296, 297, 303
Nike-X missiles, 111
Ninth Pugwash Workshop on Nuclear Forces, 40, 45, 51
Nitze, Paul, 218, 219, 229, 233
Non-nuclear war, 42, 43
Non-nuclear weapons, see Conventional weapons
North American Air Defense Command (NORAD), 363
North Atlantic Treaty Organisation (NATO), 21, 46, 51, 95, 203, 209-23, 227-30, 232, 233, 238, 240, 244, 246, 253, 255, 257, 269, 282, 287, 343, 344, 356, 363
North-South Conference of the Parliamentary Assembly of the Council of Europe, 148
North-South relations, 315, 339
Norway, 343
Nuclear accident, 35, 42, 210
Nuclear demilitarisation, 281-3
Nuclear deployments, 343
Nuclear deterrence, 41-3, 288
Nuclear disarmament, 19, 209
Nuclear discontent, 344
Nuclear disengagement, 246
Nuclear equilibrium, 53
Nuclear explosions, 48, 54, 60, 110, 117
Nuclear explosives, 53
Nuclear first strike, 19, 20
Nuclear forces, 40-54
Nuclear freeze proposals, 40-59, 75, 344
Nuclear holocaust, 348
Nuclear no-first-use policy, 347
Nuclear Non-Proliferation Treaty, 346, 378

Nuclear over-kill capacity, 328, 345
Nuclear stockpiles, 361
Nuclear terrorism, 30
Nuclear tests, 48, 49, 53, 61, 62, 66, 67, 69, 139
Nuclear threshold, 245-6
Nuclear war, 42, 43, 52, 55, 216, 348, 361
Nuclear-weapon-free zone, 206, 246, 256
Nuclear weapons, 25, 35, 60-9, 288, 336, 347
Nunn, Sam, 33, 35

Ocean reconnaissance satellites (RORSAT), 99
Ocean surveillance, 87-8
Official Development Assistance, 339
Oliphant, Mark, 362
Omnicide, 348-50
Oppenheimer, Robert, 371
Organisation for European Economic Development (OECD), 339
OTRAG rocket test, 139
Outer Space Treaty, 116-17

Pakistan, 320
Palme Commission, 203
Partial Test Ban Treaty (PTBT), 117, 119
Permissible action link (PAL), 10
Pershing missiles, 58, 219
Pershing-II missiles, 17, 24, 31, 210-14, 217, 219-22, 225-7
Persian Gulf, 323
Pesticides, 188
Phosgene oxime, 158
Photographic reconnaissance satellites, see Reconnaissance satellites
Plutonium production, 54, 62
Point Count plan, 70-5
Political factors, 14, 16, 19, 25-7, 254-6, 309
Politicans, thinking of, 363
Population distribution, 332
Population explosion, 331
Power structure effects, 362
Precision-guided munitions, 289
Prevention of Incidents on and over the High Seas, 37, 76
Prevention of Nuclear War Agreement, 32
Priroda (Nature) Centre, 86
Priroda (Nature) journal, 352

Public opinion, 343-7, 384
and scientists, 351-9
Pugwash Conferences on Science and World Affairs, see Pugwash Movement
Pugwash Council, 384
statement, 377-84
Pugwash Executive Committee statement, 37, 47, 50-4, 146
Pugwash Movement, 146, 355
amateurs and professionals, 372-3
and scientific community, 367-76
Annual Conferences, 32, 372-3
historical background, 367-8
how to enlarge, 375-6
numbers and eminence, 373-5
Pugwash Symposium on Conventional Forces in Europe, 43, 288-92
Pugwash Symposium on Scientists, the Arms Race and Disarmament, 368-71
Pugwash Workshop on Crisis Management, 37

Quarry satellite, 7

Radar technology, 141
Radiation detectors, 66
Rapid Deployment Force, 323, 337
Reagan, President, 29, 34, 36, 70, 75, 166, 218, 317, 349
Realistic policies, 349
Reconnaissance satellites, 85-6, 108, 140
Regional conflicts, 320-7
Regional Satellite Monitoring Agency (RSMA), 125, 141, 149-51
Roosevelt Center for American Policy Studies, 35

Safety margins, 43-5
SAINT (SAtellite INTerceptor), 110
SALT I, 76, 117, 222, 237, 239, 324
SALT II, 15, 48, 76, 117, 223-5, 229, 231, 236, 237, 239, 324
SALT III, 239
SALT negotiations, 3, 54, 94, 136
Salyut-6, 94, 95
Sanctuary areas, 76

Sarin, 157, 159, 160, 164
Satellite Data System (SDS)
  satellites, 90
Satellite monitoring agency,
  124-42
  tasks relevant for,
  137-41
Satellite sensors, 127-31
Saudi Arabia, 302, 321
Schelling, Thomas, 32
Schrader, Gerhard, 157, 169
Science journals, 352
Scientific American, 351,
  352
Scientists
  and public opinion,
  351-9
  education of, 368-71
  role of, 368
  social responsibility of,
  368, 371
Scowcroft Commission, 3, 4,
  44
Sea Bed Treaty, 76
Sea-launched cruise
  missiles (SLCMs), 220,
  234-7
Secrecy aspects, 64
Security concerns, 330-1
Seismographs, 66
Sensors, see Satellite
  sensors
Ship-to-ship missiles, 78
Short-flight-time missiles,
  44
Short-Range Attack Missiles
  (SRAM), 111, 228-9
Shultz, George, 219
Singapore, 300-1
Sino-Soviet border conflict,
  137
SIPRI Yearbooks, 298
Skylab, 131
Skynet geosynchronous
  system, 95
Smith, R. Jeffrey, 12
Socio-economic development,
  332-5, 338, 339
Socio-political insta-
  bility, 244
Somerville, John, 348
South Africa, 139, 318,
  323
South-East Pacific, 76
Soviet Union, 15, 24, 73,
  349, 351-3
Space expenditures, 143-5
  see also Military
  expenditure
Space militarisation,
  83-98, 107, 144, 145,
  380
  anti-satellite tests,
  93-4

Space militarisation
  (contd.)
  civilian uses, 131-3
  developments in, 125-31
  early warning satel-
  lites, 89
  existing legal measures,
  116-7
  force multipliers, 126
  geodesy, 93
  importance of, 126
  manned spaceflight, 95
  meteorology, 91
  monitoring, 124-42
  navigation satellites,
  91-3
  new proposals, 117-20
  non-aggressive functions,
  126
  number of satellites
  launched, 109, 125
  ocean surveillance, 87-8
  orbital inclination of
  satellites, 121
  origins of, 107
  photographic reconnais-
  sance, 84-6
  prevention of, 99-102
  reconnaissance craft,
  84-6, 108
  verification procedure,
  120-2, 133-7
  see also Anti-satellite
  systems (ASAT);
Space mine, 7
Space policies, 143-53
  aspects of debate, 145
  for human benefit, 145,
  147-8
  issues at stake, 144-5
Space Shuttle, 95
Space technology
  civilian applications,
  144, 146
  global effects, 147
  peaceful uses of, 144
  for socio-economic
  purposes, 147
  see also Space militarisation
SPIN (SPace INtercept), 110
SPOT satellite, 133
Sputnik-1, 83, 107
SS-4 missiles, 213-16, 218,
  221
SS-5 missiles, 213-16, 218,
  221
SS-11 missiles, 215
SS-18 Mod4 missiles, 4
SS-19 missiles, 213, 215
SS-20 missiles, 58, 116,
  209, 212-22, 225, 226,
  228-30, 238
SS-22 missiles, 24

Standing Consultative Commission, 226
Stanford Arms Control Group, 314
Stanford University, 35
Star wars, see Ballistic missile defence
Stockholm International Peace Research Institute (SIPRI), 155, 298
Strategic Air Command (SAC), 33
Strategic Arms Reduction Talks (START), 232, 239–40
Strategic bombers, 70
Strategic boosters, 5
Strategic defence, 5
Strategic deterrence, 4
Strategic stability, 14–17
Strategic weapons, 3
Stratocratisation of society, 310
Submarine-launched ballistic missiles (SLBMs), 4, 24, 44–6, 48, 76, 80, 89, 116, 215, 238
Surprise attack, 246–9
Surveillance programme, 62–5, 68, 69
Syria, 318

Tabun, 157, 159, 160
Taylor, E.P., 360
Tear-gases, 180–1
Technological destabilisation, 284
Technological developments, 3–13
Teller, Edward, 371
Tenth Pugwash Workshop on Nuclear Forces, 40, 42, 43, 46, 50
Terminal defence, 6
Terminal homing, 8
Terminology of nuclear issues, 348–50
Territorial militia, 251
Thermonuclear components, 61, 68
Thermonuclear fuels, 61
Thermonuclear reactions, 61
Thinking of politicians, 363
Third World, 29, 146, 150, 245, 295, 307–40, 346
Threshold Test Ban Treaty, 49
Titan-3C, 89
Titan-3D/Agena, 84

Tlatelolco Treaty, 76, 205
Transporter-erector-launchers (TELs), 218, 222, 225, 227
Triad programme, 113
Trident-II (D5) missile, 17, 44
Trilateral negotiations, 54
Tritium, 64
Trudeau, Pierre, 362
Tsongas amendment, 94, 112
TV programmes, 352–3

UNCLOS, 77, 80
Union of Concerned Scientists, 118, 351
United Kingdom, 237–9, 349
United Nations Department for Disarmament Affairs, 364
United Nations General Assembly, 52
United States, 15, 72, 344
United States Homing Overlay Experiment Interceptor, 8
Universities, roles of, 360–66
UNSSOD I and II, 362
Uranium production, 54, 62

Velikhov, Evgeni, 352
Vienna Declaration (1958), 367
Voronkov, Mikhail, 170
VX agent, 161–2

Warner, John, 33, 35
Warsaw Pact, 23, 203, 255, 356
Warsaw Treaty Organisation (WTO), 46, 247, 248, 257, 258, 262, 268
Washington Convention, 76
Weinberger report, 34, 35
Window of vulnerability, 44
World disarmament campaign, 364–5
World Health Organization, 333

Xenon fluoride, 113
X-ray lasers, 6, 7, 114, 115, 119
Yellow rain, 158, 168, 169

Zeus missiles, 111
Ziman, John, 368
Zone of Peace, 76
Zuckerman, Lord, 362

GPSR Compliance
The European Union's (EU) General Product Safety Regulation (GPSR) is a set of rules that requires consumer products to be safe and our obligations to ensure this.

If you have any concerns about our products, you can contact us on

ProductSafety@springernature.com

In case Publisher is established outside the EU, the EU authorized representative is:

Springer Nature Customer Service Center GmbH
Europaplatz 3
69115 Heidelberg, Germany

www.ingramcontent.com/pod-product-compliance
Ingram Content Group UK Ltd.
Pitfield, Milton Keynes, MK11 3LW, UK
UKHW041415180426
11947UKWH00007B/145